D0913134

HOW SOCIETIES ARE BORN

HOW SOCIETIES ARE BORN

GOVERNANCE IN
WEST CENTRAL AFRICA
BEFORE 1600

Jan Vansina

UNIVERSITY OF VIRGINIA PRESS
CHARLOTTESVILLE AND LONDON

University of Virginia Press

© 2004 by the Rector and Visitors of the University of Virginia

All rights reserved

Printed in the United States of America on acid-free paper

First published 2004

9 8 7 6 5 4 3 2 1

LIBRARY OF CONGRESS CATALOGING-IN-PUBLICATION DATA

Vansina, Jan.

   How societies are born : governance in West Central Africa before 1600 /
Jan Vansina

      p.   cm.

Includes bibliographical references and index.

   ISBN 0-8139-2279-8 (cloth : alk. paper)

   1. Africa, Sub-Saharan—Politics and government. 2. Africa, Central—Politics and
government. 3. Tribal government—Africa, Sub-Saharan. 4. Tribal government—Africa,
Central. 5. Political anthropology—Africa, Sub-Saharan. 6. Political anthropology—
Africa, Central. I. Title.

DT352.65.V355 2004

967′.01—dc22

2004001001

TO BEATRIX, DAVID, AND JOE
FOR DECADES OF FRIENDSHIP AND SUPPORT

CONTENTS

ILLUSTRATIONS

TABLES

FIGURE

ACKNOWLEDGMENTS

AS BEFITS A WORK BASED MAINLY ON EXISTING PUBLICATIONS, THE primary institutional contribution to its elaboration came from a library, the Memorial Library of the University of Wisconsin–Madison and especially its interlibrary loan service. In particular, I thank Dr. David Henige, who helped this internetless person week after week, month after month, to obtain the interlibrary publications required. Quite literally, without his input this book might never have been written. In addition, the University helped to bear the cost for the maps, which were prepared for publication by its Cartographic Laboratory.

Years ago, Dr. Kathleen Smythe, then my research assistant, wondered whether any of the mass of materials she was tracking down for me in the library about Angola would ever be used and to what purpose. Now she knows and she can also appreciate how helpful she has been. Over the years, colleagues in various fields related to history have shared documents and insights with me. They are Professors and Doctors Yvonne Bastin, Robert J. Papstein, Konstantijn Petridis, Evá Sebestyén, and Zoe Strother, and in particular Professor James Denbow, who not only helped me with unpublished materials about his archaeological research in the Tsodilo Hills but also took time out to read and comment on the relevant sections concerning Divuyu and Nqoma.

I owe even more to the trio of friends to whom this book is dedicated, namely, Beatrix Heintze, David Henige, and Joseph C. Miller. The first and the last of these are perhaps the foremost scholars of Angola's history in early times. They both read and commented on a first rough sketch or raw draft of the whole project, assured me it was a worthwhile endeavor, and urged me to continue with it. I can only hope that the final product will not disappoint them. As to David Henige, the well-known editor of *History in Africa,* it is his lifelong passion about the nature of evidence and the rules that should govern its use that must be acknowledged here. Our frequent discussions on various points affecting this book sometimes sounded to me rather as if Moses had dropped in for a reminder or two about one of the commandments. While this book is clearly not up to David's theoretical standards, it certainly benefitted a great deal from our discussions.

CONVENTIONS ON SPELLING AND CITING DATES

SPELLING: African words are written according to the following rules: Place names are spelled according to the national conventions as shown in the *Times Atlas of the World*. In the case of rivers that cross national boundaries, the following spelling has been chosen: *Cunene* (not *Kunene*), *Kasai* (not *Cassai*), *Kwango* (not *Cuango*), *Kwenge* (not *Cuenge*), *Kwilu* (not *Cuilo*), *Loange* (not *Luangue*), *Lungue-Bungo* (not *Lungwebungu*), Okavango (not *Cubango*).

Personal and ethnic names have been rendered by the conventions of the Africa alphabet of the International African Institute without any indication of tone. For the Bantu languages, nouns begin with a class prefix. The prefixes for populations usually are class 1 *mu-* (singular) and class 2 *ba-* or *a-* (plural). In line with a convention observed in nearly all scholarly works, *mu-* and *ba-* are omitted in ethnic designations but all other classes and other features prefixed to the main stem are maintained. Hence Kongo instead of *mukongo,* Kwanyama instead of *Ovakwanyama* or *Nyama* (the form parses as *o+va+kwa+nyama*), but *Ovimbundu,* not *Mbundu,* because the class is 7/8. This word refers to the inhabitants of the Benguela highland. But since *Mbundu* also refers to a different ethnic group living in the Cuanza basin, an exception to the rule has been made for the latter. They are *Ambundu* rather than *Mbundu.*

The names of languages are spelled according to the common conventions followed in the main linguistic sources cited. Usually, these names are cited without prefix: e.g., *Kongo* not *Kikongo, Kwangali* not *Rukwangali,* but when the prefix is a nasal, the nasal is cited—hence *Nkhumbi,* not *Khumbi.* The convention also distinguishes between the two *Mbundu* by using *Umbundu* for the language of the *Ovimbundu* and *Kimbundu* for the language of the *Ambundu.*

Other words in African languages are transcribed in the Africa alphabet with the following additions and restrictions, all of which refer to Bantu languages. Nouns are followed by the numbers of their classes. So as to not con-

fuse the reader, they are always cited in the prefix class for the singular if there
is one—even when the word refers to a plural. In addition, nouns are usually followed by one or two numbers, which refer to their classes. Hence *mu-
tumbu* (3) followed by 3/4 and not the plural *mitumbu* (4). Sometimes it is
useful to cite a noun without its prefix. In that case, the root is preceded by
a hyphen, e.g., *-tumbu* 3/4. Where it is relevant to the discussion only, semantic high tone is marked with an acute accent. With one or two necessary
exceptions, marked by a grave accent, low tone is not marked. Although contemporary Bantu languages in the study area do not distinguish between
vowels of the second and the third degree, proto-Bantu did and some other
languages still do. Where necessary, therefore, the two fully closed vowels are
rendered as *i̧* and *u̧* to distinguish them from the more open *i* and *u*. Reconstructed linguistic forms are rendered in the Africa alphabet and marked
with an asterisk (*). Nouns are accompanied by classes: e.g., *-*ntu* 1/2 "person, people."

DATES: Dates before our era are followed by BCE. Dates in our era are left
wholly unmarked unless confusion could arise from doing so, in which case
they are marked as CE.

Carbon 14 dates are approximations covering a range of years. By convention (and not because such a date would be more likely to be correct!),
the single date that is given represents the midpoint of its range at 67 percent or 99 percent certainty. The range can be added to the date in brack-
ets, usually as a + or – figure. In addition, every carbon 14 date needs to be
calibrated in order to correspond to a calendar date. Several calibrations have
been used in the past, the latest one being "southern hemisphere" (SH).
Nearly all the dates from Namibia and Botswana cited in this book are calibrated SH while most of the others have been calibrated by various earlier
methods. Still, all dates are cited, whatever the specific calibration applied to
them as ca. (*circa*) followed by the date. Uncalibrated dates are distinguished
from the above in that they are followed by "bc" or "ad" set in lowercase letters. The distinction between calibrated and uncalibrated dates is relevant
since calibrated dates with an SH correction for the first and early second
millennia of our era tend to be over a century later than the raw or uncorrected calibrated dates. Given all these factors, too much precision can be
spurious and it is usually better to discuss the chronology in terms of centuries rather than years—a situation which also accounts for seeming in-
consistencies, such as "ca. 722 ad" and a little later "in the ninth century."

HOW SOCIETIES ARE BORN

INTRODUCTION

As stars are born, so are societies, and this is a story about such a birth. It tells us how different West Central African societies emerged from the small foraging communities that preceded them and how they then grew to become what they were by 1600. It is a story worth telling for several reasons. First, the period before the sixteenth century has been hitherto neglected by historians, nearly all of whom have been content to take the societies described by the first Portuguese reports on the coast as a given or as a starting point without asking themselves how they came to be what they then were.[1] To some extent, the lack of sources, written and oral, is to blame for this situation, although it should not prevent one from trying to find other sources of evidence and tap them to discover how these societies were formed and developed later on. Hence it is useful to present a book that provides an introduction to the history of this long early period. This study draws attention to the issues involved, lays out the available information, and proposes a set of interpretations that can be proved or disproved by future archaeological and linguistic research, research that—when it comes—will in turn undoubtedly extend available knowledge, introduce new questions, and render this book obsolete, but not, one hopes, before having helped prime the pump of knowledge.

Moreover, a study of early African history should be very welcome, for, as David Birmingham puts it: "In order to understand fully the history of the centuries between 1400 and 1870 with which this volume is primarily concerned it is necessary to explore a remoter past, when the ancestors of those farming people won their living by gathering wild forest foods, by

---

1. With the exception of a general overview by David Birmingham, "Society," pp. 1–29, and some historians of Kongo and of Ndongo (the main kingdom of the Ambundu) who went back into the fifteenth or even into the fourteenth century in search of the origins of these kingdoms. See, for instance, John Thornton, "The Origins," pp. 89–120, and Joseph Calder Miller, *Kings and Kinsmen.*

hunting savanna game, and by netting fish."[2] Such a work should be all the more welcome because the pursuit of early African history in general has been rather neglected by historians of Africa and sometimes scorned as "uninteresting."[3] This dismissive attitude is worrisome and reminds one of colonial times. Hence, it is good and quite useful to have a book about an early period that reminds historians not just that such periods exist but that only the knowledge of earlier history yields the right flavor to interpretation of all subsequent history. Just as a more balanced evaluation of the Rwandan genocide can be reached only once its antecedents in Rwanda's eighteenth- and nineteenth-century history are taken into account, so too a proper evaluation of the history of West Central Africa from the advent of the Atlantic slave trade and the foundation of the Portuguese colony in Angola onward requires full knowledge of the previous era.

Granted, then, that a history of these early periods is both needed and useful, why focus on governance? Because, as a well-known Arab leader might put it: "The history of governance is the mother of all history!" Common governance creates and maintains societies, which, in turn, form the matrix in which much else flows. Any genuine society is larger than a single community and cannot exist without some form of governance to unite different communities into a larger whole. A common society also presupposes common goals, a common legitimacy, based on a common worldview, which gives a framework for common therapeutic practices, while common leadership also fosters common artistic tastes. All this makes the study of that governance which creates society a priority.

The rise of different societies and cultures in West Central Africa before the wider Atlantic world intrusively broke the relative isolation of the area in the seventeenth century is a fascinating story.[4] This study traces their growth from the time, two thousand years and some centuries ago, when every community was a society, or rather when structured societies did not as yet exist, at least not in terms of a "society" defined as a fully cohesive aggregate of people larger than a single small local community. Certainly, be-

2. Birmingham, "Society," p. 4.

3. Among the few exceptions, see the outstanding work by David Lee Schoenbrun, *A Green Place, A Good Place.* The present book complements my earlier *Paths,* although on some points my views have changed somewhat since then.

4. Although the first contacts with Portuguese traders near present-day Luanda date from before 1507, most of the area was affected only in the seventeenth century. By then European beads from the Atlantic had found their way as far away from the coast as Vungu Vungu on the lower Okavango. See Edwin N. Wilmsen, *Land,* pp. 66, 76, 88, and B. H. Sandelowsky, "Kapako and Vungu Vungu," pp. 60–61 (ca. 1630).

fore that time individuals entertained personal relationships with individuals from neighboring communities through marriage, change of residence, and some exchange of commodities, but these relationships did not entail any enduring cooperation between their communities or any collective decision making concerning matters of mutual concern. Horizons remained very limited. Local communities did not unite and form a single, fully fledged society until common overarching institutions of governance were formed. These institutions then knitted a number of communities together into a unit distinct from others and served to regulate their internal relationships on mutual concerns such as conflict resolution, common defense against aggression by foreigners, or cooperation on specific matters such as the organization of a common dry-season hunt with bushfires. Once these institutions of governance came into being, society was born.

By the seventeenth century there were still a few places in West Central Africa where "society" equaled a local community comprising less than fifty people, but, in general, societies comprised several hundred people or more settled in a cluster of village communities. There were even a few places where a single society encompassed thousands, even tens of thousands, while at least one of them encompassed well over a hundred thousand people distributed over hundreds of settled communities within a single kingdom. Such increases in scale over time are of great significance historically because the larger an internally cohesive society is, the greater the frequency of internal intercommunication; the larger the common pool of experience, know-how, and innovative ideas; the more occurrences of innovation and the greater the potential for change. Hence, in a larger society, the pace at which change occurs may well accelerate faster than is the case in smaller societies. Examining the emergence and development of common institutions of governance which underlie such increases in social scale is particularly interesting because the processes of enlargement of scale followed three different pathways. It will not do to simply assume that all of them were but the outcome of a single automatic evolutionary process from "simple" to "complex."[5] Let us, rather, ask the following questions: what were the features of the dynamics responsible for producing long-term historical change along three (and only three) well-defined pathways rather than, say, at random; and how did such dynamics produce the main features found in the

---

5. For sub-Saharan Africa as a whole, Susan Keech McIntosh (*Beyond Chiefdoms*) convincingly refutes the earlier claims by neo-evolutionary theorists that complexity was always achieved by a single stereotyped passage from band to uncentralized "tribe" to centralized chiefdoms or towns.

existing societies around 1600? Clearly, focusing on institutions of governance is necessary; this book attempts to meet that need.[6]

Sources

History must be based on evidence. How banal . . . and how true. Evidence
is derived from sources which themselves either harken back to the period
under discussion or, when of later vintage, provide at least reliable information about that period. Yet the usual sources are lacking before about
1500, for neither written nor oral materials go back far enough in time to
document all but the very tail end of the time span under consideration here.
Only archaeological evidence directly documents it, but both modern linguistic and biological data testify indirectly to those times. Languages are
legacies from the past (one may think of them as long-term oral traditions)
and historical linguistics allow us to reconstruct many of their features in a
remote past. Modern biological data, whether they apply to plants, animals
or humans, can be wholly extrapolated into the past because the requirements of specific organisms do not change over time. Unlike other data, they
need no further discussion.[7] Written ethnographic descriptions are available
only from the late sixteenth century onward. The social institutions and cultural patterns they describe obviously cannot be extrapolated without further ado into a more remote past. Yet they constitute the outcome of that
past and are essential in providing the context of meaning which attaches to
the linguistic forms with histories that can be traced. Moreover, because
these descriptions make it evident which social institutions and which cultural practices were of major significance in the seventeenth century, they
also help us to focus on the history of their antecedents.

Since most of this work is based on archaeological and linguistic evidence
combined with later ethnographic information, the reader needs to know
more about these three sets of data. A great many sites are reported from
West Central Africa, especially from Angola. One might therefore expect archaeology to contribute a great deal of evidence but that, unfortunately, is
not yet the case because far too little in-depth research has been undertaken
in the area. Even in Angola, many sites are known only from hasty surface
collections or from digging a few test pits with little stratigraphic control and

6. As I did in *Paths,* p. xii: "It [the book] focuses on institutional history, on the past
of societies."

7. For sources in general, see Jan Vansina, *Paths,* pp. 7–31, and Schoenbrun, *A Green
Place,* pp. 3–61.

without much further laboratory analysis of the items recovered. In addition, dating remains often unreliable or very tentative because radiocarbon dates are lacking for many sites. Even when such dates have been obtained from specific objects, such as charcoal somewhere on the site, the associations of these objects with the specific items one wants to date are often merely inferred. These items might or might not be contemporary with the dated objects. One must therefore agree with Manuel Gutierrez that, pending better controlled excavations, most of the available data yield very little evidence. As he concludes, "These twin results: wealth of archaeological remains allied to the poverty of the methods used in archaeological research, make it very difficult, for example, to elaborate the history of the long human occupation of the Angolan territory."[8]

Yet there have been some reliable, indeed sometimes exemplary, excavations in West Central Africa. Those undertaken in the Lower Congo are particularly useful, as are those conducted in northwestern Botswana's Tsodilo Hills by many, especially by James Denbow and Edwin Wilmsen, and in Namibia by John Kinahan and others. Furthermore, decades of research in East Central Africa, especially in Zambia, Katanga, eastern Botswana, and Zimbabwe have yielded indirect evidence about West Central Africa as well. The resulting information helps establish a chronological framework for the entire time span studied here and provides a context to interpret many of the fragmentary data stemming from the area itself. This procedure generates hypotheses that can then be tested in the future on the many known rich sites in Angola now that the war has really ended, . . . and once mine-clearing operations make it possible.

Nearly all linguistic evidence used here derives from the technique usually known as "words and things."[9] This operates by comparing words from different languages with the same form and related meanings. Such comparisons allow one to learn much about the history of such words. When a given word occurs throughout a set of modern languages known to be related, it is most probable that all variations were inherited from their common ancestral language. But when the word occurs in a number of unrelated modern languages, then these tongues must have transferred (i.e., borrowed) it at some time in the past from one of the languages in the set.[10] An essential precondition for the application of this technique is that the overall historical

8. Manuel Gutierrez, *L'Art pariétal de l'Angola*, p. 40.
9. Schoenbrun, *A Green Place*, p. 6, calls it "words and meanings."
10. See Christopher Ehret, "Language and History," pp. 276–80, for the most systematic presentation in linguistic terms.

genetic relationship between the languages involved in the comparison must be known. In our case, this means that the technique can be applied to Bantu but not to Khoisan languages, because the comparative historical study of Khoisan is not yet sufficiently developed. All the Bantu languages in the area belong to a single genetic subunit of Bantu, labeled Njila,[11] a subunit with a known relationship to other Bantu subunits and with internal subdivisions that are solidly established at all levels.[12] Thus a systematic lexical comparison of words relevant to this study has been carried out for all the Njila and other Bantu languages (but not Khoisan) in which they are attested.[13]

Some readers may not be very familiar with this technique and may well find themselves disoriented by the concrete evidence presented, usually in the form of footnotes; consequently, they may welcome some guidance to help them to evaluate such cases. Hence the additional information about "words and things" which follows. The main principle underlying the application of the technique is that if a given word is confined to a set of languages that are all part of the same genetic unit, it stems from the time when the ancestral language of that unit was still spoken and it belongs to that language. For example, when a reader is told that *kinama* 7/8 "leg" occurs in Kimbundu, Lubolo, Kisama, Songo, Imbangala, and Mbui (no reliable data exist for Ndembu), a glance at the genetic classification of languages will show that it thus occurs in the Kwanza block of languages and nowhere else. Hence *-nama* 7/8 must be proto-Kwanza and an innovation in that ancestral language. But when a given word occurs in languages belonging to different units that are not directly genetically related, it must be a loan or transfer. For example *Cínáwééj* 7, the Rund term for the supreme being or for a gentleman, is already attested ca. 1840. In Kimbundu tales of the late nineteenth century, one finds *Kimalawezi* 7 or *Kimanawezi* 7, which was the name of some "mythical dignitary, emperor, king." Kimbundu borrowed the word from Rund and adapted it to its own phonology and form of word class. An independent invention of such a complex form in the two languages is im-

11. The name derives from the innovation *njila* "birds," which is typical for this unit. Earlier authors have sometimes labeled it "Southwestern Bantu" or "Western Savanna." The former label is not satisfactory because it has also been used for only one of the subunits in the unit, while the second one erroneously evokes a relationship between this unit and the unit of Bantu languages lying to its east.

12. For the evidence, see the Appendix.

13. The lexical sources of these data are listed by language in section II of the References. Footnotes in the text mention only the specific languages in which attestations are found. Interested readers can then find the precise source of the information for that language in the References. A lack of sufficient Khoisan lexicons prevented us from checking whether these forms were also found in those languages.

probable as there were trading links between Kimbundu and Rund speakers since ca. 1750 or earlier, and the direction of the loan is indicated both by the fluctuation of the form in Kimbundu and the very imprecision of the meaning there. External evidence strongly suggests this is a borrowing from the early or mid-nineteenth century.

But the reader soon discovers from the evidence presented here that the application of the main principle and the distinction between ancestral and borrowed is frequently not as obvious as the examples just cited indicate. Thus one will encounter cases where a word may be ancestral in one genetic unit but spread at a later time to languages belonging to other units, thus being both ancestral and a loan; cases where a word may be such an early loan that it spread between different proto-languages without, however, being ancestral to the unit of a higher order which groups those proto-languages together; cases where a word may have been innovated in an ancient genetic unit only to be lost later by subsequent innovation in one of the several genetic subunits which derived from it; or cases where an innovation occurred in a language recently, well after even the lowest genetic units were in place, and then spread into neighboring languages from a different genetic unit in such a way that eventually all the languages of that genetic unit shared it, thus leaving the mistaken impression that the innovation occurred in the proto-language of the unit which actually borrowed it.

In many cases, however, further internal and external indications are available to aid correct interpretation of the data. Attention is drawn here to the two most common indicators that have been used in this study, namely, internal evidence through the use of etymologies and external evidence through the use of relevant biological data. In Bantu languages, nouns are usually innovated from existing verbs or from nouns existing in other word classes, while new verbs can be coined by using verbal extensions or by direct derivation from a noun.[14] If the etymology of a word shows that it was derived from another form with a related meaning and that this other form occurs only in a single language or subgroup within the full range of distribution of the form studied, then that language or subgroup must be the original place where that word first appeared.[15] Since the origins of most domesticated plants or animals are known from biological data, it stands to

14. In Bantu languages, common "roots" often do underlie many different verbs or nouns through the operation of verbal extensions and different sets of noun classes involving some shift in meaning as new words are coined. See Thilo Schadeberg, "Progress in Bantu Lexical Reconstruction," pp. 183–95.

15. The direction of a transfer can also be established by the deformations (skewing) its form sometimes undergoes in the language that borrows or when it exhibits a

reason that the origins of any word designating such a plant or animal which was introduced from elsewhere should lie at the closest point in its area of distribution to the place from where the plant or animal spread into the area. Even in these cases, caution is required, for people sometimes called a new plant or animal by a word they applied to another plant or animal with which they were familiar. For instance, the word used for one type of yam was later applied to the water yam when that plant became available and later still to manioc when that plant was introduced.

The greatest weakness of the technique of "words and things" is its chronological imprecision. The successive genetic splits producing a succession of language groups provide a rough relative chronology by which to seriate items that originated in the ancestral languages which flourished between splits. Linguistics alone cannot provide an absolute chronology for each split, although some linguists, especially Christopher Ehret, dispute this. They use "glottochronology," a technique which dates splits between languages or language groups by calculating the percentage of words they have in common from a given basic vocabulary on the assumption that, over the long run, the rate of replacement of basic words in any language is the same. Most linguists today, however, reject the validity of this underlying assumption and hence of glottochronology itself.[16] In the past I have used this technique, if only to give "ballpark" dates until something better came along, but I am now convinced that glottochronology is invalid and should not be used at all.[17] Hence the genetic structure of the Njila group yields only a relative chronology. Most absolute dates can be obtained only from archaeological evidence, that is, evidence which tells us nothing about the languages spoken by those whose material traces are found.

Transfers pose even greater chronological problems because, in practice, linguistic indicators do not allow for a chronological seriation of the borrowed words which fall between two genetic splits. All of these tend to col-

---

borrowed phoneme such as, for instance, an initial "b" in Rund, which does not otherwise occur in the language. But in the absence of thorough comparative and internal analyses of the languages involved, both these situations remain difficult to find. Many of the analyses needed to apply these techniques are still lacking for the languages considered here.

16. For a spirited but in the end unconvincing defense, see Ehret, "Language," pp. 287–89.

17. For my earlier position, see *Paths,* p. 16. What ultimately convinced me is Michael Mann's conclusive demonstration that different statistical procedures yield different percentages of cognation and hence different dates (see Bastin, Coupez, and Mann, *Continuity and Divergence*).

lapse into a single set. But because the periods between language splits are usually many centuries long, considerable confusion can result.[18] This is rather unfortunate because transfers play such a prominent role in this book. Since the last major genetic splits probably occurred before the onset of the last millennium (see Appendix), nearly every transfer which occurred since then belongs to a single set and internal evidence cannot tell us which among the words involved is earlier or later than the others, a situation which leaves us with a millennium of imprecision! External evidence derived from oral or written sources often helps to unravel transfers made during the last two or three centuries, but in the absence of such evidence for earlier times, one can only constitute sets of words coined during this period with related meanings to propose a tentative sequence for their relative emergence and test it. Take, for instance, the Middle Angolan words for "lineage head," "territorial chief," and "sir" (a deferential term of address for a chief). Is "lineage head" the earliest of the set as one would imagine? Further examination of the relevant forms rather supports this view because most terms for "lineage head" are innovations from the ancient kinship terminology, while the two other words are innovations from forms the meanings of which are wholly unconnected with kin or neighborhood groups, namely, "chief" from "to arbitrate" or "to surpass" and "sir" from "to be wise." While such findings do not constitute absolute proof of the proposed sequence, they do give it rather strong support.

The above information is provided with the hope that it will help readers unfamiliar with such materials to follow and evaluate the concrete evidence for "words and things" used in this book without being bewildered. At first the information given in each concrete instance is best handled in a step-by-step approach. When such an instance is met, the reader will first examine the distribution of the items under discussion (and assume that the author has provided a complete distribution insofar as the sources allow), then check with the Appendix whether the languages involved form a single genetic unit or not, then check whether any etymologies or external evidence are provided, then evaluate the conclusions reached by the author, and finally decide whether these are justified or not.

No complete set of full ethnographic descriptions establishing a single overview of the whole area at a single date before the early 1900s exists, so

18. In theory, a detailed study of internal change within each language should allow one to seriate loanwords between moments of language split. Yet not only do we lack such studies for all the languages involved except for Rund, but, rather than preserve them in their original shape, borrowers also tend to "translate" transferred forms into their own phonology and morphology, thus erasing the relevant chronological indicators.

at first glance it does not seem possible to establish a chronological baseline earlier than that.[19] On the other hand, even the earliest writings contain some information about economies, polities, and religion, while the earliest comprehensive ethnography was composed in the 1650s and 1660s by Giovanni Antonio Cavazzi, whose work concerned the Ambundu.[20] Yet a comparably full description for the Ovimbundu of the Benguela plateau, or *planalto,* was first composed in the 1850s.[21] By that time, significant ethnographic observations had also been gathered about the Herero of Namibia and the Nkhumbi of the lower Cunene.[22] In the following decades, full descriptions become available first of peoples of eastern Angola and later of those living in southern Congo (Kinshasa).[23] Nonetheless, one has to wait until the 1970s to obtain such a description for the Kongo Dinga of the Kasai and Lweta Rivers.[24] Still, once one takes oral traditions into account, excluding traditions of genesis, which are not reliable as historical sources, the information available reaches into the seventeenth century. Hence one can set up a common chronological baseline in that century after all.[25] This is important be-

19. The earliest more or less solid, complete ethnographic overview for Angola (and thus for most of the area) is José de Oliveira Ferreira Diniz, *Populações indígenas de Angola.*

20. I do not cite it in the rare original but in the well-annotated Portuguese translation by Graziano de Leguzzano, *Descrição histórica dos três reinos Congo, Matamba e Angola.*

21. Ladislaus Magyar, *Reisen,* translated from the unpublished Hungarian by Johann Hunfalvy.

22. J. Irle's *Die Herero* is based on his own observations since 1871 and on those gathered by his Rhenish missionary predecessors since 1845. The trader António Nogueira settled among the Nkhumbi in 1852 and lived with them for a decade. Although his *A Raça negra* is not organized as such, its contents and his remarks elsewhere amount to a formal ethnography. The first formal monograph for the neighboring and related Nyaneka is by A. Lang and C. Tastevin, *La tribu des Va-Nyaneka,* the content of which consists mostly of notes gathered before 1890 by the missionary Dekindt and later expanded by Lang.

23. For the core of the Lunda Commonwealth in the northeast, the earliest systematic ethnography is Paul Pogge, *Im Reiche* (data gathered in 1875), but the richest observations were made by Henrique Augusto Dias de Carvalho in the 1880s and published in a series of volumes. See, for instance, his *Ethnographia e História Tradicional dos Povos do Lunda.*

24. See Joseph Ceyssens's *Pouvoir et parenté.*

25. Reliable oral traditions and a few written data about the Ambundu lands reach back to 1500 or a little earlier. On the planalto and in the south, they include most of the seventeenth century. In the northeast, they reach back to ca. 1600 for the Rund and, by implication, the Lweta speakers. In Mixico, and among the Pende of the middle Kwilu, they reach back to dates within the seventeenth century. While there are some written data for the lower Kwango-Kwilu region from the seventeenth century, information that refers unambiguously to the lands of the middle Kwilu there appears only by the late eighteenth century.

cause by the end of that century at the latest the new Atlantic trade began to exert its influence on nearly everyone in the entire area.

Although the reliability of these ethnographic descriptions varies from author to author and is not uniform throughout but varies a great deal from point to point, most of the ones that were written before the standard ethnographic genre became prevalent are of surprisingly good quality.[26] Although most authors generalize their statements, their ethnographies are often accompanied or supplemented by information about actual persons and concrete situations. Many were written by persons with several years of local experience and with considerable command or at least interest in the local language. Still, each author comes from his (there were no women among them—it shows in the databases!) own professional background and has prejudices and foibles that must be considered in any evaluation of their trustworthiness. Most were missionaries, but there were also some (military) administrators, such as António Cadornega in the seventeenth century or Henrique de Carvalho in the nineteenth, traders such as A. F. Nogueira, the occasional physician (for example, Paul Pogge), or the professional explorer. To assess their work one cannot be content with just this. One must look into the particular background of each author and discern the effects produced by his nationality, upbringing, education, professional experience, literary sophistication, and personal opinions expressed in the work or elsewhere.[27] With regard to specific items one should, wherever possible, cross-check such information with data derived from other relatively contemporary authors, which, to my surprise and delight, has quite often been possible and fruitful. It turns out that despite the diversity of the authors and the spirit of their times (*Zeitgeist*) most of these ethnographies can serve as a solid basis of information, a finding all the more important in that the full meanings of the words used in "words and things" stem from these ethnographies and that ultimately the quality of semantic comparisons also depends on the quality of these underlying sources.

Constructing a History

The first step in the research strategy used for this study was to establish both an initial situation and a final situation to be compared with the first one. In

26. For a general introduction to the issues involved, see Beatrix Heintze and Adam Jones, *European Sources for Sub-Saharan Africa before 1900,* and for this area, see Vansina, *Paths,* pp. 23–31.

27. For some nineteenth-century explorers, including Pogge, see Heintze, *Ethnographische Aneignungen,* and Johannes Fabian, *Out of Our Minds.*

this case, the initial situation was the time of the introduction of the first ceramics and of the first attempts at horticulture. It was reconstructed by using
the relevant proto-Njila vocabulary. Indeed that is the major reason why the
areal extent of "West Central Africa" is nearly identical to that of the Njila
languages in this book.[28] As the study progressed, it became increasingly obvious that the initial proto-Njila speakers were but a tiny fraction of the total
population in the area and therefore that the initial conditions were not representative for the great majority of people living at that time—very little
can be said about that majority for lack of sufficient linguistic evidence.
Later, Njila-speaking societies came to include an overwhelming proportion
of the whole population as the result of language shift and fusions between
proto-Njila–speaking communities and others.

The final situation was the onset of the seventeenth century before most
of the area came to be profoundly influenced by trade from the Atlantic
world.[29] It was reconstructed in part from contemporary written ethnographic information and in part by oral traditions of later vintage. By then
most of the inhabitants of West Central Africa were farmers and herders and
were organized in societies of varying scale and of considerable diversity. Yet
significant numbers of non–Njila-speaking foragers were still roaming over
the southern half of the area and Njila speakers were still encroaching on
their lands in the southeast of the area.

Once established, the initial and final baselines provided a framework in
which the available evidence could be ordered. The "outcome" could then
be used as a foundation for "upstreaming."[30] This technique derives from the
observation that any situation observed at the end of a period must be the
outcome of a process that started from the known earlier, simpler situation.
Hence the outcome contains clues which can allow us to describe that
process. However, to reconstruct the whole sequence backwards from the
final outcome to the initial situation yields only a view of what logically
should have happened, not necessarily of what actually happened. It is not

28. Although the savannas of West Central Africa also encompass the Kingdom of
Kongo and the lower Kasai basin where languages other than Njila languages were spoken, these societies, languages, and cultures were closely linked with those of their
neighbors in the equatorial African rain forests. Hence they were included in *Paths* and
we do not need to consider them again except for their interactions with Njila-speaking
peoples.

29. The economic and political history of the area after the seventeenth century is
well known from a host of studies. The best introduction to this period still remains that
of Joseph Calder Miller, *Way of Death*.

30. William N. Fenton, "Ethnohistory and Its Problems," pp. 1–23.

evidence. The evidence comes from both archaeological data and the testimony from "words and things" and it must be ordered chronologically. In the absence of other means, archaeology has provided enough carbon 14 dates to establish a full temporal grid, albeit a rough one, since the smallest "moment" it can discern is only a little less than a century as even the best carbon 14 dates available do not allow for more precision than that. Historians accustomed to a grid that dates "moments" to the year or even the day may well be disconcerted at first. Yet they soon discover that the rough archaeological grid works perfectly well for the purposes for which it is used, namely, to provide a seriation of various technological innovations and to date the appearance first of stable villages and later of towns. These data can then be correlated with the technological information and the social developments indicated by the "words and things" method. In this fashion one obtains a consistent narrative history, despite a plethora of remaining lacunae. This constructs a narrative which constitutes a hypothesis that can be tested in the future by the addition of further evidence derived both from archaeological evidence and from further linguistic analysis.

A history of this sort runs the risk of becoming a mere narrative of successive technological introductions that "diffused" or "spread" into the area—one whereby social institutions evolve more or less predictably from small-scale social groups to larger and more intricate ones. Yet such a narrative would be spurious because it excludes people. After all, the agents of historical change are individual persons. Technologies do not spread by themselves like an oil slick, nor do social institutions unfold their latent potential automatically. One should never forget the doings of human actors. Technologies are adopted and institutions built through concrete decisions and then actions taken by conscious individuals. Individuals decide to imitate something new seen elsewhere, to try out something new which one has figured out for one's self or merely to join a person or group who advocates such a novelty. In each case, these decisions involve speculations about a better future and include some thoughts about potential side effects or drawbacks. Novelties must be worked out through trial and error until their advantages and disadvantages become fully evident to those who are affected by them. At that point, these people then make a choice. Hence the weight given in this work to the pros and cons of introducing new technologies as well as the attention given to etymologies linked to words denoting social innovations since, usually, etymologies tell us something about what the actors imagined about the innovation in question. Moreover, decisions are always choices and whenever a clue can be found, one should think of such choices not just in terms of an imaginary standard person representing a whole community or society, but also in terms of one who represents appropriate subgroups within that community. Thus certain choices affect mainly women, others mainly elders or just elites, and so on. In rare cases it is even possible to consider the impact of a decision on individual careers. No doubt such an approach will always remains fairly iffy, but in the absence of concrete evidence about individuals and their actual doings, it may well be the only way to bring back actors into a record that has erased them.

The history of the area, as the sources allow one to reconstruct it, falls into two major periods; thus, this book is divided into two parts. During the first period, which ended around 800–1000 CE, a series of identical technological innovations, relating to the production of food, were adopted everywhere and affected everyone in the area. These provided the necessary preconditions for different communities to construct societies of larger scale, either by becoming sedentary or by becoming nomadic herders of cattle and sometimes of sheep. The second period began after these technologies had been internalized and were leading to an increase in the scale and the internal intricacies of most societies in the region. In different parts of the area, various local societies then created their own larger scale social organizations by internal innovations, with the consequence of greater differentiation among them, a process known as divergence. However, as the internal intricacies of these societies increased further, neighboring societies in similar environmental conditions and with similar fundamental values began to copy various institutional features from each other and thus tended to become more and more similar over time, a process known as convergence.[31] The outcome of the tug-of-war between the dynamics of divergence and convergence was the emergence of the restricted number of regional patterns of governance attested to by or before the seventeenth century, the endpoint of this narrative.

The Stage

West Central Africa is limited by the masses of tropical rain forests to the north and the tropic of Capricorn to the south and extends eastward from the coast to about latitude 24°S (map 1).

31. New developments after 1600 were accompanied by convergence on such a scale that it tends to obscure what the social organization of the populations had been before 1600. Much of the observed social and cultural homogeneity in the region may well be recent, a creation of the forces unleashed from the eighteenth century onward. This situation makes the task of the historian particularly difficult because the flood of transfers generated by convergence after 1700 usually cannot be distinguished from those that occurred before 1700.

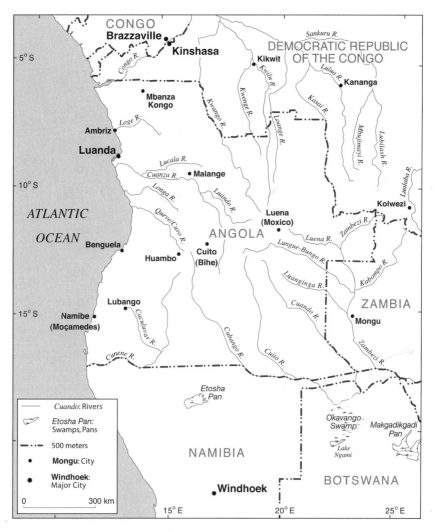

MAP 1. General Orientation

As the geological makeup of the environment changes only at a glacial rate, the major features of relief remained virtually unchanged over the entire period covered by this study (map 2). Its dominant characteristic are two high ridges above 1,500 meters or so. From a knot on the Benguela plateau, or *planalto*, one of these runs north to south and separates the coastal plains from the uplands of the interior, gradually in some places, by steep escarpments in others. The other ridge runs west to east and separates the basin of the Congo from the southward sloping lands toward the Okavango basin. This disposition generates the general direction of rivers which, interrupted

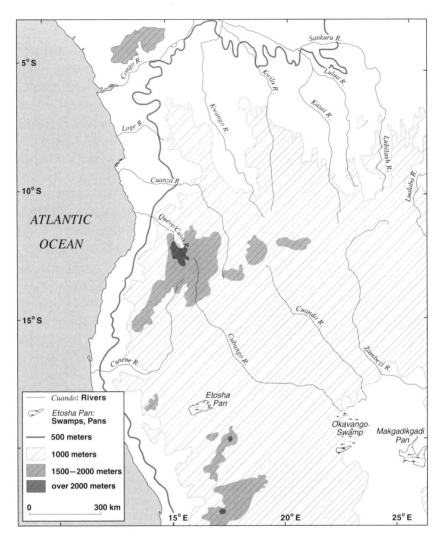

MAP 2. Relief

by waterfalls, flow either directly toward the coast, or for those in the deeper interior, from both sides of the interior ridge in a general north-south direction, whether south-to-north for the Kasai and its affluents, or north-to-south for the Cunene, Okavango, and Zambezi systems.

The most significant distinction between the soils of the area concerns their fertility and distinguishes between the gray or white sands, dubbed Kalahari Sands, found in much of the south and the east of the area and all others because Kalahari Sands are almost wholly unfit for agriculture (map 3).

While geological features were permanent over the period studied, cli-

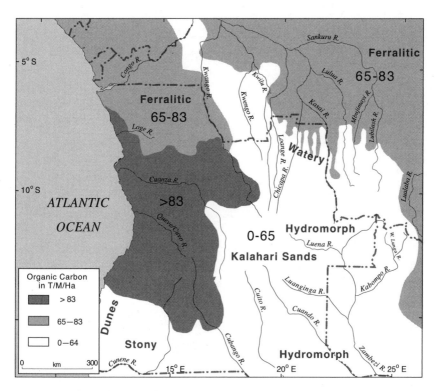

MAP 3. Soil Fertility

mates, determined by temperature and rainfall, have varied. Still, at all times, climate is accounted for by the position of the area on the globe, north of the tropic of Capricorn but well south of the Equator and due east of the south Atlantic and its cold Benguela current. Different climates succeed each other by latitude. Yet at each point the height above sea level influences the local temperatures and the degree of rainfall. The amount and the annual distribution of rainfall was crucial because most agriculture was rainfed. A seasonal monsoon originating in the southwest Atlantic regulates precipitation and divides the year into dry and wet seasons. From north to south, the duration of the main dry season becomes longer (map 4).

Moreover, the overall amount of precipitation per year, the amount of rainfall from year to year, and the date at which the monsoon sets in become more and more irregular, and hence less predictable, as one moves from north to south (map 5).

Because the amount of rain and its predictability are crucial to agriculture, the level of anxiety among farmers about rainfall also increases from north to south. The most crucial isohyetal line was the one of 700 milli-

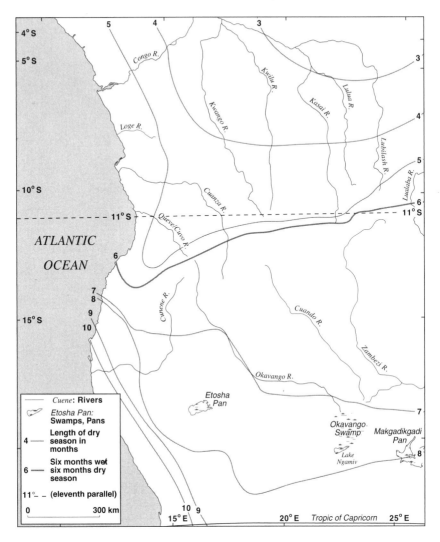

<small>ATLANTIC OCEAN</small>

MAP 4. Length of Dry Season

meters, below which rainfed agriculture is no longer possible, but the line of 1,200 millimeters was also significant because of its impact on types of vegetation. During wet phases in the past, both of these lines were located farther southward than they are now.

In general and as a first approximation, the vegetation of the area is also disposed in latitudinal belts (map 6). Going from north to south, one crosses first savannas or open woodlands, then denser dry *miombo* forests, then

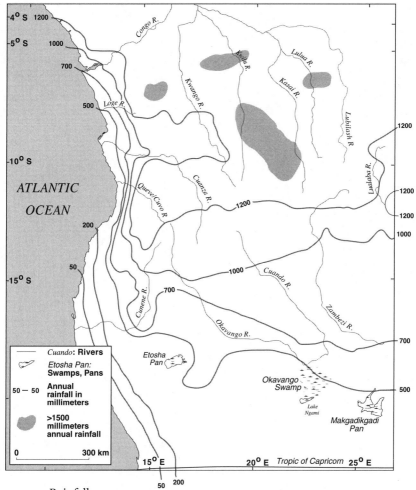

MAP 5. Rainfall

grasslands, and finally steppes. But near the coast this disposition is altered. There the cold Benguela current combined with the relief reduces rainfall so that desert appears in Namibia and parts of southern Angola while the steppes and grasslands reach much farther north along the coast than elsewhere.

Historically the most important boundaries have been around latitude 11°/12° S and latitudes 16°/17° S. South of the first one, domesticated palm trees and most cultivated yams would not grow while south of the second one exclusively rainfed agriculture becomes impossible. A closer look reveals

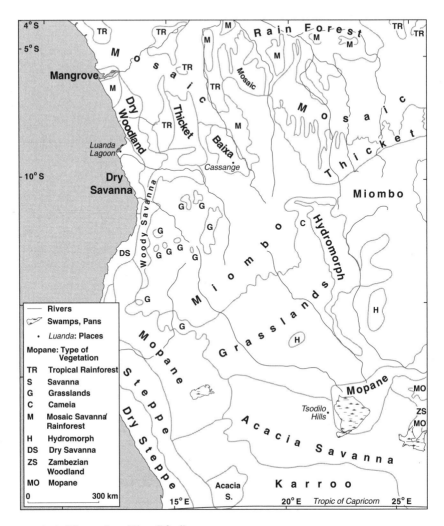

MAP 6. Vegetation (Simplified)

that the major groupings of vegetation are themselves internally diversified under the influence of more local physical situations.[32] They consist of sets of related microenvironments, a few of which became quite significant historically as they affected potential sources of food and the strategies used to exploit them. Thus the Luanda lagoons with their shellmiddens or the stands of *mongongo* nuts (*Rhicinodendron rautanenii* Schinz) in the southeast (for instance, at the Tsodilo sites in northwestern Botswana) and southwest were

32. See, for example, L. A. Grandvaux Barbosa, *Carta Fitogeográfica de Angola*.

already highly significant during the Late Stone Age. In later times, the different types of grasslands of the lower middle Cuanza, in the basin of Cassange, and around the Cameia, as well as the locally higher rainfall in the middle Kwilu and the lower Lweta regions also exerted a significant impact on the local populations.

But climate and vegetation change over time. In the north of the area covered by this study, the main climatic fluctuation during the period was the shift from a very wet period before 1000 BCE to a drier period which still perdures.[33] In the south, more precise information relates directly to the basin of the Okavango and the Kalahari immediately west of its delta. Indirectly, these data can be extrapolated for much of the planalto around the headwaters of the Okavango and for adjacent parts of the Kalahari but definitely not for the coastal areas or for the whole northern half of the area. At first, from about 500 BCE to ca. 900 CE, the climate was wet, perhaps wetter than it is now. Then followed first a drying interlude from 900–1200 CE and then a short wet period, around 1200 CE, after which the climate gradually became drier and then stabilized with very minor fluctuations around the state reported by 1950.[34] During the wetter episodes, the isoplethic line of 700 millimeters may have shifted several degrees farther south, perhaps even as far south as the northern edge of the delta, while the line of 1,200 millimeters probably shifted much less, by perhaps one or two degrees. More will be said on these potential shifts when we evaluate the effects of the environment on historical trends or events.

Besides these major shifts, significant climatic changes of durations shorter than a century but still encompassing several decades and affecting smaller regions were common but have not yet been documented in the area before 1600. These climate changes nonetheless did exert a dramatic impact on the life of the people subject to them; so did droughts or excessive rains lasting several years but often to a lesser degree. Moreover, when evaluating today's landscapes one must keep in mind that, during the period under study at least, humans have had greater effect than did climate change, especially in places of relatively dense and stable populations. But then, sometimes human action also induced changes in climate.[35]

33. J. Maley, "Conclusions de la quatrième partie," pp. 383–84.

34. See, for instance, James R. Denbow, "After the Flood," pp. 184–86, 196.

35. E.g., the case of Diosso near Loango where a sudden humid interlude occurred ca. 1350/1450. It only lasted a few decades and may or may not be the result of human action (deforestation). See Schwartz, Guillet, and Deschamps, "Études de deux flores forestières," pp. 290–92.

Finally, even the same environment did not always affect people in the same way because changing technologies altered the significance of land-scapes and natural resources. Sometimes technological change or a change in patterns of consumption led to the abandonment of old resources and/or the introduction of new ones. For instance, while the exploitation of mol-lusks around the Luanda lagoons has continued unabated ever since the Late Stone Age, the mining of specularite minerals in the Tsodilo Hills was aban-doned after dozens of centuries of intensive exploitation by foragers and food producers alike. At one time, this iron-holding mineral powder was highly prized as people rubbed it into their skins to enhance its appearance. But eventually that practice fell out of favor and specularite was no longer mined. Mastery of metallurgy led to the exploitation of copper and iron ores and the dissemination of these metals over huge distances. But truly inten-sive mining and smelting of iron ores flourished only in earnest after the in-troduction of a form of cereal agriculture, which created an insatiable de-mand for iron hoes. The effects of technological change reached much further than this, however; they also resulted in the transformation of social institutions to be discussed in the following chapters.

PART ONE IN THE BEGINNING THERE WERE ONLY FORAGERS in West Central Africa. They lived in small nomadic communities whose members communicated and intermarried with individuals from the outside but they did not develop any social aggregate larger than the community itself. Some time after 500 BCE, a few communities began to adopt a series of technological innovations which allowed them at first to expand the range of gathered foods that were edible and later to produce food rather than just gather it by practicing agriculture and/or the herding of domestic animals. This allowed them to aggregate in larger settlements and to become sedentary wherever farming made this possible. These new communities, sedentary or pastoral, were considerably larger than the foraging households had been and their members began to create new overarching institutions to bridge the social divide that existed between the different local communities. Such institutions allowed them to better cooperate with each other in some economic or social endeavors where this was advantageous to all of them. Such practices of common governance created genuine societies, that is, social aggregates larger than a seasonally unstable set of local households. By the ninth century CE or so, small societies were becoming the norm which opened the way to processes by which governance could become gradually more intricate and the scale of society could gradually increase to the situations described by outside observers from the sixteenth century onward.

Part One deals with the period from about 400 BCE to 900 CE, during which the basic innovations were adopted that made all the rest possible. It is divided into two chapters. The first one tells of the introduction of ceramics, horticulture, and the early use of metals over nearly a millennium before 500 CE, whereas the following chapter deals with the transformations wrought during the four following centuries by the introduction of cereal crops, a more intensive use of iron tools, large herds of cattle, corporate matrilineages, and dispersed matriclans.

1

PRELUDES

 WHEN THE EARLIEST SIGNS OF A SET OF NEW TECH-
nologies that would lead to the creation of larger and more
complex societies appeared during the second half of the last
millennium BCE, small communities of foragers were roaming the savannas,
woodlands, and steppes of West Central Africa south of the rain forests just
as they had done since times immemorial. The first harbingers of change
were the adoption of ceramics, accompanied or followed by that of horticulture and husbandry of small domestic stock. The use and fabrication of
metal objects followed half a millennium later. Compared with the pace of
change in earlier times, these innovations were abrupt, even if they unfolded
over some thirty generations, that is, over three-quarters of a millennium.
Indeed, at least in part of the area all three developments may well have occurred within a single lifetime.[1] Abrupt or not, the changes were radical. For
they concerned something essential: the preparation of food and its availability in a way which made its supply more reliable and eventually more
abundant. They also allowed communities which grew crops to become
sedentary and in the fullness of time they fostered population growth and
its aggregation into larger societies.

None of these technologies were invented by the inhabitants of the area.
All were demonstrably introduced from elsewhere, which makes one wonder whether they were carried there by foreign immigrants. One suspects
this all the more so because the Njila set of Bantu languages began to diffuse
into the area from the earlier part of this period onward. Proto-Njila speakers produced pottery, practiced horticulture, and kept goats. It would seem
logical to attribute the spread of these innovations as well as the later spread
of metallurgy to their expansion. But the matter is not that simple. At least
in the southernmost part of the area and well before the first Njila speakers
ever arrived there, foragers did adopt ceramics and the herding of sheep from

---

1. See Raymond Lanfranchi and Bernard Clist, eds., *Aux origines.*

other foragers who spoke languages related to theirs.[2] Could foragers then not have borrowed from other foragers elsewhere in the area as well without any immigration at all? We probably will never know for certain because archaeological sites do not disclose which language was spoken by those who once lived there.

Late–Stone Age Foragers

Humans first appeared in the record of West Central Africa well over a hundred thousand years ago and they have been present there ever since.[3] By the Late Stone Age, that is, from well over ten thousand years ago, their tools and their rock art are found all over the area wherever archaeologists or other specialists (such as geologists) have looked for them (map 7).[4]

What ordinary mortals see only as small scatters of ordinary stones, specialists discern as tools that can be studied, and they will search for and often find other debris, such as remnants of animal bones or shells others do not even notice. In contrast, larger telltale shards of pottery which dot later sites are more easily recognized by laypersons. Since few archaeologists worked in West Central Africa, one would therefore expect known Late–Stone Age sites to be quite rare. Yet the number of known sites is greater than expected, which suggests that there once were many more people in the area than the layperson now imagines. It is reasonable to think that the number of foragers by the end of the Late Stone Age was at least as large, and probably larger, than their number by the middle of the twentieth century, especially since pastoralists or farmers have long dispossessed foragers of their most productive lands. Thus, we may accept that several tens of thousands foragers or more lived in the area on the eve of the introduction of ceramics.[5]

2. See James Denbow and Edwin Wilmsen, "Advent," p. 234, 1509–10; Wilmsen, *Land,* p. 65; Ralph Vogelsang, "Archaeological Investigations," pp. 27–28. Rainer Vossen, "Studying the Linguistic and Ethno-history," pp. 24 and 33, indicates that proto-Khoe practiced some agriculture and pastoralism some two thousand years ago.

3. Carlos Ervedosa, *Arqueologia;* See also Gutierrez, *L'Art,* pp. 18–29, for a summary including maps.

4. See Ervedosa, *Arqueologia,* pp. 149–66, for a summary in Angola. So far only one rock painting has been directly dated. See Guttierez, *L'Art,* pp. 190–92, re Opeleva (Tchitundo Hulo), where the paintings date from the first century CE.

5. In the south, Manuel Viegas Guerreiro, in *Boximanes,* pp. 35–37, recalls the persistent underestimates made before the 1960s and estimates that there were 10,000 foragers in southern Angola by the 1960s, while Tobias counted over 50,000 of them in Botswana and Namibia. For the difficulties involved in counting, see Richard B. Lee, *The !Kung San,* pp. 42–44. He observed a 20 percent increase over four years, which is more

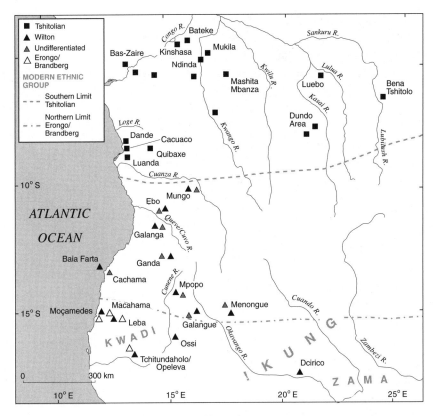

MAP 7. Late–Stone Age Sites in Angola and Congo

The ancient forager's way of life is known for the most part by the uses of their stone tools, the only tools which do not decay, as well as by durable remnants of their food such as nuts, while information about the practices of recent foragers in the region helps to interpret these finds.[6] These people survived by gathering plants and hunting game. In recent times, the gath-

a result of improved counting than of real population growth. Although all foragers have by now disappeared from the larger and more fertile northern half of West Central Africa, they must have been more numerous there and even a guess of several tens of thousands is likely to be a gross underestimate.

6. While the socioeconomic environment and makeup of recent foragers is wholly different from what it was well over 2,000 years ago, still they have to cope with the same physical and ecological constraints which once confronted foragers from Stone Age times and they may well cope in ways that are still similar to the strategies used by those foragers. That makes ethnographies such as those of Wilmsen (*The Kalahari Ethnographies (1896–1898)*, Guerreiro (*Boximanes*), and Lee (*!Kung*) quite suggestive to the historian.

ering of edible plants constituted the mainstay of the daily diet, and it probably has always been so, even though previously game was perhaps one hundred times more abundant than today. Today !Kung women still gather
about one hundred species of plants, a good dozen of which can be called
staples. Even two or three thousand years ago women, who were the main
gatherers, already knew a great deal about which plants were edible, which
ones were useful for what, where and when they could be found, how they
should be processed and so on.[7] All of this was the fruit of hundreds of generations of experience. Today, and formerly as well, such edible plants include tubers dug out of the soil with digging sticks weighted by bored stones
(or *kwe*); fruits and nuts, some of which, such as the *mongongo,* are still
found by archaeologists; melon, squash, pumpkins, calabashes, gourds such
as the *tsamma,* which still is a main staple in the arid south, and the seeds
of a few grasses crushed on grinding stones. Tubers were the most important as they provided the bulk of the carbohydrates, although pumpkins and
melons were also crucial in drier areas and seasons because of their water
content.[8] Plants were so important to the food supply that one may think
that in most places their availability was more crucial than that of game dictating where a camp was to be located and how long people would stay there
before moving on, which implies that women had a major voice in making
such decisions. And as plants tend to grow in the same spots year after year,
camps may well have returned to the same locales year after year. Indeed
their very exploitation also tends to assist their propagation by the scatter-
ing of nuts and seeds, and perhaps Late–Stone Age women were also already
sticking tuber cuttings back into the ground. In this way even foragers leave
ecological fingerprints on their environment.

While women gathered, men hunted. Game was abundant, especially in
the grasslands where ruminants moved about in large herds. This not only
stands in sharp contrast with the situation today but also contrasts favorably
with its availability in the equatorial rain forests, whether one counts in
terms of biomass overall, the number of species available, or the average
weight per animal. Most meat was procured by hunting rather than by trapping, although the latter was also practiced. As the stone arrowheads and
spearheads tell us, game was hunted by bow and arrow and by spearing. In
most places the preferred animals seem to have been small- or middle-sized

7. Women still are the main gatherers everywhere in central Africa and have probably always been so.

8. For plant resources, see Guerreiro, *Boximanes,* pp. 67–78, and especially Lee, *!Kung,*
pp. 158–204. For *mongongo* in archaeological context, see Lawrence Robbins and Alex
Campbell, "Prehistory of Mongongo Nut Exploitation," pp. 37–41.

antelopes, although Richard Lee observes that big game, mostly larger ruminants such as elands, calculated in yield per weight per year contributed
perhaps as much as half of the meat consumed. If the actual place where a
camp was located was dictated by the supply of plant food, the seasonal
roaming territory of that community was certainly dictated by the habits
and presence of game.[9] In most places away from the coast fish was but a
minor source of food. Most of it was speared by harpoons. As to nutrition,
plants were essential in providing carbohydrates, lipids, vitamins, and minerals while meat or fish were crucial for their proteins and salts.[10]

Because of their mobility, foragers owned rather few objects and most of
these were made from organic materials that have not survived. But scrap-
ing stones show that they processed skins into leather fabrics for garments
or bags, while trapezoidal or triangular microliths, probably glued to a
wooden support, once were the cutting edge of knives, and heavy bifacial
elements suggest axes and adzes for cutting and working wood. Containers
certainly included calabashes and perhaps woven bags, string bags, and
slings. Then there were ornaments such as stone or shell beads and perhaps
lumps of vegetals or minerals such as redwood or specularite powder that
were used as oils to protect and beautify the body.[11] Some of these were exchanged over long distances. But none of these objects were considered to
be just belongings with an objective value independent of who their owners were. Rather, all of them were thought of as mere extensions of the person who used them.

In most parts of West Central Africa, foraging provided a reliable, not
too arduous, and perfectly satisfactory way of life as long as every day everyone obtained the expected plant and animal food. But nature is not a su-
permarket. Some women found more plant food while some of their neighbors might have an unlucky day. Some hunters were more skilled or luckier
than others and bagged a large piece of game whereas some of their fellows
returned empty-handed. Then some adults were too ill or too old to forage.
Such uncertainties could be and were effectively eliminated by sharing. Sharing seems to have been the central value of all foragers then as it still was in
the twentieth century. Those who had gave to those who had not, so as to
even the score. But sharing was not giving. If one received today, one was

9. Territory then only meant lands over which people roamed and not lands to
which they claimed exclusive access. Even in recent times, men belonging to different
bands hunted on the same land.
10. On hunting: Guerreiro, *Boximanes,* pp. 79–123; Lee, *!Kung,* pp. 205–49.
11. Lanfranchi and Clist, *Aux origines,* p. 121; Robbins et al., "Intensive Mining,"
pp. 146–48.

expected to return the gift tomorrow. Rather than giving, we are talking here about a delayed exchange, a notion usually called *hxaro* after its designation in !Kung. Sharing created an ongoing relationship between the giver and the recipient, be they adults living within the same camp or not, be they related by kinship, as most were, or not. Sharing brought an indispensable predictability to foraging and turned this way of life into a highly satisfactory one, so satisfactory that it has been called "the original affluent society."[12] For did it not bring plants into the kitchen without the hardship of farming and meat into the larder without the trouble of herding? Did people think about their way of life and their communities in these terms? Unfortunately, the messages they left behind in the shape of paintings and engravings do not tell us, for they can only be interpreted, not understood.[13]

Be that as it may, there were, alas, side effects to this kind of affluence. Settlements had to remain both small and nomadic. Moving was difficult for the less mobile, old, or sick and it shortened their lives. Moving was also hard on pregnant or lactating women who could only cope by delaying a childbirth until the previous child could easily walk on its own. This trade-off thus entailed a significant demographic cost. It also entailed a considerable social cost, caused by the small size of all settlements. These were communities with intense face-to-face relations. These were certainly based on relationships of kinship and neighborhood. Everyone knew and dealt daily with everyone else. Most people were kin, and everyone behaved as if they were or were about to become kin. They all formed a single family in which rules of descent mattered only to define the boundaries of incestual relationships and hence of permissible marriage alliances, for there was nothing to inherit or to succeed to. The size of residential aggregates or camps was quite flexible and fluctuated according to seasons while individual mobility between various camps was high for men as well as for women. Except for sharing, an essential activity to alleviate risks, there was no incentive in this kind of community to develop more intricate social institutions on a larger scale.[14] One could label these social organizations (vaguely enough) as egalitarian bilateral systems but even such a vague label is misleading. It hints at

12. On sharing, see Pauline Wiessner, "*Hxaro,*" pp. 118–52; On "The Original Affluent Society," see Marshall Sahlins, *Stone Age Economics,* pp. 1–39.

13. Guttierez, *L'Art.* For dating, see p. 192. (Only two sets of rock art are said to be certainly of Late Stone Age.) See also Janmart's Lunda plaque in Ervedosa, *Arqueologia,* pp. 151, 342.

14. Kinship relations, rules about incest and marriage, and relations with neighbors are "universals" attested to in all human societies. For the inferences of flexibility, mobility, and the need to share, see the convincing argument in Lee's *The !Kung San.*

corporate groups that probably did not exist and it suggests the observation of invariant uniform rules in all matters regulated by descent, which was certainly not true then, just as it was not true among foragers in recent times.[15]

Despite the general identity-kit just drawn, it would be a grievous error to lump the foragers in the entire area together as if their way of life was the same everywhere, if only because different environments had produced different adaptations. Some foragers, for example, lived off the sea. Shell-middens are found along the Angolan and Namibian coasts. On the !Khuiseb Delta, communities lived mainly on white mussels and wild melons,[16] while along the shores of the lagoon south of Luanda City people relied mostly on a bountiful supply of other mollusks which throve in the shallow and calm warm waters of the lagoons.[17] In this last case, the strategy was so successful that, as their shellmiddens attest, they probably had become nearly sedentary, the only foragers in all of West Central Africa to have done so. Indeed their adaptation was so successful that this way of life has survived nearly until today. Well after 1600 a tiny group of people north of the mouth of the Cuanza River, known as the Nambiu or Nambwa, still lived exclusively from fish, seafood, and the sedges of the local papyri.[18] Besides these cases there also must have been considerable variation inland as some, especially in the north with its wealth of tubers and poorer fauna, relied more heavily on gathering, while elsewhere hunting big game or fishing in inland waters may have played a bigger part. In some cases, especially in the south, seasonal movements must have been considerable, while in others, such as in the lower Kwango area, movements may have been limited to moves from valleys to hillsides.[19]

15. For rules of descent and the situation among recent foragers, see the discussion about matrilinearity in the next chapter.

16. See John Kinahan, *Pastoral Nomads,* pp. 87–95 (the earliest from shortly after the beginning of our era).

17. The earliest shellmiddens date to the "Second Intermediate Period." See Lanfranchi and Clist, *Aux origines,* p. 123. Nearby coastal Tshitolian sites without shells were located in Luanda City, at Cacuaco, and somewhat farther north at the mouth of the Dande River. Any associated shells in Luanda at least and probably at Cacuaco had certainly been removed to make lime by the time archaeologists looked at the sites. See Ervedosa, *Arqueologia,* p. 152.

18. António Brásio, *MMA,* 3:181–82 (letter from 14 January 1579), 8:121; 9:377, 522; Heintze, *Fontes,* p. 184; Cadornega, *História,* 2:383 and 3:58–60, 64, 68, 248; Heintze, "Historical Notes on the Kisama," p. 410.

19. Sheryl Miller, in "New Look," p. 87, cites an adjacent hill (Mukila) and valley (Ndinga) facies in the Kwango area. But David Cahen and Georges Mortelmans, *Un site tshitolien,* pp. 40–41, thought that it was still premature to make such distinctions between transient camps and more permanent sites.

Indeed, in some places they may have been entirely absent. Besides these variations, others certainly existed as well. Thus, in the northern half of the area, every single regional site where archaeologists have worked, displayed significant variants of the same industry.[20]

Far more significant is the major difference found between the northern and the southern halves of the entire area. The savannas and woodlands of the well-watered north were the home of the so-called Tshitolian industry[21] while the more open and drier south was dominated by the Wilton industry and its derivations.[22] This indicates that West Central Africa did not yet exist as a single historical region at the time, since Wilton is typical for southern and parts of eastern Africa and Tshitolian for equatorial and northern central Africa. This division appears to correspond with a difference between northern and southern autochthonous inhabitants, which Njila speakers seem to have been deemed essential despite the fact that they applied the same term Twá to all autochthons.[23] Those foragers—later called pygmies by Europeans—lived north of roughly latitude 12° S while those later called Khoisan lived farther south. Mbunda oral traditions remember and clearly distinguish between both the *tumonapi* "pygmies" in the north and the Sekele and Zama groups of San in the south.[24] Such a distinction between northerners and southerners certainly underscores that the foragers of West Central Africa did not participate in a single culture or speak dialects of a single language or even of genetically related languages. The very existence of Kwadi in southern Angola proves this. So far Kwadi remains unique and cannot be linked to any other Khoisan language or other tongue.[25] Furthermore a map of the distribution of contemporary Khoisan languages still shows the presence in northern Namibia and Angola of languages belonging to at least two entirely different families of Khoisan, namely, Khoe and

20. Six major variants are known, namely, those of Lower Kongo (Tumba), Kinshasa, western Kwango, Bibanga/Bena Tshitolo (Kasai), Lunda, and Luanda. See Miller, "New Look," pp. 87–89.

21. Lanfranchi and Clist, *Aux origines,* pp. 118–22, 127–28; Miller, "New Look," pp. 86–89; Ervedosa, *Arqueologia,* pp. 149–52 (note on p. 151 a single plaquette with geometric ornamentation typical for the Congo).

22. For Wilton in general, see Raymond Inskeep, "Southern and Eastern Africa," p. 80; For Angola, see Ervedosa, *Arqueologia,* p. 165 (map) and pp. 153–63; Gutierrez, *L'Art,* p. 25, fig. 5. In Namibia, see Kinahan, *Pastoral,* pp. 17–18 ("Damaraland Culture").

23. Note *-tʉ́a* 1/2, CS 1804–5, is early Bantu for "autochthon foreigner." CS stands for "Comparative Series in Malcolm Guthrie's *Comparative Bantu,* vols. 3–4. See List of Abbreviations in References for a full citation. Cited hereafter as CS.

24. Cheke Cultural Writers, *The History,* pp. 9, 10, 23.

25. See Tom Güldemann and Rainer Vossen, "Khoisan," p. 100 and map.

Ju.[26] It is quite likely that many of the tongues spoken in the area two to three millennia ago have died out both through language shift and in some cases because the number of speakers was too small to allow for the long-term survival of their language. The linguistic diversity of the foragers roaming throughout West Central Africa during the Late Stone Age was therefore certainly far greater than it is now and, although language and culture are not identical, such a situation still suggests that the sociocultural diversity among foragers at that time was also greater than it is now. One must therefore accept that when most of these foragers were eventually absorbed into Njila-speaking communities, they contributed significantly different inputs of ideas, values, practices, and artistic expressions to the makeup of the different societies in which they fused. Hence it is absolutely wrong to think of all the resulting societies as consisting of a single invariant forager input and a single input of Bantu-speaking agriculturalists.

Of Pots, Fields, and Flocks

When ceramics, domestic food crops, small domestic stock, and even metallurgy first appeared in the area, its northern and southern halves still remained completely different historical regions just as they had been during Late–Stone Age times. In the northern half, all these innovations arrived from farther north, from the rain forests of equatorial Africa, a diffusion that was quite separate from the arrival of similar innovations in the southern half to which they came from the grasslands of eastern Africa.[27] Hence these developments must be kept separate. Ceramics and the cultivation of food crops need not diffuse together and they did not do so in the southern half.[28] In the north they apparently did with one possible exception.[29] The earliest set of relevant sites are those of the Sakuzi and Ngovo industries in the Lower Congo, where ceramics first appear ca. 400 BCE together with polished stone tools. Most direct evidence for horticulture is lacking apart from fragments

26. Ibid., pp. 102–3. The languages of the northern autochthons have totally disappeared. They may not have been related to Khoisan languages at all.

27. For the northern origins of ceramics and horticulture, see Lanfranchi and Clist, *Aux origines.*

28. See Vogelsang, "Archaeological Investigations," p. 27, and his "Archaeological Survey," pp. 22–24; evidence from the Tsodilo Hills in Botswana dates only to ca. 600 CE. See L. A. Murphy et al., "Pottery from the White Paintings Rock Shelter," pp. 3–5.

29. The exception is the isolated and very early 1382–1340 or 1320–1020 BCE date at Kwimba (Lower Congo), which may well be a fluke. See Pierre de Maret "Le néolithique," p. 449.

of nuts of both the elais oil palm and *Canarium schweinfurthii* Engl., although indirect indicators suggest that horticulture was practiced.[30] At least in Sakuzi, a settlement had become sedentary enough to use pits for the disposal of the rubbish. By 270 BCE ceramics are also reported in Kinshasa, albeit without other materials.[31]

Only indirect evidence is available because, unlike stone tools, ceramics and metal products, botanical remains, apart from tree nuts, charcoal, and sometimes pollen are not easily spotted on sites. Thus with the exception of the Tsodilo Hills in northwest Botswana, there still are no direct botanical data for documenting food crops on early sites in West Central Africa. All that is known about the specific plants introduced from the north stems from linguistic data. These refer to one or more species of yams, the Livingstone potato, perhaps the Hausa potato, groundnuts, cowpeas, various cucurbits, amaranth and castor oil, oil palm trees, *Canarium schweinfurthii* Engl. trees (again for oil), and kola (*Cola acuminata* Schott/Endl. and *Cola ballayi* M. Cornu).[32] Archaeologists infer horticulture from indirect indicators such as the larger size of a settlement and the presence of pits filled with trash along with ceramics and polished tools. A combination of all these indicators is found at Sakuzi and renders the inference credible. Where only ceramics occur without any other indicators one cannot postulate horticulture. Thus the claim that horticulture was practiced at Benfica, a second century (140 CE) site on the Luanda lagoon, was based on the finding of ceramics and of the shellmidden, which show that the settlement was not ephemeral. But that claim is not credible since Late–Stone Age lagoon sites in the vicinity, without ceramics and without horticulture, are just as sedentary.[33]

What prompted the foragers east and south from the Lower Congo to adopt these innovations? What were their advantages? As containers, ceramics are rather poor substitutes for baskets to store dry goods or calabashes to hold liquids, for they weigh more and are more breakable. But they have one great advantage: they make cooking and the preparation of broths and soups possible. While root crops, nuts, berries, and even seeds could all

30. See de Maret, "Le néolithique," pp. 447–57, and his "The Ngovo Group," pp. 103–34; also, Marie-Claude Dupré and Bruno Pinçon, *Métallurgie*, pp. 38–39. The pits themselves were probably dug to extract earth for building wattle walls.

31. See de Maret, "Le néolithique," p. 453 (the Funa site contained only charcoal and a single potshard); Dupré and Pinçon, p. 39.

32. See Roger Blench, "Linguistic Evidence," pp. 83–98, for very early times. Hibiscus, Gnetum, fluted pumpkin, and sesame may not have been known at all to proto-Njila speakers.

33. Ervedosa, *Arqueologia*, pp. 150, 152; Guttierrez, *L'Art*, p. 26; Lanfranchi and Clist, *Aux origines*, pp. 123–24.

be grilled, roasted under cinders, or roasted on a platform over cinders, leaves could not be roasted.[34] Leaves, like many fruits or berries, could only be eaten raw. But most leaves are not very edible that way, which explains why so few of them occur in catalogues of plant foods among foragers in contrast to the prominent place they occupy among those who make and use pottery.[35] That was the main attraction of ceramics for women in both their capacities as the main gatherers and those who prepared food. They acquired pots first as exotic curiosities from neighboring communities where the craft was already practiced, but soon the usefulness of such vessels led them to learn how to make them. Ever since, women have been and still are the main potters nearly everywhere in the area.[36] Girls acquired the necessary skills as part-time apprentices from a woman potter who also taught them the repertoire for ceramic decoration, a repertoire that was no doubt derived from designs elsewhere, such as on mats, baskets, calabashes, or even body decoration. When such girls married, they were integrated into the communities of heir husbands and brought their craft with them, thus spreading it from place to place. The newly arrived potter either continued to decorate her pots in the manner she had learned as a girl or created different designs inspired by designs common in her new community.[37] Hence the major factor in the speed of diffusion of the technique and in the evolution of ceramic decor was probably the frequency of intermarriage between communities.

Women also introduced the first domestic food crops. Earlier they may already have practiced some vegeculture by sticking parts of roots used for food back in the ground in the hope for later regrowth or by weeding patches of ground around useful wild plants to foster their growth. They were also quite familiar with a great number of plants, including a whole set of wild

34. For recent cooking practices among some foragers in the Kaokoland, see H. R. MacCalman and B. J. Grobbelaar, "Preliminary Report," pp. 9, 17, 25. They could not prepare and did not eat grass seed. Previously they had made pottery but not at this point because no one knew any longer how to make it. Wooden vessels could not and did not replace them for cooking.

35. See Lee, *!Kung,* pp. 165–67 (only 6 leafy greens eaten raw as salads out of ca. 100 plants); Guerreiro, *Boximanes,* p. 72 (2 sorts of leaves), p. 73 (1 sort of leaf); Thayer Scudder, *Gathering among African Woodland Savannah Cultivators.*

36. By the nineteenth century, the exceptions were the following: only men were potters among the Lwena, Mbunda, and Mbukushu, while among the Cokwe and Lucazi both men and women practiced the craft.

37. N. M. Katanekwa and John H. Robertson have stressed the inspiration for ceramic designs from decorations on other earlier objects. See, for instance, Robertson, "Early Iron Age Archaeology," p. 175.

yams and other tubers that were similar to the new domestic plants. They
probably learned to plant by experimenting with a few specimens, which
represented little risk since food crops were only a small experimental part
of the total food supply. Only later did the risks increase as such crops became staples.

But horticulture is more than putting a plant into the ground and here
the drawbacks begin. Serious production required the clearing and fencing
in of a field before planting as well as weeding later on. Since fields were
hacked out of forest land, the women required the help of men to cut trees
and to build fences sturdy enough to keep out warthogs as well as antelopes.
The women also had to learn the intricacies of the agricultural calendar, including planting, weeding, harvesting, learning which plants could be put
together in one plot, and recognizing soil exhaustion. Substantial yields may
not have impressed a small foraging community very much for, given their
nomadic way of life, they did not require much surplus food, and it may not
have been self-evident that horticulture made their food supply more secure.
Moreover, horticulture lessened overall mobility since women at least had
to stay near their fields for much of the year, a practice that actually may have
slightly increased risks of food shortage. In addition, the required tasks significantly altered the usual division of labor by involving men more directly
in the production of plant foods. Above all, it had to be clear to everyone that
this involved a lot of extra work and drudgery, far more work than foragers
usually spent on gathering. Given such drawbacks, one easily understands
why foragers would not be interested in horticulture. The long-term advantages, such as the possibility of living in larger groups and becoming sedentary, were probably not even perceived at first by them. All these are cogent
reasons to think that full-fledged horticulture, unlike ceramics, was not welcome at all. Some women may well have planted a few individual domestic
plants here or there, just as some men may have propagated palm trees or
Canarium trees to gather the bunches of palm nuts, calabashes of palm wine,
and oil-bearing nuts.[38] Thus it rather looks as if fully fledged horticulture came
into the area from the outside by immigration. Indeed immigration from the
north best explains the sudden and simultaneous appearance of ceramics, polished stone tools, and arboriculture which occurred in the Lower Congo.[39]

38. Women still are not allowed to climb trees and probably never were. Because tree
climbing is a male task and because trees were not planted in "fields," i.e., orchards, the dynamics of the diffusion of this arboriculture were quite distinct from those relating to horticulture. Perhaps the chronology of their introduction may also have been different.

39. Although this simultaneity may be an effect of the serendipity of the finds, in this
case, the number of sites found seems to be large enough to accept that it is genuine.

Although no bone has been recovered from any of the sites, the linguistic evidence maintains that the horticulturalists kept goats. The universal ethnographic practice in Central Africa suggests that married women aided by their young children kept them and that in most cases no community flock was established. While some foraging women may well have adopted a few goats from time to time as a curiosity or as an occasional substitute for the common goat-sized antelopes, substantial goatherding was probably out of the question since the fundamental ethos of sharing and exchange would soon lead to the depletion of the flock. Moreover, in the prevailing game-rich environments, goats certainly did not contribute enough to the whole food supply to force a change in this ethos.

The diffusion of horticulture south and eastward from the Lower Congo and Malebo Pool still remains almost unknown for lack of sites, especially dated sites. The only early dated sites with ceramics in the northern half of the study area are Kapanda in the middle Cuanza region at ca. 80 CE and Benfica at ca. 140 CE (map 8).[40] Whether horticulture was practiced at either of these sites remains unknown. If future research confirms these dates to be typical for the arrival of ceramics there, the rate of diffusion of ceramics between Kinshasa and the lower Cuanza basin would have been about 1.6 kilometers per year (570 kilometers in 350 years), a rate compatible with a process of diffusion by the marriages of women potters. Given the lack of comparative ceramic analysis and of dating, that is all that can be said for the moment. We can only presume that the craft continued to spread farther south and eastward. The linguistic evidence suggests that horticulture, like ceramics, also spread south but not farther than a climatic boundary which now lies around latitude 11° or 12° S but which in the period of higher rainfall before 500 CE lay several degrees farther south, perhaps as far as the latitude 16° S.[41]

Neither oil palms, raffia palms, the gourd *Cucumeropsis edulis* Cogn., domestic yams, or their usual wild relatives grew farther south than that

40. See J. R. Junior dos Santos and Carlos Ervedosa, "A estação arqueologica de Benfica," pp. 33–51; Gutierrez, *Archéologie et Anthropologie,* pp. 59–60. Whether or not the associated "stones" were tools remains unclear.

41. For the climate, see Denbow, "After the Flood," pp. 183–86, and also somewhat different results in Robbins et al., "Intensive," pp. 145–46. As the climatic boundary was also conditioned by factors other than rainfall, such as soils, the latitude given here is very approximate. It is based on an estimate of the amount of increased rainfall before 500 CE. For the approximate southward boundary of elaïs today, look at "Major Vegetation Zones" in Régine Van Chi-Bonnardel, *The Atlas of Africa,* p. 39, but note that elaïs was also found around Novo Redondo.

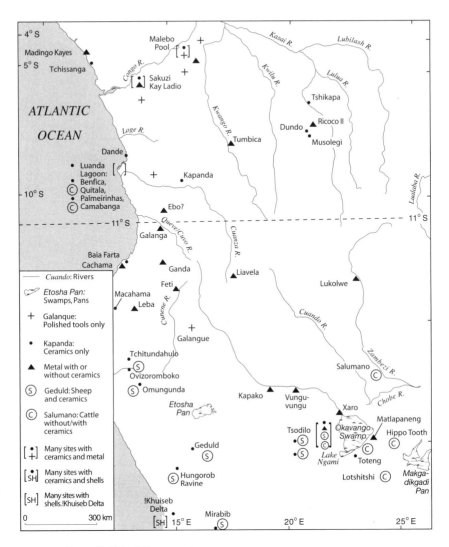

MAP 8. From Polished Stone to Iron

boundary, and as yams were the staple around which the whole system was built, systematic horticulture could not spread farther. Beyond the boundary, local inhabitants adopted a few suitable crops, especially groundnuts, beans, cucurbits, and castor oil but in a piecemeal fashion and only as useful adjuncts to their usual foraging way of life. Indeed, in the regions where *Ricinodendron rautanenii* Schinz. grew they were probably of less significance than *mongongo* nuts.[42] Moreover as beans, groundnuts, or pumpkins mature

42. See Grandvaux Barbosa, *Carta*, pp. 231–34, for a partial distribution.

quickly and do not require constant tending, a few months of sedentary life by women farmers in the community would suffice. Men need not even have stayed in the settlement and could still roam about in pursuit of big game,[43] while during the long dry season the whole community could continue to lead the nomadic life to which they were accustomed and forage wherever conditions were the most favorable. Pastro-foraging fitted well into this lifestyle and did nothing to make communities more sedentary. And as the climatic boundary retreated northward after 500, so did horticulture. Any community beyond the present boundary that had earlier adopted this way of life was then gradually forced to revert to foraging or to adopt cereal agriculture, which seems to have been spreading in the region by 500. Thus while horticulture in the north facilitated the rise of more sedentary and probably larger settlements that could potentially engender larger scale social organizations, this did not occur in the south. There people remained foragers. Hence the spread of horticulture did not affect the earlier Late–Stone Age division between northerners and southerners.

Historical change in the deep south had nothing to do with the developments just outlined. Here changes, when they came, were of a very different sort and came about in a very different way. The first ceramics appeared here around 1 CE or perhaps somewhat earlier. They were introduced by pastro-foragers, nomadic sheepherders without any form of horticulture or agriculture, and without any tendency toward sedentarization.[44] Ceramics and sheep came from areas farther east, the earliest attestation being Bambata Cave in modern Zimbabwe around 200 BCE.[45] They spread eastward to northern Botswana and northern Namibia and southward as far as the Cape where they are also reported in the first century CE.[46] Northward they settled into southern Angola where ancestors of today's Njila speakers acquired them from Khoisan herders and borrowed the Khoisan term to designate sheep as far north as the southern part of the planalto, that is, once

43. For Zambia, see John H. Robertson and Rebecca Bradley, "A New Paradigm," pp. 312–13.

44. See Vogelsang, "Archaeological Survey," pp. 22–24, and his "Archaeological Investigations," pp. 25–28; Kinahan, *Pastoral*, pp. 87–90, 123–24, 149–52; Wilmsen, *Land*, pp. 64–68; Karim Sadr, "Kalahari Archaeology," pp. 104–12.

45. On the Bambata cave ca. 195 BCE, see Denbow and Wilmsen, "Advent," p. 1509, fig. 1511; Wilmsen, *Land*, pp. 65–67. For an even earlier date, see C. Britt Bousman, "The Chronological Evidence," p. 137. But the early date and the originality of its pottery is still much disputed in literature.

46. See Kinahan, *Pastoral*, pp. 127–28; Sadr, "Kalahari," pp. 107–11; Sadr, "The First Herders," pp. 101–32; Bousman, "The Chronological Evidence," pp. 133–50.

again more or less as far as the climatic boundary between the two halves of West Central Africa.[47] Eventually sheep would be adopted farther north and goats would be south of the boundary, but not in large flocks and without pastro-foraging.

The available dates suggest a very rapid spread of sheep and ceramics from northwestern Zimbabwe, along a route south of the then much larger Makgadikgadi Pans and of the Okavango Delta, which was then two or three times as large as it is now and included the Lake Ngami depression among others. From there the nomadic sheepherders then moved all over the *mopane* grasslands, which provide excellent fodder, deep into what is now the Kalahari. The original inhabitants of the regions into which the pastro-foragers were expanding gradually followed their example and adopted ceramics and sheepherding.

But the introduction of a herd of sheep into a foraging community caused a major problem. For keeping flocks of sheep soon had to come in conflict with the fundamental ethos of sharing. As long as anyone was free to slaughter any animal at any time, the reproduction of a flock remained haphazard since to achieve this goal animals in their most reproductive years must be spared from slaughter. Once it became an accepted practice to exclude such animals from sharing, the underlying ethos was bound to change. At the very least, some animals were no longer available and were set apart from all other goods. Still, because all sharing was based on the principle of delayed returns, even these animals could still be given away but only for raising more stock and with the understanding that at some time in the future some of their progeny would return to the donor. Even so, setting sheep apart from all other goods introduced a new principle of property which then in turn raised questions as to ownership (community or a leading man?) and inheritance (male or female descendants?). The disposition in these matters in turn had a strong impact on the prevalent social organization. There is no way of knowing how this process occurred or over what period of time. All one can say is that adult men probably became the owners since among the eighteenth-century Kwandu of southern Angola only men were the managers, owners, and heirs of sheep.[48]

<hr/>

47. The relevant root *-gwii/-jwii* was borrowed from a Khoisan *-guu*. See John Argyle, "The Linguistic Evidence," pp. 27–31, and "Proto-Khwe" in Ehret, *An African*, p. 217, table 40b. See Dciriku and Mbukushu *ndj'wìì;* Nkhumbi *ngwi;* Nyaneka *-ngi;* Kwanyama *-di;* Kwambi, *nji;* Ndonga *ngswi;* Herero *-ndu;* Mbunda *-ngi;* Lui and Luyana *-ngu;* Umbundu *-ngwe/-ngi.*

48. Kinahan, *Pastoral*, pp. 40–48, 125, 128, proposes an imaginative scenario to account for the process. The transition from sharing to personal property would have been

Thus in the last centuries BCE, or around the turn of the era, the technology and the use of ceramics arrived twice in West Central Africa: once from the north and once from the south. Ceramics were accompanied by horticulture in the north and by sheepherding in the south. Although these innovations then spread toward each other in Angola, the earlier great divide between southern and northern foragers remained intact. Horticulture did not cross to the south and pastro-foraging was not adopted in the north, even though some southerners adopted goats and minor crops from the north, while some northerners raised a few sheep. Without further research, however, one cannot be more precise about either the exact location of the geographic boundary between north and south or about the extent of intermingling between northerners and southerners in the boundary region. All one does know is that the main innovations of the age did not manage to bridge the divide.

Proto-Njila Speakers and Their Society

Today Njila speakers occupy nearly all of West Central Africa. These languages all stem from a single ancestral tongue which we may label "proto-Njila." Proto-Njila and its daughters spread from a single community or a group of neighboring communities throughout the entire area. This diffusion can therefore be seen as yet another innovation comparable to the ones we have already discussed. Yet, this is wholly different because it is not just a matter of adopting a new technology but of introducing a new medium of communication. That is a much more fundamental change because a new language alters the whole worldview of those who adopt it and also transforms the quality of their relationship with others since a common language greatly facilitates the flow of information and ideas between the communities who share it, while a difference in language creates a substantial barrier to intercommunication. Hence the dispersal of the Njila languages merits a separate presentation, and all the more so because the prevailing assumptions about this dispersal hopelessly confuse languages and the people who speak them. One still reads summaries such as "Proto-Herero speaking Bantu peoples entered the western part of southern Africa roughly 2,000 years ago."[49] This phrase informs us that a massive migration brought "proto-

---

imposed by shamans whose supernatural powers gave them the authority to dictate this. On gender, inheritance, and sheepherding in the eighteenth and nineteenth centuries, see Carlos Laranjo Medeiros, *Vakwandu*, pp. 18–21, 65.

49. In his summary, Duncan Miller, *The Tsodilo Jewellery*, pp. 14–15, follows the views of the linguist Bernd Heine, "Zur Genetischen Gliederung," pp. 164–85.

2

HOW SOCIETIES ARE BORN

Herero" people straight from the Lower Congo right to Namibia, nearly 1,000 miles (1,600 kilometers) away as the crow flies, across various climatic zones, at an average speed of one mile (1.6 kilometer) per year and kept this up for a whole millennium. Can one really believe that something like that truly happened?

The linguistic evidence about the Njila language family is set out in the Appendix and in section II of the References. It clearly shows that such a family exists and it allows us to locate the region in which the ancestral language, proto-Njila, was first spoken. Njila's closest links are with the Western Bantu branches of Kongo and Pool-Kasai (B East). The small Lweta group in the present province of West Kasai (Democratic Republic of Congo) is its nearest indirect relative. According to the principle of the least moves, this means that the original language arose on the margins of both Kongo and Pool-Kasai languages, west of and next to the Lweta group.[50] According to the earliest known distribution of these languages,[51] proto-Njila took shape in the Middle Kwilu region. Its speakers probably lived in or near the equatorial rain forests which border the valleys of the rivers with their fertile soils rather than on the grasslands of the interfluves covered by sterile Kalahari Sands. Because proto-Njila has words to designate these activities, the language came into being after its speakers had acquired pottery and horticulture, but before metals reached them, for the metallurgical vocabulary is not proto-Njila. In the absence of any relevant archaeological evidence whatsoever in the middle Kwilu region itself, and in the present state of the evidence, proto-Njila emerged after the appearance of ceramics at Kinshasa ca. 300 BCE and well before 400 CE when metal appears at the Pool.[52]

Proto-Njila word forms allow us to present a sketch of its speakers and of the major features of their society during the last centuries BCE. They were horticulturalists since there are common words for both fields cut out in the

50. The argument "of least moves" is an application of the principle of Ockham's razor, which holds that the most probable among several alternatives is the one that introduces the fewest presuppositions—in this case the one that accounts for a geographic dispersion by the least number of possible movements.

51. For Kongo and Congo-Kasai, directly before 1600; for Lweta, estimated ca. 1600. To use present-day language distributions can obviously be risky as language domains can expand or contract as happened to Lweta. But in general the domains of whole language groups do not fluctuate so easily. Hence, I feel justified in using this procedure here.

52. The dates around 1000 BCE, which had been proposed earlier derive from glottochronology and are therefore unreliable. The date of ca. 300 BCE relies on the 270 BCE date for the appearance of ceramics around Malebo Pool. Only more intensive future research, preferably in the middle Kwilu area itself, will alter this calculation. The 300 BCE date is that of the first appearance of metallurgy at Gombe (Kinshasa).

forest (*-*gunda* 3/4, 5/6, 7/8, 9/6, 9/10, CS 897[53]) and fields laid out in grass-land (*-*pįá* 5/6, CS 1506).[54] There they planted root crops, especially various species of yams (*-*kuá* 7/8 [CS 1166],[55] *-*dingu* 7/8,[56] -*cádi* 7/8,[57] -*gamba* 5/6, 14/6[58]—all terms referring to one of *Dioscorea rotundata/cayenensis* Lamk., *D. Dumetorum* Pax, *D. bulbifera* L.), as well as the Livingstone potato, i.e., *Coleus dazo* A. Chev. alias *Plectranthus esculata* (*-*tamba* 9/10, *-*koda* 14/6[59]), and the Hausa potato, i.e., *Sphenostylis stenocarpa* Harms (*-*camba* 9/10[60]). They also grew *voandzeia* groundnuts, i.e., *Voandzeia sub-terranea* Thouars alias *Vigna subterranea*,[61] cowpeas, i.e., *Vigna unguiculata* Walp. (*-*kúnde* 5/6, CS 1222[62]), *Dolichos lablab* L. beans (-*kanza* 6),[63] and the leaves of *Amaranthus caudatus* L. (-*mbua* 9/10[64]). No less than six different

53. CS followed by a number refers to the dictionary of "Comparative Series" as used by Malcolm Guthrie in his *Comparative Bantu,* volumes 3 and 4.

54. Proto-Njila or somewhat earlier. See CS 1507 ("burnt grass") and 1508 ("fire") for the etymology of *-*pįá* showing that it was an innovation made necessary when fields began to be cultivated in the grasslands. CS 1506 is quite incomplete. Reflexes (corresponding forms) are also attested to in Kongo, Yaka, Lwalwa, Mbala, Pende, Kimbundu, Sala Mpasu, Ndembu, Umbundu, Nyaneka, Kwanyama, Kwambi, Ndonga, Lucazi, Luvale, and Cokwe ("home").

55. Most of the reconstructed forms for plants are still provisional and a great deal of further research needs to be done. Dictionaries only list the most common crops and many names can refer to different plants in different languages while they may shift from one crop to a similar one introduced later. For Angola I relied on John Gossweiler, *Nomes indígenas.* Thus *-*kuá* is attested to for various root crops in Kongo, the Kimbundu group, and Umbundu. It is just possible that !Kung !Xwa (Fockea sp) for a water root is related (Lee, *!Kung,* p. 164).

56. Attested in Kimbundu, Umbundu, Cokwe, and the Ngangela cluster. Is -*dungi* 7/8 in Rund and Ndembu perhaps related to this?

57. Attested in Kongo, Kimbundu (*D. praehensilis* Benth.), Holo, Rund, Lwena (wild yam).

58. Attested in Kongo, Kimbundu, Umbundu (*D. dumetorum* Pax).

59. *-*tamba* in Kimbundu, Umbundu, and the Ngangela group and see also next footnote; *-*koda, in the Ngangela group. Guerreiro, *Boximanes,* p. 73, mentions that the Sekele !Kung find these in the wild.

60. *Ohamba* 9/10 in Umbundu; -*sambi* 3/4, 14/6 in the Ngangela cluster. Perhaps Libolo *kajamba* is related to this. *Thamba* 9/10 in Pende, Cokwe, Lwena, and -*tamba* in Rund and Ndembu, all designate the sweet potato.

61. They are now designated by a great variety of terms, which attests to a very complex history.

62. Attested to in practically all the languages of the area except for Mbala. Beside these beans, proto-Njila speakers may also have planted *Cajanus cajan* Druce for its peas and other legumes as well.

63. Attested in Kongo and Kimbundu and perhaps only cultivated there.

64. Attested in Kongo, Kimbundu, and for *A. spinosus* L. (a weed) in Umbundu and Nyaneka.

cucurbits were also cultivated. They include the calabash, i.e., *Lagenaria vulgaris* (*-bindá* 9/10, CS 128), the pumpkins *Cucumeropsis edulis/Mannii* Cogn. (perhaps only in Kongo country), and *citrullus vulgaris* Schrad. (*-tanga* 5/6, CS 1676[65]), the colocynth, i.e., *Citrullus colocynthis* Schrad. (*mbumba* but only in Kongo), squash, i.e., *Cucurbita maxima* Duch. (*-nyangwa* 5/6[66]), the melon *Cucumis ficifolius* A. Rich both wild and cultivated (*-tanda* 5/6[67]), plus terms for a calabash bottle (*-cúpa* 9/10, 14/6?, CS 426[68]), and a calabash flask (*-cadį* 9/10, CS 253[69]). Another legume was okra, i.e., *Hibiscus esculentus* L. (*-ngombo* 7[70]). Besides this there were oil-bearing plants such as the castor oil plant, i.e., *Ricinus communis* L. (*-bóno* 3/4/*-móno* 3/4, 11/10, CS 166/CS 1320[71]), *Canarium schweinfurthii* Engl. (*-pápu*?[72]), and *Elaïs guineensis* Jacq., the oil palm (*-bá* 5/6, CS 1, and -*gadį*, CS 767[73]). Indeed *-yadį* 6 "oil," CS 1898, which is derived from *-gadį* 9/10, CS 768, "palm nut," became the universal designation for "oil, fat" in the entire area, including far to the south of the extreme limits where the tree could grow— indeed into the very Kalahari. Finally, there also was *Raffia textilis*, Welw. and related raffia palms (*-toómbe* 5/6),[74] which provided wine (*-dogų* 6, CS 649), building materials, and fibers. All these crops were planted (*-kún*, CS 1217) rather than sown, with the help of a toolkit that included digging sticks and ground stone tools, probably the same kit which foragers around them used as well. In this context one must mention that relatives of nearly all the

65. Attested in Kimbundu, Umbundu, Nyaneka, Nkhumbi, Kwanyama, Ndonga, Herero, Ngangela, Kongo (but there *Cucumerops edulis/manni*) but not in the Moxico or Lunda groupings.

66. Attested in Kimbundu group, Kete-Ipila, Ndembu, Cokwe, and Ngangela.

67. Attested in Kongo, Umbundu, Ngangela, perhaps Cokwe 7/8.

68. Attested in Holo, Sala Mpasu, Rund, Ndembu, Lwena, Cokwe, Ngangela, Kwanyama, Ndonga, Herero, Umbundu.

69. Attested in Cokwe, Lwena, Ndembu.

70. Attested only in Kimbundu and Cokwe, but most lexicons have no entry for this plant. The Kimbundu form produced the common American word *gombo* or *gumbo*.

71. The form *-móno* is attested in Kimbundu, Rund, Ndembu, Lwena, Cokwe, Ngangela, Umbundu, Nyaneka, Kwanyama, Ndonga, Herero and *-bóno* in Kongo.

72. Modern form *mbafu* 3/4. Attested in Kongo, Kimbundu, and Cokwe. Cf. Gossweiler, *Nomes*, pp. 174–75, but the word may have diffused recently under colonial influence. Also well known in Katanga, e.g., Luba *umpàfu* 3/4 "wild olive."

73. Henceforth, once a CS number is given, the languages cited there are no longer provided.

74. Attested in Pende, Holo, Kongo, Kimbundu, Imbangala, Cokwe. In Umbundu, the attestation -*tome* refers to "palm leaf" only and this was then borrowed into Nyaneka. The older Common Bantu *-bondo* 5/6 (Vansina, *Paths*, pp. 288–89) has been preserved in the Lweta and the Rund group languages.

plants mentioned grew wild in the area and in the Late Stone Age foragers may well have gathered most of those already.

Besides horticulture, fishing was evidently important to proto-Njila speakers. They used canoes and practiced most of the methods of fishing that are still in use. Older proto-Bantu words were still used in proto-Njila for "fish," "to fish with line," "fishhook," "canoe," "to row," and "paddle" while fish traps and fishing with baskets were probably in use as well.[75] Ethnographic evidence suggests that their technology was more developed than that of foragers and hence that fish as food was more important to them than to foragers, except along the coasts. At the same time, proto-Njila speakers, like the local foragers, also obtained most of their meat from hunting and trapping,[76] although they supplemented this by raising goats (*-búdį 9/10, CS 185). Despite the produce of their gardens, all year-round gathering still remained essential to them and provided additional edible or useful plants (especially leafy plants), mushrooms, and insects as well as honey.

The proto-Njila speakers were also potters (*-búmb- "to mold a pot," CS 199[77]), obtained salt (*-o(n)gúá 3/4, CS 2176[78]), worked stone tools[79] as well as wood,[80] and plaited or wove (*-túng-, CS 1847, "to sew, to plait," and, CS 1848,

75. Cf. Vansina, Paths, p. 288. The term for trap probably was *-támbo 3/4, CS 1661, and was also used for trapping game. In the east and southeast, many new terms (e.g., "paddle" and "river," and perhaps "fishtrap," "creel," "fishing net," and "fishing poison") were later borrowed from the upper Zambezi area. Internal innovations later developed along the northern coast (e.g., "canoe," "sweet water fish," "shark," "whale") and in the whole northern region from the coast to the middle Kasai as well (e.g., *-jadį 9/10 "river"). No comparative study of names for different species of fish has been made to date.

76. Considerable linguistic innovation took place later in these domains no doubt in part at least under the influence of foragers from whom knowledge and new techniques were borrowed. Still *-kónga "to hunt" and the usual derivation "hunter" are proto-Njila. The word is found in the Kongo group, and in every subgroup of Njila, except for the Lunda subgroup. I did not find it in Herero (but omukonge "a tracker"), Pende (but kongo 9/10 "track"), Rund, Sala Mpasu, Kete-Ipila, Lwena and Ndembu (but konga 5/6 "snare" later borrowed in Lwena and also -konga "to gather"). Proto-Bantu terms for "bow" (but not "arrow"), "spear," and "dog" are also attested everywhere (cf. Vansina, Paths, pp. 282–83, 290).

77. Add Nyaneka omumi "potter."

78. Guthrie, *-yungúá. Later a technique to make salt from the ashes of grasses by straining them was developed in the East Central African savannas. This new salt was called *-kédé 3, CS 1031c (from CS 1030 *-kéd "to filter"), and was borrowed into Mbala, Umbundu, Lwena, Cokwe, Ngangela, and Ndembu.

79. The most telling term is the one now used for "to forge" (*-tụd, CS 1861; Vansina, Paths, p. 294). Its reflexes attest to all the later phonological transformations of the notorious initial "*tụ."

80. See *-cong, CS 385, "to carve" (not just "to sharpen"). Widely attested in the Njila area.

"to build"[81]). By these and other processes they produced a wide range of products ranging from leatherwork to bark cloth (probably) and a wide variety of wooden and stone tools, baskets, mats, and nets.[82] As the communities became more sedentary, their houses became larger and better built. The range (and the weight!) of manufactured goods became far greater than it had been among nomadic foragers and that, in turn, fostered the development of new conceptions of property and the limits of sharing. Proto-Njila *-yéné in class 1/2 means both "owner" and "self to the exclusion of others" and in all other classes "self-same" (CS 1970/1[83]). The term could be linked to goods, places, or people and stressed that these belonged to this and no other person, rather than that such goods or people were an extension of the self-hood of the person, as was the case among foragers.

Even a cursory comparison between the lists of plants grown by the earliest proto-Bantu speakers and by proto-Njila speakers some two millennia later and some 1,500 kilometers farther south reveals a considerable expansion in the number and variety of the crops cultivated, especially among the yams and the cucurbits. Unsurprisingly, horticulture became more sophisticated over such a lapse of time. But the comparison also reveals that most of the newly added crops could also be found in the wild, which indicates that the proto-Njila system resulted from a fusion of the experience of earlier gardeners with that of foragers. While much of this was undoubtedly already old by proto-Njila times, the creation of grasslands gardens, fertilized by burning, as well as most of the set of cucurbits were then recent innovations, which came about when some of these communities began to settle on grassland. This burning technique and the crops associated with open grasslands were certainly obtained from the local foragers, who had "always" burned the grasslands as a hunting device and knew its regenerative effect on plants. Their inputs were responsible for the perfect adaptation of this system of horticulture to its environment, a system which was productive enough to allow for the kind of sedentary settlement found at Sakuzi and hence potentially for a considerable increase in the scale and the internal

81. See CS 1848; this is almost universal among the Njila languages. Building in this region implied plaited wattles sewn unto a wooden framework.

82. A thorough comparative study (including the vocabularies) for most of these processes and their many products still needs to be done and would be of considerable value to historians as well as archaeologists.

83. Both meanings attested in all the languages involved. Some time after proto-Njila, the form evolved in most languages to *-éné. The form given is valid for proto-Njila. For proto-Bantu, Meeussen reconstructed *-inị 1/2 "owner" and -ényé "self" but the latter is probably *-énị + a.

complexity of society. With the exception of fishing techniques, the role of aboriginal foragers as teachers was also crucial in all matters of hunting and gathering in which detailed knowledge about the local environments, fauna, and flora was essential. Hence one cannot but conclude that aboriginal foragers collaborated in the development of the technology of horticulture as it spread and that without them this achievement would have been impossible. It is not at all fanciful to imagine that some of their communities might well be tempted by this new mode of life were it not for the drudgery and extra work gardening entailed.

Something is known about the social organization of the proto-Njila speakers from their nomenclature for different social and territorial aggregates. Still as each of the later societies which use Njila languages underwent a great deal of change since proto-Njila times, so did their social vocabulary and it is not always easy to establish whether a word (form and meaning) is proto-Njila or arose at a later time. Keeping this in mind and starting with the local residential community, one encounters three terms for local residence, none of which existed in earlier times, but only one of which is undoubtedly proto-Njila. The other two are *-jĳko 5/6 "household,"[84] innovated from the earlier meaning "hearth" (CS 828 + 2056), which refers to people living in the same compound, and *-jóoto/a 5/6 "councilhouse" as well as "household, descent group,"[85] innovated from "fire in the hearth" and proto-Bantu *-jót- "to warm oneself (CS 2136)," which referred to all the inhabitants of a village. Neither term specifically refers to descent. Indeed *-jĳko probably included anyone living in the compound since by 1600 its attestation in Kimbundu had become a term reserved for the local group of slaves born as such in the household of a leader, a meaning also found in Mbala. Whether or not either term is proto-Njila with the meanings given, one can hardly doubt that households and village communities existed. The village itself was *-gigumbo 5/6[86], an innovation that is certainly proto-Njila

84. Attested in Pende as "local lineage," Rund as "local bilateral descent group," Mbala and Kimbundu as "group of slaves belonging to the local household," Cokwe as "household including domestic slaves," and way southeast in Mbukushu (didhiko) as "household." But the extension from "hearth" to "household" may have occurred independently in the north and in the southeast. Hence one cannot be certain that the term is proto-Njila.

85. Attested as "reception place" in Cokwe, Rund, and Nkhumbi (glossed as "sala"), Kongo-Dinga "patrilineal group," Pende "sacred place for chief," Kwandu "shrine and name for deceased patrilineal ancestors." Were it not for Nkhumbi, the term certainly would not be considered proto-Njila.

86. The form *-gĳmbo is attested in most languages, but the form reconstructed by Homburger (Meeussen) in the southern languages of the Kunene group is *-gumbo 5/6,

and replaced the older term *-gị 5/6 "village" (CS 818 + 936). This reconstruction suggests that villages were now fenced in by bushes as a defense against either predators or enemies. The last relevant term is *-páta 3/4, 5/6, 9/10 (CS 1456) "tract of land pertaining to a village or a ward in the village."[87]

Several other words attest to groups larger than the local village community, two of which are territorial while three others relate to groups that were perhaps composed of kinsfolk, perhaps not. The proto-Bantu term *-ci 9/10 "country" or "territory" (CS 330, 331) was still in use but during or soon after proto-Njila times its meaning came to be restricted to a stretch of land or a landscape. Later innovations were coined to designate a common political territory.[88] The fact that proto-Njila abandoned the form *-ci 1/2 + personal noun "group of X" and substituted *-kwá 1/2 + personal noun ("at + X") for the same meaning supports this interpretation.[89] Moreover proto-Njila lost an earlier word for leader, namely, *-kụ́mụ́ 1a/2.[90] It also lost *-dịmu 1/2, 3/4, CS 619, "ancestral spirit." This implies that leadership roles were now less prominent than had been the case earlier. The whole suggests that proto-

---

and 3/4 "house" 11 "enclosure" are derived from *-gumb (CS 893) "to enclose with bushes." The attempted reconstruction given here adds *-gumbo "enclosure" to *-gị "village" and assumes that the second syllable was elided in the northern languages and the first one in the Kunene group. The word occurs in every language, except in the Lunda group (Sala Mpasu, Kete Ipila, Rund, Ndembu), although in Cokwe the meaning is any "capital, chief's village." Yet in the same region, Mbal Kasai and Lwalwa do have the form. The form *-gumbo is attested in Nyaneka, Nkhumbi, Kwanyama, Ndonga, and Kwambi.

87. Certainly proto-Njila (Vansina, *Paths*, p. 273). The meanings vary from "political domain" in Rund to "ward" in Nkhumbi and Nyaneka, "bilateral group" in Umbundu, "neighborhood" in Ngangela, "kitchen, family" and (with prefix 7/8) "garden" in Kwangari, "home" in Dciriku, and "small village, house" in Kimbundu. The original meaning is established by reference to meanings in other Western Bantu languages.

88. Attested with the meaning "ground" in all languages and also "district" in Kimbundu, Holo, Pende, and Mbala as in proto-West Bantu. Replaced by -fuci 7/8 "crowd, political territory, region" in Kimbundu (-fushi), Mbala, Pende, Cokwe, Lwena (where the same form is also in class 5/6), and Sala Mpasu with the meaning "stranger." Then -futi or -huti 7/8 in Lucazi, -futi 5/6 in Mbunda, -kuti 7/8 "chief's enclosure" in Nyemba, -kuti 9/6 "field" in Herero and Ndonga. All these *may* ultimately stem from a common form because of the transformations undergone by *k/p/t before *-ụ. Related to -kutu 7/8 "family, group of families" in Herero, or even -puta 7/8 "clan" in Pende? The words for "political territory" in other languages are unrelated to this set.

89. Vansina, *Paths*, p. 274. One sees that *-kwá 1/2 occurs in nearly all the Njila languages but was apparently innovated shortly before proto-Njila emerged.

90. The attestation in Kimbundu is a later loan from Kongo while attestations in Pende and Mbala stem either from Kongo or from the lower Kasai region. Those in the Lweta languages are recent loans from Luba-Kasai.

Njila speakers abandoned an earlier recognition of overarching formal districts consisting of several villages. Still society did not completely shrink to the level of single-village communities. For *-gandá 5/6 "large social group" (CS 779) is also certainly proto-Njila.[91] Moreover, the same form but in the classes 9/6, 9/10 (CS 780) referred perhaps originally to a village more important than others. If so, that would point to the existence of a territorial hierarchy beyond the village. But this meaning may not have been the earliest as the meanings associated with this form came to vary a good deal in the different subdivisions of Njila, no doubt to accord with divergent social developments after proto-Njila times. Thus the form acquired meanings ranging from "hunter's camp" or "ordinary village" to "capital."[92] Finally, proto-Njila had *-cok "to be equal," from which words for "kinsfolk (as opposed to others)" derived, namely, *-coko 14 "relatives, kinship," as well as "quasi-relatives, interclan allies" in classes 7/8 and "settlement composed of relatives" in classes 3/4. Although most of these terms are clearly later regional innovations, the abstract form in class 14 may be proto-Njila.[93]

Taken as a whole these words tell us that proto-Njila speakers were aggregated in households, several of which made up a village. They also recognized at least two larger social groups, one based on kinship in general (*-cok-) while the other (-gandá 5/6) may have expressed the notion of an association on a larger scale than the village community without specifying the criteria for membership. An earlier organization into formal districts led by chiefs was abandoned during proto-Njila times. The overall impression these data leave is one of a social organization in which village communities may well have been of about the same size as those of neighboring foragers

91. Vansina, *Paths*, pp. 268–69, "House." In proto-Njila, however, the group was larger than a village community and membership was not necessarily based on kinship. Thus *rianda* 5 "company, group, association" in Kimbundu. Attested in Kongo, Mbala (7/8), Holo (7/8) Kimbundu, Nyaneka, Nkhumbi, Herero, Kwandu and -*ngandi* 9 "kinsman" in Umbundu.

92. Vansina, *Paths*, pp. 268–69. Attested in Pende as "small sacred house [of chief]" and in plural (6) "nobility"; in Kimbundu, "hunters's camp" and "place for discussion"; Cokwe "chief's court" and in plural Cokwe and Lwena "courtiers"; in Lwena, Ndembu, Lucazi, Mbunda, (Nyemba?) "capital"; in Rund and Kongo-Dinga "political territory"; in Bushong and Mbagani "big village" and in Kete Ipila and Herero "village."

93. In class 14 "family, kindred, relationship" and in the plural class 6 "relative, relation" in Cokwe, Lwena, Ndembu, Ngangela group, Nyemba and -*shoko* 14 "generation" in Mbunda; in class 7/8 "clan allies" in Kwandu, Nyaneka, Hanya, Umbundu, and "kinsfolk" in Nyemba; in class 3/4 Rund, Luba Kasai, Songye, and Herero "family, ethnic group" and Pende *musoga* 3/4 "new residence and its founder." Includes perhaps also -*sówú* 5/6 "name of the patrifamily" in Mbagani.

and more similar to them than to earlier Bantu-speaking societies because the previously existing political institution which bound village communities formally together had withered. But the same terminology also betrays traces of considerable fluidity in meaning, which tells us that these social institutions probably underwent some changes during proto-Njila times as well as considerable and complicated changes after these remote times. Of particular interest is how meanings of the same forms in different languages sometimes designate local and territorial aggregates and sometimes other social groups usually based on kinship. This indicates that forms easily shifted from one set of meanings to the other and suggests that an aggregation based on locality, albeit of related folk, and not an aggregation based exclusively on kinship, irrespective of locality, was the most fundamental form of social grouping. This throws doubt on the existence of clans of any sort whether unilineal or based on double descent.[94] It strongly suggests that the kinship system was bilateral and based on territory. From the point of view of each person, an individual recognized all relatives living in or stemming from the villages in which one's ascendants had been born as forming a single group. At the same time, however, from a "detached" point of view the inhabitants of each village or in each neighborhood of villages were considered to constitute a block of kinsfolk.

Nothing in the proto-Njila system of kinship terminology as it can be reconstructed indicates whether it fitted with either a unilineal or a bilateral kinship system. The terms were arranged in a hierarchical order by generations and within a generation by age and in the first ascending generation and the zero generation (Ego's) by gender. The set included what is called bifurcation in the first ascending generation by designating a mother's brother as "male mother" and (less evidently) father's sister as "female father" while

94. Contrary to what one might deduce from Ehret (*An African*, pp. 149–50), there is no term for "large unilineal descent group" in proto-Njila. The forms *-dongo 5/6, 7/8 and *dungo* 5/6 were no longer in use in proto-Njila times although *-dong-* "to arrange, to heap, to pack," CS 657–59, from which they are derived, was. According to Ehret, this etymology proved that the early Bantu system was one of unilinear descent. In the Njila branch, however, *-dongo 7/8 is attested only in a single compact block, namely, the languages of the Kunene group plus Nyengo and Kwangwa beyond the frontier (according to Johnston) with the meaning "country" (in Herero only "place where one can live") and seems to be due to borrowing from the east. That evidence is insufficient to posit the form in proto-Njila. However, proto-Njila had *-dongo 3/4 "line, rank," CS 664, another derivation from the same *-dong-* verb. Note that the idea of "a linear arrangement" is not part of the original meaning of the verb and hence need not be present in *-dongo 5/6, 7/8 and *dungo* 5/6 "large social group." Hence these were not necessarily unilineal as Ehret claimed.

in the zero generation it distinguished between siblings of opposite sex by calling them *-*páángi* 1a/2 and assimilated all cousins to siblings. Because cross-cousins were not distinguished from others, it is clear that the opposite sex sibling designation and those in the ascending generation had more to do with actual and potential marriage alliances than with descent.[95]

A comparison of the religious vocabulary found in the languages belonging to the *njila* group shows that this underwent a great many changes since proto-Njila times. Only a few words survived from earlier times in proto-Njila, namely, *-dog-* "to bewitch," CS 644, and its derivations for "witch" and "witchcraft," CS 646, as well as *-ganga* 1n/2, 9/10 "ritual/medical specialist, healer," CS 786, and its derivation for "charm," CS 787.[96] The words applied to spirits of the deceased were those used to designate old living persons as well. There remains the ambiguous case of *-kítị* 3/4, 5/6, 9/6 "charm," its "shrine" and its causal "spirit," CS 1072. Although this form is attested everywhere in the area barring only the Okavango languages, it is not proto-Njila because the present range of its meanings is huge, because the different languages do not conserve an identical semantic core, and because the variants are geographically well defined. The situation is better explained by diffusion from language to language than by common inheritance. Moreover the word also diffused from this area into most of the languages of the east central savanna. Hence it is not an ancestral item but an ancient loanword.[97]

95. In general, proto-Njila kinship terms, with the exception of "grandchild," are easy to reconstruct, despite later changes. As to *-páángi* 1a/2, (i) it occurs in all the languages of the area, except for the Ambo and Herero groups as well as Ndembo. But (ii) *-paanga* 5/6 "friend" occurs in the Herero group, Nyaneka, Nkhumbi, and Nyemba. Hence a nominal form applied to people and derived from the well-known verb *-pááng-* "to divide in two" or (in Herero) "to join" was universal. Third (iii), opposite-sex siblings are distinguished everywhere in the area except among the Ambo, modern Ambundu (but they were in the seventeenth century), Holo, Mbala, and Pende with a curious feature in Ndembo. There women use an opposite sibling term but men do not! Last (iv), wherever it is used, *-páángi* 1n/2 refers to opposite-sex siblings, except in modern Kimbundu, Kongo, Yaka, Suku, Pende, and Holo, where it refers to all siblings, and except in the Moxico languages, where *-panyange* 1n/2 (contracted from *pangi* + *yange* [mine]) designates cross-cousins. The present situation is best explained by positing proto-Njila *-páángị* 1n/2 "opposite-sex sibling" with semantic derivations and replacements following later.

96. The term *-gang-* included the ambivalence of a force thought to destroy as well as to heal. In the eastern and southern part of the region, *-ganga* 1n/2 later acquired the meaning "witch," while *-ganga* 14 (e.g., *bwanga*) seems to have included sorcery as well as medicine from the outset.

97. *Contra* the implication in Vansina, *Paths,* p. 297, but the diffusion is clearly not recent as attestations were already reported ca. 1600. Some contemporary meanings

Thus, the proto-Njila speakers maintained a somewhat more complex economy than the autochthons. The size of their settlements may have been somewhat greater than that found among foragers if the terms for household, hearth, and village assembly place around a fire are indeed proto-Njila. But one sorely needs archaeological data from the Middle Kwilu area to establish whether village size was indeed greater than the size of foraging encampments. The relationships between people living in different villages were more institutionalized (e.g., *-gandá) than was the case between settlements among foragers.[98] On the whole, though, one gains the impression from the admittedly sparse linguistic evidence that the society of the proto-Njila speakers had become less structured than earlier Bantu-speaking societies to its north had been through the loss of formal overarching institutions concerning both leadership and political territory. If this impression is borne out by future research, then one can certainly attribute this loss of formal complexity to an increased influence of the foraging way of life on horticulturalists as a result of the emergence of proto-Njila speakers into new environments so different from their familiar equatorial rain forests.

The Dissemination of the Njila Languages and Its Consequences

Linguistic data indicate that the Njila languages dispersed from their cradle in the Middle Kwilu region and eventually came to be spoken over all of West Central Africa, but there is little or no evidence as to how this happened. As John Robertson and Rebecca Bradley have conclusively shown for Zambia, Bantu languages did not and could not have spread as the result of a massive population movement.[99] And just where would all those people have

within the area are: "spiritual being" (*mukita* 3/4) in Kimbundu, "chief's ancestor" (*ekisi* 5/6) in Umbundu, "circumcision mask" (*mukhisi* 3/4) in Pende, "ancestral spirit" (*mukishi* 3/4) in Ndembu, and both "ancestor" (*mukisi* 3/4) and "nature spirit" (*likisi* 5/6) in Lucazi, as well as "suit in netting of masked dance" (*mukisi* 3/4) in Nyemba, "epidemic" in Herero (*omucithe* 3/4), and "an epidemic disease of boils" in Nkhumbi in Quilengues (*mukifi* 3/4). It is also evident that the form with the linked meanings of "mask," "masked dancer," and "dangerous spirit represented by the dancer" have all diffused together in the whole eastern part of the area as part of the spread of the initiation masquerades. Note that Kongo *nkisi* 3/4 "object containing a spiritual being" differs significantly from all of the above, including Kimbundu.

98. Only future excavations will be able to tell us whether the settlements were larger than those of foragers or their houses better built. Robertson argues that in Zambia during the Early Iron Age they were not. See Robertson, "Early," pp. 147–81 (esp. 179).

99. Robertson and Bradley, "A New Paradigm," pp. 287–323. For an increased awareness of the problems involved in postulating mass migrations, see Stefan Burmeister, "Archaeology and Migration," pp. 539–67 (pp. 548–52 for the exemplary Anglo-Saxon case).

continued to come from during so many centuries? Hence the languages must have been disseminated by language transfer since at least some of the local communities speaking other languages must have adopted the Njila language. Sociolinguistic studies show that such a transfer was a slow process lasting several generations. First, important people in the affected communities became bilingual. They not only learned to speak Njila to outsiders but also began to introduce some Njila words and expressions into their own language when their dependents and followers who imitated them also became bilingual. As the attraction of the Njila language continued, the descendants of the now bilingual community then began to use the Njila language more and more frequently and gradually forgot some of the finer points of their own speech until their descendants, several generations later, eventually became wholly Njila-speaking. Anecdotal evidence for this process abounds in the literature dealing with the relations between Khoisan-speaking foragers and Njila-speaking farmers in recent times.[100] A systematic study concerning the transfer from Yeyi to Tawana (both Bantu languages) around the Okavango Swamps documents the process in detail and shows that after two centuries of contact, and despite Tawana domination, Yeyi speakers have not yet completely shifted over to Tawana.[101] An alternative or complementary scenario is suggested by recent interrelations in the Kaokoland between Cimba foragers and Himba herders. It documents how even in a land of nomads a sedentary settlement does become a magnet that will attract foragers. So it is quite reasonable to expect that at least a few small individual families of foragers would come to live in the vicinity of a sedentary village and eventually shift over to the Njila language.[102]

Another major means of fostering language shift, and perhaps the most frequent one, was intermarriage between Njila speakers and others. Not only did the spouses in such a marriage become at least somewhat bilingual, but the numbers of bilinguals rose sharply in the next generation as their children grew up, and this just as much in the non–Njila-speaking communities as in the Njila-speaking ones, unless the exchange of women was un-

100. See Guerreiro, *Boximanes,* p. 211 (children are given two names—one San, the other Njila); p. 276 (Njila influence on kinship terminology). Almeida, *Bushmen,* p. 19 (both Zama or Kwengo and Sekele speak several Bantu languages besides their own).

101. Sommer, *Ethnographie.* The transfer remained slow despite the close linguistic relationship between Yeyi and Tawana. In the Lozi case nearby, Kololo (Lozi) did not succeed in completely ousting Luyi despite missionary and administrative action in its favor. Indeed, recently Lozi itself is becoming more and more influenced by Luyi rather than the reverse.

102. MacCalman and Grobbelaar, "Preliminary Report," pp. 1–32.

balanced in favor of the Njila communities and/or unless Njila-speaking communities only used the Njila language while foragers used both languages. Certainly some migrating communities in recent centuries were very much aware of the impact of sexual liaisons on linguistic and cultural assimilation. Thus during and even after the end of their migration in the hinterland of Namibe (Moçamedes) any Kwandu who had sexual relations with any of the Kwisi among whom they migrated lost his identity as a Kwandu. By strictly enforcing this rule the Kwandu succeeded in maintaining their identity.[103] Perhaps then in early times also any Njila-speaking man marrying a non–Njila-speaking woman was supposed to impose Njila in his household or become an outcast, while Njila-speaking women marrying non–Njila-speaking men were also supposed to teach Njila to their children and use the language in their compound. Who knows? As the reader senses, a great deal of speculation, none of which can be tested, is needed to develop a full-fledged scenario of how the Njila languages spread. Better then to bluntly admit that all one knows is that most Njila languages disseminated by language shift and that the precise processes by which this shift occurred were certainly not uniform over so many centuries but rather contingent on different concrete situations.

Language shifts are only induced if there are strong and enduring reasons for the people who shift to do so. Most commonly these tend to be political, as when a group is dominated by another one, as in the Tawana case, for example, or economic when a *lingua franca* becomes extremely important, as happened in early times when some East African coastal people adopted Swahili. Language shifts can also occur in any situation in which the community of the donor language is perceived as more prestigious even if the donor speakers are in the minority in relation to recipient speakers in the region surrounding their settlements. Still, it is hard to see why speakers of very different languages in the Middle Kwilu area would have been attracted to the proto-Njila spoken in a few novel villages that had appeared in their midst. Why should proto-Njila speakers enjoy any special prestige? Yes, they were perhaps better at fishing, they probably were somewhat better housed, and they used more manufactured objects. But these people came from a rain forest environment and they needed the local inhabitants to teach them how to adapt to the local savanna environment. Foragers had to work less than horticulturalists and could easily gather wild plants similar to those the villagers raised in their gardens, plants which they had had probably long before horticulturalists appeared. In addition, it would not

103. Medeiros, *Vakwandu*, pp. 22, 28, 31.

escape notice that life in sedentary villages was less healthy. Fields bred mosquitoes and hence malaria, while continued residence in a single spot facilitated both the transmission of malaria and favored the occurrence of helminthiases and diarrhea.[104] On the other hand, sedentary villagers need not have applied such stringent birth control as foragers did, thus allowing for somewhat faster human reproduction. Sedentary life was certainly better for the longer survival of the elderly and of their memories. Their experience was undoubtedly a positive asset to cope with environmental crises recurring at longer intervals. Still none of this would have prompted foragers to adopt proto-Njila. I rather imagine that the decisive factor that favored the proto-Njila speakers was the existence of a network of more formalized associations (*-gandá) between their villages, which allowed them to assemble larger and more efficient work parties for endeavors which required them.

The dissemination of the Njila languages occurred in two stages (map 9). At first, the use of the proto-Njila language spread slowly southward from community to community mainly by language shift, occasionally assisted by the relocation of existing villages until a line running from the coast north of Benguela over the planalto to the uppermost Cuanza and beyond the upper Kasai was reached. At that point, the tract of territory in which proto-Njila was spoken had become so large that direct intercommunication between the inhabitants at its extremes was so rare that their local dialects became mutually unintelligible and turned into two daughter languages, one for the northern unit and one for the southern one.[105] The location of this southern boundary region happens to coincide more or less with that of the ecological limits of the horticultural system, based as it was on yams and oil palm, which suggests a connection between the two diffusions.[106] In any

104. See Robertson, "Disease and Culture Change in South Central Africa," pp. 165–73.

105. The simplest possible scenario for the dissemination is given by the "the principle of the least moves." It is derived from the genealogical tree of the Njila languages as is its chronology. Each successive node or split in the tree is located on the map at a line or point on the mutual border of the tracts *now* covered by the daughter languages. The lines or points of chronologically successive nodes yield a dissemination path. See Ehret, "Language and History," pp. 286–87. But the contemporary map of languages can be misleading. In the case of the Njila group, considerable change occurred from the eighteenth century onward and for the Lweta languages even a century earlier than that. One uses, therefore, the earliest known situation rather than the contemporary one. Moreover, splits on the tree correspond in fact to fissures in an area originally covered by the ancestral language. Such fissures occurred at first well beyond the later frontiers between daughter languages on the map.

106. Indeed, the very fact that the splitting of the northern and southern units seems to have occurred in this place suggests that the spread of Bantu languages was held up for a long time in this area.

case, although not every community that took to horticulture necessarily adopted the Njila language, still many (perhaps all?) who adopted the language also seem to have taken to horticulture. Hence concern about gardening conditions (rains and soils) probably influenced the overall pattern of diffusion of both. The infertile soils due south of the middle Kwilu region were not of interest. They only allowed horticulture along the forest galleries fringing the main rivers. But from the middle Cuanza basin southward lay vast tracts of quite fertile lands attractive to horticulturalists and therefore to Njila speakers as well. Major rivers were another focus of attraction, this time for fishing people. At first, rivers such as the Kwango, Kwilu, and other affluents of the Kasai probably attracted fishing folk southward, but later the Cuanza and its major affluents drew others westward as far as the coast, which they then explored both northward and southward from the Cuanza Estuary.

The second phase of the dissemination began when the languages of the new northern and southern units began to fissure themselves and spawn daughter tongues. In the north, the inhabitants of the richer lands of the middle Cuanza lost contact with the little islands of Njila speakers in the poor lands to their northeast so that the northern unit split into the Middle Kwilu and Kwanza Blocks. A similar process in the south led to the emergence of the languages of the Eastern and Kunene Blocks. Here the southward dissemination of the Njila languages east of the uppermost Cuanza nearly came to a standstill more or less along the latitude of the upper Lungue-bungo River, which was also near the ecological limits of horticulture. The Eastern Njila language then disseminated eastward as far as the headwaters of the Zambezi and later northward downstream along the Kasai, Lulua, and other rivers teeming with fish.

Meanwhile some Kunene languages continued to be disseminated southward in the Cunene basin and along the Okavango River well beyond the limits of efficient horticulture. The reader will remember that the main domestic crops could not be grown south of the environmental barrier, which now lies along latitudes 11° to 12° S, but was farther south before 500 because the climate then was wetter. Nevertheless, even then much of the internal Cunene basin, the whole Cuvelai basin, and the banks of the lower Okavango were well beyond the ecological boundary. Attestations of old word forms or oil palm and domestic yams of any sort do not occur in the Njila languages south of that barrier. In these climes, products of wild palms and tubers substituted for palm oil and yam tubers. Palm oil was first replaced by the oils found in the nuts of local trees and by the use of castor oil. Yet it is telling that *-gadú, the old Njila word for the palm nut and its fat,

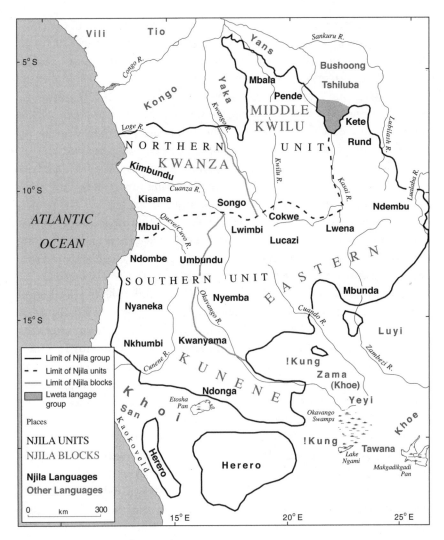

MAP 9. The Spread of the Njila Languages

was retained despite the absence of such palm nuts and was now applied to all oils and fats.[107] Some of the cucurbits of the north were lost and were replaced by a wide choice of wild gourds, melons, and squashes. Hence the cultivated crops in this region were limited to beans, groundnuts, perhaps the

107. Compare *-gadi 9/10 "nut" and 6 "fat" (maji), CS 768. In Lwena and Cokwe, the form refers to the oil palm, its nut, and its fat. The form for fat is attested in virtually every language. For the south, e.g., in Umbundu, Kwangari, and even in Mbukushu and Yeyi, Nyaneka, Nkhumbi, Kwambi, Kwanyama, and Ndonga, but not in Herero.

Livingstone potato, and several varieties of cucurbits. As a result, the cultivation of domestic plants became less important than gathering. The rise of gathering naturally led to the adoption of seasonal transhumance despite the fact that villagers did continue to lay out fields, in contrast to pastro-foragers, who might plant the occasional plot of cucurbits or groundnuts but did not stake out fields. Newcomers here had to adopt nearly the whole way of life of the local pastro-foragers, including sheepherding, with the result that both groups, language apart, became nearly indistinguishable.

Under such circumstances, speakers of other languages could not be expected to shift to a Njila tongue, so the dissemination of these languages must have been caused by immigration, probably by already assimilated communities from farther north. The geography of the region suggests that such immigrants were fishing folk who founded villages here and there along the lower Okavango and a few communities on the Chela highlands and perhaps along the Cunene River. But these would have been so dispersed and so few in number that one would rather expect these folk to shift to a Khoisan tongue predominant in the wider region than the reverse and that probably began to happen. There is, after all, nothing inherently superior to a Bantu language as such, and some Njila speakers have evidently lost their language to adopt one of the San tongues, as witnessed by the Bergdama and the so-called Black Bushmen of northern Botswana.[108] An example of just how easily language in a small community can change is the case of the Dciriku, whose language underwent profound change as a result of a single Tawana attack ca. 1900.[109] By all expectations then, the Njila language in southern Angola should gradually have become extinct. Yet it did not happen because the introduction of cereal agriculture from the southeast followed shortly after the arrival of the Njila speakers and saved their languages from extinction. For, unlike others, they still made fields; hence, it was easier for them to take to cereal farming than it was for other pastro-foragers.

Dating the dissemination of the Njila languages still remains vague. On present evidence, this process began during the third century BCE and Njila languages reached the lower Okavango by about 500. They were in use there before cereal crops and cattle herding appeared in the region because the terminology of cereal farming and cattle pastoralism in the Njila languages is

---

108. The Bergdama are the best-known case. See Vedder, *Bergdama* 1:153–54; Almeida, "Dos Kwadi"—*Garcia*, pp. 772, 775–76; Almeida, *Bushmen*, pp. 13–16, 19 (Zama or Kwengo black Khoe speakers); Livingstone, *Missionary Travel*, pp. 78–79 (Black Bushmen); Denbow, "Material Culture," p. 116. Such cases existed, then, all along the southernmost Bantu border.

109. Möhlig, *Die Sprache der Dciriku*, pp. xxiii–xiv, 52–54.

borrowed from Bantu languages without any Khoe intermediary.[110] The earliest cattle bones in the area proper date to ca. 600 at Divuyu in the Tsodilo Hills just south of the Okavango River. They are somewhat later than 290 at Lotshitshi, well east of the Okavango Delta.[111] The whole dissemination process of the Njila languages seems then to have taken some eight centuries at the most or between 25 and 30 generations. Given the distance between the middle Kwilu and the lower Okavango (ca. 1400 kilometers) and the slow rate at which language shift occurs, this is actually a rather fast expansion, which in turn suggests that Njila speakers did not settle on the lower Okavango long before 500.

The dissemination of language is perfectly possible by language shift or by the movement of a few persons between communities. But languages do not shift and disseminate just by themselves and for their own sake. Other elements are always involved and language shift itself is usually only one effect of a wider assimilation process. At the very least it is accompanied by the acceptance of those particular sociocultural features of the donor community which impressed or attracted the recipient community to begin with, for instance, its sedentarity, its horticulture, or its patterns of intersettlement coordination.

But although language shift and the transfer of social organization often occur together in a process of assimilation, the dynamics of the actual language shift and sociocultural transfers are very different from each other because sociocultural organization and language are totally different things. Language is a single, integrated, and arbitrary system of communication while sociocultural organization is a congeries of more or less integrated institutions which regulate actual living. It follows that while sociocultural assimilation is often quite gradual as one feature and then another are borrowed without affecting the framework of the receiving community very much, language shift is all-or-nothing. To borrow bits or pieces of grammar or syntax is literally nonsense because without the whole arbitrary framework no common meaning can be construed from any utterance. Hence language shift means the adoption of the whole framework and not just one feature or another. The consequences of all this can seem strange: Thus it is true that all Njila languages today grew out of a single proto-Njila language,

110. See the next chapter for the terminologies involved. This conclusion goes against Wilmsen, *Land*, p. 71, as his authority, Ehret, changed his views to claim that all transfers were directly from Bantu to Bantu languages, which also agrees with our findings. See Ehret, *African*, pp. 271–73 and table 45. He adds that the influence of Khoe on Bantu cattle vocabulary occurred later.

111. Wilmsen, *Land*, pp. 65–66; J. Denbow and E. Wilmsen, "Advent," pp. 1509–15.

but it is false to say that all the societies and cultures of Njila speakers today developed out of a single primordial proto-Njila–speaking society. It is a fallacy to hold that a whole distinct sociocultural system diffused along with each Njila language group, but it is correct to hold that the dissemination of the Njila languages was accompanied by that of important sociocultural features, most probably linked to sedentarity and horticulture or cereal agriculture, and it is that quality which makes this dissemination truly significant for the social historian. Thus while the equation language = culture = society is a fatal if all too common error—still language is not wholly disconnected from culture but forms a part of it.

The story of the dissemination of Njila languages and the accompanying assimilation processes does not end on the lower Okavango ca. 500, and not just because Njila languages were eventually to spread as far south as present-day Windhoek. Moreover, when the lower Okavango was reached that does not mean that the whole area between there and the middle Kwilu, or between the ocean and the upper Zambezi, was by then solidly Njila-speaking and wedded to a single set of cultural ways. Far from it. Njila speakers were still very few and far between in the southern half of the area and foragers still occupied much of the infertile land in the north, perhaps even in the middle Kwilu. One must imagine Njila-speaking settlements as rare, scattered over the landscape like islands in an ocean, isolated and strewn at random here, arrayed in a line there, bunched into an archipelago elsewhere, all according to the lay of the richer land or the direction of the rivers. One must therefore separate the first appearance of Njila speakers without any special prestige, from a renewed expansion of the languages in a much later period when Njila-speaking communities had become technically and socially so advanced as to impress or even force their non–Bantu-speaking neighbors to assimilate and to abandon their own tongues. Only at that point did a general process of Bantuization begin. That point would not be reached before 900 CE when Njila-speaking communities had become full-fledged cereal farmers, after their populations had increased many times, after they had begun to develop more intricate sociopolitical institutions, and after a grid of flourishing trading routes had been formed between Njila-speaking population centers all over the area.

Metallurgy

The art of smelting and working metal came late to West Central Africa, later than anywhere else in Africa except for Namibia and the western Cape area. Moreover metallurgy entered the area twice, just as had happened in the case of ceramics, namely, once from the north around 400 and once from the south a century later. So even at this late date the northern half still belonged to a northern historical area and the southern half to a southern one, just as it had been during the Late Stone Age, even though the dissemination of Njila languages was beginning to blur the gap.[112]

Metalworking came first to the northern half of the area from the Lower Congo, where it appeared ca. 1 CE when the Ngovo industry was succeeded by the Kay Ladio industry. Iron smelting began around the same date on the Bateke plateaux north of Brazzaville. But in Kinshasa evidence for the use and smelting of metals appears only at Ngombe by the fourth century.[113] In the middle Kwilu region, the first use of metals may have occurred even later. Thus metallurgy was introduced four centuries or so after the first ceramics appeared in the Lower Congo and six centuries after they appeared in Kinshasa.[114] Despite all the loose references to Early Iron Age sites in the literature for any site with ceramics but without stone tools,[115] no dated site with direct evidence for iron earlier than the eighth century has been found so far between the Lower Congo and the Tsodilo Hills in the far south.[116] Iron

112. Despite the two quite separate introductions of metalworking into the area, the vocabulary referring to forging is similar nearly all over the Bantu-speaking world and also in this area. It consists of *-tμ́d- "to forge by pounding" and *-cámb- "to sharpen by forging through elongation of the metal" (many references, besides the few in CS 268 *cámbo 9/10, 11/10 "wire"). The word *-tμ́d- is "forge" and is clearly derived from an earlier "pounding," probably to knap stones. A similar change of meaning for *-cámb- could be "to make a point," although perhaps not "sharpen by grinding." In general the vocabulary for metallurgy supports a single origin for the technology. See also Nsuka-Nkutsi and de Maret, "Étude comparative," pp. 731–42. Yet the terminology is complex and also reflects considerable borrowing and innovations in later times (smelters!) even though Duncan Miller did not find any significant change in the techniques used at Divuyu and recent practices in southern Africa.

113. Kanimba Misago, "Zaire," p. 213; Dupré and Pinçon, Métallurgie, pp. 39–42.

114. Dupré and Pinçon, Métallurgie, pp. 39–42; Lanfranchi and Clist, Aux origines, p. 213 (for Gombe and Iron Age pits at Sakuzi).

115. Gutierrez, L'Art, pp. 33–34, noted this unwarranted assumption. None of the sites so labeled is well described. They all mostly contain just a scatter of pottery.

116. The oldest known ceramics stem from the scatter at Kapanda near Pungo aNdongo and from the lagoon site of Benfica. See Santos and Ervedosa, "A estação," pp. 48–51, plates 24–35 (date to ca. 140 CE). The ceramics differ from those of the north and date to ca. 80 CE. See also Gutierrez, Archéologie, pp. 59–61; Lanfranchi and Clist, Aux origines, pp. 180–219. The sites are not associated with stone tools, polished or not, nor is there any evidence of much stability of settlement, although Lanfranchi and Clist, Aux origines, p. 179, accept the presence of the shellmidden at Benfica as such, nor is there any sign of an incipient food production. Thus these sites are nearly a half-millennium later than the first appearance of ceramics in Lower Congo at a time when the first

has been found on a site dated to 760 at Dundo in northeast Angola, a sculpture, shaped by an iron tool, was found at Liavela (sources of the Cuanza) and dates to 750, while the date ca. 720 at Feti on the planalto may or may not be associated with iron objects found there.[117]

Given this situation, one understands why recently some archaeologists have prudently stated that metallurgy only reached Angola as late as "the second half of the first millennium of our era."[118] It seems therefore that Angola and Namibia were the last large portion of the continent to acquire this technology. Moreover, the introduction of cereal farming and the first acquisition of cattle in the southern half of the area followed so closely on the heels of the introduction of ironworking that it may even have been contemporaneous. For in the south, metallurgy first appeared ca. 600 on the then new settlement at Divuyu in the Tsodilo Hills of northwestern Botswana. At that time, smelting of iron and of copper was well known a considerable distance away from Divuyu because the people there imported the bloom from sources at least 200 kilometers away.[119] But in contrast to the north, metal may have been used there mainly to make beads and other portable ornaments and the whole appears here in a context of incipient herding of bovine cattle. Hence its introduction is best presented in the next chapter.

The metal objects found at the early Lower Congo sites are rather small but there may have been larger objects as well. In the beginning, iron was

---

evidence for the use of metals occurs there. Despite this chronological overlap and the absence of stone tools, we cannot not accept the interpretation of the latter site (179/219) or, for that matter, Kapanda as Early Iron Age.

117. Lanfranchi and Clist, *Aux origines,* p. 220 (Ricoco II (1010 BP = 840 CE); Feti (1240±100 BP = ca. 710 CE), but Ervedosa, *Arquéologia,* p. 220, has Dundo 760 CE, Feti 720 CE, and Ricoco 940 CE. The sculpture at Liavela dates to ca. 750 CE. See Van Noten, "La plus ancienne," pp. 133–36. The Feti date based on a Yale lab determination is also given in a letter by M. G. Childs to M. Herskovits, of which I have a copy. Ervedosa, *Arqueologia,* pp. 151–62, 197–220, gives five sites without evidence of iron near Luanda, in Lunda, in the center west and in the southwest: Mahura and Lue have stone tools and ceramics; Leba C6, Quitala, which is another lagoon site, and Mussolegi only ceramics. With evidence of iron, there are another five: Luxilo 5 (stone and iron); Galanga (microliths, pottery, slag); Ebo and Ganda I (slag and stone tools); and then probably late: Macahama (stone, ceramics, beads of which 14 are European, 2 local) and Tchitundo Hulo (stone, beads both European and local). Most of the sites mentioned here are clearly much later than Kapanda or Benfica. See also Gutierrez, *L'Art,* pp. 27–29. Several supposedly Urewe pots found near Tshikapa should not be considered. See de Maret, "Les trop fameux pots," pp. 4–12.

118. Oliveira, *Projetar o passado;* Gutierrez, *L'Art,* p. 171.

119. Denbow, "Congo to Kalahari," p. 161; Miller, *Tsodilo,* p. 95 (diversity of ores used).

rare and copper even more so; thus one would expect extensive recycling of the larger tools once they were worn out. The few objects that have been recovered include fishhooks, arrowheads, and an adze, i.e., all utilitarian items linked to fishing, hunting, and cutting—in sharp contrast to the profusion of beads and ornaments found at Tsodilo in the far south. Here in the north nearly every adult was interested in acquiring iron tools to replace the various stone-edged, or polished stone objects used until then. Despite this, however, demand for iron remained at first fairly flat because larger tools such as knives, machetes, or axes were recycled, because some items such as spearheads or even adzes wear out only slowly, and because most arrowheads are recuperated. Nevertheless, even this situation created a need for smiths and even for smelters in many communities, as is shown by the rapid spread of smelting during the first half of the first millennium on the neighboring Bateke plateaux.[120]

The process of transmitting the know-how and practice of metallurgy differed greatly from those of the earlier innovations. To begin with men, not women, were its main actors since the ethnographic record everywhere intimates that only men were metalworkers. Smelting and smithing became as much a badge of masculinity as hunting and perhaps stone knapping or waging war had been before. Second, this transmission was far from being a straightforward matter because the practice of metalworking does not just consist in handing over a set of recipes about smelting and forging—and both sets of operations were certainly not carried out in every settlement— if only because suitable ore was not available everywhere.[121] The main principles of the art of forging metal over an open fire were the easiest to learn and may have been acquired first. As a single man (all smiths later were men) or a man with a single aide could carry out this task and also cut the wood and prepare charcoal for the fire, no special organization of labor was needed. It was a task that required year-round apprenticeship with an experienced smith but perhaps not for many years. The acquisition of forging may thus well have preceded that of smelting, even if the raw metal was acquired from afar by trade, as may have been the case, for instance, at Divuyu from some 200 kilometers away.[122] Even so, raw metal had to be produced by a smelting operation somewhere.

120. Dupré and Pinçon, *Métallurgie*, pp. 42–43. Here slag heaps are easily detected on the flat open plateaux.

121. When considering these matters, Colleen Kriger's *Pride of Men* is the indispensable work. For this section, see pp. 29–157.

122. J. Denbow, "Congo," p. 161.

The art of smelting was far more difficult to transmit. A smelter required a great deal of knowledge ranging from identifying good ores or good wood for making charcoal capable of producing high temperatures, to building an efficient furnace which itself required some knowledge about pottery making, to melt the metal itself, and then to hammer the impurities out of the product. All of this could be learned only through many years of dry-season apprenticeship. Moreover, smelting, on any but the tiniest scale, required a considerable input of labor to perform the required ancillary tasks of mining ore, drying and milling it, building the furnace, shaping ceramic tuyeres, making and transporting charcoal, blowing the bellows, and fueling the burning furnace. Smelting was a dry-season occupation and, given the small size of the camps or villages, smelting operations were bound to entail a thorough upheaval of the usual dry-season hunting routines, which did deter many communities from adopting this pursuit. Finally, the apprentice could only learn his craft during a few months per year in the middle of a round of frantic activity under the tutelage of a very busy master smelter. Hence the transmission of the art of smelting and metalworking in general remained a rather slow and often uneven process, just as it had earlier been in Gabon, Cameroon, and Congo Brazzaville.[123]

One must therefore imagine the advancing frontier of the spread of metallurgy as a landscape where iron tools and jewelry were used ahead of the frontier of smithing, and smithing was far ahead of the frontier of smelters. Smiths remained in contact with smelters and probably also with other smiths, both to acquire raw metal and to exchange know-how. Finally, smelters did not move from village to village but from one good deposit of ore to another one some distance away. The front of their diffusion advanced then by occasional leaps and bounds rather than steadily year by year. It is very likely that smelters maintained their own communities and that the expansion of their operations implied the movement of a whole community. Because most good ore bodies are not quickly exhausted, a move usually occurred after a long period of time when an original community had become large enough to split. Attracted by a newly found promising ore body and/or repelled by internal quarrels among ambitious men in the original community, a portion of that community then moved to a new site. Young smiths, on the other hand, probably moved individually, attracted to new communities who wanted a smith in their midst by inducements such as the offer of a wife and by the likelihood that they could become a more important personage in that community than they could be at home. Along with the

123. Lanfranchi and Clist, *Aux origines,* p. 225.

diffusion of metallurgy there thus appeared new networks of communication along which smiths kept in contact with smelters and obtained raw iron or perhaps even iron ore.[124]

The introduction of metallurgy was soon followed by significant indirect economic and social effects. As new iron and copper ore deposits were discovered, such places began to attract people from sometimes far away to obtain either metal ore or the raw metal that was smelted there. Such places then reshaped the perception people had of entire regions around them by providing new foci and new travel routes. That altered the patterns of spatial mobility that had hitherto been current in the region. Moreover, the new activity created new links between different communities because of the now necessary interaction between smelters and smiths. The need for raw ore or refined metal and metal products favored the blossoming of exchanges not just between communities but also within them since only a very small number of people were knowledgeable and experienced enough to make metal goods. This is very different from the acquisition of the earlier technologies, including ceramics, which many people could hope to master. The use of metal objects thus signalled a loss of self-sufficiency. In order to obtain them, something had to be given in return, a requirement which promoted both exchange and a more developed sense of personal or familial property.

These effects were modest as long as metallurgy produced only small ornaments or tools. In the beginning, the impact of metal objects in the northern half of the area was linked to their utilitarian value as substitutes for less efficient stone or organic tools. Axes and bush knives were forged to clear gardens for root crops and legumes, knives for all sorts of cutting and carving, spears and arrowheads to hunt big and small game, and "ceremonial" items were made for prestige. At that time, small objects for hunting and cutting were personal property in the sense that, like other earlier ornaments and tools, they were perceived as an extension of the personal individuality of the person who had them, despite the fact that even then, such objects had to be acquired by exchange. They were acquired new, but once in use they were not resold. We can only surmise which goods were given in return. At the outset nothing was standardized and, according to the needs and surplus of the moment, a large a variety of goods could be exchanged for personal use, such as goats, food, other types of finery such as beads in other materials, or manufactured items such as furs, bark cloth, baskets, mats, etc. Bulkier

124. Kriger, *Pride*, p. 91. A few instances (Hungaan in Kwilu, Kwambi in the Chela Mountains) are known of parties of smelters touring the countryside in the dry season to smelt or forge as required.

objects, such as axes or large bush knives, were always more than an extension of a single person. Like dugout canoes or drums in earlier times, they may at first well have been communal property shared by all the adult members of the community in which they were fashioned and may not have been acquired by exchange with outsiders. But the more everyone needed these heavier tools at the same time to clear and prepare farmland, the more they also became personal property and they were directly acquired from smiths. Such objects were no longer tied to the personality of their users but became commodities which could and were transferred to all. Hence the quality of their ownership was also different. From then on, ownership began to be understood as exclusive control over a transferable commodity, a concept that soon spawned the notions of wealth and poverty.

The full impact of metallurgy was to come only later, after the practice of cereal agriculture established the dominance of the iron hoe over the wooden digging stick. Thus the introduction of metallurgy only held the potential of accelerating the advent of a larger scale society by favoring more trade, a stronger expression of status distinctions, and the possibility of concentrating power. But this potential could fully blossom only in concert with other innovations, of which cereal farming was the most important. One is tempted to speculate that this technology with its great potential was acquired by Njila-speaking horticulturalists only and was the key that later ensured the supremacy of their languages over all others. And, yes, it does seem that the transfer of the technology both in the north and in the southeast via Divuyu occurred between Bantu speakers, for there is no evidence of any distortion in the words that would indicate passage of the terminology through a non-Bantu language.[125] Still nothing prevented foragers from acquiring these skills at the same time as the Bantu speakers did. Indeed, during the nineteenth century some foragers as well as pure pastoralists, all speaking Khoisan languages in Namibia and in southern Angola, mined, smelted, and forged metals. Why not in early times as well? If early foragers did so, though, the volume of metal needed would have remained small since they required only portable objects, such as arrowheads, jewelry, and ornaments. Metallurgy was not of great importance until the adoption of farming, especially cereal farming, which introduced the hoe. Then the realization of its full potential was to benefit farmers far more than foragers and

125. The vocabulary relating to ironworking includes a series of terms, common all over the Bantu-speaking area, which seem to have originally applied to the working of stone (e.g., Guthrie, *Comparative Bantu* 1:132, 139, topograms 19, 26). Others stem from regional innovations of much later date.

since most farmers, especially in the south, were Njila speakers, that development did benefit the further dissemination of Njila languages.

Toward the Formation of West Central Africa

During the Late Stone Age, what is now West Central Africa formed part of two different areas. Its northern half was part of an equatorial area and its southern half of a southern African one. But the first stirrings of a new way of life that had taken root in the tropical rain forest country of western equatorial Africa reached the Lower Congo area around 400 BCE and slowly spread into the northern half of the study area from there. Ceramics and horticulture based on root crops appeared, more or less in tandem with the Bantu tongues, one of which was proto-Njila. While horticulture was the crucial technological innovation with the potential to create a sedentary way of life and genuine societies, proto-Njila–speaking communities introduced a few novel ideas and values as well as one or two formal social institutions that overarched the individual local residential community and thus constituted a first step on the road to constructing such societies. Women played the crucial role in these processes. They adopted and adapted the new technologies and they were the decisive agents in language shifts because they chose which language to teach to their small children. Through their marriages, many women physically bridged the gap between neighboring communities and thus carried innovations from their childhood homes to their homes or successive homes as spouses and perhaps elsewhere again as widows. More than any other factor, these ceaseless movements of women were the force that propelled these diffusions. Hence, even though we do not know what the rules which governed marriage prohibitions and preferences were, we must accept that they were probably the most crucial variable regulating these diffusions.

Both the technologies and the new language communities, more or less intertwined, then spread southward but only as far as the environmental barrier which then lay one or a few degrees south from latitude 11° or 12° S. Horticulture and its promise for more sedentary and larger human aggregates could not spread farther so that the division between the northern and the southern half of West Central Africa remained essentially unchanged. Meanwhile, from the last century BCE onward, the deep south saw significant change when sheepherding accompanied by the use of ceramics reached these lands from the east. But these innovations did not foster sedentarity nor need they have affected the size of the local community. Communities simply changed from being foragers to being pastro-foragers. Here men as

sheepherders seem to have been the main actors of change, and their ceaseless quest for more reliable rain and water supplies as well as richer grazing
grounds, usually on *mopane* lands, ensured the diffusion of sheepherding.

So horticulture could not move south of the ecological boundary, and
while agroforaging reached the same boundary from the south, it does not
seem to have crossed it. Thus the northern half of what is now West Central Africa seemed destined to remain part of an equatorial African area and
the southern half part of a south African one. That was still the case during
the first half of the first millennium, for the twofold introduction of ironworking did not alter the situation. And yet a few centuries later, by 800 or
900, all of West Central Africa had become a single coherent cultural entity,
despite the ecological boundary. This unification of the area resulted from
the combined effects of the dissemination of the Njila languages with the
cultural baggage they carried and the spread of cereal farming as the mainstay of food production over the whole area. Thus even though there were
no "Bantu migrations," the slow dissemination of the Njila languages from
person to person has been highly significant for the later social and cultural
history of West Central Africa. Still, without the adoption of cereal foods
everywhere, the entire area probably would not have been unified. Be that
as it may, it is very clear that the first ferments of change, the introduction
of ceramics, horticulture, goatherding and sheepherding, and metallurgy
had no decisive immediate impact on sedentarization, settlement size,[126] or
even food production in the south. The turning point, the subject of the next
chapter, would come only with the advent of cereal agriculture and cattle
herding on a large scale.

126. There is no evidence at all during this entire period for the appearance within
the area of "village sites," i.e., larger and more sedentary settlements than the temporary
encampments or the more stable lagoon settlements found earlier. But the large
Early–Iron Age site of Sakuzi in Lower Congo dated to the first century CE has been interpreted as a village site. See Gosselain, *Sakusi*; de Maret, "Le contexte archéologique,"
1:118–38, and references in Lanfranchi and Clist, *Aux origines*, pp. 213, 235.

2

EARLY VILLAGE SOCIETIES, 700–1000

 SUDDENLY—LIKE A SPECIAL EFFECT IN A MOVIE—TWO features that would play a decisive role in the future long-term history of all of West Central Africa appear simultaneously around 680 at a single, totally new settlement in the far southeastern section of our area of study. The features are the sedentary village and domesticated bovine cattle. Given the present state of knowledge, the settlement of Divuyu is so significant that one does well to open the subject by describing the finds there in some detail. Moreover, such a description will familiarize the reader with the concrete archaeological evidence that provide the foundation for the overall historical interpretations which flow from these finds.

Divuyu

Forty kilometers northwest of the great Okavango Delta in the steppes of the Kalahari, three hills (known as the male, female, and child), the components of the Tsodilo Hills, rise above the landscape. Late–Stone Age foragers were attracted to them because of the specularite deposits, which they mined to produce cosmetics.[1] There they also found abundant supplies of easily stored *mongongo* nuts, which contributed significantly to their food supply.[2] And it is also at Divuyu, on the top of the middle hill (the female hill), that in the late seventh century a wholly different community of immigrants suddenly appeared from nowhere.[3] At that time, the local climate was either still quite

1. Robbins et al., "Intensive Mining," pp. 144–50. My descriptions of Divuyu and Nqoma owe a good deal to some unpublished information and especially to comments made available by James Denbow. I am very grateful to him for his assistance. Still any errors of fact in this account are mine, not his!
2. Robbins and Campbell, "Prehistory," pp. 37–41.
3. Dates in Wilmsen, *Land*, p. 66. The calibrated dates are 667, 679, 705, 879, 892. The gap between 705 and 879 may only be apparent, however, as the sigma values overlap between 779 and 790 CE and the dates come practically from the same spot.

humid or just beginning to dry out. In any case, it was still much wetter than it is now and there were more sources of water nearby than is now the case. Indeed the local inhabitants may even have been exposed to schistosomiasis.[4] The Divuyu site itself was located on a hilltop plateau that was difficult to reach, small, and waterless. The nearest spring flowed in a ravine to the southeast. The Divuyans arrived bringing not only a novel type of ceramics, but also cowpeas, goats, and bovine cattle, as well as the art of forging metal, although they did not smelt it. Given the present state of research, it certainly looks as if these particular people really were immigrants who imported all these technological innovations at once, in contrast to other places where the advent of such innovations was staggered. Moreover, Divuyu was no longer an ephemeral camp, such as the earlier ones in the region, for this rather small spot was nearly continuously occupied for five to six generations or about two centuries. It was a permanent village from the start, albeit not one of great size, containing two living areas with substantial pole-and-daga houses and well-defined spaces for living, storage, and waste disposal.[5]

The lack of stone tools on the site indicates that the newcomers did not mingle much with the autochthons who worked in the nearby mines, and the site on a plateau was probably chosen by the immigrants for defensive reasons. Still, some remains of Divuyu pottery and a few scraps of iron on contemporary Late–Stone Age sites only a few kilometers away suggest that both groups participated in mutual exchanges.[6]

The faunal assemblages tell us that the Divuyans obtained 66 percent, or nearly two-thirds, of their animal food from goats or sheep,[7] 20 percent from animals hunted in the plains below the hills, 7 percent from fur-bearing animals, 4 percent from fish brought there from the river to the north or from

4. Robbins et al., "Intensive Mining," p. 146. On bilharziosis, see Robbins et al., "Archaeology," p. 1109 (schistosomiasis).

5. This information is from Denbow, who informs me that the full site reports for Divuyu, Nqoma, and other sites are now nearly complete and should be published soon. As of now, however, one still has to rely on the available statements made by the main excavators James Denbow and Edwin Wilmsen. For example, while an exact plan of the layout of Divuyu is not yet available, one does know that some 44 pits, each of one square meter, were excavated in two areas labeled "Baobab" and "Acacia." So even though nearly all the relevant data are available now, some of my interpretations will have to be qualified once the full site report is published.

6. Murphy et al., "Pottery," pp. 2–7; Robbins, "Intensive Mining," p. 149; Robbins "Archaeology," p. 1110.

7. See Gil Turner, "Early Iron Age Herders," pp. 7–17. One cannot distinguish between most bones of sheep and goat.

the delta to the southeast, and only 3 percent from cattle.[8] Too little remains of vegetable food have been found to establish a similar diagram, but there are cultivated *Vigna* beans and gathered *mongongo* nuts.[9] Given the permanence of the village, it is evident that, besides *Vigna,* other crops must have been cultivated. At the time when Divuyu flourished, sorghum or millet was cultivated at Matlapaneng on the other side of the Okavango Delta; both cereals were also present at nearby Nqoma—but still no trace of them has been found at Divuyu, although one strongly suspects that Divuyans cultivated these crops as well. Salt was not obtained from mineral deposits, which, given the climate then, may well have been more rare than today, but by filtering ashes since colanders used for this purpose have been found.[10] Despite the fact that Divuyans no longer relied on stone tools, 75 percent of the iron and copper objects found were jewelry and only 7 percent were small tools (arrowheads, points, and possibly blades, punches, and staples). The largest of these finds was a chisel approximately 5 centimeters (2 inches) long. Still, once worn out, larger utilitarian objects may well have been recycled into jewelry, for there are traces of iron slag, at least in the upper levels of the site.[11] All the raw material was imported, probably as blooms, ingots, larger objects used as ingots, or even metal scrap rather than ore, despite the local presence of specular hematite ore. The copper stemmed from several sources, the nearest being the Qwebe Hills nearly 300 kilometers south of the site and the Tsumeb Mountains in Namibia more than 400 kilometers to the west, while the nearest source for iron lay eastward at Shakawe on the western edge of the Okavango Delta 70 kilometers away.[12]

The inhabitants of Divuyu were traders from the time of their arrival onward, and they very likely became more involved in such activity over the generations. Apart from metal objects, the main imports were pottery,[13] fish,

8. Denbow, "Material," diagram 120, and compare with his "Congo to Kalahari," diagram 165, for less rounded percentages.

9. Miller, *Tsodilo,* p. 15, citing Wilmsen. No domesticated plants besides *Vigna* have been found at Divuyu. Denbow, personal communication, 2002, confirms this.

10. Denbow, "Material," p. 119, and Miller, *Tsodilo,* pp. 12, 15.

11. Miller, *Tsodilo,* pp. 14, 20 (11 pieces of probably smithing slag from 50 centimeter depth upward—hence not from the beginning at 200 centimeters); pp. 23–26 for descriptions; pp. 78–84 for evaluation.

12. Miller, *Tsodilo,* pp. 82, 95, on diversity of sources; Denbow, "Congo," p. 161, and his "Material," p. 12. Denbow informs me that one copper bead seems to have come from eastern Botswana or South Africa because of its high nickel content, which occurs only in ores found there.

13. According to Denbow, personal communication, 2002, one-third of the pots contain marl or partly burned reed fragments, thus indicating an Okavango origin.

river mussels, some beads made from such mussels, and water fauna from
the Okavango. Two shells from the faraway Atlantic coast attest to indirect
trading links spanning a huge area. The exports are unknown. They may well
have included specularite (obtained from Late–Stone Age miners nearby),
furs, and ivory, since ivory was found on the site.[14] Their main trading partners were certainly foragers or pastro-foragers, but perhaps the Divuyans
were in contact with one or more other agricultural settlements as well.

All one can say about the internal social structure of the Divuyans is that
they lived in small households grouped into two distinct agglomerations.[15]
Despite the fact that Stone Age foragers worked in the specularite mines and
at the Depression rock shelter near the base of the hill only about a kilometer away from the site, Divuyans did not mix with them, for only two stone
tools have been found at the village site.[16] Yet there must have been some contacts because pottery shards and small bits of iron have been found in the
mining area while no less than 111 ostrich shell beads were found in the village.[17] In addition, cattle could not be kept on the exiguous plateau where
Divuyu was located. They had to be obtained elsewhere, perhaps from
nearby pastro-foragers, although so far there is no contemporary trace of
such anywhere in the vicinity. All of which tells us that although villagers and
foragers were separate, they interacted as equals. Divuyans clearly did not
dominate foragers, a fact which also explains why they chose to settle in such
a strong but uncomfortable defensive location.

From where did these people migrate? The clues that might answer this
question are contradictory and confusing. James Denbow points out that the
pottery shares some stylistic elements with the ceramics he uncovered on the
Loango coast and with that at Naviundu in Katanga, but that does not mean
that the Divuyans migrated directly from either the Loango coast or
Katanga.[18] In any case, the pottery at Divuyu is unusual in that it is charcoal
tempered, a characteristic shared with ceramics in northern Botswana and

14. Wilmsen, *Land,* p. 70, ivory and shells, p. 71; the shells were *Cerithiidae.* Denbow,
"Congo," pp. 161, 164. See Miller, *Tsodilo,* p. 20, for specularite; Robbins et al., "Intensive
Mining." Denbow makes the point about furs (personal communication, 2002).

15. Denbow informs me that most pots had a capacity of 2 liters or less, which suggests that the amount of food prepared or served in them was suited only for a small
household.

16. Denbow, "Congo," p. 164; Denbow informs me that there were also two stone
tools.

17. Murphy et al., "Pottery," pp. 2–7; Robbins et al., "Intensive Mining," p. 149; Robbins et al., "Archaeology," p. 1110. Denbow, personal communication, 2002 (ostrich shells).

18. Denbow, "Congo," p. 161. Denbow, personal communication, 2002 (no "direct
movement").

adjacent areas but not with that found in any other areas.[19] Yet the Divuyan ceramics contrast on nearly every other point to those of Zimbabwe or Botswana to the east and southeast. In any case, about one-third of them were in fact made in what was then Okavango swampland. But the cattle and—if there were any—the cereals clearly originated from somewhere to the east. One can only conclude that the Divuyans immigrated from an unknown place not very far away from Tsodilo, probably from across the lower Okavango River to the north.

Divuyan ceramics have been found at only two other sites: (1) in an undated layer at Xaro to the north of Tsodilo on the Okavango River and (2) among remains dating to the late eighth and ninth centuries at Nqoma two kilometers or so away from Divuyu on a lower, larger, and more accessible plateau.[20] Divuyu itself was abandoned around 890 at about the same time that the outpost at Nqoma also vanished. Thus the Divuyans settled first in a main village and a century later established an outpost about half an hour's walk away at Nqoma. No further splitting occurred during the next century and there is little evidence for continuous population growth. These data do not support the conventional migration scenario of "Bantu expansion." According to that model, new settlements should have been founded nearly every generation, rather than once per century, and the population should have grown continuously. Hence the model should be dismissed.

Divuyu is the earliest site in southern West Central Africa where metal objects been found. These first objects of metal probably entered into the community as small exotic items, mainly as iron or copper beads. At least this is what the finds suggest since mainly jewelry and no large pieces of metal have been found.[21] The jewels may be the product of recycling as the metals were probably rare, especially here where there is no evidence for smelting. Not much metal was needed for such purposes, the level of technical skill required was adequate, and production was probably quite small. Contrary to the recycling hypothesis, one could also claim that iron and copper smelting were adopted in the Divuyu region as a new technique to make beads from imported bloom smelted *in situ* to produce metal sheets which were then cut into beads. The new exotic jewelry would then just be a part of the general demand for beads, and several generations may have passed

19. Regarding the charcoal temper, see Wilmsen, *Land*, p. 331, nn. 4 and 5; Murphy et al., "Pottery," pp. 3–4.

20. Both Divuyu period dates at Nqoma stem from the central area. They are 779 and 879, the total range being 669–968 with an overlap at 779–874. The two last dates at Divuyu are 879 and 892 with a combined range of 779–986.

21. Miller, *Tsodilo*, pp. 20, 23–26.

before smiths learned how to fashion more massive utilitarian objects. This interpretation finds some support in the observation that, in contrast to these objects from Divuyu, tools as well as beads were fashioned in the Lower Congo and on the Loango coast. Hence the original overall impact of metal-working at Divuyu remained rather limited until the time when extensive cereal agriculture with its demand for hoes became common.

In contrast to the situation with regard to metalworking, the presence of cattle and the suspected presence of cereals at Divuyu is the earliest on record in the entire area covered by this study. These innovations amounted to a revolution in the daily business of making a living and became an essential foundation for the subsequent elaboration of more complex societies, not the least because they did lead to sedentarization. Hence they warrant the following detailed discussion. The considerable changes in social structure that occurred concomitantly with this revolution are examined in the concluding section of this chapter.

Agriculture

The acquisition of cereal agriculture, more than any other factor, allowed the people of West Central Africa to become fully sedentary, within the limits of shifting cultivation, which required shifts over small distances every few years (between three and ten years in most cases) within the same territorial domain where the village was located. Sedentarization made a more complex social organization possible as it allowed for the numbers of people living together in a village to rise from a dozen or at most fifty people per settlement to an average of around one hundred and sometimes many more. The effects of cattle herding on social organization would be equally significant once large herds were introduced. These appeared first in combination with agriculture, and later, in some cases, as part of nomadic pastoralism. This way of life in particular soon led to significant social stratification and the elaboration of groups larger than residential communities. Finally, farming and herding were accompanied by an increase in trade and travel between communities as well as an increase in the range of distances reached by trade. Traders and other travelers also fostered a more frequent and wider exchange of ideas, values, and practices, which would later facilitate the development of social complexity.

It has long been known that the cereals cultivated in the area are of eastern African origin.[22] They are sorghum (*Sorghum caffrorum* Beauv.), millet

22. See J. M. J. de Wet, "Domestication," pp. 15–27 (figures 3, 5); Ehret, "Agricultural," pp. 15–18.

(*Pennisetum typhoides* Stapf and Hubbard), and finger millet or eleusine (*Eleusine corocana* Gaertn.). In addition, an unrelated plant, sesame (*Sesamum indicum* L.) was also adopted as an oilseed plant. Direct archaeological evidence for their spread in southeastern Africa is still very rare. In Zambia, sorghum has been found at only two early sites, Mteteshi, ca. 100, and at Mondake, ca. 600.[23] The find at Mteteshi is also the earliest anywhere in southern Africa. Somewhat later finds come from Ngamiland first at Matlapaneng (680 at the earliest) and later at Nqoma (ca. 997).[24] Evidence for millet is even rarer. The only one reported (*Pennisetum americanum* not *typhoides*) comes from Matlapaneng.[25] Even more rare, thus far, are early finds of finger millet anywhere in southern Africa, with such evidence being restricted to Natal and Zimbabwe, while sesame has, so far, not been found at all. Hoes, which are the only relatively unambiguous indirect evidence for agriculture in general, are also rare finds. The earliest ones in Zambia come from Kumadzulo in southern Zambia and date to the sixth or seventh centuries.[26]

The linguistic evidence is richer. Everywhere sorghum as a generic name was *-caa* 5/6, but later—in the Kwanza Block and in the languages of the Middle Kwilu and even as far as Ndembu—it produced a derived form: *mu-saa* 3/4 "bread."[27] Over time new varieties of sorghum became available and needed to be distinguished. In the Kwanza Block and in Kongo this was done by appending a name for the variety to *-saa* 5/6. Thus the most cultivated variety became *ma-sambala* 5/6 or *ma-saa* + *mbala* 9/10. The compound word was later adopted by the Portuguese, who spread the usage all over Angola as far away as the Kwanyama language. In other parts of the area, specific names later ousted attestations of *-caa*. The most common ones were *pondo* 5/6 in the north and *-púngu* 5/6 in the southwest.[28] Millet was desig-

23. See Robertson, "Early Iron," pp. 153, 157.

24. See Denbow, "Congo," p. 166, and his, "New Look," p. 14. The earliest finds at Nqoma come from the Society site.

25. Denbow, "New Look," p. 14. For the date, see Wilmsen, *Land*, p. 66.

26. Roberts, *History of Zambia*, pp. 45, 47.

27. The form could also be *-ca*, but *-caa* is more likely with the long vowel indicating the loss of a consonant. The form is not attested in the east, although it would be tempting to relate this to *-caka* 5/6 were it not for the unexplained loss of *-k-* and for the fact that the distribution area of the latter term does not even come close to West Central Africa.

28. In both cases the meaning was later transferred to maize. Attestations of *-pondó* occur in Suku, the Middle Kwilu, and the Lweta languages, in Sala Mpasu, and Kete Ipila, as well as in Luba Kasai, Songye, and Bushong (in a skewed fashion). Attestations of *-púngu* 5/6 occur in Lwena, Cokwe, Nyemba, Ngangela, Umbundu, Kwangari, Dciriku (skewed form), Nyaneka, Nkhumbi, Kwanyama, Ndonga, and Kwambi.

nated everywhere as *-*cangu* 5/6,[29] including the languages of the floodplain of the upper Zambezi River. The evidence about the third cereal, finger millet (eleusine), suggests that it was a much later loan. Hence its case is deferred for now. Moreover, the evidence indicates that sorghum as well as millet spread into West Central Africa from a single point of origin. This was probably somewhere in the area near the middle Zambezi River, which is also the region of origin suggested by the agroclimatic and the archaeological data.[30] In any case, sorghum must have been introduced into the area from the east or southeast, because only one major variety of sorghum (Kafir) is found in West Central Africa and that was developed in or south of Tanzania.[31] One concludes that sorghum was the first cereal to be introduced, closely followed by millet, since the present distribution of both plants suggests that they must have been introduced together with a local relative preponderance of one over the other according to the amount and the reliability of local rainfall. But the climatic conditions, at least in the southern part of West Central Africa, were much wetter during the first millennium than now so that it is actually more likely that sorghum was introduced first and that millet spread somewhat later when the area became drier.

The routes by which cereals could come from eastern to western Central Africa are suggested by modern maps. These maps, based on modern climatic conditions (FAO 1980), indicate that, while nearly all of East Central Africa would be suitable, the best conditions for both millet and sorghum existed in a band or corridor on the southern edge of the area from southern Zambia to southern Angola. Given the local topography and the wetter conditions prevailing there until 500, that corridor lay somewhat farther to the south, that is, south of the middle Zambezi River through northern Botswana, south of the then much larger Okavango Delta to the Tsodilo Hills and then farther west to the bend of the Cunene River. Divuyu, of course, is situated in that corridor.[32]

The introduction of sorghum and millet involved much more than the adoption of two more crops.[33] As a dozen new terms attest, growing cereals

29. CS 2931–32, 294. The term derives from proto-Bantu *-*cangu* 5/6 and 9/10, CS 294, for "grass seeds." See also Ehret, "Agricultural," p. 16, and his *African*, p. 272.

30. This is accepted by Ehret, *African*, p. 274 (map).

31. De Wet, "Domestication," pp. 23–24.

32. But the climatic conditions did not preclude that these crops could also have been carried from east to west along the grasslands of eastern Angola on a broad front from the Sioma reach of the Zambezi to north of the lower Okavango—albeit over very poor soils. Even recently there were no farmers at all in southeastern Angola with the exception of enclaves along the banks of the major rivers.

33. See Ehret, "Agricultural," pp. 17–18.

involved the acceptance of a wholly new agriculture based on sowing rather than planting, which fostered the use of the hoe rather than the bush knife or the digging stick and involved reaping, threshing, winnowing, plus the necessary tools. This was followed by new food preparations: pounding grain for flour and using the flour for cooking porridge and for brewing beer. New terms were introduced for these activities, tools, and products, including a general one for working in cereal fields.[34]

Moreover cereals differed from earlier root crops in that, once ripe, they had to be harvested without delay, thus introducing a sudden demand for labor that far exceeded requirements at any other time of the year. Relying on cereals as staples tended to lead to an annual season of scarcity as supplies ran out before the harvest, despite the use of granaries. To cope with this, it was necessary to obtain a larger than usual amount of food from other sources just at the time when all available labor was needed for the harvest and none could be spared for additional gathering. Thus both the labor bottleneck and the seasonal constraints ensured that cereals could only become staples if all food-producing activities were harmonized into a single agricultural calendar. The practices of interplanting the existing older crops with cereals and crop rotation from season to season so as to maintain the fertility of the soil and hence ensure good yields also required such a unified calendar. In this regard, beans and groundnuts were particularly prized because they helped yields by fixing nitrogen in the soil. Hence one soon learned to sow small plots of these crops as ancillary food. While this practice may well have diffused rapidly from neighbor to neighbor, turning cereals into the main staple food required a truly revolutionary reorganization of all food production, and that at a considerable risk of crop failure.[35] This required much new knowledge and more experience, so that cereals as staple crops were probably only adopted locally as staples after at least a generation of

34. Over a dozen words have been identified, especially by Ehret, but I have not traced their precise areal distribution. Hence some may be later loanwords. The correct forms are given by Emiel Meeussen in *Bantu Lexical Reconstructions* and cited here rather than the form in the CS itself. The words are: "to cultivate" (*-dim-*, CS 568), "to sow" (*-bé(j)ad-*, CS 99), "to winnow" (*-pépet-*, CS 1488, and *-pung-*, CS 1601, and *-jed-*, CS 1955), "to thresh" (*-púúd-*, CS 1590), "to grind" (*-ped-*), "hoe" (*-témo* 5, CS 1705/1706), "mortar" (*-nu* 7, CS 1377), "pestle" (*-jici* 3, CS 2076), "mush, bread" (*-kíma* 10, CS 1081), "millet beer" (*-jad-ua* 14, CS 1892/1901), "broth" (*-cudi* 3, CS 405), "winnowing tray?, threshing floor" (*búga* 7, CS 191, but from meaning "open space," CS 190), "chaff" (*-bungu* 3, CS 2174). See Ehret, "Agricultural," pp. 4, 17, 18; Ehret, *African*, p. 272, and his "Patterns," tables 35–44.

35. That the two cereals did become the mainstay of the whole food supply in the southwestern lands is betrayed by the fact that they came to be called there the "edibles" par excellence.

trial and error. Hence their diffusion as staple crops was quite slow as each community cautiously began to imitate more prosperous neighbors who had already adopted the new system of agriculture.

Since no cereals have been found as yet at any other site, we ignore when they were adopted in the whole of West Central Africa. One might make a guess by analogy with the spread of cattle, which is attested at Camabanga near Luanda ca. 830.[36] The first use of cereals near Luanda might well be of comparable date but it certainly took longer to integrate the whole new agricultural system than it did to introduce cattle so that it would be imprudent, at least until further notice, to date the general acceptance of cereal agriculture everywhere in the area much before the end of the first millennium. This is especially true for the lands north of latitude 11° or 12° S where a satisfactory horticulture based on a staple of yams was, by then, a long entrenched habit. Yams had good yields, could be harvested year-round, and provided a satisfactory flour for the basic menu. Moreover, it was more difficult to integrate cereals into the existing system of horticulture than was the case farther south, if only because yams were planted in the same season during which cereals had to be sown. In any case, even after the adoption of cereals, root crops still remained quite significant here as is shown by the adoption of a water yam (*Dioscorea alata* L.) in large parts of the northern regions around 1000.[37] Nevertheless, early written sources for the northern coastal areas make it clear that, even there, cereal flour had become the main staple by the 1500s, except during months of scarcity before the harvest when root crops still retained that position.[38]

Given the difficulties involved in successfully transferring the complex technology of cereal agriculture, one may well wonder if all of this just diffused from neighbor to neighbor or if new immigrants were involved. The Divuyans were immigrants to the site, but perhaps they did not come from very far away; later on, some Nqomans also seem to have been immigrants. One could also point to the considerable phonetic, morphophonemic, and morphological influences of Eastern Bantu languages on those of the Kongo and Njila units as evidence for the arrival of numerous immigrants from East Central Africa, were it not that these transfers occurred independently from each other at least as far as morphological features, tone, and phonetics are concerned, that the process lasted over a very long period of time (the great

36. Lanfranchi and Clist, *Aux origines,* p. 220, give the uncorrected date as 1120 BP or 830 AD. The genuine date probably fell in the ninth century.

37. Water yams are one of the crops introduced from the Indian Ocean.

38. See William Randles, *L'ancien royaume du Congo,* pp. 65–67, for a short, competent, and well-annotated summary.

sound changes involved several successive transfers), and that they evidently spread from neighbor to neighbor. Hence these influences probably were not attributable to migrants but only indicate that, like agricultural fashions, linguistic fashions from the east have been highly appreciated in the west for many centuries.[39] It would be unrealistic, however, to claim that there never were any small population movements back and forth across the linguistic boundary between the Njila group and Eastern Bantu. There probably were, but they never were numerous enough to fully blur the boundary between the two linguistic groups.

The adoption of cereal agriculture had a profound impact on iron production, on trade, indirectly on the accumulation of wealth, and on gender relations. It all begins with the replacement of the wooden digging stick with the iron hoe used in cereal farming. Metal hoes were made by men and acquired by men, yet women used them. Whereas women had until then fashioned their own wooden digging sticks and other tools for gathering or for horticulture, now they had to receive the hoes they needed from men. Moreover those same hoes also acquired a significant economic value. These developments made women economically dependent on men in a way that had never been the case before. That in turn upset the social balance between the sexes. For dependent soon meant inferior; henceforth, gender relations became unequal or far more unequal than they had been hitherto.

Cereal agriculture spawned an insatiable demand for metal hoes. These wear out after a year or two, much faster than any other iron object barring perhaps bush knives, and most hoes do contain a substantial amount of iron. As a result, the volume of metal production had to increase in step with the expansion of cereal agriculture. A higher volume of smelted metal led, in turn, to the provision of heavier axes, larger bush knives, and more substantial spearpoints. At this juncture, owning metal tools became crucial for one's social standing, one's security, and one's power and these tools, especially hoes, began to be used for all important social payments ranging from the payment of bridewealth to that of judicial compensation. That situation transformed the older notions of ownership. In proto-Njila, ownership was rendered by the form *-yéné, "self" and "owner, master."[40] This implied that

39. See Bastin et al., "Statistiques lexicale et grammaticale," pp. 375–87 (especially 381, 383), and Bastin et al., "Statistique grammaticale et classification des langues bantoues," pp. 17–37. A number of morphological features as well as major shifts in tone (tone reversals), vowels (from seven to five vowels), and consonants (spirantization) were borrowed from east to west.

40. The form constitutes a famous conundrum in proto-Bantu. See CS 1301–2, 1970, 1971, 1972, 2015, 2070, and Meeussen, who for his part, distinguished *-inj 1/2 "master,

the "owned" objects or persons were an extension of one's personality, i.e., objects for personal use that normally were not transferred, or persons (such as children or a spouse), who were also considered an extension of one's personality. But in the new economy, ownership of some objects was divorced from personal use, became highly transferable, and any link with "self" was severed. As a result, many Njila languages began to differentiate in some way between "owner" and "self."

In addition, new hoes also became a staple of trade, a favorite medium of exchange, and sometimes a currency of account. Metal became the measure of wealth and people began to hoard metal objects as a means to achieve security and power over others. Over time, the effects of this development became quite considerable. The person or group who controlled the hoard of some 400 hoes at Feti around 1200 or earlier must have wielded considerable power there.[41] No wonder then that wealth came to be measured by the size of a hoard or that the status of smelters and smiths rose to great heights.[42] Is it then so surprising that four centuries or so later on, the Ambundu tradition of Genesis still celebrated a smith or smelter as their civilizing hero, namely, Mbumbabula, the founder of the Kingdom of Ndongo?

The heightened production of iron led to an increased trade in hoes especially and to the rise of a denser and more frequently used network of communication between specialists in metallurgy. The emergence of trade on a large scale ca. 900 on the Congo River upstream of Kinshasa in the far north may well have been due, in part at least, to the adoption of cereal agriculture. Thus, once in place, cereal agriculture reshaped the perception of the landscape locally, not only by distinguishing between good and bad farmland, but also by creating more sedentary villages—that is, more fixed points in space with dependent territories around them. Cereal agriculture also remade landscapes by making some hitherto unremarkable spots famous because they were repositories of salt, iron, and copper, or of other special resources necessary to all. Finally, agriculture fundamentally altered the social landscape because the steady production of agricultural food eventually led to increases in population size, especially on fertile soils but also elsewhere, which then fostered increases in the social scale of institutions.

owner" from *-*ényé* "self" but considered both to be related. Ethnographers still report the notion of ownership as an extension of "self" among foragers.

41. See Ervedosa, *Arqueologia*, p. 214 (75 hoes in a single package, 400 in all).

42. See de Maret, "Ceux qui jouent avec le feu," pp. 263–79; Kriger, *Pride of Men,* pp. 230–32; Beatrix Heintze, *Studien*, pp. 65–66; Antonio da Gaeta, *La maravigliosa conversione*, pp. 134–35. For Mbumba, see Luc De Heusch, *Le roi de Kongo*, pp. 259–85.

On a less exalted note, the introduction of cereal farming did not signal the end of agricultural innovation in the area. To the contrary, soon after cereals were adopted the domestic fowl and a series of minor crops, mostly from the East African coast and ultimately of Asiatic origin, began to arrive from the east and continued to do so, one after the other, until the very end of the period studied here. At the same time, more and more refined agricultural techniques, such as the double-handed hoe, green manuring, farming on river-flooded tracts, and finally even full irrigation systems were perfected, especially in regions of high population density. Yet all these later changes should be interpreted as mere refinements of an economic system that had been put in place with the adoption of cereal agriculture.

Bovine Cattle

Although cattle ultimately stem from northern East Africa they probably first arrived in West Central Africa from the southeast. The wetter climate at the time and, hence, the greater extent of the lakes and swamps as well as of the presumed tsetse-fly belt help us to understand why cattle were not introduced earlier and why they did not come directly westward from the Zambezi Valley where cattle bones dating back to approximately the third century BCE have been found at Salumano.[43] Closer by, one finds cattle teeth first at Lotshitshi ca. 290 CE, then a few domestic bovine remains at Divuyu and many more such remains at Matlapaneng ca. 680–90.[44] Transfers of cattle herding from the southeast westward occurred between Bantu speakers because the form for "cattle" *ngombe* 9/10 remains identical in all the Bantu languages and differs from the Khoe forms.[45] A few other words from the pastoral vocabularies, namely, "calf," "to pasture," and perhaps "dung" may also have been borrowed at the same time.[46] Hence despite ancestors of Khoe

43. David Phillipson, *African Archaeology*, p. 194, dates Salumano to the third or second centuries BCE, while the inventor Katanekwa, "The Iron Age in Zambia," p. 14, gives a range from 380 BCE to 1 CE.

44. Denbow, "Congo," p. 159; dates in Wilmsen, *Land*, p. 66; see also Denbow and Wilmsen, "Advent," pp. 1509–10. Details are in Turner, "Early Iron Age," pp. 7–12, 14, 16, and in her "Hunters and Herders," pp. 25–29, 32–33.

45. See Argyle, "Linguistic Evidence," pp. 18–25; Ehret, *Classical*, pp. 135–36, 271–73; Denbow, "Congo," p. 144, for words designating cattle and sheep terms south of Angola.

46. "Calf," *kana* 12 (*tana, thana* invarious classes) is derived from *-jána* 1 "child," CS 1922, with a diminutive prefix *ka-* or *tu-*, and "to pasture" *-lisa, -risa* is the causative of *-dí* "to eat," CS 550. "Dung," *-pumba* 5, attested among the languages of the Middle Zambezi and in Kwangari, Ndonga, and Nyaneka, could have been introduced before *-dombo* 5, which occurs in Mbukushu, Nyemba, and Umbundu. Today the pastoral

speakers in the same region also becoming pastoralists at about the same time as Bantu speakers did, they did not transfer cattle herding to their Bantu-speaking neighbors. Although the language spoken by the Divuyans is unknown, one can still say that, about the time when cattle appeared there, they were transferred between speakers of Eastern Bantu and speakers of the Njila group probably somewhere near the Okavango River in southeastern Angola.

At Divuyu, cattle made up only a small portion of the meat consumed as compared to that from goats or sheep.[47] Divuyans ate some beef, but there was no place for cattle on this small plateau. The animals had to be brought there in small numbers from unknown places presumably within easy traveling distance. This situation and the duration of the settlement itself suggests that the Divuyans had not developed a full herding economy and probably did not drink milk. True pastoralism and its consequences would arrive only later on.

North of Divuyu, cattle bones are first reported very far away at Camabanga near Luanda, where they date to the ninth century.[48] This date is far too early to assume that the animals came from Divuyu. Hence cattle must have spread westward from western Zambia but south of the tsetse belt at an early date and may well have reached the inner Cunene basin in southern Angola at about the same time as they reached Divuyu. Even so, a diffusion from the inner Cunene basin to Camabanga would still have had to occur at a remarkably fast rate and would only have been possible because the routes

---

vocabulary is the result of a complex history characterized by successive new introductions (the last ones from Tswana or Sotho), in which shifts in the meaning of some forms occurred over time (e.g., between "cow," "sweet milk," "butter") and in which internal innovations also appeared. These dynamics resulted in the considerable diversity of the terminology found among Njila languages today. The contrast with the stability of the agricultural vocabulary is striking. This nest of terms needs to be further disentangled, however, before any more conclusions can be drawn.

47. Denbow, "Congo," pp. 165, 171. Not enough cattle bones were found to establish the profile by age of the cattle killed and thus establish whether the Divuyans were intent on building up herds by saving young breeding cows. They did not do so with regard to goats and sheep. Either they had such large flocks of small stock that the practice did not matter, or, more likely, they obtained each time a few animals from a great many different flocks all around their settlement. This situation differs sharply from that of Lotshitshi, where the inhabitants retained a predominantly hunting economy (Turner, "Hunters," pp. 26, 33) despite the introduction of cattle.

48. Lanfranchi and Clist, *Aux origines*, pp. 51, 219–20 (dated to the ninth century). The uncorrected date given without the sigma range is 1120 BP = 830 AD. The next dated site with cattle in the Luanda area is Quitala from the thirteenth century.

followed remained in very similar vegetation zones, which required little if any acclimatization of the cattle to new environmental conditions. In contrast, if genuine, the earlier slow rates of diffusion between Salumano and Lotshitshi or even Lotshitshi and Matlapaneng are to be explained by the difficulty of moving cattle into new feeding and disease environments—that is, if they are not a spurious result caused by the vagaries of archaeological discovery.[49]

Many years ago the geographer Frederick Simoons had already observed from the ethnographic record ca. 1900 that roughly north from a line running to Caconda and eastward, people such as the northern Ovimbundu and the Ambundu did not drink milk or milk their cattle, which they kept only for their beef. Indeed the northern limit of milking is also the limit to which agropastoral systems prevail.[50] Beyond this line, cattle, however much prized, remained unimportant compared to farming. The existence of this border then makes it clear that there were two different sorts of acquisition concerning cattle, in which Divuyu and Camabanga represent the earlier one but not the transition to true pastoralism (map 10).

Full-fledged pastoralism was based on keeping cattle in herds, typically from 30 to 50 head each, cared for by boys or young men.[51] To keep such herds, a wholly new pattern of production based on transhumance was required. According to the seasons, the herds stayed near the settlements or were moved farther away. In the northern areas blessed with more rain, cattle remained at home near the settlements during the wet season and grazed nearby, but during the dry season they were sent away with their herdsmen to roam about in search of surviving pastures with good grasses near rivers or at higher altitudes where wetter conditions still prevailed. In the best environments of the inner Cunene basin, the distances between the dry season cattle posts and home varied only from one to a few days walking. During transhumance the herdsmen survived only to a small extent on milk or beef

49. For the evidence concerning East Africa especially, see Diane Gifford-Gonzalez, "Animal Disease," pp. 95–140.

50. See Frederick Simoons, "The Non-Milking," pp. 58–66; Wilfrid Hambly, *The Ovimbundu*, pp. 153–54.

51. See Ehret, *African*, pp. 271–72; *-tangá* 5/6 "herd" is only attested in the area as "cattle pen" and occurs only in the languages of the Moxico group and in Ndembu as a transfer from languages in the Zambezi floodplain, perhaps at a late date. In the agropastoral regions of the southwest, the term is absent. For "cattle herd" there was: Nyaneka and Umbundu *-mbamba* 5, Kwanyama *-uana* 7/8 or *-fita* 14 ("flock"), Ndonga *-ngunda* 7/8 and Herero *-panda* 11/6. One does not see any influence from Eastern Africa in this. The terms were, in part, newly coined and may, in part, have been taken over from "flock of small stock."

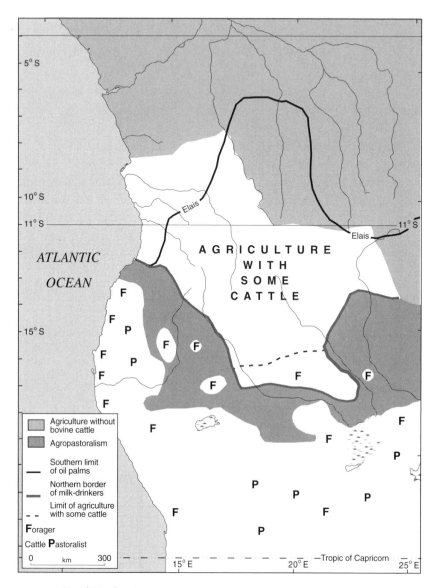

MAP 10. Food Production, ca. 1000

and depended mostly on hunting. In drier areas, the herds stayed also not very far from home during the wet season but lived dispersed at cattle posts. In the dry season, the herds were then led on grazing expeditions to the higher elevations of Angola and eastern Ovamboland at distances from 80 to 160 kilometers away. In some years it could happen that some herds would stay away from home for up to eleven months out of the year.[52] As we shall see, in the very dry areas of Namibia the herds were dispersed during the short rainy season and concentrated at waterholes near home during the dry season. One easily recognizes that transhumance requires a reorganization of labor and leads to an annually recurring scission between two groups of men in every community, namely, the young herdsmen and the older heads of farming households. To appreciate the extent of this pattern, one must recall that the dry season even in the most favored parts of southern Angola lasted about as long as the wet season did and lasted even longer farther south.

Moreover it was not wise to keep all one's cattle (or sheep) together because they could all be wiped out by a single epidemic. To avoid this risk, a number of them had to be dispersed. One could do this by placing them in the herds of trusted relatives living in other settlements. The ideal persons to leave them with were maternal relatives since they lived dispersed in a number of other settlements whereas paternal relatives all lived together in the same place or in adjacent settlements. Hence this was the solution adopted by pastoralists and agropastoralists alike in recent centuries.

Large herds and the practice of transhumance brought with it some changes in social structure. Sizeable herds fostered a new notion of wealth and gave new meaning to notions of ownership (e.g., as distinct from possession for use) while transhumance over long distances raised questions of security since herds become more vulnerable to raiding when they are moved beyond the existing circles of interrelations between kin and neighbors. This threat could be met in the short run by using companies of young herdsmen to protect their herds by force of arms, but in the longer run it also required another social innovation, i.e., the creation of long-distance alliances.

This new pattern of full-fledged pastoralism, in the sense of keeping large herds whether or not agriculture was also practiced appeared first ca. 700 at Matlapaneng just southeast of the Okavango Delta, near the area studied, and then about a century later at Nqoma, the successor to Divuyu in the Tsodilo Hills.[53] At both places it was apparently introduced by immigrants

---

52. See Lang and Tastevin, *La tribu*, pp. 86, 89–91; Edwin Loeb, *In Feudal*, pp. 147, 149–50; Carlos Estermann, *Nhaneca-Humbe*, pp. 183–84 (grasses and water), and his *Ambós*, p. 173; Kinahan, *Pastoral*, pp. 51–53, 76–86 (early transhumance for small stock).

53. Cereals were cultivated both at Matlapaneng and at Nqoma. See Turner, "Early Iron Age Herders," abstract, p. 7 (Nqoma "by 800 AD"), and her "Hunters," p. 25. Wilmsen, *Land*, p. 66, has 680–990 as the earliest dates for Matlapaneng and 730 as the earliest for Nqoma still associated with Divuyu-like ceramics. Typical Nqoma ceramics and abundant remains of cattle date from 800 or later, the earliest associated date being 850.

from westernmost Zambia if one is to judge by their style of ceramics and their avoidance of fish.[54] In the past, many anthropologists have been struck by the cultural and social parallels between pastoralists in southwest Africa and others (especially Nilotes) in eastern Africa and have interpreted these as traces of a large-scale migration from East Africa over the Kafue region in Zambia (Ila) to southwest Africa.[55] But many parallels can simply be technical or functional requirements for pastoralism. The role of groups of young herdsmen, the use of sturdy light vessels, such as baskets, calabashes, or wooden pots, rather than heavier and more breakable ceramics, are such features and they are found in nearly every fully pastoral society that refuses transport by pack animals. A second set of parallels can be explained as a natural psychological adaptation to this mode of life. This includes features such as the importance paid to the coloring and the shape of the horns of the cattle, praisenames or songs for cattle, the use of cattle as "sacred" animals, and the emotional identification of a specific animal and his master, features which are also found among pastoralists elsewhere. When further incorrect parallels, such as a taboo on fish or on women milking, taboos which do not exist in southwestern Africa, are excluded, few concrete common features remain—although some do, such as the prohibition to mix milk with meat.[56] Still one need not postulate any mass migration from far away or nearby to account for the remaining features. They may well have been an unquestioned part of the essential pastoral techniques learned by those who became pastoralists. One may well ask, just as we did with regard to agriculture, whether all the know-how (including the veterinarian practices) required to start a successful pastoral economy could be acquired just

54. Matlapaneng pottery belongs to the Gokomere-Dambwa tradition. See Denbow, "Congo," pp. 164, 166. The absence of fish also points to immigrants from the southeast. See Turner, "Hunters," p. 26.

55. M. Herskovits, "The Cattle Complex," pp. 230–72, 361–88, 494–528, 633–64, established the special features of the eastern African pastoralists and was prompted by a suggestion of Bernard Struck, who later added Southwestern Africa to his "East African cattle area" in his "The Culture Areas of Africa," pp. 67, 71–72. His views were widely accepted and somewhat elaborated by later culture historians, until this whole approach was abandoned altogether. The last major proponents for this region have been Loeb, *In Feudal*, pp. 10–21, 315–17 (1962), and Hermann Baumann, "Die Südwest-Bantu Provinz," 1:473, 476, 479, 486–90, who detailed parallels between Nilotes and Southwest Africans which he felt to be particularly convincing.

56. See George Murdock, *Africa*, p. 371 (the taboo segregating women from cattle did not spread to the southwestern Bantu), yet p. 369 for his "unquestionable" conviction that they "acquired the cattle and the milking complex" from the "Middle Zambezi Bantu" and p. 371 for a Nilotic parallel.

by a few instructions and fleeting observation or not. In that context, one easily imagines the immigration of a small number of expert foreign communities as happened at Matlapaneng and then again at Nqoma.

The new techniques also spread by gradual migration, as the transhumance of some herds led to the occupation of new and better pastures, at least until the limits of the better pasturelands had been reached at the upper edge of the planalto or on the crest of the Chela Mountain Range. It is useless to guess how long it would take to reach those limits, but this could not happen in the blink of an eye because it required a profound transformation of the economy. On the other hand, it need not have taken a great many generations, for pastoralism is a mobile way of life that facilitates its spreading. On balance, one may think that it took well over two centuries and probably even three. In that case, an agropastoral way of life would have become characteristic for most of the good grasslands in southern Angola during the eleventh century. Thus we may think that by ca. 1100 the boundary between full-fledged pastoralism with milking and nonmilking areas had emerged.

Once established, this divide between milkers and nonmilkers acquired lasting significance because the subsequent sociopolitical developments in both the milking and nonmilking areas diverged radically in some ways. Simoons correctly attributed the emergence of this divide to a situation in which settled farmers acquired cattle merely as an additional source of meat even where their environment allowed for full-fledged pastoralism.[57] In addition, it is now well known that the absorption of milk depends on the physiological capacity to absorb lactase, a trait largely diffused in a milk-drinking population as the result of natural selection. This implies that intolerance toward milk would remain high elsewhere, which was the case all over Western Central Africa since neither goats nor sheep were milked there either. The introduction of cattle and cereals changed this pattern. Despite the prevalence of lactase intolerance, a cereal/sour milk gruel did become the main dish in the southern part of the study area, the very region where horticulture had earlier been halted by environmental conditions. But farther north, root crops had apparently long provided a satisfactory flour-based diet so that, even though cereals were accepted, people were still not interested in replacing their basic menu with milk-based gruels. Once in place, the new dividing line remained a major sociocultural divide in the area of study ever since.

57. See Simoons, "The Non-Milking," pp. 58–66.

Overarching Institutions: Corporate Matrilineages and Dispersed Matriclans

The practice of cereal agriculture and agropastoralism required the creation of new social institutions to accompany the novel ways of obtaining a living. Sedentary villages contained larger aggregates of people than had been the case earlier and hence needed more formalization of relationships among kinsfolk and somewhat better defined patterns of leadership, while ownership (especially of metal goods and cattle) created wealth, unequal statuses, relations of dependence, and raised issues about inheritance and succession. In addition, the increased frequency of links with other communities through trade, transhumance, and the need to disperse cattle to avoid the ravages of epidemics required formalized overarching institutions to span the gap between communities. Such requirements could be and were met by the creation of various institutions, none of which turned out to be more ideally suited than corporate matrilineages and the resulting network of dispersed matriclans. These two institutions were so successful that they spread throughout the entire area.

Today a huge continuum of peoples organized in corporate matrilineages and matriclans stretch from ocean to ocean all across Central Africa. This is the famous matrilineal belt that has attracted the attention of many an anthropologist.[58] In these regions, only descent through the mother's line was used to establish corporate lineages, usually headed by the oldest man of the group and not by the oldest woman. He was succeeded by the next man in the uterine line. Yet, at the same time, matrilineal descent was accompanied by virilocal residence, as wives went to live in the villages of theirs husbands, a situation that has been called disharmonic because its consequence was that a matrilineage could never be entirely congruent with a residential unit, since different women of the same matrilineage found themselves scattered in different villages with their children while the wives of male lineage members in every village belonged to other matrilineages. The members of the dominant matrilineage within each settlement included only the head of the lineage, his uterine brothers, their unmarried or widowed sisters, and those among their sister's sons who chose to return to live with their mother's mother's brothers or their mother's brothers.

This disharmony entailed several undesirable but inexorable side effects. The matrilineage became more and more dispersed from generation to generation as its women were married in villages farther and farther away from

---

58. The latest one is Trudeke Vuyck, *Children of One Womb*.

the lineage's point of origin. Second, the corporate matrilineage was always struggling for survival as it had to convince its younger men to abandon the villages of their fathers or other relatives and return to the lineage home. Every sister's son who did not do so became himself the founder of a new lineage in another settlement, even though he and his sister's descendants still recognized their relationship with the original lineage. It was possible to partially overcome the disharmony between rules of descent and rules of residence by arranging marriages between residents of the same village, or in such a fashion that upon their marriage the children would return to the village of their mother. Marriages between close kin, especially between cross-cousins who lived in the same settlement or in the same neighborhood, achieved this goal best and were much preferred nearly everywhere.

Nevertheless, most lineages remained small since they consisted only of members of two or three adjacent generations, while related lineages were scattered over a wide area. Still all such related lineages continued to recognize their common descent and formed a dispersed, noncorporate aggregate, the matriclan, The clan was only an entity that provided a common identity to all the lineages who recognized a common origin, whether through a remembered genealogy or more often by claiming a common ancestress. Clan members also shared a common name, praisename, and food avoidance. Hence it was possible for a matriclan to incorporate previously wholly unrelated lineages once they adopted the signs of a clan's identity: the name of the ancestress, the clan name, its praisenames, and its food avoidance. The practical advantage of common clan membership was that it greatly facilitated cooperation between the constituent matrilineages.

The most significant consequence of the disharmony between descent and residence was that it contained the germ for the rapid emergence of various unequal social statuses and of a territorial structure distinct from that of the residential lineage. For the disharmony entailed that local residential communities had to be carefully distinguished from the local sections of lineages which lived there. This easily led to distinctions within a community between those who were members of its leading matrilineage, that is, the one which was supposed to have first founded the settlement, and those who did not. Further gradations of social status then arose by distinguishing those who were only one step removed from full status as children of that matrilineage and those who were several steps removed or perhaps not related at all. The leader of the founding lineage could only establish a claim of leadership over all others in terms of their residence in his settlement, that is, on the basis of a territorial principle, not in terms of common descent. It followed that all those who were not members of the founding lineage were second-class residents while only those born into the lineage (or sometimes the matriclan) were rightful "owners of the land." Thus the members of the founding matrilineage emerged as a ruling "dynasty" of "nobles" as opposed to "commoners" In this lay the germ for the development of further territorial political organizations.

From time to time, historians have wondered how the great matrilineal belt came into being. Was it a common legacy of great antiquity, a legacy that had died out elsewhere? This is the opinion of Christopher Ehret, which I think is not well founded.[59] Was it repeatedly invented independently in various parts of that vast area? Or did corporate matrilineages and the ensuing matriclans develop somewhere within the belt and were then borrowed from neighbor to neighbor all over Central Africa? The fact that the matrilineal belt occupies a single uninterrupted area where corporate matrilineages and virilocality are found points to an origin by diffusion either from a single center or from several independent centers of origin. I argue that this has in fact been the case and that the invention and spread of the corporate matrilineage is to be linked with the development of farming or herding. But that certainly does not mean that the whole set of institutions concerning descent and residence was borrowed in every detail as a single blueprint from a single village, as if the corporate matrilineage could be introduced without taking any locally pre-existing patterns of kinship relations into account. Before pursuing this argument, we must first consider what such pre-existing patterns might have been.

The earlier patterns of kinship relations among foragers a millennium and a half ago cannot be directly known because all observed evidence relates only to the nineteenth or twentieth centuries. The sole contribution such studies bring us is to give us parameters, that is, a fan of possibilities. For instance, modern Kua San communities are said to consist of an aggregate of families, an aggregate that waxed and waned in size and composition according to the seasons and other circumstances. The sharing of foods and goods is crucial for the well-being within and between communities while relationships by marriage or the exchange of goods could obtain between groups living far from each other. The core of each family usually consists of a group of brothers, their immediate families, and a few more real or puta-

---

59. Ehret, *African*, p. 155, argues for double descent since proto-Bantu times, the matrilineal part of which was preserved only in the belt. His argument is based on *-gandá 5, a local bilateral group or "household," which he interprets as a matrilineage and on the common use of "belly" or "womb" to designate local matrilineages (pp. 150–51). In my *Paths*, pp. 75–76, 252, I proposed that the descent system was bilateral among early Bantu speakers, vague as that designation is.

tive distant relatives. Kinship terminology is bilateral and marriage virilocal. There are no permanent leaders and decisions are reached by consensus.[60] Should this be dubbed an egalitarian bilateral system of descent?

But then among the Kwisi foragers of Angola it is the maternal grandfather who solemnly confers a name and hence an identity on a newborn, while the oldest son inherits both the tools to hunt and the family's rights over a hunting territory.[61] Should we label this "double descent"? Are the Kwadi (Kwepe) pastro-foragers "matrilineal" because the overall heir is the son of the oldest sister and the domestic animals are inherited by the maternal brothers of the deceased, or are they also "double descent" because the father plays a significant ritual role, inherited by the son?[62] And what about Bergdama, also pastro-foragers? Here mothers leave their goods, which can include goats, to their daughters, and fathers leave theirs to their sons, but daughters inherit the family name of their father and sons the family name of their mother.[63] Certainly this is also "double descent" but of a very different variety. Finally, among the Kwandu pastoralists of Angola the eldest son inherits sheep and most other goods from his father, but the cattle went to a sister's son and when Kwandu women tilled fields the produce was inherited from mother to daughter. Besides a category of patrilineal relatives (*veto*) the Kwandu recognized matriclans (*eanda*) and a category of matrilineal relatives (*himo* "belly").[64] So "double descent" again? If so, it is yet again quite different from all the other examples.

Such ethnographic records tell us above all how variable social organizations among foraging communities can be and how unwise it would be to attribute a detailed specific pattern of social organization to any foraging community nearly two millennia ago. Second, the record tells us that labels such as bilateral, patrilineal, matrilineal, or double descent, which take only principles of descent into account and not specific institutions or patterns of succession, inheritance, name-giving, or exogamy are wholly inadequate

60. See Laurence Bartram, Jr., "Southern African Foragers," p. 190 (all according to Renée K. Hitchcock). !Kung communities correspond to this sketch, although a set of brothers are less common than two- or three-generation deep families, and leadership, however temporary, may have been more pronounced than among the Kua. See Guerreiro, *Boximanes,* pp. 265–86, and Lee, *!Kung,* pp. 333–64, but also Wilmsen, *The Kalahari,* pp. 147–48 and 199–204.

61. Baumann, "Die Südwest-Bantu Provinz," 1:483; Estermann, *Ambós,* p. 52.

62. Baumann, "Die Südwest-Bantu Provinz," 1:483.

63. Hirschberg, "Khoisan," 1:403–4; Vedder, "The Berg Damara," pp. 71–72, and his *Die Bergdama* 1:48–49, 143–46.

64. Medeiros, *Vakwandu,* pp. 18–21.

as summary descriptions of entire social organizations. At best, such as in the "matrilineal" Kwadi case, the label designates only one "dominant" principle among others; at worst, there are instances such as that of the Bergdama where all the labels are misleading.[65] Nor will it be of any avail to dismiss cases such as the Kwisi, Kwadi, Kwandu, or Bergdama as irrelevant oddities due to the influence of neighboring Bantu-speaking pastoralists, in contrast to the Kua or !Kung cases, since the social organization of the latter is also only known from recent descriptions and has also been influenced by neighboring Bantu-speaking farmers and agropastoralists.

It is nevertheless of interest to point out that some of these practices could have led early foragers to become aware of the several principles of descent, including combinations of them. Thus among the recent !Kung, Kwandu, and the seventeenth-century Xam foragers near the Cape, brideservice was common. A young man went to live for a number of years with his wife's parents and among the Xam this situation could last for a lifetime.[66] In that case, this created a core residential unit among the women which we perceive as a matrilineage. The Xam may or may not have observed this and they could have abstracted a notion of matrilineage and of the principle of matrilinearity from this situation.[67] But all that is still a far cry from organizing corporate matrilineages or recognizing matriclans.

It is striking that corporate matrilineages are not found at all among any of the foragers in the ethnographic record, while they are universal among farmers and pastoralists. Inheritance or succession (given the fleeting nature of leadership in all small communities[68]) were of little importance among

65. To label them as "double descent" would be equally wrong. As far as is known, there is no other system like the Bergdama one anywhere in the world, although the separation of boys and girls recalls the "rope system of descent" reported from New Guinea.

66. Hirschberg, "Khoisan," 1:392 (Xam); Lee, *!Kung,* p. 452; Guerreiro, *Boximanes,* pp. 238, 243–44; Medeiros, *Vakwandu,* pp. 18, 21. Recently, the "double descent" Goba of Zimbabwe also practiced perpetual brideservice and thus produced residential matrilineages around women. See Chet Lancaster, *The Goba,* pp. 167–73, and his "Brideservice, Residence, and Authority among the Goba (N. Shona) of the Zambezi Valley," pp. 55–58.

67. But royal succession in the Netherlands has been from mother to daughter for over a century since 1890 and could be perceived as matrilineal (rather than bilateral) but no Dutch person has interpreted it as such.

68. On this subject, Lee, *!Kung San,* pp. 343–48, is very convincing. An office of headman would perpetually set one person apart from all others in the context of a lifetime of face-to-face relationships with the same small circle of interlocutors. It is easy to understand, as studies of small-group behavior have repeatedly shown, that in such a context a headman will disappoint all his interlocutors.

foragers, while those issues are precisely essential in defining corporate line-ages. In these matters, the advantage of a unilineally defined corporate group was to limit the number of claimants and to arrange them in a certain order of succession. Succession or inheritance and the regulation of marriage are interlocked, however, for it is typical everywhere in Africa south of the Sa-hara that the groups from which one inherits or succeeds to are never those in which one can marry. With regard to marriage, the advantage of unilineal descent was to create sharply delimited exogamic groups even while en-couraging marriage just beyond the limits, such as cross-cousin or similar unions between some close kin, all of which are excluded in a less discrimi-nating bilateral system. There is no doubt that the corporate matrilineage was a response to the increased importance of goods, claims, obligations, positions, and statuses, and hence of their inheritance or succession, a situa-tion which could only obtain after farming or a reliance on herds had be-come of paramount importance. This is also the view of the Kwandu, as re-ported by their ethnographer. They say that when they became farmers and cattle-keepers, rather than pastro-foragers after having lost their flocks of sheep to a devastating epidemic in the nineteenth century, they also adopted corporate matrilineages. Whereas sheep had been and still were strictly in-herited by men in the patrilineal line, cattle were inherited by the sister's sons, and whereas women could never inherit stock in earlier times, they now could inherit farm produce and some cattle.[69]

So the adoption of the corporate matrilineage followed the adoption of farming and of herding and could have occurred several times. The Kwandu case has the merit of drawing attention to the link between cattle herds and both corporate matrilineage and diffused matriclan. This reminds us that in the recent past and anywhere in southwestern Central Africa, cattle have been inherited only in the matrilineal line, in sharp contrast to sheep in the same regions and also to cattle in southeast Africa, which were inherited in the male line. This strongly suggests that matrilineal descent was associated with cattle herds right from their introduction into southwestern Central Africa and that matrilineal descent had not been so before the arrival of cattle in eastern Central Africa. Rather than being linked to cereal farming, corporate matrilineages and dispersed matriclans either accompanied the adoption of cattle in southern Angola and northernmost Namibia or they were "invented" there as a consequence of that introduction.

69. See Medeiros, *Vakwandu*, pp. 18–21, 65–66. The case is not as straightforward as it looks. For in earlier times sheep were also dispersed among matrilineal relatives and matriclans were recognized, but formal matrilineages were not.

How can one check whether or not such a diffusion actually occurred? Credible evidence can come only from the relevant vocabulary shared between the different societies involved. Given that words are rarely invented from scratch, such terms would have to be metaphors implying the idea of mother and descendant and applied to lineage groups.[70] Such a term in most of the matrilineal belt, including the whole area studied, is a local reflex of *-búmo 5/6 and its variant *-bímo, meaning "abdomen, womb" to designate a lineage.[71] But on reflection this does not prove much. For to use the metaphor of "womb" to describe a matrilineal group is so obvious that even if matrilineages had been developed independently several times over, the use of the metaphor "abdomen, womb" was very likely to have accompanied it.[72] Indeed the connection between womb and descent is not limited to matrilineal descent. Even in patrilineages, small groups of close kin were also called by a word meaning "abdomen."[73]

As it happens, there are two cases in which a less obvious yet unmistakable metaphor was used, providing much stronger evidence for diffusion. The first one links "navel cord" to "matrilineage or matriclan." In Nyaneka both are rendered by onkhova 9/10 "intermediate matrilineage." The same form with the meaning "navel cord" is found in many subgroups of Njila barring only the Umbundu and Middle Kwilu groups, while in East Central Africa, it is attested only in Mbukushu, Nkoya, Lamba, and partly in Lenje.[74] In many languages of Zambia, however, including Lenje and Lala, but not

---

70. All these terms have been coined from previously existing forms with a different meaning, such as, for instance, "branch" or "origin."

71. CS 299, which is western Bantu but also includes the Luban and most Zambian languages. The term appears nearly everywhere but note that in Bemba at least it was not used to refer to a corporate lineage. See also Ehret, African, pp. 150–51, 253.

72. The use of the most crude and direct expression "those of the vagina" as opposed to "those of the penis" in use among the populations of Lake Mayi Ndombe is not found anywhere else, probably because it offended notions of modesty.

73. Thus today diifu 5 in Luba Shaba, Kanyok, and Luba Kasai is used for "belly" and for "smallest patrilineage" and perhaps earlier for bilateral descent group.

74. The regional proto-form *-kóba "umbilical cord" 9/10, 5/6, or 11/10 is also attested in Kimbundu hoa, the Ngangela group including Nyemba as nkova or nkoua 9/10, as inkova 5/6 in Lucazi and Mbunda, and as -kowa 9/10 in Lwena; it is skewed (*-kóga) in Herero ongua 9/10, Ndonga (olu-a-ngoga 11 (pl. omalu-a-ngoga 6), Kwangari nkoga 9/10, Mbukushu kakoghatji 12/13, "navel cord" and mukogha 3/4, "womb") and skewed (*-kóba/-kóbu) in Ndembu, mukwá 3/4, Rund múkw 3/4, and Cokwe mukuvu 3/4 "end of umbilical cord." In the east, the word occurs in Nkoya nkôwa 9/10, Lamba umukowa 3/4, and in part Lenje lukowa 11/10 but also lúshalilo 11. Lala umukowa 3/4 has the form for "navel," which shows that it borrowed the form.

now Lamba or Nkoya, the term, always in class 3/4, is also used for "clan" and "lineage" and even "nation," while in the Njila languages it occurs only in Nyaneka and in slightly skewed form in Ngangela. In both cases, the term does not mean "clan" but is a synonym (archaism?) for "lineage."[75] The meaning "family, lineage, clan" is certainly derived from "navel cord" and not the reverse, while "navel cord" itself is an innovation in the Njila languages that ultimately derives from proto-Bantu "skin."[76] The innovation of the meaning "group of matrilineal descent" must have occurred in a language that had the meaning "navel cord" and hence must have arisen somewhere in southern Angola, even though the form and meaning "matriclan" is far more widespread in Zambia than in Angola. On present evidence, one concludes then that matrilineages developed first in southern Angola, probably in relation to the management and inheritance of cattle herds, and then spread to Zambia where the term then acquired the further meaning "matriclan."

When did this occur? Following the reasoning outlined above, it only happened when items such as hoes or cattle became highly valued property and a means to accumulate wealth. It is tempting then to link the emergence of corporate matrilineages to the early acquisition of cattle. As the agropastoral economy at Nqoma seems clearly derived from southeastern Africa, where in all matters bovine patrilinearity was to obtain later, the very fact that cattle were inherited in the matrilineal line everywhere in southern West Central Africa indicates that this mode of inheritance predates the arrival of large herds. Thus the corporate matrilineage may have been first established in this region during the eighth century.

The second case is apparently a similar one. It concerns the word *mukoka* 3/4, which occurs in many of the northern Zambian languages where it only means "matriclan."[77] But in Cokwe the item means "clitoris," and in Lwena it is an obscene term for "female genitals." Thus one meaning of "matriclan" is found only in one area and the meaning that explains the metaphor only in the other. Still the appearance here may be misleading because until recently the word "clitoris" was considered unprintable and it does not occur in any of the Zambian dictionaries or word lists available to me. Without further data one cannot conclude anything except that in these matters a

75. In Ngangela *cikoua* 7/8 "lineage," but *inkova* "umbilical cord."
76. *-kóba* 3/4, 5/6, 7/8 (CS 1095). E.g., see Cokwe *-kôwa* 6, 7/8 "living skin," also used as an insult for "penis."
77. This word spread well after *mukowa* "matriclan" had been established since it cuts across the distribution of *mukowa* in the copperbelt area and must therefore be later.

relationship existed between a portion of eastern Angola and northern Zambia.

One should not conclude from the above that the development of all corporate lineages or clans in the whole matrilineal belt resulted from a straightforward diffusion starting in southern Angola. The very diversity of the vocabulary linked with these institutions in various parts of the belt is already a sign by itself of a complex institutional history in which some words are quite ancient and were originally not linked at all to matrilinearity, for example, *eanda* 5/6 "matriclan" in Nyaneka, which is the local attestation of *-gandá* 5/6 "a form of association" and only later came to be used for "matriclan." Some other words are more recent replacements for older ones, such as Lucazi *cikota* 7, which is replacing *cikoua* 7, or on a larger scale *mukoka* 3/4 for "matriclan" in Zambia replacing the older *mukowa* 3/4. Every change of this nature is a trace left by a historical event affecting the institution or idea it designates and we are far from having even identified all of these.

The ethnographic record also shows us that such a diffusion would not have been a straightforward matter. Matrilineages and matriclans are not the only institutional framework or even the dominant one in the whole matrilineal belt. In recent centuries matrilineages and matriclans were the dominant institutions among the agropastoral peoples of the southwest and to a lesser extent also among most farmers in eastern Angola, but the nomadic pastoralists of the far south and southwest developed dual descent, namely, patrilineages of various depths that were especially important in ritual matters alongside matrilineages and matriclans to regulate herds and their inheritance. On the planalto, they divided their relatives into two main bilateral groups, a residential one on the father's side and a dispersed one on the mother's side to regulate the inheritance of wealth and, in part, succession to political office. Farther north among the Ambundu, the Kongo and the Tio matrilineages competed to varying degrees with bilateral descent groups. Societies in the Lweta-speaking region of West Kasai Province and in the northeast of the Njila-speaking area had been organized around bilateral groups with matrilineal descent playing only a very subordinate role. Similar situations can be found elsewhere in the belt.

Once adopted, corporate matrilineages and matriclans had to be fitted in an existing, often less discriminating (more bilateral) framework of social organizations and once they were, the new framework would again be remodeled under the impact of a host of further changes ranging from demography and security to sociopolitical development. On the other hand, the impact of such factors of change in some places could also have led in some instances to an independent reinvention of matrilineages or clans elsewhere.[78] Thus the matrilineal belt probably resulted as the coalescence of the areas of different diffusions from several independent centers. Southwestern Angola was only one of these centers, albeit an important one whose area of diffusion included most of Zambia and reached beyond into Katanga. Another one probably arose in farming villages of the Kongo-speaking regions far to the northwest and again probably spread from there to the Middle Kwilu.[79]

The appearance of more stable villages with larger aggregates of population and corporate matrilineages also involved the creation of a better defined leadership at the lineage and village levels. In the beginning, the terminology to designate such leaders was still drawn from the vocabulary of existing kinship terminologies and hence appeared independently in many different places. Within the matrilineage, the leader was the oldest man (either the most senior one genealogically or/and the oldest one in age) who emerged naturally from the matrilineal dispensation. Such a leader was still called by relevant kinship terms such as "male mother" (mother's brother) for the head of a lineage or "old father" (grandfather or oldest of fathers) for the head of a settlement. Even today there are still places where leaders are merely "mother's brother" (*inanu*), or "grandparent" or, "father" (*se*).[80] In Kimbundu one finds *kota, makota* "elder brother," a term indicating pure seniority that came to be used to designate the head of the lineage. Soon afterward, many communities felt the need to invent new terms, still mainly derived from kinship terminology, which allowed them to distinguish between leaders and ordinary relatives, especially where a distinction between the head of a settlement and an ordinary grandparent or where a mother's mother's brother was concerned. Thus *sekulu* ("oldest father" yet used for the "oldest mother's brother") or *sukulu* in Nyemba, Umbundu, Nyaneka, Kimbundu, and others. In northern Kimbundu, one finds *nkuluntu* "oldest person." The same terms or more simply *mukulu* "the elder," "the adult" also signified "ancestor" since the leaders and their forebears were the protec-

78. For instances from equatorial Africa, see Vansina, *Paths*, p. 421, "matriclan."

79. Vansina, *Paths*, pp. 152–55, but note the erroneous rendering of *ngwa nkhazi*, which should be "resident at my mother's place" (*nkhazi* from -*kàla* "to reside" not *nkázi* "wife"). As to Middle Kwilu, while some Mbala terms ("lineage," "clan," "mother's brother") correspond to Kongo, the others correspond to Pende, in which the terminology is in part innovative ("clan") and corresponds in part to Kimbundu. That also holds for Holo. Overall, the evidence is too ambiguous to reach any firm conclusion.

80. We have *onkuntwe, ongundwe* "mother's brother" in Dimba and Herero and *nikontswe* in Sala Mpasu, but Ndonga has *osyinakulu*. Today Mbala calls the head of the lineage *ngwashi* as happens farther north and west—e.g., *ngwakazi* in Kongo.

tive ancestors par excellence.[81] At a later time still, completely new words, unrelated to any kinship terms, would be invented to designate various leaders and these will be examined as needed in the following chapters.[82]

Becoming Food Producers

The introductions into West Central Africa of cereal agriculture and full-fledged pastoralism were not one or two revolutionary events that happened perhaps in the sixth century; rather, they were processes. We have taken pains to stress the magnitude and the complexity of this transition from foraging to farming and pastoralism, which required a transformation of the entire economic basis of making a living. Such a transformation could not happen in the blink of an eye. It took at least three or four generations and probably more before it was complete and well adapted to local ecological conditions even in the places where cereals and cattle first appeared. Moreover, the gradual expansion of this completely new way of life over the whole of this vast area also took centuries to accomplish. Taking the date of Camabanga into consideration, stable sedentary villages, based on solid systems of food production supported by an increased production of metal tools, appeared in most of West Central Africa only around the tenth century or so. Compared with other parts of Africa, even in the adjacent lands of what is now Zambia, the slowness of the process of transition is not exceptional at all, but the late date for the first introduction of cereals and pastoralism is and hence also the late date for the completion of the process.[83] Once this was achieved, however, the road was open for subsequent population growth in harmony

81. The word -kúlu 1/2 (*-kúdu, CS 1195–98 from CS 1190) is still used as a term for "[protective] ancestor" in Mbala, Rund, Lucazi, Mbunda, Nyaneka, Nkhumbi, Ndongo, Herero, most of the Lower Kasai and Kongo languages, and in Ngwii.

82. To understand how this could occur, consider how himi or kimi came to mean "mother's brother." It was an honorific term normally added to the proper kinship term to distinguish the leader from all other mother's brothers, but subjects or dependents alike used it for their own mother's brother as well and began to drop the kinship term proper. Consider in Mbui: kimi or kime "senhor"; in Umbundu ocime "master"; in Hanya ihimi (Alfred Hauenstein, Hanya, p. 98), Nyaneka himi and Nkhumbi hime, "mother's brother" usually added to the specific term; the etymology of the term is unknown but in 1893, Kimbundu kimi meant "being in the state of . . ., being in the situation of . . ." (e.g., waria-kimi "state of age," uko-vakimi: "state of parent in law").

83. See Jan Vansina, "A Slow Revolution: Farming in Subequatorial Africa," pp. 15–26; Robertson, "Early Iron Age," pp. 177–79. Large stable villages appear there only after 500, yet, on present evidence, in Angola they are still evolving another two centuries later.

with the different environments and thus also for the development of the larger scale societies, the histories of which will be traced in Part Two.

We have also seen why and how the development of full-fledged cereal farming and pastoralism also required a major overhaul of social institutions. New divisions of labor by gender and age and new patterns for the coordination of labor were necessary, the new metal goods and cattle, around which most exchanges turned, widened the concept of individual ownership, fostered a novel notion of material wealth, and made the emergence of classes based on wealth possible. The corporate matrilineage with virilocal residence was probably first introduced as a result of the adoption of herds of bovine cattle and was adopted elsewhere later on. The institution brought some formalization of leadership and succession as well as an orderly pattern of inheritance of the new wealth and created alliances based on claims to common clanship while it also contained the potential to differentiate social groups into unequal status categories and to develop leadership based on the criterion of territory.

The spread of cereal agriculture, of matrilineal institutions, and the dissemination of Njila languages across the great divide, which until then had separated the northern and the southern halves of the area, erased that divide and unified West Central Africa as a cultural region, despite the appearance of a new cultural boundary of some importance between milking and nonmilking areas. Actually the appearance of this new milking boundary is an early sign that henceforth further innovation in the different regions within the area was to occur predominantly as a consequence of new local inventions, whether they were adaptations to growing population density, local environments, or the products of a common regional social imagination. From then on until the irruption of the Portuguese around 1500, the diffusion of new features from outside of the area was no longer the main impetus for change.

PART TWO By the tenth century of our era, most inhabitants of West Central Africa had chosen to adopt farming and/or herding and were actively building common overarching institutions between autonomous local communities, among which diffuse matriclans may have been the first. In other words, the inhabitants were now beginning to build societies. Once they had fully mastered their rejection of foraging and nomadism as a way of life, the possibilities for further development inherent in the new technologies and novel social institutions could begin to unfold. And unfold they did after ca. 1000, albeit not as a bud automatically expands into a flower. That metaphor implies an ineluctable progression toward a preordained goal, which was not the case here. There never was a single inherent program that automatically forced people to expand the scale of their societies continually and continuously from village to region so as to wrest power relentlessly from a multitude of villages in order to concentrate it in a single capital. Nor was it a matter of taking authority away from the many family heads to centralize it into the hands of a single paramount, even though some societies did end up as large kingdoms. What happened was that in different regions people developed their incipient societies by recognizing and implementing additional choices as further solutions to issues of common governance. As these choices and solutions were different in each region, each region went its own way.

Certainly those choices and solutions were still concerned with and constrained by the physical environment, but in each case the collective imagination of different societies came up with different outcomes. The available evidence makes this clear and invites us to distinguish between three different major sociocultural regions in the area. Nevertheless, these regions are in fact congruent to a large degree with different amounts of rainfall, different qualities of soils (fertile loamy or poor sandy soils), and different conditions for herding bovine cattle. Moreover, such conditions largely account not merely for different patterns of aggregation among the populations in the area but also for the major differences in population densities between the regions from the beginning of the second millennium onward. Later directions of development resulted not from automatic environmental effects but were inspired by the operation of the collective imagination shared by the members of a given society. The planalto, for instance, was well suited for keeping large herds of cattle; thus, people there kept some cattle but relegated herding to a subordinate place and did not even drink milk. On the so-called Kalahari Sands in the east, all societies developed sodalities as institutions of common governance but some refused to accept any form of monocephalic rule while others recognized common neighborhood chiefs as spokespersons for and living emblems of their neighborhoods. Actually, the three major sociocultural regions were characterized above all not by objective environmental differences but by major differences in the subjects which mesmerized people. Thus in one region all minds and imaginations were enthralled by cattle, in another they focused on initiations and social position, and in the third everyone dreamed of the splendors of sacralized leaders and the possibilities of participating in such splendors.

How did these differences between the regions develop? In earlier times, the great innovations had affected nearly the entire area in a roughly similar fashion and this allowed us to discuss the whole area all at once. But once sedentarization had been achieved, the population of some settlements in privileged places, blessed with a favorable environment, gradually increased, probably both by migration and by natural increase, as the villagers became more knowledgeable about their disease environment and found ways to mitigate its effects. As such settlements grew larger, they split so that sets of related neighboring village communities began to form larger societies. After several generations, this process led to the emergence of a pocket of relatively higher population density in such places.[1] Greater interaction between a larger number of people within each pocket then further fueled more rapid sociocultural change. As these pockets were rare and at sizeable distances from each other, the shared ideas and social practices within each of them began to drift more and more away from those current in another. As each of these pockets grew, they increasingly became centers of attraction for the scattered small settlements or camps in their hinterland so that in due time these peripheries were assimilated into the social and cultural way of life of each central population node.

Njila speakers played a major role in the formation of each of these pockets just as they had played a major role in attempts to become more sedentary through the practice of horticulture and cereal agriculture earlier on. That they were also prominent in the development of each population node is evident from the outcome since Njila languages ousted all others among sedentary populations in the area and most others among nomadic cattle

1. As we shall see in each case, the localization of each cluster can be deduced by the main differences in population density as known from data after 1600. The chronology of their appearance will remain unknown as long as intensive archaeological research has not been undertaken. The only dates available at this time are the eighth and the thirteenth century ones associated with the complex site of Feti on the planalto.

herders. This linguistic assimilation or Bantuization of most of the inhabitants in the entire area formed part and parcel of the cultural assimilation of the peripheries. At first different communities, even within a population node, used different languages but soon those who did not speak the predominant Njila language became bilingual and, later still, sometimes after a century or even two had elapsed, they abandoned their own tongues to adopt the locally dominant Njila language.[2] The same occurred later as non–Njila-speaking communities in the peripheries were gradually drawn into the culture of the central nucleus. Ultimately, the Njila languages triumphed nearly everywhere in the area but we do not know precisely when, how, or even why Njila speakers achieved their dominant position in each case.

In the heartland of each node as well as within isolated stable commercial or political centers, such as Nqoma for instance, strong internal dynamics led to vigorous internal sociocultural innovations. These first emerged in the confrontation between different local ideas and practices, which gradually were fused into a single homogeneous way of life, in stark contrast to the dynamics that had fueled momentous change in earlier times when all known relevant innovations had been triggered by external inputs, which then diffused the entire area. Such common inputs had tended to make local societies more similar all over West Central Africa, a process which has been called convergence.[3] But from the beginning of the second millennium CE, this trend was reversed because the new dynamics of clustering fostered cultural divergence; this would be the paramount trend at least until the irruption of the Portuguese around 1500, when convergence became once again paramount everywhere. Thus, while it made sense to follow the successive developments in the earlier period from a global perspective for the entire area, it no longer does so once the dynamics of divergence predominate. Hence, Part II of this study discusses the history of each major region in turn. Indeed, we will follow each region separately during the first half of the second millennium rather than subdivide the presentation into separate chronological segments.

By organizing the narrative in this way the reader gains the impression that a huge break occurred in the historical dynamics involved in both periods. It looks as if at first everything comes from outside the area while afterward and until the Portuguese arrival nothing came from there. Indeed the dynamic emphasis did shift decisively in favor of regional divergence but borrowing from outside continued as well. The difference is that none of

2. On such a process, see Gabriele Sommer, *Ethnographie.*

3. For the use of the terms convergence and divergence, cf. Michael Bisson, "Continuity and Discontinuity," pp. 43–46, and John H. Robertson, "A New Iron Age Pottery," pp. 59–64.

these later loans was momentous enough to affect the fundamental economic and social framework of the societies in the area in the same way as they had done during most of the first millennium. While the break between the periods is therefore of paramount importance, the choice of presentation tends to erase the fact that borrowing from outside the area continued unabated during the whole second period even though the newly imported features were now but additions to the framework that had already been laid down. After all, such additions continued to enrich, amplify, and strengthen that framework. Hence, some are mentioned as needed in the following chapters. For now, it may suffice to briefly sketch the paths of entry by which these later innovations entered the area. To appreciate this issue, the story of the domestic chicken is perhaps particularly apposite.

This humble fowl, which is of Asian origin, reached West Central Africa at about the time large cattle herds and widespread cereal farming became common there. Chickens are reported in and near East Central Africa from the eighth century onward.[4] From there, they were introduced into nearly all of West Central Africa, probably during the next century.[5] Unlike cattle or the early cereals, they were not imported from a single point of entry into West Central Africa but through three different "gates," namely: one from southern Zambia to southern Angola and from there to central Angola and then farther north;[6] another one from the copperbelt in Zambia to the head-

4. Namely, at Bosutswe (Botswana)—Denbow, "Material Culture," p. 114, and Ina Plug "Domestic Animals," p. 517; Ndondonwane or Kwagandaganda (Natal) in Plug, "Domestic Animals," p. 517, and Clutton Brock, "The Spread of Domestic Animals," p. 62; Sanga (Katanga)—de Maret, *Fouilles archéologiques,* 1:132, 167. Until recently, no finds earlier than the eighth century had been reported from the east coast itself (see Mark Horton, *Shanga,* p. 384, for Shanga and Chibuene). Now Felix Chami, "Chicken Bones," pp. 90–91, concludes that chickens found on a site in Zanzibar date at least to "the end of the last millennium BC" and in his "Response," p. 648, he arrives at "800 BC or earlier." The dating, however, is uncertain since 80 BCE, 800 BCE or 2838 BCE all seem nearly equally likely. Given the importance of the find, one hopes that AMS dating on the bones themselves will be undertaken.

5. Assuming that they were adopted within two centuries after their presence at Bosutswe around 700. Their introduction did not affect the essentials of food production. The whole ethnographic record for eastern central and southern Africa shows that domestic fowls were not kept primarily for their eggs, nor for their feathers, and perhaps not even directly for their meat, but for their ritual value. Their meat and blood was then the most common of all sacrifices and chickens were often used in divination. This suggests at least that fowls may have been first adopted for their value in divination and as sacrificial animals.

6. Note *-cúcú/cúcua 9/10 (CS 402 and partial series 125) (onomatopaea); *-sangi 9/10 in Middle Angola is a later innovation (Malcolm Guthrie, *Comparative,* 1:137 and topogram 24).

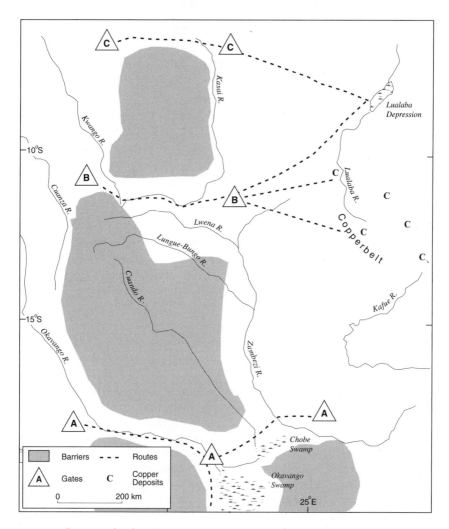

MAP 11. Communication Routes

waters of the Zambezi and into eastern Angola;[7] and finally a third one around latitude 8° S across the Lubilash from Lubaland to the lands in the northeast where the Rund Block of languages and Lweta are spoken (map 11).[8] Subsequently, all later linguistic introductions into West Central Africa from East Central Africa continued to pass through the three gates indicated

7. Note that *-cumbi 12/13 (CS 415) includes Lamba, Lala on the copperbelt, but not Nkoya.

8. The word *-jódo (nzolo/u) 9/10 or "white bird" is an innovation from the Luba languages. See topogram 24. Finally, the Mbala and Dciriku forms are derived from *-kuku 9/10 (CS 1203), which was the original form on the east coast, with CS 1203 representing the change from seven to five vowels.

by the terminology for "chicken" rather than all along the long border between the two areas.[9]

Elsewhere, barriers prevented communication and borrowing and these
remained in place during the entire period. One lay west of the floodplain
of the upper Zambezi River, another between the upper Lulua and the uppermost Lubilash Rivers, and a third one between the upper-middle Kasai
and the upper Kwango Rivers. Such barriers resulted from sizeable uninhabited or nearly uninhabited stretches of land, whether in the infertile barren
sands of the uplands in the east or along the steep escarpments running
along the coast from the latitude of Benguela to the lower Longa River. They
blocked those easy and frequent communications from neighbor to neighbor which favor linguistic borrowing and appear therefore on specialized
language maps.[10] Their overall effects explain why influences from East
Central Africa, while strong in eastern Angola, did not percolate readily into
central Angola to its west and why northwestern influences would easily
spread from Kongo speakers into middle and southern Angola but not often
into northeastern Angola. Thus even though convergence was active within
the area, the gates and barriers to communication both limited and channeled its flow.[11]

9. The terminology for various plants introduced from the east between ca. 800 and
ca. 1400 bears this out. But some features entered West Central Africa from the northwest rather than from the east. This includes some plantains and bananas. See Gerda
Rossel, *Taxonomic-Linguistic Study.* A recent report claims to have identified plantain phytoliths in Cameroon ca. 1500 BCE but on unconvincing evidence. See Christophe Mbida
Mindzie et al., "First Archaeological Evidence," pp. 1–6. Moreover, this claim flies in the face
of all other evidence elsewhere in Africa. Most likely the phytoliths identified are *ensete.*

10. Such as those elaborated by Michael Mann in Bastin et al., *Continuity,* p. 75; the
heterogram 3.1.4 line of similarity of less than 30 percent between neighboring languages. The Zambezi floodplain barrier starts there between K33 and K31 and ends between L35 and K22. The northern barrier is less clear and shows up only around Mbagani. Note a second less hermetic barrier (at 15 percent) between Umbundu and the
Moxico languages, which corresponds in part to the empty lands east of the upper
Cuanza mentioned by nineteenth-century travelers, for instance, "Ladislaus Magyar's
Erforschung," p. 228.

11. Further archaeological evidence informs us that after 1200 features from southeast Africa no longer directly entered this area through the southern gate, which henceforth only provided access to the lower floodplains of the Zambezi and its middle
course. The study of loans shows that most of the innovations through the middle gate
came directly from the copperbelt until after ca. 1600, when the majority stemmed from
the main Luba Katanga Kingdom and that communications via the northernmost gate
in the northeast were more frequent with Luba Kasai speakers on the lower Lubilash
than with the famous polities of the Lualaba depression.

3

OF WATER, CATTLE, AND KINGS

 THE CONSTRAINTS OF THE PHYSICAL ENVIRONMENTS are the most evident and seem to be the most severe in the southernmost of the three great regions that make up West Central Africa. The region can be delimited to the north by the line between those who milked cattle and those who did not, for this practice is a reliable indicator of the wholly different impact of the environments on the socio-cultural developments that occurred to the north as compared with that of the south. The farther south of the milking line one goes, the scarcer and less reliable the rains. In southern regions where rainfall was less than 700 mil-limeters a year, the minimum amount of annual precipitation that allows for rainfed agriculture here, the only permanent rivers were the Okavango, the Cunene, and their tributaries, which also come down from the well-watered planalto.[1] The farther south one goes, as well as nearer to the coast, the cli-mate becomes increasingly drier while surface water becomes more rare, at least for most of the year, so that eventually there remains neither sufficient water nor grass to raise cattle.[2] The specific distribution of the population was dictated by the availability of water and it was low nearly everywhere. The way people made a living was determined by rainfall in combination with orography and, in some measure, with soils. These features dictated where settled agropastoralists could thrive, where nomads could keep cattle, where other forms of nomadism were possible, and where no one could survive. The present distribution of the three main subdivisions within the

---

1. As an anonymous reader remarked, the unavailability of surface water in the Kala-hari Sands region was more significant than the amount of rainfall by itself, since in southeastern Africa dry-land farming did occur in regions with rainfall between 450 and 700 millimeters rainfall but with good surface water availability. Indeed P. W. Porter, "Environmental Potentials," pp. 402–20, has demonstrated that annual rainfall must be at least 500 millimeters annually to be suitable for crops.

2. The word "cattle" in this chapter refers to bovines, not to goats or sheep. For An-gola, see Alvin Urquhart, *Patterns of Settlement,* pp. 2–8.

Cimbabesian group of the Njila languages largely corresponds to these ecological zones and shows that they are of very long standing. Thus, most cattle nomads now speak Herero-related languages, agropastoralists Nyaneka-Nkhumbi tongues in one ecological zone and Ambo languages in another, while in recent historical times at least nearly all foragers and sheepherders, save for some Herero speakers in the Kaokoland, spoke different San or Khoe languages or Kwadi.

To the degree that the physical constraints on human settlement increase with a corresponding lack of available water, their influence on possible social organizations and their attendant cultures becomes greater and greater, with the result that environments become more determinant here than anywhere else in the area. But the introduction of cattle and milk drinking altered the equation between people and their surroundings by creating a new potential for increases in the internal social intricacy of communities as well as increases in the size of societies. Thus environmental conditions have stamped the sociocultural history of the entire southern region to such an extent that any analysis of the history of governance in those parts must consider each ecological zone separately. Given the decisive role of cattle in these developments, it is best to first present the earliest evidence for greater pastoral activity and a more complex way of life than that of Divuyu. That evidence is found on the site of Divuyu's successor: Nqoma.

Nqoma

Late in the eighth century some Divuyans left their exiguous site on top of the female hill at Tsodilo to settle at Nqoma[3] on a larger and more accessible lower plateau two kilometers away. A little over a century later, new immigrants arrived and absorbed them into a new village, which attained its fullest development between ca. 1000 and 1180. Nqoma was then abandoned as was the contemporaneous small site of Kapako situated to the northwest of Tsodilo on the Okavango River.[4] The Nqoma site covered about 100 × 200 square meters or about two hectares and comprises six sections.[5] It was

3. Also spelled N!oma. The nasalized consonant is a click. See Denbow, "After the Flood," p. 190.
4. Dating after Denbow, personal communication, 2002. For Nqoma in general, see Wilmsen and Denbow, "Advent," pp. 1511–12; Denbow, "Material Culture," pp. 119–21; Denbow, "Congo to Kalahari," pp. 164–66; Denbow, "After the Flood," pp. 190–92; Turner, "Early Iron Age Herders"; Miller, *Tsodilo*, especially pp. 12–13, 15–6, 21–22, 26–30, 89–91. Publication of a full site report on Nqoma is underway.
5. That is 20,000 square meters. See Turner, "Early Iron Age Herders," p. 7. This surface comes in addition to previously excavated test squares as per Denbow, "Early Iron

sampled at regular grid intervals with a series of excavations of one square meter each for a total of 127 square meters. Excavations were made in ten-centimeter spits and revealed evidence for several occupations. The middle levels, that is, the ones between 50 and 80 centimeters depth, correspond to the entity which has been labeled Nqoma.[6] Among the finds one notes four burials and at least one housefloor. From the available data it seems that, during its heyday in the eleventh century, the site was large enough to contain a village divided into quarters and comprising sets of households with a total population in the lower hundreds.[7] Unfortunately the overall shape of that settlement (circular, oval, square?) remains unknown.

One novelty at Nqoma is its pottery, which is quite different from that found at Divuyu, although there are a few continuities. These ceramics, mainly shallow dishes, have also been found at smaller sites to the southeast of Tsodilo and similar ones appear at Kapako. The decor of a portion of the pottery is new and stems in part from the Gokomere-Dambwa tradition that arrived here, probably from western Zambia or adjacent parts of Angola northeast of the delta.[8] To some extent, many of the pots and their decors also recall those at Sioma in Zambia some 200 kilometers to the northeast but a very few others apparently have been inspired from pottery styles near the Shashi/Limpopo confluence.[9] Far more cattle and metal jewelry, especially copper, were found at Nqoma than at Divuyu. Cattle remains constitute about one-third of all faunal remains here against only three percent at Divuyu, while 2,600 mostly small iron and copper artifacts were recovered, as well as evidence of local forging and resmelting operations, although no primary smelting occurred here despite the nearby mining of specularite for other purposes. Thus either the raw metal or larger metal

Age Remains," pp. 474–75, and his "Prehistoric Herders and Foragers," p. 181, and Denbow and Wilmsen, "Iron Age Pastoralists," pp. 405–8. The Divuyan settlement at Nqoma occurred in the section called Central A. The Nqoman occupation includes the sections labeled Periphery, Outpost, Central B, Blacksmith, and Society. Among these, Society was the earliest, followed by Blacksmith and then simultaneously by the three others.

6. See Denbow, "Congo to Kalahari," p. 164; Miller, *Tsodilo*, pp. 15, 21. In addition to the names for the earlier test squares (Outpost I, Outpost II, and Society) different names have also been given to different portions of the site. As far as is known at present, these are Sandfringe, Midden, Blacksmith, Rockhouse, Burial, Periphery, and Mbukushu. For details, wait for the promised site report.

7. Blacksmith, Midden, Society, Outpost I, Outpost II, and Rockhouse were apparently all occupied in ca. 950–980 and the following evidence derives from these portions of the overall site.

8. See Denbow, "Congo," p. 166. Denbow, personal communication, 2002, stresses the similarity in ceramics with Matlapaneng.

9. See Denbow, "After the Flood," p. 192.

objects had to be imported from elsewhere. Glass beads, marine shells, and even a replica of a conus shell in ivory indicate trading contacts with the east coast. The presence of ivory also points to long-distance trade. But Nqomans were not cattle nomads since evidence of dung heaps is absent and cereal crops and melons as well as wild plants, including large quantities of *mongongo* nuts and *moretlwa* seeds, remnants of game, and fish and mollusk shells from the Okavango River are present. Finally, and in contrast with finds at Divuyu, moderate numbers of stone tools were also present.[10] The most telling find was a two-liter mass of carbonized sorghum and millet seeds, two smithing tuyeres, much copper and iron, cane glass beads, marine shells, ivory, and a large number of chert tools (chert may have been an object of trade) all found in neighboring units surrounding the floor of the "Blacksmith" house.

Compared with that of Divuyu, the numbers of cattle present at Nqoma had increased dramatically. The abundant cattle remains also indicate a considerable consumption of meat. Indeed, approximately one-third of all meat consumed came from cattle as opposed to only three percent in Divuyu.[11] This meat came both from a number of young animals (mostly young steers) and from the carcasses of old cows that had been killed or had died at the ends of their productive lives. Such a distribution agrees well with nineteenth-century pastoral practice in central Namibia where, except for a few young steers, no young animals were killed just for eating because milk was a staple; hence, the herd had to be preserved because wealth was counted by the size of one's herd and not, say, by the size of one's hoard of metal objects.[12] Yet when one looks at the high frequency of cattle sacrifices, especially among the Herero, it is clear that actually much meat from cattle of all ages was consumed.[13] Since the data from Nqoma are also similar to the situation of the Ambo in the nineteenth century, they do not rule out the notion that the site was inhabited by an elite.[14] In any case, the patterns of meat consumption at Nqoma are practically identical to those found on most sites in eastern Botswana during the same centuries. There they have been interpreted as survival strategies to cope with sudden loss of large livestock caused by droughts, epizootic disease, or warfare.[15]

10. See Miller, *Tsodilo*, p. 15; Denbow and Wilmsen, *Metallurgical*, p. 10.

11. See Denbow, "Congo," p. 165.

12. See Irle, *Herero*, p. 139.

13. Ibid., pp. 81–86; Hendrik Luttig, *Religious System*, pp. 27, 38–40.

14. Even though Ambo nobles did slaughter cattle for meat, this only occurred on festive occasions according to C. H. L. Hahn, "Ovambo," pp. 13, 34–35. See also Hermann Tönjes, *Ovamboland*, pp. 70–71.

15. See Andrew Reid and Alinah Segobye, "Politics," p. 60.

A more detailed study of the age of these cattle when slaughtered found a bimodal pattern of culling that is consistent with culling young males and seven- to eight-year-old cows. That reflects a typical management strategy in which the breeding potential of the herd as well as the production of milk were both fully preserved while the culling saved on herding labor and provided more pasture land per head of cattle.[16] This suggests that, in contrast to Toutswe, Mapungubwe, and later Zimbabwe, the Nqoma consumers were not powerful enough to command a perpetual supply of *prime* beef, even though they did obtain a good amount of beef. The Nqomans therefore either exploited their own herds or bargained on equal terms with other herders. As no remnants of kraals have been found at Nqoma itself, the herds must have been grazed on the plains away from the hills and managed from dispersed cattle posts.[17] Hence seasonal transhumance must have been practiced between permanent water along the Okavango Delta margin and the grasslands surrounding the Tsodilo Hills, although tsetse infestation may have prevented that and, in any case, no direct evidence about this has been found. Nor is it known whether the Nqomans owned these herds and maintained their own cattle posts or if the herds were owned by others.

Similarly the location of the fields remains unknown. They were probably not placed on the Nqoma plateau itself. It is very likely that they were worked by Nqoma's women, who were assisted by their children, who also cared for small stock. Finally, the sharp increase in the consumption of game, as compared with that of Divuyu, parallels a considerable increase in stone tools found on the site. This suggests an increase in daily social interactions between foragers and the Nqoman settlers. Perhaps some foragers even lived on the site, but whether they did or not, they certainly had easy access to it in order to exchange meat, skins, occasional furs, and other products from the veld for local goods.

This brings us to another major characteristic of Nqoma: the evidence for trade. Nqoma was the main economic hub for a large region (map 12). Trade with the southeast, as far away as the Indian Ocean is directly documented by imports such as glass beads and marine shells, while the major exports may well have been ivory and specularite, which, in contrast to the evidence for Divuyu, is quite abundant on the site. One can trace the trade route southeast from Nqoma in some detail by the appearance of foreign

16. See Turner, "Early Iron Age," pp. 10–11, for the model; Denbow, "Congo to Kalahari," pp. 170, 171, figure 16b.

17. Cattle posts of this period have been found in eastern Botswana; see Reid and Segobye, "Politics," p. 60.

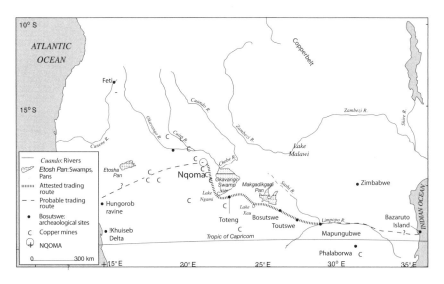

MAP 12. Nqoma Trading Contacts, ca. 900–1100

objects found along the way stations. Thus some Ngamiland pottery turned up at Bosutswe. In turn, Bosutswe ware appears at the Shashi/Limpopo confluence, which was directly linked to coastal trading posts.[18] Evidence for other distant links include places where copper and iron was mined and smelted. Copper is much more abundant at Nqoma than it was at Divuyu and its trace elements indicate that it came from several different sources. Most possible sources are quite distant, however. Of these, the Qwebe Hills mines in Botswana are the closest, the Otavi and the Tsumeb mines in Namibia are farther away but richer. Duncan Miller even mentions very distant possible sources such as Phalaborwa in the Transvaal or the Zambian copperbelt.[19] What could the Nqomans have given in exchange for these metals? Metal in general was precious (resmelted!) and therefore had to be traded for something equally precious, such as livestock or jewelry made with the metal. At Nqoma itself, jewelry was produced and may well have been exchanged for metal and livestock. Specularite was mined there intensively as well, although perhaps not by the villagers themselves, and probably traded to eastern Botswana just as it was during the nineteenth

18. See Denbow, "Material Culture," p. 114 (Ngamiland bowl at Bosutswe). See also Reid and Segobye, "Politics," pp. 59, 61 (pottery from the Shashi confluence on a Toutswe site and vice versa).

19. See Miller, *Tsodilo*, p. 89; Reid and Segobye, "Politics," p. 62 (Zambia—but may be too affirmative).

century.[20] Whatever the counterpart exchanged for the metal, Nqoma had plenty of it since this settlement differed from all others in being the center for the large-scale production of metal beads and other finery, a production that goes far to explain its commercial preeminence in the whole region.

Nqoma was not just a regular player in long-distance trade. It also was the hub of a complex regional trading system wherein items from different ecological environments were directly exchanged for each other by the parties who needed them in a manner that may well have been similar to the *hxaro* practice still attested to in the nineteenth century.[21] In the *hxaro* arrangement, a set of partners practiced preferential, reciprocal, obligatory, and delayed exchanges among themselves and these partnerships were inherited from generation to generation.[22] In the nineteenth century, the distances involved were usually under 90 kilometers but some exchanges covered distances as far as 270 kilometers. Because *hxaro* was a stable inherited arrangement, trust between partners was assured and that was essential to making delayed exchange possible. The exchanges themselves, as Polly Wiessner stresses, were an important strategy in reducing environmental risk.

This system of exchange involved a wide range of regional commodities, such as salt, game, ivory, furs, hides, rhino horn; useful wild plants, perhaps *Cannabis,* and ocher from foraging milieus; domestic animals such as calves, goats, some sheep and perhaps milk from cattle posts; ceramics, goats, and cereals from farming settlements; fish, mollusks, mats, baskets, and perhaps local plants from the Okavango River and Delta milieus; while specularite for ointment was mined at Tsodilo itself. In Denbow's reconstruction of this system, all these products flowed to and through Nqoma.[23] To Nqoma because some of them, such as salt or cattle, were needed there for local consumption, while others, such as ivory and specularite, for instance, were used to sustain the long-distance trade with its metals, cattle, ivory, chert, agate, glass beads, and marine shells. To Nqoma rather than elsewhere because it was a central place where persons from a given hinterland could find the whole range of commodities they needed, and to Nqoma because the place lay between localities with different but complementary ecologies.

20. See L. Robbins et al., "Intensive Mining," pp. 147–49; Denbow, personal communication, 2002, for the abundance of specularite at Nqoma and for the nineteenth-century trade.

21. H. Luttig, *Religious System,* pp. 87–89 misses the main rationale of the *oupanga* link between friends, namely, to form a chain for exchanging goods; P. Wiessner, *Hxaro.*

22. See E. N. Wilmsen, "Exchange," pp. 98–109 (105–7).

23. See Denbow, "Congo to Kalahari," pp. 168–70.

Contrasting this model with the one Denbow elaborated for eastern Botswana, he shows that although Nqoma obviously enjoyed "economic and political primacy," its regional system was clearly less centralized than the emerging chiefdoms (and principalities) in southeast Botswana, which, among other signs of strong centralization, exhibit a hierarchy of settlement sizes. Although he speaks of "those in authority" at Nqoma, of "politico-economic stratification" and "political leveling," he still maintained that for well over two centuries Nqoma remained the hub of an economic regional system in which all participating partners enjoyed "autonomy" and "mutual support."[24] For him, Nqoma was not the heart of a chiefdom, yet its elites still somehow dominated the entire regional arena.[25]

Data about meat consumption as well as the profligacy of jewelry suggests that some people at Nqoma did form an elite.[26] Yet this elite did not derive its status from political centralization. There is no evidence at all, no sumptuous residence, no splendid tomb, no regional exploitation, to suggest that Nqoma was the seat of a chiefdom. Indeed even its rather small size and the modest number of its inhabitants militates against the idea of a centralized polity as does the geography of its surroundings. Something else must therefore account for the signs of well-being found there. As it happens, the only exceptionally rich housefloor found was not that of a lordly residence but that of a blacksmith. This suggests that perhaps all this jewelry may have been intended as exchange for cattle rather than just to be flaunted locally. Indeed the extent of its production is such that one may well think of Nqoma as an industrial settlement of blacksmiths and a trading emporium.[27] The

24. Ibid., p. 168 for "Political and Economic Dominance"; pp. 170–72 for other quotes and for the whole argument.

25. Denbow, "Material," p. 113, enumerates the power which wealth in cattle can procure. The use of patron-client relationships and straight loans of cattle are two obvious pathways by which to dominate others.

26. See Turner, "Early Iron Age," p. 10; Denbow and Wilmsen "Advent," pp. 1511–12. The jewelry especially impressed Denbow, who, in "Material," p. 119, speaks of its intentional use to construct social distinctions and, on p. 120, to possibly "encode differences in status, power and wealth."

27. It is the richest site in metal of Southern Africa: 2,600 metal items (992 beads) were recovered there. Cf. Miller, *Tsodilo*, pp. 89–90. That this metal was not smelted from raw ore on the spot should not be surprising. The local vegetation was insufficient to furnish the quantities of charcoal that would have required. As it was, the fabrication of charcoal required for blacksmithing and modest resmelting may already have exceeded local possibilities and hence may have been partially imported. One wonders why during these centuries no competing centers arose. Environmental location, long-standing social relationships with far-away smelting and trading communities, and manufacturing secrets (especially concerning copper beads), to mention but the obvious, were probably all factors to explain why it was so.

settlement probably consisted of an elite of a few master smiths linked by kinship, surrounded by apprentices and perhaps also by a few menials as well as "hangers-on" intent to benefit from the ongoing trade. Indeed there seems to be just enough evidence for differences between various household belongings (e.g., in the amount of stone tools) to suggest differences in the way different households lived and also some heterogeneity in the composition of the population. While the elite were blacksmiths, the lesser folks were agropastoralists, hunters, and the occasional immigrant trader from far away.[28]

This commercial emporium flourished for well over two centuries before it suddenly vanished around 1100, as did the small satellite settlement at Kapako. What could have provoked this sudden demise? Was it a major shift in demand by the east coast trade from ivory to gold, concomitant with the decline of Mapungubwe? Was it some unknown factor such as the rise of a successful center for beadmaking elsewhere? Or was it a deterioration of local climatic conditions?[29] The manner of the demise itself is easy to envisage, considering the relatively small size of the settlement, the heterogeneity of its society, and its commercial *raison d'être*. Most smiths vanished in search of opportunities elsewhere, and once they left, the site lost its attraction, although it was not wholly abandoned, as small quantities of ceramics and metal continued to be produced there.[30]

Was Nqoma just a flash in the pan that left no visible legacy at all? True, no archaeological trace of the destination of its smiths has been found, but their special knowledge of copper smelting and beadmaking as well as their trading activities may have survived after all. When written information becomes available, nearly 700 years later, it tells us of Bergdama all over Namibia who were smelting and forging beads and bangles of copper and iron, jewelry that was in such demand that they traded it over considerable distances, and that they exchanged beads not just for goats but also for

28. As a somewhat heterogeneous community, Nqoma was probably polyglot. Varieties of San, Khoe, and Bantu languages were probably common there although the dominant tongue was that of its elite blacksmiths, and we cannot even guess at what sort of language that actually was!

29. On the change of demand from ivory to gold, see Denbow, "After the Flood," pp. 184–86, and "Material," p. 121; on the effects of the demise of Mapungubwe on all sites in Botswana, see Reid and Segobye, "Politics," p. 66; on the climate, see Robbins, "Intensive Mining," pp. 145–46, and "Archaeology," pp. 1108–9. For Denbow, "After the Flood," pp. 184–86, the climate became steadily drier from 900 or so onward until ca. 1200. By 1100 it might have become too dry to stay at Nqoma. But Reid and Segobye, "Politics," p. 63, citing Thomas Huffman, assert that in eastern Botswana the climate was wetter between 900–1050.

30. See Denbow, "After the Flood," p. 196; Denbow and Wilmsen, *Metallurgical*, p. 16, for later occupations.

cattle.[31] Similarly, information about the Ndonga of northern Namibia tells us that among all the Ambo only their smiths knew how to fashion jewelry from copper mined and smelted near Otavi, also one of the probable sources of Nqoma copper 700 years earlier.[32] Is there a link between Nqoma smithing and these later smiths? Future archaeological research could tell us whether any copper found at Tsodilo did stem from Otavi and as yet unfound sites of later date could shed light on the hypothesis of a link between Nqoma smiths and later metalworkers who happen to be Bergdama.

The fate of Nqoma forcefully reminds us of the vulnerability of a settlement located on the edge of environments where farming could not be practiced. As soon as long-distance trading activity was disrupted, Nqoma collapsed because, despite its role as a hub for local exchange, it no longer was the central place to acquire cattle and metals, the two commodities crucial to the local society. Without these, the place lost its appeal to herders and foragers who reverted to a fully nomadic life. To fully understand its demise one must remember that professional trade for material profit makes no sense in societies where wealth consists in control over others. While acquiring or hoarding jewelry allowed one to claim increased respect and establish relative status, its appeal paled compared to that of owning cattle. Cattle offered not only the means of leading a different way of life, but they were wealth that increased over time. Moreover, its mere possession and even more its hoarding created a strong social hierarchy in which its masters controlled clients who herded cattle for them while both groups lorded it over their cattleless servants, whose livelihood lay totally in their hands. The social advantages of cattleowners were further enhanced by the fact that an exchange of cattle was essential for a wide range of social transactions, such as marriage or the payment of fines and debts. Hence, when all is said and done, it was cattle herding that made the long life of the Nqoma emporium possible.

31. See John Kinahan and Joseph C. Vogel, "Recent Copper-working," pp. 23–62, and Kinahan, *Pastoral*, pp. 43–44, and his "The Rise and Fall," p. 383, for trade-beads and cattle so that a store of beads can be seen as the equivalent of a herd of cattle.

32. See Heinrich Vedder, *South West Africa*, pp. 27, 29, 35, 67, 175. (Vedder's identification on p. 28 of Kawebs with Ambo is sheer fancy. The smelters were probably Bergdama from the neighborhood of Rehoboth.) For Ndonga, the earliest information dates to the 1840s. See the sources cited by Harr Siiskonen, *Trade*, pp. 61–62, and Heintze, "Buschmänner," pp. 45–56. But in 1852, Magyar mentions a settlement of coppersmiths among the Kwanyama. See "Ladislaus Magyar's Schilderung," p. 1002.

Cattle Nomads and Their Societies

Of all the ways of life discussed in this book, nomadic pastoralism was perhaps the most closely conditioned by environmental constraints for it developed only wherever watercourses were intermittent and where suitable grasses for cattle or sheep and/or shrub for goats were available but where sustained agriculture could not be practiced. Moreover, a striking correlation suggests that where rainfall was less than 200 millimeters annually, cattle were rare or absent as compared to sheep and goats. Cattle nomads congregated on or near pastures in or near the valleys of the intermittent rivers or near permanent waterholes. As the alternation of short wet and long dry seasons dictated the successive concentration and dispersal of cattle and their keepers, adequate social institutions had to be developed to cope with this annual rhythm. Since a similar rhythm also dictated the movements of nomads with small stock, foragers, and indeed even game, as well as the appearance of edible plants (*veldkos*), bovine cattle and their masters were thus inserted in a landscape where earlier inhabitants had long been attuned to such conditions and where newcomers were taught how to survive in such circumstances.

Cattle are first reported in larger numbers from 1000 or slightly earlier at Nqoma, not far from a zone in which agriculture was also possible. The animals soon may have multiplied in part by natural increase, as happened in central eastern Botswana, and in part by acquisition from the southeast, so that large-scale cattle herding expanded in nearby regions suitable for farming in southern Angola. There agropastoralists came to be established rapidly as far as the planalto. But only future archaeology will tell us exactly how rapidly agropastoralism spread to all the landscapes where this way of life could be sustained. Since keeping cattle on a small scale was already known, there was no major obstacle to the spread of acquiring larger herds, so one may suggest that it took only a little over one to two centuries for agropastoralists to become established all over the zone where they were later found.[33]

Perhaps Khoe speakers were the earliest groups to perfect a pastoral nomadic way of life with cattle, but unfortunately all that is known about them is that they migrated southwestward or southward from the Okavango Delta

33. Hence by 1100 or 1200. The rapid increase in cattle in the Toutswe zone of east central Botswana within a single century is well known. See Denbow, "A New Look," p. 15. Still one cannot take a rapid unproblematic multiplication of cattle for granted wherever they are introduced. See Clifford Gonzalez, "Animal Disease," pp. 95–139.

to eventually reach the Cape, where some of them were present at least since the late fifteenth century.[34] It is still not clear whether at first aboriginal local residents in southwestern Africa gradually introduced more and more cattle into their existing flocks of sheep over time to gradually turn into cattle no-mads or whether Khoe-speaking cattle nomads actually migrated all the way toward the Cape, nor is it when such an eventual migration might have hap-pened. So far, though, all the early pastoral nomads identified in central Namibia kept only small stock.[35] It is tempting, however, to imagine that full cattle nomadism came about when agropastoral cattle herders expanded deep into the northern Kalahari during wetter times when there was always water in some pans. Once the rains became more rare and the pans dried up, these people were trapped. They had to abandon farming and chose to be-come pastoral nomads.[36] But only further archaeological discoveries and environmental research can assess the plausibility of such a scenario.[37]

Adopting a fully pastoral nomadic way of life clearly required consider-able social adaptations. The requirements for the efficient management of a herd from which everyone's livelihood depended were stringent and in-consistent with many of the earlier practices and values current among for-

34. See Sadr, "The First Herders," pp. 101–32. (Sheep at Blombos dated to 155 BCE by AMS date arrived by diffusion, not migration; see p. 116 for evidence of migration, pre-sumably by Khoe speakers, that would date to ca. 750–1050—but again, did they have cattle?) Bousman, "The Chronological Evidence," and Andrew Smith, "Early Domestic Stock," pp. 97–156. Smith maintains that the first cattle known from the Cape and Namibia are those that are mentioned in the written record, from the early sixteenth century onward. For dating, see Robert G. Klein, "The Prehistory," pp. 5–12. Herders pre-sumed to be Khoe speakers are attested to there ca. 1000 CE, but apparently these people herded only sheep. It is still not known when the first cattle herders appeared there, al-though Khoe-speaking cattle nomads were prominent in that region by the sixteenth century. It is quite possible that the introduction of cattle from northern Botswana met with epidemiological barriers that slowed down further expansion until herders had learned to cope with this. See Diane Gifford-Gonzalez, "Animal Disease," pp. 95–139, esp. 104–5, map 1 (p. 112) and map 4 (p. 124). Buffalo and especially wildebeest posed major risks (pp. 110–11; 116–17). Cattle were not directly acquired from southeast Africa, how-ever, because Namibian cattle belong to a different variety, one which seems to have de-veloped locally.

35. See Kinahan, *Pastoral*. All these sites had less than 200 millimeters rain per year. The first evidence for cattle there dates only as of the late eighteenth century (see photo 104).

36. On climate change, see Robbins et al., "Archaeology," p. 1110; Robbins et al., "In-tensive Mining," p. 146; Denbow, "After the Flood," pp. 183–86.

37. Thus the remains at Hungorob Ravine in central Namibia, dated to ca. 1200, seem to have been left by pastoral nomads but they apparently were only sheepherders. See Kinahan, "The Rise and Fall," pp. 374–81 (Hungorob Ravine 730 BP = 1220 CE) and his *Pastoral*, pp. 14–86.

agers. Some of the major social consequences included new conceptions of property and hence new dispositions for inheritance and succession. Cattle herding introduced the notion of wealth and led to an alteration of the relative status of the genders as well as to profound social stratification. It also necessitated the development of novel institutionalized relationships between individual communities as a strategy to avoid the risk of epidemic loss. To appreciate how considerable the consequences of this way of life were on the organization of society, just consider for instance the change in transhumance patterns required by cattle compared to the patterns practiced by foragers or keepers of small herds of sheep or goats—all because cattle need more water than do sheep or goats. Therefore in many places deep waterholes had to be dug for them during the very long dry season and a sufficient labor force had to be found to do this. But once that was done, the animals could then be left completely untended in the vicinity since they had to return daily to the waterhole anyway. To the contrary, in the short wet season when there was abundant surface water the cattle had to be dispersed to profit from all the new grass but also needed to be closely supervised as the animals tended to wander off on their own. Hence their herders established outposts in the bush and corralled the cattle at night.[38] It is easy to see that this transhumance cycle necessitated new divisions of labor and novel groupings of laborers to the point that it required a profound transformation of society. All of this must have happened to those Khoe speakers who abandoned foraging and small stock to become cattle nomads, but unfortunately none of it can be documented. The necessary ethnographic detail is missing, except for the Nama farther south, and not only has intensive archaeological research been carried out only in regions to the west of the wooded grasslands where most cattle herds flourished, but comparative studies of Khoisan tongues have not progressed far enough to trace the development of nomadic pastoralism among them.

Such evidence is available in the case of some Njila speakers who adopted pastoral nomadism (map 13). It is true that we cannot directly trace how these societies actually evolved step by step from foraging communities, if only because all these Njila speakers were already agropastoralists before they became nomads and therefore had already developed overarching institutions well beyond the wholly autonomous communities that characterize a foraging way of life. Still one can use nineteenth-century descriptions to

38. See Estermann, *Herero*, pp. 133–34; Frank Vivelo, *Herero*, pp. 85–88. For the varying transhumance patterns of San foragers in northern Namibia, see the summary in Bartram, "Southern African Foragers," p. 191.

learn which specific solutions these people adopted to meet the social requirements imposed by the practice of pastoral nomadism and also to go
backward in time by scrutinizing the history of the vocabulary associated
with these solutions. As it happens, rich ethnographies and good linguistic
data about the Herero of Namibia based on observations beginning in the
1840s allow one to do just this, although it must be kept in mind that the
observations date to a period of great turmoil.[39] Oral traditions and linguistic data also allow us to reconstruct an outline of the history of their
forebears.

Independently of the Khoe, a second transition from agropastoralism to
nomadic herding occurred in the drier coastal lands of Angola west of the
Chela Mountains and in the adjacent Kaokoland in Namibia. There some
speakers of Ndombe and of the languages of the Herero group turned to cattle
nomadism, probably around 1300, as an overspill of the earlier agropastoral
expansion.[40] Centuries later, some among them then migrated from this zone
into lands hitherto held by Khoe speakers, as far south into Namibia as
Windhoek and as far east as Ngami and Ghanzi in Botswana. The descendants of the bulk of these immigrants are now known as Herero, and their
oral traditions, backed by religious practice, unambiguously claim that they
originated in Kaokoland.[41] A date for this migration can be suggested only
by Herero oral traditions. Traditions concerning the forebears of Maharero
place this in the sixteenth or seventeenth century but others may have preceded them. For Maharero's traditions refer merely to his own family, which

39. The works of Luttig, Irle, and Vedder are a good first introduction to nineteenth-
century Herero ethnography, an ethnography that by now counts perhaps five hundred
titles. In addition, related Cimbebasian speakers in Angola are considered in the Herero
volume of Estermann, as well as in the contributions of Leroux and Laranjo Medeiros.

40. The suggested date is inferred from that of the known climate change. Agropastoralism in the inner Cunene basin of southern Angola had just been established by
the time of the short wetter period, which began ca. 1200, so that agropastoralists established themselves well beyond the western borders of where rainfed farming is now
possible. When the climate turned dry after a century of good rainfall, they were trapped
and turned to cattle nomadism.

41. See Irle, *Herero*, pp. 53, 75–78; Brincker's dictionary discusses this under the rubric
omumborombonga, "the ancestral tree"; Vedder, *South West Africa*, pp. 131–45; Silas
Kuvare, "Kaokoveld," pp. 191–92. However, discussions about more remote origins
in such texts are sheer speculation inspired by the Hamitic theory. The linguistic evidence backs the oral traditions on this point and is incontrovertible. All the languages
directly related to Herero are spoken in southwestern Angola and the whole group links
up with the Nyaneka and Ambo linguistic groups of the inner Cunene and the Cuvelai
basins.

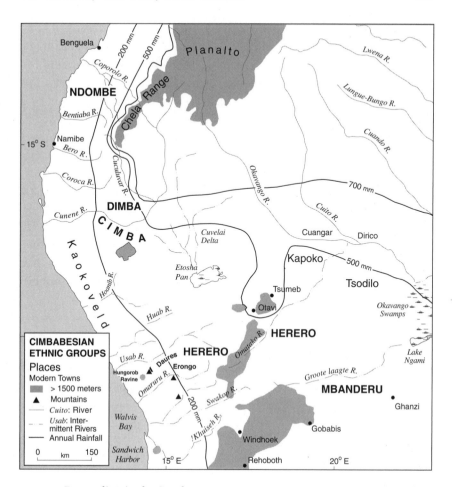

MAP 13. Pastoralists in the Southwest

became prominent only during the nineteenth century.[42] Still they make it clear that a migratory current was underway around 1600.

The lands in which these cattle nomads settled were already occupied by foragers, some of whom also herded sheep. While the newcomers introduced a wholly new social framework in the area, they also copied a great deal from the autochthons, including their transhumance patterns and a good many local social and cultural specifics, just as the latter also adopted some of the habits and beliefs of the newcomers. As a result, the details of many practices and beliefs mentioned in the ethnographic record concerning San for-

42. Vedder, *South West Africa,* pp: 147–48, 151–53.

agers, Bergdama, Herero speakers, and even Nama are quite similar or even identical.[43] While these ethnographies document only the outcome of many centuries of interaction, they still show that for many centuries past no community in these areas had been isolated from the others. Hence even if the focus remains on the social developments of Herero speakers, historians should still consider and interpret the region as a whole of interrelated populations, irrespective of their ways of living and of their languages.

From the later eighteenth century onward, cattle began to be exported in large numbers from the Namibian coast while the demand for cattle and skins also grew in adjacent areas of South Africa. This provoked an intensification of cattle rustling, which triggered hostilities to such an extent that the whole of central Namibia lapsed into a generalized state of war well before the 1830s when the region becomes better documented. One of the effects of this state of affairs was the rapid concentration of political power in the hands of a small number of warlords.[44] Nevertheless, the findings from central Namibia agree largely with those later found among the Kuvale and other Herero-related people in southern Angola who had been exposed to different pressures. Hence they can be taken as representative for all Njila-speaking cattle nomads.[45] Most of the key vocabulary of the social relationships involved still remains identical today in the language continuum stretching from the Kuvale in the far north to the Herero in the south, which implies in most cases that the features described from the 1840s onward in Namibia were already present when the Herero began to immigrate in the 1500s.[46]

43. Similarities include some fundamental commonalities in worldviews, notions about spirits, and a moon spirit in particular, the practice of healing by sucking out objects, the use of trance in divination, initiation rites for girls and for young men not involving circumcision, the presence of a sacred fire, the status of hunters, and their protecting spirits, such as Huvi! All of these features are found together over a large area and isolated features of this suite of features can be found all over western Angola as far north as Luanda and even as far as the mouth of the Congo River. For a general orientation and overview, see Baumann, *Völkerkunde,* 1:473–648.

44. See Wilmsen, *Land,* pp. 86–89, 91–96; Kinahan, *Pastoral,* pp. 98–122; for the conflicts and warlords by midcentury, see Brigette Lau, "Conflict," pp. 29–40; Vedder, *South West Africa,* pp. 146–47, 169–220, 47–57, and his "Herero" pp. 166, 189, but the reader must not forget his strong Christian and Eurocentric biases.

45. The Kuvale and related people in Angola formed part of a regional system centered on the Chela highlands and on the relations between chiefs there and the coast near Namibe. A few sources shed some light on the conditions in the late 1700s, mainly *Relaçam da Viagem* and *Relatório de Gregório Mendes.* See also the ethnographies by Estermann, *Herero;* Leroux, "Quelques coutumes," pp. 52–61; and Medeiros, *Vakwandu.*

46. The only key Herero terms missing in the north are intermatriclan alliance (*otjikutu* 7, 8), patrilineal descent group (*oruzo* 11, 10), servant/slave (*omukarere* 1/2),

Moreover a number of key items are also found in the Njila languages spoken in the inner Cunene basin, including designations for matriclan (*eanda* 5/6),[47] clan names on the pattern *ekwa* 5/6 + noun, subclan/lineage (*omuhoko* 5/6), wealthy person (*omuhona* 1/2), and permanent trading partner (*epanga* 5/6). Finally, all the Cimbabesian languages share the designations for rich person (*orutumbo* 1/2), poor person (*-si(g)ona*), and initiation comrade (*ekula* 5/6) as well as a host of ordinary words. All this confirms that the social organization and culture of Njila-speaking cattle nomads diverged directly from that of the agropastoralists of the adjacent inner Cunene basin and not from that of the Ambo farther east and that at an earlier time all the agropastoralists shared a common social and cultural framework. One can therefore use the Herero ethnographic record because one can identify which elements in it are innovations, which ones are recent, which ones go back to after the arrival of the Herero in Namibia, which ones go back to the emergence of cattle nomads in southwestern Angola, which ones go even further back to the onset of agropastoralism (e.g., *ohambo* 9/10 "cattle post"), and which ones preserved Njila group forms that go back to a time before cattle were kept at all.

Herero cattle nomads were settled in small and tightly organized residential units (*onganda* 9/10) that moved every few years, just as villages did elsewhere. The well-being of their inhabitants depended on the state of the herd which fed them. It belonged to the local leader (*omukuru* 1/2) and its management was crucial for everyone's survival. Ideally, the settlement formed a circle of houses inhabited by a group of kinsfolk with a kraal for calves and small stock in the middle. The sacred fire (*okuruo* 9/6) with the place of offerings to the ancestors of its leader lay to one side in front of the

---

while among the Dimba and Kuvale the term for sacred fire, *okuruo* 9/6, which is derived from *mukuru* 1/2 "local leader," itself from -*kura* "to be fully mature," became *elao* 5, which means "good fortune" in the Nyaneka from which it was borrowed and even *masululo* 6 in Kwandu. See Estermann, *Herero*, p. 198. In the case of "descent group," "sacred fire," and "servant," the etymologies show that they are old Herero innovations, from proto-Bantu stems. The case of "sacred fire" suggests that the north dropped the older *okuruo* under Nyaneka influence, while *omukarere* from -*karera* "to serve someone," itself from -*kara* "to dwell, to be in a given situation," a proto-Njila form (CS 974), is clearly a Herero innovation dating to after the split—given the prevalence of slave trading from the 1700s onward. The oruzo-type descent groups were probably also Herero innovations after the split since no such formal patrilineages are recognized in the north.

47. We remind the reader that all Bantu nouns are cited in the singular even if the meaning is plural.

house of his main wife.[48] Most of the cattle were kept in outlying cattle posts (*ohambo* 9/10), which moved frequently as needed by the state of the pastures and the availability of water. These posts differed from others in the region in that whole families settled there and not just young cowboys. In catastrophic droughts—that is, droughts worse than those which occurred roughly every decade—not just the *ohambo,* but even the onganda was moved sometimes as far as 100 kilometers away from the previous site.

While residence in a given settlement was always justified in one way or another by kinship, most of the men there belonged to a single exogamous patrilineage (*oruzo* 11/6) into which all married women were also incorporated on their arrival.[49] In practice, the oruzo was residential, although several settlements in a neighborhood shared the same oruzo name and its food prohibitions and could derive their sacred fire from a single source.[50] Given the nomadic way of life, settlements of the same oruzo could even be found all across the country but they did not collaborate with each other in any way. The foremost sign of belonging to the oruzo lay in participation by all the residents of the settlement in a common and intensive worship for the ancestors of its leader. This took place at the sacred fire hearth where the leader, who at that moment was deemed to bodily incorporate all his deceased male predecessors, ritually tasted and distributed the prescribed daily ration of milk to everyone. The milk for each family within the settlement came from designated cattle and was milked in special calabashes. Moreover, prescribed sacrifices of cattle took place frequently since they occurred on 16 to 20 different prescribed occasions. The sacred fire was tended by the leader's eldest daughter and the supposedly eternal fireplace lay in front of the house of his main wife, in which individual representations of each of the ancestors were kept in the shape of sticks. In addition, the cult also involved a sacred ox, almost an

48. See Irle, *Herero,* p. 78; Luttig, *Religious,* pp. 32–34; Estermann, *Herero,* pp. 95–97, for settlement plans and p. 97 for a Kuvale case with kinship links between the inhabitants. P. Leroux, "De quelques," pp. 53–56; note a slightly different disposition in Medeiros, *Vakwandu,* pp. 59–60.

49. *Oruzo* 11 from -*za* or -*zaa* "to originate from somewhere, to descend from the place where the speaker is, to come from [a place] by birth" and even "to go away" in Irle, *Herero,* p. 87, as well as in Peter Heinrich Brincker, *Wörterbuch,* and F. W. Kolbe, *English-Herero Dictionary.* Hence *tu za mumwe,* "we are relatives." Note the stress on *place,* which gives an impression of bilateral descent rather than a strict patrilineal one. On this issue, see Gordon Gibson, "Double Descent," pp. 109–39.

50. See Estermann, *Herero,* pp. 121–22; Luttig, *Religious,* pp. 59–63 (dispersed clan) yet pp. 63–64 (a local group incorporating even inmarrying women); Gibson, "Double Descent," pp. 116, 118, 121. To speak of a "district," a term which implies a specific territory, is not indicated in such mobile communities and "local lineage" is more appropriate than "clan."

alter ego of the leader, as well as sacred cattle, that is, cattle dedicated to a specific ancestor or to commemorate a relationship between specific kinsmen, and everything that had even the slightest connection with this ancestor cult was inherited patrilineally. The fireplace was also the site where all communal discussions and consultations took place. Hence the expression "the fire has been extinguished" meant that a community had been exterminated.[51] But such consultations pale into insignificance next to the nearly absolute powers of the Herero *omukuru* 1/2. These were based on his role as the manager of the indispensable cattle herd, not on his "priestly" position as the early missionary observers claimed, for that position was a consequence rather than a cause of this style of leadership. Thus the need to manage cattle led the tightly regulated Herero community far away from the egalitarian ethos prevalent in local foraging communities.

Even though the term *oruzo* has not been documented for other Herero-speaking peoples such as the Kuvale, they all practiced similar rituals with patrilineal inheritance. Indeed the Kuvale and Cimba are renowned for the great number of categories of sacred cattle involved. Each category contained one or more head of cattle as living reminders of a certain social relationship and circumstance involving an ancestor. For instance, a nephew received one at his mother's brother's funeral, a son one from his living father, a previous husband from a later husband of his divorced wife, and so on. The Kuvale had six and the Cimba no less than eleven such categories.[52]

Like other cattle herders, the Herero held that it was not wise to keep all one's cattle in a single herd for fear of the ravages caused by epidemic disease.[53] One had to disperse some of them in other settlements and in other herds, and the herds of close relatives on one's mother's side were best suited for this. This may well have led to the emergence of dispersed matriclans, for Herero society was divided into only eight named and exogamous clans (eanda), supposedly founded by the eight daughters of a common ancestress, descent of whom was the badge of identity of being Herero—that is for those who had cattle.[54]

51. Irle, *Herero,* pp. 77–86.

52. Estermann, *Herero,* pp. 139–48.

53. They even dispersed some of their children among nonresident relatives for the same reason. See Vedder, "Herero," p. 177.

54. Irle, *Herero,* pp. 87, 89–93; Luttig, *Religious,* pp. 58, 64–67; Vedder, *South West Africa,* p. 50, and his "Herero," p. 187; Theo Sundermeier and Silas Kuvare, *Mbanderu,* pp. 113–18; Kuvare, "Kaokoveld," pp. 204–19; Estermann, *Herero,* pp. 109–19; Medeiros, *Vakwandu,* pp. 48–49. For a structuralist functionalist interpretation, see Gibson, "Double Descent," pp. 117–18, 128, 130–32, but a number of his supposed lineage levels seem to be theoretical fabrications. Note that *eanda* (plural *omanda*) has the same root *-ganda* as in *onganda,* for *g-* falls away after a vowel.

Some eanda had subdivisions (*omuhoko* 3/4), and in two cases at least clans were paired. Such an alliance was referred to as *otjikutu* 7/8, "a big sheaf," a term also used to designate a nuclear family.[55] Each clan had a common myth of origin and perhaps a common oath.[56] The small number of clans and their dispersal meant that when cattle posts were scattered over a wide area, their herders often met herders from another onganda and that some of those who met shared the same clan, which greatly facilitated relationships between them. Moreover, some cattle were always placed with close male matrilineal relatives. The most important formal function of the eanda was to regulate the inheritance of all valuable goods, such as beads and especially cattle herds. Only a small minority of cattle was "forbidden" or "sacred" while the rest were inherited in the matriclan with each herd going to a single heir. Because keeping the herd together was the top priority under these circumstances, and a minimum-sized herd of at least 15 to 20 head was a sine qua non condition for survival as a cattle nomad, a single heir was necessary. The ratio of cattle to people among Cimba and Dimba in far from optimal surroundings was from 4 to 6 cattle *per person,* that is, a herd of 16 to 24 head minimum for each monogamous household with two children.[57]

Thus one ends up with the following anomaly: local leaders were succeeded by one of their sons and local patrilineages were sustained by the ownership of a herd, but cattle were inherited in the matrilineal eanda and a son could not keep the herd that had maintained his father's patrilineage. The solution to this conundrum was to consistently practice cross-cousin marriage, preferably with a father's sister's daughter.[58] Then the succeeding son inherited a herd from his mother's brother but his son inherited both the spiritual powers and the herd of the grandfather. The inheritance of herds would thus alternate between only two settlements and, every second generation, their leaders found themselves in the same position as their grandfather. Such a policy resulted in pairing two matriclans together and

---

55. Innovation from -*kuta* "to tie" (also in Nyaneka), and *omukuta* 3/4 "sheaf," "package" (*okankhutunkhutu* in Nyaneka). Neither exist in Ambo.

56. See Irle, *Herero,* pp. 87, 89–93. Each clan name was formed by *ekwa* + substantive. Only two or three of these clans were also found among Herero speakers in Angola. See Estermann, *Herero,* p. 112 (see detail on alliances there), on oaths pp. 118–19. Northerners also kept food taboos but the Herero did not. They may have lost this feature.

57. See Estermann, *Herero,* pp. 131–32. Data gathered by Van Warmelo in 1946.

58. Father's sister's daughter marriages were preferred among all pastoral nomads in the Herero group. See Gibson "Double Descent," pp. 132–34 (even 41 percent of modern Mbanderu marriages were with father's sister's daughter); Estermann *Herero,* p. 88; Medeiros, *Vakwandu,* pp. 51–55.

opposing them to all others, a situation well known to the Herero.[59] In case of persistent cross-cousin marriage with the mother's brother's daughter, however, the number of settlements involved in the cycle became equal to the number of existing clans, that is from six to ten.[60] But as this type of marriage was not nearly practiced as much as the one with a father's sister's daughter, the number of clans linked by such matrimonial alliances seem to have only involved three or four clans.

Kinship relations were supplemented by individual friendships between males (epanga), just as cattle-keeping was supplemented by trade. Epanga were clearly of greater importance than the ethnographers have acknowledged, but they were not interested in this matter and hence very little is known about this institution, except that epanga had access to each other's wives and that long-distance trade seems to have been conducted at least in part along a chain of individuals related by epanga rather like hxaro relationships among foragers.[61] While at first sight it does not seem that trade mattered much for the maintenance of the herds, it still was of considerable importance as a mechanism for the transfer of cattle via the medium of copper beads and similar exotica. Cattle in excess of the capacity of available pastures or labor could be exchanged for other necessities, such as iron weapons, or for commodities such as copper beads, which eventually might be redeemed again for cattle when needed. From far or from nearby, iron spearpoints and perhaps knives, calabashes, stone pipe stems, ostrich shell beads, specularite, iron beads, and ceramics were all in demand by one group or another and trading partners passed these on from one community to another. In addition, by the nineteenth century, small caravans were also active, perhaps in response to the general lack of safety engendered by widespread turmoil. By the 1830s, Herero parties were trading with Europeans on the coast north of the Cunene River for glass beads and iron knives and somewhat later one hears of Ambo parties trading iron spears and ornaments for cattle while Herero went to the Cuvelai basin to exchange cattle

59. See Irle, *Herero,* pp. 91–92, for the pairing of clans #4 and #5 as well as #6 and #7. See Estermann, *Herero,* pp. 119–120; Kuvare, "Kaokoveld," pp. 208–15.

60. See Irle, *Herero,* pp. 89–93 (8 main clans); Vedder, "Herero," p. 187 (6 main clans); Estermann, *Herero,* p. 112 (10 clans); Medeiros, *Vakwandu,* p. 50 (9 clans).

61. See Brincker, *Wörterbuch,* rubrics *epanga, oupanga;* Luttig, *Religious,* pp. 87–89; Sundermeier, *Mbanderu,* pp. 118–19; Estermann, *Herero,* pp. 139, 141, 143 (Dimba and Chimba: *otyipanga* "head of cattle of my friendship"). *Epanga* "friend" is also reported in Nyaneka, Nkhumbi, and Umbundu. The distribution of this term suggests that it resulted from borrowing along trading channels rather than from a common ancestral term.

and ostrich shell beads (most of which they obtained from their neighbors in Namibia) for metal goods.[62]

But descent and friendship were not all that mattered in Herero society. Social stratification was at least as important and that was again closely tied to cattle pastoralism because cattle were property par excellence and because caring for a herd was quite labor intensive. John Kinahan has eloquently argued that even the adoption by hunters of the nomadic herding of small stock presupposed a fundamental shift with regard to the notion of property. Sharing among earlier foragers was essential for survival and hence individual property seems to have been limited to a small number of items worn by a person, such as for adornment (ostrich shell beads) and for strictly personal use, and even that is not certain. In order to even constitute flocks, the free access to and killing of livestock by anyone who fancied to do so had to be curtailed. Thus a wider exclusive notion of property appeared with the attendant consequence that henceforth people could be divided into rich and poor. One can certainly accept this, even while one remains skeptical of the rest of his scenario, which attributes this shift of values to the actions of much-respected shamans.[63] Once domestic stock became individual property, the same notion also came to be applied to other valuables, especially copper beads and cowries, as the cache of valuables found at the False Rock Shelter site in the Hungorob Ravine convincingly shows.[64] The same cache also points to another essential feature of cattle nomadism, namely, exchanges between communities over longer distances.[65]

62. Gibson, "Bridewealth," pp. 618–24, thoroughly documents exchange and trading. Outside the family, exchanges occurred between *epanga*. The proto-Bantu form *-dand "to trade," CS 490, is found in all of southern Angola and must have been in use near Benguela when Portuguese first began to trade there around 1600. Its present distribution was certainly strongly influenced by the Atlantic trade, and because of this one is not certain that it was used in proto-Herero. The word -*pimba* "to exchange" and its derivative -*pimbasana* may have been the older form in use. The word -*mana* is the form in Nyaneka and Kwanyama. The word -*pa* is "to give" (CS 1404) in Herero and in all the Cimbebasian languages. But "to give a present" is -*jamba* in Herero. The derived word "present" *ondjambi* 9/10 also occurs in Ndonga and Nyaneka but not in Kwanyama. Hence this could be older than -*pimba*, which seems to be an Herero innovation (-*pa* "to give" + *imba* [demonstrative] those people"). Still even if -*jamba* was older, this does not explain why an innovation was needed.

63. See Kinahan, *Pastoral,* pp. 43–46.

64. Ibid., pp. 40–41. For dating, see pp. 28, 54, 151 (1220±70), that is, 1200–1400.

65. Thus, ibid., p. 96. Point Midden, an undated but early site in the !Khuiseb Delta, contained specularite in a pot, a cosmetic mineral imported from far away, perhaps even from as far as the Tsodilo Hills! These exchanges may well have been similar to the *hxaro* exchanges of later times.

Under such conditions, the impact of cattle herding on the social stratification within and between communities was bound to be considerable. Everyone's survival depended on herds, yet herds were owned by individuals and hence everyone else came to be dependent on them. That cattle herding was quite labor intensive aggravated the situation.[66] Cattle needed to be led to pasture, watered, and milked, and they required manpower at all times to protect them from raids by animal and human predators. In the short wet season, the cattle posts were at their busiest as the search for new pastures and leading the cattle to them was constant. In the nine-month-long dry season, water was the problem. Many meter-deep wells had to be dug or constantly cleaned with mere digging sticks and the liquid hauled out in buckets to water the cattle. The need to fragment herds into small groups to protect them from the risks of epizootic disease, drought, and raiding prevented any economy of scale in this regard and further increased the amount of labor required to keep them. Thus keeping cattle required the input of both clients who were given cattle to herd and servants who had none. The lot of the servants in particular was very hard, as a chilling matter-of-fact comment indicates. In his dictionary, Peter Heinrich Brincker gives an example of "bad luck": "I am unlucky with my cattle; he is unlucky with the servants (*omukarere* 1/2). They keep dying on him."[67] Some had become *omukarere* by being taken as booty during cattle raids, and others had been born as such. Whether or not they technically should be labeled slaves does not matter much in such circumstances. What mattered was that they had no access to cattle and could not call on kin in the vicinity to loan cattle to them. Being cattleless turned them into despised people.

The relevant vocabularies and ethnographies make it abundantly clear that cattle nomadism was accompanied by highly pronounced social stratification between rich and poor. In every settlement, only one man owned the herd on which everyone was dependent for a decent life. The owner had clients who received cattle on loan for herding. They kept the milk and sometimes an agreed-upon number of heifers as well so that they could also build up or rebuild their own herds. Then there were the servants or serfs attached to the previous groups, without access to cattle even for their own use, but who performed the menial work for others. Even ethnicity was based on access to cattle. Those without cattle, even people who once had herds but had

66. Clifford-Gonzales, "Animal Disease," p. 127 (citing Dahl and Hjort), claims that sheepherding was even more labor intensive and would, in consequence, have had to involve foragers in client relationships.

67. See Brincker, *Wörterbuch, verbo omupia* (p. 250).

lost their cattle, were despised as "miserable" Twá irrespective of the language they spoke and whatever their status and their identity had been previously.[68] For, whatever else they had, they lacked cattle. Therefore they could not lead a civilized way of life, for how could they be married, buried, or even fined properly without the cattle one needs for such transactions?[69] Because of the vagaries of the weather, the dangers of raiding, and of cattle epizootic disease, one could easily lose one's herd. Hence, in addition to other measures of risk management, one also insured against this eventuality by dispersing a few cattle each among various clients in various localities and/or by acquiring copper beads or the equivalents (e.g., cowries) with which one could acquire new cattle later on when needed.

At the other end of the scale were the rich. They were powerful since everyone's survival depended on access to their cattle. Hence those rich in cattle had many dependents. When nineteenth-century rumors speak of owners of over ten thousand head of cattle, such persons probably had between one and two hundred client families, at least as many servants, and occupied a very large grazing territory to match.[70] Hence the term *omuhona* 5/6 "rich person" also designated a political leader. Yet, while material wealth was inherited within the matrilineal eanda, spiritual and ideological power was vested within the patrilineal oruzo while the best way to preserve both as far as possible was marriage to the father's sister's daughter. Hence, whenever possible, the person chosen as a successor to an *omuhona* was issued from such a cross-cousin marriage and married himself to at least one of his patrilateral cousins.

Local leadership, based on alliances between pairs of eanda and backed by the power of the ancestor rituals on a small scale, appeared at an early date, but the mobility of the population and their need for flexibility and autonomy in economic decision making prevented further developments until the late eighteenth century. From that time onward the increase in raiding accompanied the loss of cattle to the European trade on the coast and Jonker

68. Brincker, *Wörterbuch, verbo omutua*, and pp. 347–48 (applied to Nama); Estermann, *Ambos*, pp. 55–60, and his *Herero*, p. 130; Medeiros, *Vakwandu*, pp. 18, 25; Gibson, "Preface"; Vivelo, *The Herero*, p. viii; Kuvare, "Kaokoveld," p. 198; António de Almeida, *Bushmen*, p. 28; Vedder, "Berg Damara," p. 40; *Túá* 1/2 (CS 1804, 1805 and partial series 467) was applied in common Bantu to foragers as well as those who did not speak Bantu languages or followed a completely alien way of life.

69. All the ethnographies attest that cattle herding was the only proper way of life for civilized people.

70. Gibson, "Bridewealth," p. 618, after Hahn, "Ovaherero," p. 237.

Afrikaner's advance from the south and began to require defensive alliances on a much larger scale than may have existed before, such that by the 1840s five or seven leaders had come to dominate all of Hereroland.[71] Even under these circumstances, the increase in the scale of power of those leaders did not lead to much ideological or institutional elaboration. The ritual of installation remained basically what it was for any omuhona who succeeded to an onganda.[72] Nor did a warlord's rule differ in any way from that of any head of an ordinary onganda.[73] A fixed capital would scarcely have been possible in this environment but there was no traveling capital either—no court, no officials, no tribunal, no taxes or tribute. At the local residential level, Herero leaders had more autocratic powers than anyone else in Central Africa since they could refuse even basic food (milk) to their subjects, but their despotic powers stopped right there. Hence, even if one uses the term "chief" to designate a warlord, one cannot speak of chiefdoms and even less of structured and centralized government.

Cattle remained the unwavering single focus of interest for all cattle nomads whose livelihood and very identity depended on these animals. No wonder then that the only special know-how that was thoroughly appreciated, apart from healing, was that of the person who knew all about the qualities and varieties of grasses.[74] All their rituals and ceremonies revolved around cattle, men's personal oxen shared in their personal identity, oral art never ceased to celebrate the shape, color, and movements of their beasts, and a luxuriant vocabulary described them. People's imaginations and emotions were fully enwrapped with cattle and their relationship to these animals, to the exclusion of any abiding interest in other avenues of governance, including the development of monocephalic rule.

71. See Vedder, "Herero," p. 166 (seven "great priests" among the Herero and one among the Mbanderu), and p. 189 (later only five major warlords by 1904).

72. Thus the main emblem conferred at a chief's installation of wealth and power was a large seashell (*ondjii* 9/10), according to Vedder, "The Herero," p. 188. But under the rubric *ondjii*, Brincker tells us that these were obtained through trade from the Ambo, and he adds that they could also be worn by all men rich enough to acquire one.

73. Although Vedder, "Native Tribes, pp. 187–90, attempted to describe a government with councilors, messengers, vassals, powers over life and death (but no tribunal!), the upshot is that in peacetime chiefs lived just like ordinary men. They became important only during wars when they coordinated and led the combined fighting forces of large numbers of less important omuhona. See also Irle, *Herero,* pp. 139–41.

74. Estermann, *Herero,* p. 132.

Agropastoralists

Two major differences between the cattle nomads and agropastoralists of West Central Africa have struck every foreign observer from the time of the earliest written records onward: the difference in environments and the difference in governance. Let us discuss the environment first. In general, natural environments were far less restrictive in the lands inhabited by agropastoralists than those where cattle nomads roamed because they enjoyed more rainfall and had more access to water year-round. Beyond this, the most striking feature of the region they inhabited is that it is not a single unit. Rather it consisted in two different and sharply demarcated ecological zones, namely, the inner basin of the Cunene River with the rim of mountains that surrounds it from the planalto in the north to the Chela Range in the southwest, and then the Cuvelai seasonal floodplain east of the Cunene (map 14). The first zone is limited roughly by the planalto to the north, the Cunene River to the east, the Caculovar, an intermittently flowing river, to the southwest, the low steppes coastward from the Chela Range in the west and the well-watered lower lands along the permanent Coporolo and Catumbela Rivers and their affluents to the northwest. Nearly everywhere, rainfall exceeds 700 millimeters excepting the lowlands near Benguela. Most of the population seems to have been settled from the outset in a big semicircle near or on the uplands where the best land for farming lay, leaving the dry stretches between the Caculovar and Cunene Rivers in the middle of the basin to San-speaking foragers. The richest pastures of the zone, however, lay not there but were situated all along the right bank of the Cunene River and along the edge of the planalto while those on and near the Chela Range or along the Caculovar were somewhat less desirable.[75] These characteristics of this ecological zone have had a long-standing and profound impact on the populations who settled there because the zone corresponds strikingly, if not exclusively, with the extent of the languages of the Nyaneka group. Still, in the far northwest on the outer rim of the basin, some speakers of the Ndombe group were also agropastoralists while the lush grasslands on the very fringes of the planalto were occupied by Umbundu- and Nyemba-speaking agropastoralists. The overall pattern leaves the impression that in this zone Nyaneka speakers were the initiators of agropastoralism.[76]

---

75. Estermann, *Nhaneca-Humbe*, p. 182.

76. Ibid., p. 148. The ethnic groups Estermann discerns are mainly geographic labels to which an ethnic content was given. These names are at least as old as written records about them are.

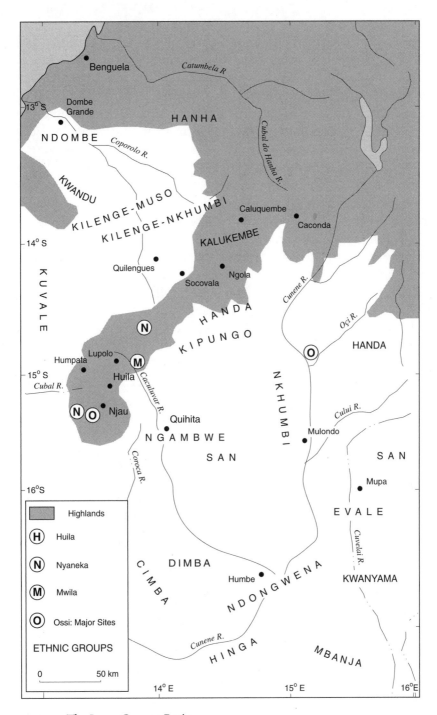

MAP 14. The Inner Cunene Basin

In contrast, for most of the Cuvelai basin (map 15) east of the Cunene River, rainfall is less than 700 millimeters and, moreover, precipitation rapidly decreases from north to south. As a result, the Cuvelai River and its tributaries only flow year-round in their uppermost course; in this basin, cereal agriculture is only possible in or on the edge of the main riverbeds. These run dry for most of the year and form a huge delta of interbraided channels that run in the direction of the Etosha Pan. When the climate was wetter, as indeed it was during a century or so after 1200, these channels held water that fed the Etosha Pan and turned it into a lake. At that time, the Cuvelai Delta must have been a prime location for agropastoralists. When the climate became drier again, a century or so later, its population adapted to a regime in which, during most years, surface water was available only for a few weeks. As a result of the great annual variability of rainfall, there was often either no flood at all or, to the contrary, the entire delta would be flooded.[77] Life in such a unique environment with cattle and some farming required extensive seasonal mobility over large distances. It was also characterized by the need to dig extensive large water reservoirs, a task carried out collectively by a large labor force.[78] In this case, the correlation between the spatial extent of the Ambo languages and the Cuvelai basin is practically perfect. It suggests that the Ambo division within the Cimbabesian languages arose there and that its speakers have remained there ever since.[79]

77. Siiskonen, *Trade,* pp. 35–41; Estermann, *Ambos,* pp. 79–80. Between 1924 and 1953, there were five great, seven medium, and four partial floods as well as ten years in which the water did not reach the delta and three years in which only the uppermost part of the river held water. Great droughts and famines are known for 1877–78, 1908, and 1915; see Tönjes, *Ovamboland,* pp. 13–22 and 22–23, for the annual outbreaks of malaria that accompanied the floods.

78. Siiskonen, *Trade,* p. 45. In 1883, Duparquet saw 300 men digging a storage reservoir.

79. As Ambo, Nyaneka, and Herero are three equidistant branches of Cimbebasian, they must have differentiated at roughly the same time. Just as I have argued earlier that the wet episode of the thirteenth century and the following desiccation led Njila speakers first to expand into new lands and then forced them to become cattle nomads, something similar seems to have happened in the Cuvelai basin. While Njila-speaking agropastoralists may have been established much earlier there, the Ambo languages differentiated from the others only after the desiccation began. Just as in the case of the Herero-speaking cattle nomads, their new way of life became then different enough to hinder an untrammeled flow of population between the inner Cunene and the Cuvelai basins and that led to the emergence of the three new language branches. Therefore we can roughly date their emergence at around 1300.

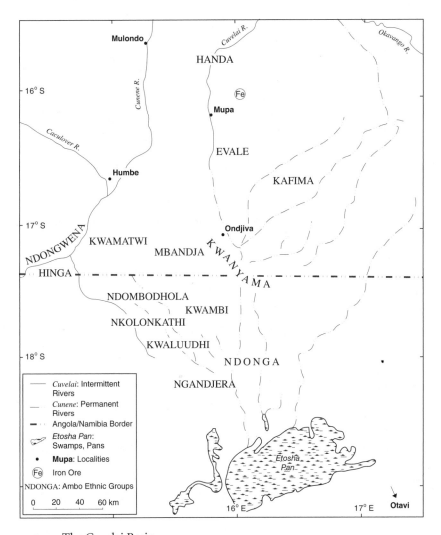

MAP 15. The Cuvelai Basin

Their environments explain why agropastoralists, in contrast to cattle nomads, could be sedentary farmers as well as pastoralists. In addition and in sharp contrast to nomadic pastoralists, most agropastoralists were also organized in chiefdoms or principalities,[80] that is, forms of centralized gov-

80. Some of the westernmost Ambo groups were not organized in chiefdoms. See "Hugo Hahn's Reise," p. 297 (six of the most westerly Ovambo groups had no chiefs), and Siiskonen, *Trade*, p. 45.

ernance under the direction of a single overall leader.[81] But centralization and rule by a single leader are by no means an ineluctable outcome of sedentarization. Hence the appearance of this form of governance among agropastoralists needs to be accounted for. Previous authors have done so by claiming that monocephalic government was imported into these regions lock, stock, and barrel by emigrants from the kingdoms of the planalto and have supported their claims by reference to oral traditions found among the Nyaneka, in Quilengues (Otyilenge) in Caluquembe, among the Nkhumbi and in the Kwanyama, Evale, and Kafima kingdoms.[82] Many institutional similarities as well as similarities in the exercise of governance seem to support such a claim. Yet these oral traditions relate only to the past of the ruling dynasties while the similarities in governance found all over agropastoralist lands should not blind one to the significant differences that existed especially between the two ecological zones. Rather, how was it possible for a whole complex system of governance to be transferred wholesale from a

81. Technically these like kingdoms are all "monocephalic polities." In this text, I use the terms principalities and lords for larger entities, chiefdom and chief for smaller ones, whatever their internal makeup, even though in theory the distinction between chiefdoms, headed by chiefs, and principalities, headed by lords, consists in the number of territorial layers within a single polity. Chiefdoms were made up of villages and principalities of chiefdoms. Thus chiefs ruled directly over village headmen or headwomen while lords ruled over chiefs. By this definition, kingdoms comprised yet another layer. They consisted in principalities, which encompassed chiefdoms, which in turn consisted of villages. Such distinctions can be made at any individual moment in time but not diachronically because political control waxed and waned over time since principalities were so unstable in this region. Thus several chiefdoms might at one moment recognize a superior lord but reject that recognition at another. Principalities rose very quickly but dissolved with equal rapidity because beyond the recognition of a supreme leader no additional institutional ties of centralized governance developed here.

82. Already in the 1850s, according to Nogueira, *Raça*, p. 256: "The Ba-Nhaneka like the Ban-Kumbi have a tradition that they arrived here from the north, from the side of the Nano [planalto] from where they were expulsed by the Bin-Bundo [Ovimbundu]." Also his "Lun'kumbi," pp. 185, 188; later Hermengildo Capello Roberto Ivens, *De Angola*, 1:214–16, but see mainly Baumann, "Die Südwest-Bantu Provinz," pp. 491–92, 501, and his "Die Frage," pp. 118–19, 122, 124–27; Lang and Tastevin, *La tribu*, pp. 4–10; Estermann, *Ambos*, pp. 80–83, and his *Nhaneca-Humbe*, pp. 28–31, 39–46, based in part on *Ovanthu vatetekela*, a five-page manuscript text translated by Julio b Henrique and found in Baumann's papers; Alfred Hauenstein, "L'Ombala de Caluquembe," pp. 48, 59–61, and his "Le serpent," pp. 221, 224. These citations include Nyaneka traditions, traditions from Quilengues (Otyilenge) and the area of Caluquembe, from the Nkhumbi and from the Kwanyama; Loeb, *In Feudal*, p. 22; Tönjes, *Ovamboland*, pp. 35–38. All these traditions obviously refer only to the movements of a few elite people, not to mass migrations.

country of farmers to one where livestock was extremely important? It cannot be assumed then that the monocephalic form of governance from the planalto was imported; we must investigate how and when similar forms of governance have arisen among agropastoralists.[83] A new sort of leadership superior to that of the homestead arose and chiefdoms appeared fairly soon after the introduction of large cattle herds. Later, the early common institutions of governance became more intricate, leading to larger chiefdoms or principalities. At the same time, the polities of the inner Cunene basin and the Cuvelai Delta began to diverge more from each other under the influence of differing ecological constraints. Concomitantly or perhaps only later, interactions with polities of the planalto also began to exert some influence over the growth of some agropastoral polities. At this time, however, even a tentative chronology of all of these developments remains hazy. We only know that chiefdoms and principalities in the region existed in the seventeenth century and we may assume that they arose only well after large herds of cattle began to flourish here, probably during the tenth century.[84] Only further archaeological research can establish a better chronology, once some of the numerous sites with stone ruins in and around the Chela Range and at the edge of the planalto are excavated. The huge site of Ossi at the confluence of the Oçi and Cunene Rivers seems especially promising in this regard.[85]

For several centuries before large cattle herds arrived in the agropastoral zones, their inhabitants had already been sedentary cereal farmers who also kept flocks of goats, probably managed by women, and flocks of sheep herded by men. The Njila speakers among them lived in large homesteads dispersed across the landscape and inhabited by as many as 20 or 30 people. Internally, homesteads were divided into households that were related mostly by kinship ties.[86] Although sheep, which constituted another source of wealth, were probably inherited from father to son, there is no evidence that this practice had

83. Although some written documents become gradually available for the western parts of the agropastoralist zones from the early 1600s onward, more detailed written data are obtainable only as of the 1840s and 1850s. The standard ethnographies go back to information from the 1860s for Ndonga and from the 1880s for the other parts of the zones involved. Still, oral traditions about the ruling lines of the various kingdoms make it evident that kingdoms or principalities existed in the northwest by at least 1600 and elsewhere in the eighteenth century.

84. That is, soon after they were established at Nqoma ca. 900.

85. On Ossi, see Ervedosa, *Arqueologia*, pp. 409–13; de Almeida and Camarata Franca, "Recintos mulharados," pp. 109–24.

86. The forms used to designate "large homestead," "household," "kinship group," and similar features are proto-Njila with similar meanings.

led to the existence of unilineal corporate lineages.[87] Each large homestead was led by a *hekulu* 1n/2 or *sekulu* 1n/2 "grandparent," to whom, no doubt, most of the inhabitants were linked by various bilateral ties of descent.[88] In each settlement a common sacred fire and the rituals that may have been attached to it protected its inhabitants and expressed their common identity.[89]

Large herds of cattle first appeared in this milieu during the tenth or eleventh centuries. The increase in the number of larger herds was rapid, not just because this zone contained quite desirable pastures, but because the local people were familiar with cattle and had already kept a few of them during the preceding century or two. Moreover, they had much experience in herding flocks of sheep and goats. So agropastoralism developed wherever there was a minimum of 700 millimeters of rainfall a year or an adequate sizeable seasonal supply of water made it possible.[90] The management of cattle herds was easily integrated with the previous practice of cereal agriculture to produce the essential patterns of agropastoralism still in use in recent centuries. It was easy because raising cattle and farming were juxtaposed rather than fully integrated into a single system. Mutual integration was limited to letting cattle feed on the stubble after the cereal harvests, to allowing the establishment of new fields in abandoned corrals where manure abounded,

87. On agriculture, see Urquhart, *Patterns,* pp. 65–104. Among eighteenth-century Kwandu, sheep were only tended and owned by men and inherited by sons, whereas sister's sons inherited cattle. See Medeiros, *Vakwandu,* pp. 18–19.

88. *Sekulu* 1n/2, literally "his mature father," from two proto-Bantu roots. The compound arose probably in proto-Kunene to designate a grandfather or male elder and spread also to Kimbundu. In the beginning, it carried the strong implication that authority was legitimized by father-child ties. Later, it came to be extended to the male head of any homestead or local lineage, including mother's brothers even though *se-* denotes a father! Finally, the later use of the term spread throughout Angola because the Portuguese called any local leader *seculo.* Found with the meaning "grandfather" and "elder" in Kwanyama, Umbundu, Nyemba, Nyaneka (generic), and Nkhumbi; with the meaning "mother's brother" and "elder" in Kwambi, Kwanyama, Kwangari, and in the Kimbundu group.

89. In recent centuries, sacred fires were kept in every community in Angola and northern Namibia whether of foragers, small stock herders, cattle nomads, or agropastoralists, and whatever language they spoke, suggesting that this was a very ancient usage in the region, adopted by everyone who came to live there, although it is also possible that the practice was copied by everyone from prestigious cattle-keepers with large herds. Be that as it may, such fires expressed the identity of the whole group that shared one, be it a San camp, a Bergdama homestead, a Herero neighborhood, or an agropastoralist community. In every case, the extinction of such a fire meant the destruction of its community.

90. See Urquhart, *Patterns,* pp. 1–128, for a general orientation, but his study does not consider conditions which obtain farther south in the Cuvelai floodplain of Namibia.

and, in Nkhumbi, to providing for the fertilization of fields by manuring them.[91] Patterns of transhumance for cattle during the dry season posed little problem in the better watered northern parts of the inner Cunene basin as the distances involved were not great. Consequently, the notion of neighborhood domain here soon came to include large tracts of wasteland for dry season pasture.[92] But in the dry south, the distances involved were too large to include such extensive territories into a local domain. Moreover, where water was truly rare, as in the Cuvelai Delta, many different homesteads had to send their cattle to the same waterholes with the result that during the dry season large cattle posts with several thousands of head of cattle sprang up there.[93]

Once the inhabitants became agropastoralists and because cattle were to be inherited in the matrilineal line, they organized themselves in exogamic corporate matrilineages[94] under the leadership of a senior mother's brother.[95] Patrilateral cross-cousin marriage, that is, marriage with father's sister's daughter or the equivalent soon accompanied this dispensation in order to ensure continuity of local leadership in the paternal line.[96] But the creation

91. Ibid., p. 80. On use of manure in Hanya and Ngola, see pp. 84–87, 89.

92. Estermann, *Nhaneca-Humbe*, pp. 182–84.

93. Siiskonen, *Trade*, pp. 54–55, n. 32 (three to four thousand head of cattle at a single post in 1851).

94. Nyaneka, *onkhova* 9/10: "navel cord"; and Kwanyama: *epata* 5/6: "settlement ward." Both terms are innovations in meaning from older forms. *Onkhova* is quite old given its presence in Lucazi as well as in Nyaneka.

95. Nyaneka and Nkhumbi *himi* 1n/2, Hanya *ihimi* (Hauenstein, *Hanya*, p. 98) often prefixed to the proper kinship term "mother's person." The form is related to Kimbundu *kimi* 1n/2, an honorific term added to another substantive, and Mbui *kime* 1n/2 "lord," Umbundu *ocime* 1n/2 "master." The form seems to change its meaning from a general honorific term applied to a senior mother's brother and later to all mother's brothers in Nyaneka, Nkhumbi, and Hanya rather than the reverse. Its application to "mother's brother" may have been late, but its etymology remains unknown. Its adoption indicates an increasing role of governance for mother's brothers. For a comparable process, see the evolution of *lemba* 5/6 "leader" in the north of the area.

96. All the sources stress this form of preferential marriage. For instance, see Maija Tuupainen, *Marriage*, pp. 36–38, Cross-cousins are *cepwa* 1/2 [not class 7/8] in Kwandu, Nyaneka, Nkhumbi, Hanya, and Umbundu. Despite the superficial final similarity of its second syllable, this form cannot be derived from or linked to proto-Eastern Bantu (CS 2091) *jįp(ú)á*: "cross sibling's child." A local innovation, it probably derives from the passive of a thus far unknown verb -*cepa*, and it is not very old since it was coined after the language separation in this region was complete, most likely in Nyaneka. Later, nearly all Nyaneka's immediate neighbors were to borrow it. In the Cuvelai basin, Kwambi and Ndonga used different terms while Kwanyama had recently outlawed cross-cousin marriages and abandoned the special term that designated them. See Loeb, *In Feudal*, pp. 99, 107, 273, 283; Estermann, *Ambos*, pp. 120–21. In several of the languages, cross-cousins of different sex also used terms such as "husband," "wife," or "bull."

of matrilineages concerned with the inheritance of material goods did not alter the strong spiritual ties that existed between fathers and their children and their inheritance. These bonds were usually expressed by dedicating individual heads of cattle to the commemoration of father/child relationships and to have them inherited by sons. Nevertheless, and contrary to what was to happen among cattle nomads, formal patrilineal groups did not arise among agropastoralists nor were local settlements explicitly based on patrilineal principles, even if that was often the case in practice. Finally, the reader will not be surprised to hear that here too the introduction of larger cattle herds gave rise to the social inequalities and the demand for servile labor already mentioned among cattle nomads.[97]

These matrilineages soon began to aggregate themselves as equals into noncorporate matriclans, that is, clans without any common activities and without a designated leader; these came to be dispersed over large regions, irrespective of ethnic grouping.[98] The main relevance of clanship was that it constituted a set of exogamic units, that when clan members belonging to different settlements met they provided mutual assistance to each other, and that common clanship between the heads of homesteads easily led to an alliance between their settlements. Over time, the number of clans seems to have varied as large ones split into two and allowed marriages between the two halves, while in other cases several small clans turned into subclans as they fused into a single larger clan.[99] Such processes of fission and fusion

97. Hence forms for various terms, such as "rich person," are common to Nyaneka and Herero, "to be poor" in Herero, Ndonga, Kwanyama, and Nkhumbi, "master" everywhere except in Kwambi, and "servant, to serve" in Herero, Ndonga, and Kwanyama, while a form "to be needy, poor" is common to Nyaneka, Kwanyama, and Ndonga.

98. *Eanda* 5/6: "subclan, clan" in Nyaneka and Nkhumbi; *epata* 5/6: "lineage, clan" in Kwanyama; *eswimo* 5/6: "lineage, clan" in Ndonga. All these forms are proto-Njila (original meanings "association," "local group of settlers," "belly"), which acquired new meanings, an indication both of the novelty of matrilineages and of their emergence after the main languages in the region had already partly separated but still probably before ca. 1300 when the Cimbebasians began to move southward. For their description and spread, see Estermann, *Nhaneca-Humbe*, pp. 147–54, and his *Ambos*, pp. 141–49; Tupainen, *Marriage*, pp. 25–28, 30, 140–44, 163; and Loeb, *In Feudal*, pp. 99–103.

99. The first process is reported more for the Ambo (Loeb, *In Feudal*, p. 102; Tupainen, *Marriage*, p. 26); the second specifically for the Nyaneka (Lang and Tastevin, *La tribu*, p. 46). In the two examples he gives, each *ombunga* 9/10 superclan grouped five *eanda* subclans. To seek special significance in the fact that the numbers of clans per ethnic groups varied greatly between the inner Cunene basin (Nyaneka, 40 clans) and the Cuvelai basin (Ndonga, 14; Kwanyama, 18 or 29) makes little sense, both because of the more transient nature of ethnicities and because of the differences in the dynamics of clan fusion and fission.

show that today's clans are not merely the automatic outcome of a series of exogamic marriages with virilocal residence but that they are, above all, the expression of dynamic networks of alliances and counteralliances reflecting changing force fields in the political arenas of the region.

At some time after matrilineages emerged and perhaps at the very time that matriclans began to take shape, another major innovation, the creation of territorial chieftaincies, changed the political landscape, as is shown by the coining of two new terms *ohámba* 1/2 for "chief" and *ocilongó* 7/8 for "territory," which occur in all the languages of the agropastoralists. *Ohámba* is derived from the proto-Bantu root *-cámba* "to leap over, to surpass" and the corresponding verb *-hámba*, from which the noun is derived, is still used in Herero and Ndonga.[100] *Ohámba* thus means "he who surpasses all others." The first chiefs were those "who surpassed all others" because their homesteads contained more people. The invention of the term *ohámba* and hence the rise of chiefs cannot be dated, but the use of the word probably began to spread at approximately the same time that another word for "chief," *somá, sobá, homphá* began to spread among the farmers of the planalto to its north, perhaps in the eleventh century. Hence ohámba must have been invented soon after large herds became common in the agropastoral zone. *Ocilongó* 7/8 "land, territory, domain" was also coined at an early date.[101] It is probably

100. Proto-Bantu *-cámba:* "to leap over, to surpass" occurs in Meeussen citing Meinhof and Homburger. Guthrie does not list this root. The Herero and Ndonga verb forms are attestations in this region of this form and meaning. In addition to the known citations, see Bushoong: *-shyáám:* "to overcome, pass by, surpass." That this is the basic meaning is also evident from the general construction of the numeral seven as *-cámbwadi:* "surpasses [five] by two" (CS 270 with Herero forms in CS 269, and correct tone) as well as the occasional one of six as *cámbanu* "surpass [five] by one" (CS 266, add Sala Mpasu and Bushoong, and correct tone). Extensions of the basic meaning of the verb include Lunda: *samba, sampa* "to jump, to play," in Cokwe, "to acquit," and in Rund, "to plead in court." All the Moxico languages refer also to "winning in court" and "to judge"; in Cokwe, it is "to acquit," in Rund, "to plead in court," related to Pende, Mbala, Kimbundu (all with *-sáámb* forms) "to recount events in court" and from which all these languages, as well as Holo and Mongo, derive the further meaning "to pray." A further extension "to judge" is attested in Mongo, Rund, Sanga and the western Great Lakes languages. The geographic distribution of the form suggests that Umbundu *-sambo* 7/8: "main chief" is a transfer from a southern language rather than the reverse. Note that ohámba, "chief," has no relation whatsoever with *ohàmbo,* "cattle kraal."

101. The form occurs in Nyaneka, Nkhumbi, Kwanayama, Kwambi, Ndonga, Kwangari, as well as in Umbundu (but as *ocilonga*) and Herero. But it may only have been common in southern Umbundu because the usual form there is *ofeka.* In Herero, *ocirongo* means "place where one can live." If this was the original meaning, then the form would be Cimbebasian and antedate the separation of the three subgroups ca. 1300. But Herero might also have borrowed the form from its Ambo neighbors at a later time.

derived from a proto-Bantu noun, but exactly from which form remains unclear.[102]

We will never know how it came about that certain leaders attracted many more people to their settlements than others. Possibly such leaders had accumulated more cattle than their peers, perhaps as the result of successful raiding, which then attracted more clients and servants to them. Yet even then, and certainly in later times, chiefs claimed lordship over others not because of any claims of ownership over the herds of others, but because of their claims of ownership of a landed domain. Like the nineteenth-century local "chiefs of the land," the early chiefs were owners of their territorial domains and their individual title was *mwene* 1/2 + *X* "possessor of *X*," in which *X* was the name of their domain. Anyone who had settled on their land became their subject and as a visible sign of this status, such homestead leaders could only light their fires with firebrands obtained from the sacred fire at the chief's place.

One may imagine that these early chiefdoms were rather similar in overall size and organization to nineteenth-century districts or cantons: units comprising less than 1,000 people or so living in scattered homesteads within its territory.[103] Succession soon became strictly matrilineal and one may well wonder whether it was a stress on ownership of the land that led agropastoralists, unlike people to the north, to consider succession to the office of chief as if it was similar to the inheritance of cattle herds. Be that as it may, the effect of this succession rule was to split the ruling elite class into two sets, namely, those of the aristocrats (all of which were also called ohámba) and of a group consisting of the children of the ruler, who were nobles only during his or their lifetimes.[104]

102. The proto-Bantu form of *ocilongó* would be **-dongó* 7/8 if the reconstructed tones are correct. Now **-dongó* 5 and 14 "clay, soil" (CS 667–68) and even **-dongó* 7/8, 9/10 "pot" (CS 669) would fit were it not that these are clearly exclusively Eastern Bantu innovations without any attestations anywhere in the Njila area. Were it not for the tonal difference in the second syllable, one could derive *ocilongó* "country" from **-dongo* 5/6, 7/8, 14 "large social group" (Vansina, *Paths*, p. 268, with CS 665 and indirectly CS 714), which has many attestations in Western Bantu, including one in Pende. The question must be left open.

103. A rough calculation yields a little less than 1,000 per district in Nkhumbi lands as in Estermann, *Nhaneca-Humbe*, p. 167 (80 districts and population before 1915), and Lang and Tastevin, *La tribu*, p. 6 (has 80,000 before 1910); Brochado, "Descripção," p. 207, estimated the population of Nkhumbi proper in the 1840s at 50,000 to 60,000 and of all the Nkhumbi lands at 65,000 to 78,000 inhabitants (pp. 205–7), and all Nyaneka at 73,000 to 89,400. Nogueira, *Raça*, p. 256, estimated in the 1850s at 140,000 to 150,000 for the combined Nyaneka and Nkhumbi. Siiskonen, *Trade*, p. 47, tells us that the larger districts in the Cuvelai basin encompassed about twenty homesteads.

104. For social classes in the 1850s, see Nogueira, *Raça*, pp. 263, 266–68.

Another effect of the succession rule was that, once in place, chiefdoms certainly began to exert a considerable influence on matriclans by attracting matrilineages of various homestead leaders to affiliate with them to the point that in later times it was believed that every single clan had a chief somewhere—in other words, no matrilineage was affiliated with any clan that did not have a chief somewhere.[105] From then on the composition and size of various clans waxed and waned with the evolution of the power relationships between chiefdoms.

The main tasks of these chiefs probably consisted in those expected of the leader of a homestead, namely, to regulate the agricultural and pastoral calendars and perhaps also tasks pertaining to the periodic initiation rituals for boys and girls (and thus regulating the latter's marriages), to carry out rituals to obtain rain, rich harvests, and the maintenance of human and animal fertility. Chiefs also presided over tribunals to resolve local disputes, were supposed to protect their subjects from foreign attacks or cattle raids, and maintained peaceful or warlike relations with other chiefs. As owners of the lands, they were probably entitled to specified portions of game while, in return for their stewardship, their subjects provided free corvée labor for the maintenance of the chiefly homesteads and perhaps for some work in their fields as well.[106]

Once the first chiefdoms had been established, they were adopted by most inhabitants in the entire agropastoral zone, a process which resulted in the creation of a stable balance of power between a very large number of equally strong small chiefdoms. This situation lasted perhaps for centuries, until there came a time when this equilibrium was broken when one or a few chiefdoms became stronger than their neighbors and were able to subjugate and incorporate them as districts or cantons. The imbalance of power which came to exist then eventually led to the extension of principalities over nearly the whole of the agropastoral zone, although among some western Ambo groups resistance to the loss of local autonomy prevented their establishment or even led to the later dissolution of existing principalities.[107] The main

105. Lang and Tastevin, *La tribu*, p. 47, "Each clan formerly had a chief or *soba* who was king of a whole land."

106. For lack of sufficiently precise data, much of this scenario must remain vague. The only concrete description of local chiefs in action dates from the 1850s and relates to the handling of legal issues and of an accident. See Nogueira, *Raça*, pp. 121–23, 126–35. For a relation to girls' marriages, see "Ladislaus Magyar's Schilderung," p. 1003. For generalities, see Estermann, *Nhaneca-Humbe*, pp. 167–69 (tribunals, corvée, gifts).

107. See Brochado, "Descripção," pp. 195–96; Estermann, *Nhaneca-Humbe*, p. 161; Clarence-Smith, "Underdevelopment," pp. xv (map) and 98 (Mbalantu had a king once but dispensed with him).

linguistic traces left by this development are the coining of a new meaning for *omukunda* 3/4,[108] formerly "field" and now "district, subordinate chiefdom," as well as the introduction of two words for district head, namely, *onkhinyi* 1n/2[109] in the principalities of the inner Cunene basin and *elenga* 5/6 in those of the Cuvelai basin.[110]

We will only know approximately when principalities were formed once archeological research has been carried out in and around the large stone ruins, such as at Ossi, which abound in the region. Still even the earliest Portuguese reports for the region, from the seventeenth century, mention principalities in the Quilengues area and farther south on the Chela Range. In 1680 Cadornega mentions "Angolo, sova da Provincia de o Hila," in which Huila is a known place name (*mwila* means pasture land) and Angolo is a ruler of what later became Lupolo.[111] He further mentions Quipungo, "a great lord," now on the southern edge of the planalto and Quilengues "with many lords." Earlier he had already told of a Portuguese defeat inflicted around 1637 by a coalition involving some of these Quilengues lords.[112] The overall

108. *Omukunda* 3/4 is derived from *-gunda* 3/4, CS 897, "field established in a forest" still attested to in Umbundu, *-ngunda* 9/10 "newly cut field"; Lwena, *-kundu* 5/6 "wilderness with little vegetation"; and perhaps Mbala, *muguundú* 3/4 "field of manioc." This term was only used in Nkhumbi- and Ambo-speaking lands and had not spread to Nyaneka. Hence the districts were "the fields" that generated revenue for the court.

109. *Onkhinyi:* Nyaneka under "chefe da terra" or "sobeta [small chief]." According to Lang and Tastevin, *La tribu,* p. 59, n. 1, the term is derived from *-khinya* [not *-kinga*] "to subjugate, to dominate." Hence the word means "ruler, dominator" and does not seem to refer to a local rather than to a paramount chief.

110. *Elenga* 5/6 "noble person," "local chief": in Ndonga, Kwambi, Kwanyama, and Kwangari. It is derived from the related verb in Kwanyama and Kwangari, *-lenga* "to assist, to promote," and hence clearly refers to a subordinate chief for he is the "promoted one." However, see also Cokwe, *-lénga* "to rule," from which *mukalenga* "sir, lord" in Cokwe, Kanyok, and Tshiluba. Note further the derived meaning "well-dressed noble person" in Nyaneka and "beauty, elegance" in Herero.

111. See Cadornega, *História,* 3:168, 172, 218, 250. Nogueira, *Raça,* p. 125, mentions the specific titles given to the ruler in each of the various Nyaneka and Nkhumbi principalities. Thus Nangolo is the title of the ruler of Lupolo.

112. The governor of Benguela, Lopo Soares Lasso, was killed in 1637 by a coalition of lords of the Quilengues region led by Ngola Njimbu. See Cadornega, *História,* 1:201–2. Ngola Njimbu is also described as a major Umbundu-speaking ruler in Cadornega, *História,* 3:172, 250 (since he was a "Gram *Feque,*" in which *Feque* is Umbundu *ofeka* "country"), separately from the many lords of Quilengues and the great ruler Quipungo as well as others. In the 1840s, the main power in the Quilengues region was the ruler of Sukubala (Socovala). See Brochado, "Noticia," p. 204; Estermann, *Nhaneca-Humbe,* pp. 162–63.

political evolution of the principalities in and around the Chela Range becomes better known from ca. 1770 onward. According to a report from that year, "Injau" had recently become wealthy by trading with the bay of Moçamedes (now Namibe) and was reported to have rebelled against "Canina," his overlord and ruler of Lupolo. Fifteen years later he was practically independent. By then, several lords ruled in the Chela Range, none of whose lands was very extensive, at least if one disregards their obviously unrealistic claims of overlordship over the peoples living between the range and the coast.[113] Still, before the 1770s, Lupolo seems to have included most of the other principalities and must have ruled over several tens of thousands of people. Judging by size and population at that time, one may call it a kingdom.

Despite claims made by the Portuguese in the later eighteenth century that Nkhumbi was then a single large kingdom, this was not so. Their assumption that it then encompassed the whole valley of the middle Cunene seems to rest nearly entirely on the heading of two legends "Terras do Humbe" and "Terras do Humbe grande" on the map which Pinheiro Furtado began to draft from 1786 onward.[114] Yet there was no such single large kingdom in the 1840s. Then there were three principalities called Nkhumbi, and neither oral traditions nor early travelers or settlers in the region claimed that there ever had been only one.[115] One must conclude therefore that in Furtado's time a geographic or perhaps ethnic name Nkhumbi had been erroneously understood as referring to a single polity.

The size of each principality waxed and waned over time. Some grew to be so large in size and in population that they could be called kingdoms. Polities comprising 20,000 inhabitants or more in the 1840s included

---

113. *Relaçam da Viagem* . . . written by João Pilarte da Silva at Huilla on 9 September 1770 and published in Felner, *Angola*, 1, #8:177–86; The long report of 1 January 1786 by Gregorio José Mendes of 1785 can be found in Delgado, *Ao sul*, 2:562–75; Nogueira, *Raça*, pp. 255–56, summarizes the oral traditions current in the 1840s as follows: "Formerly Lupollo, Njau and Humpata formed the single state of Mwila, the collective name still given to these peoples and which we give to Lupolo for it was there that the old lords of Mwila lived, from whom the present inhabitants of Lupolo descend."

114. *Carta geographica da Costa occidental da Africa* . . . *desenhada pelo Tenente Coronel Eng. o L. C. C. Pinheiro Furtado em 1790. Gravada em Pariz por Ordem do Major João Carlos Feo Cardozo de Castellobranco e Torres em 1825.*

115. The first nineteenth-century authors to claim this were Capello and Ivens in 1886 (in their *De Angola*, 1:213–17), yet their narrative makes it clear that their views did not rest on oral traditions but were cobbled together from general speculations about large-scale migratory movements in Africa.

Ngambwe and Nkhumbi in the inner Cunene basin,[116] and Kwanyama, Mbandja, Ndonga, and perhaps Ngandjera still, in the Cuvelai basin, even though none of them encompassed very large territories.[117] Yet at the same time other principalities were not larger than the older chiefdoms they replaced as they counted scarcely more than 1,000 inhabitants each. The most striking characteristic of the political landscape was in fact not the size of the largest polities but the instability of all of them. The oral histories and descriptions from the 1840s and 1850s about them are replete with stories about overthrown dynasties, fiercely contested successions, and frequent secessions either as a consequence of succession struggles or when an enterprising local chief grew rich enough and attracted enough followers to secede.[118] While the reported cases of instability were certainly exacerbated by the effects of the Atlantic slave trade, a certain lability may have been an enduring characteristic of this sort of polity. The absence of any intermediary or parallel institutions of governance between the small central courts of each principality and those of the chiefdoms, now called "districts," which they included, suggests as much. Thus, for example, Nkhumbi proper incorporated eighty different chiefdoms, all of whose leaders reported directly to the king alone and were instructed by him. The importance of the personal quality

116. Brochado, "Noticia," pp. 204–7, has 80,000 to 100,000 for Sucubala in the Quilengue regions, 50,000 to 60,000 for Nkhumbi, 10,000 to 12,000 for Mulondo, 5,000 to 6,000 for Kamba (but 7,000 to 8,000 "like Evale" in his "Descripção," p. 194) but only 3,000 to 3,500 for Mwila, and 1,000/1,200 for Hai, and Quihita. Nogueira, Raça, pp. 255–56, gives a more modest global estimate of 140,000 to 150,000 inhabitants for 10 independent polities, of which Ngambwe and Nkhumbi were the most populous, while Lang and Tastevin, La tribu, p. 6, gave 200,000 for the whole basin before 1912 and the 1960 census gives 191,861 for the same area (Redinha, Distribução Etnica, p. 8).

117. Population estimates for the Ambo polities in H. Siiskonen, Trade, pp. 42–43. Those of Brochado, "Descripção," pp. 191, 194–95, established in 1850 are clearly strongly inflated by comparison. He has Kwanyama 120,000 to 130,000, Evale 6,000 to 8,000, Handa 2,000 to 3,000, Ndonga 50,000 to 60,000, and Ngandjera "like Kwanyama." Clearly the estimate of 800,000 for Kwanyama or even for all Ambo speakers in "Ladislaus Magyar's Schilderung," p. 1003, is not credible.

118. In the Cuvelai basin, for Brochado, "Descripção," p. 196, as well as "Hugo Hahn's Reise," p. 293, Ndonga and Kwambi had seceded from Ngandjera and were still "in a certain sense" colonies of Ngandjera. For instability in and around Kwanyama in the middle 1850s, see Silva and Franco, "Annaes," p. 486, "Hugo Hahn's Reise," p. 290, and "Ladislaus Magyar's Schilderung," p. 1003; Estermann, Ambos, pp. 77–78, for Ndonga and Evale. In the inner Cunene basin, the breaking up of ancient Lupolo is summarized in Nogueira, Raça, pp. 255–56. For some other contestations and secessions, see Lang and Tastevin, La tribu, pp. 7–11, 57, and Estermann, Nhaneca-Humbe, pp. 30, 40–46; Petermann, "Die Reisen," pp. 195–96.

of the relations between each chief and the king is quite clear from A. Nogueira's experiences. Chiefs appreciated by the king "got away" with much more than those who were not.[119] Although the overlords usually managed to maintain their control by approving the local appointment of all chiefs or by replacing them with others who were not even related to the local lineage of the earlier ones, and even though they usually appointed their own relatives (frequently their own children) to such posts, all of this still remained insufficient to maintain effective centralization in the absence of other parallel structures.[120]

Governance by an overlord consisted as much, if not more, in his ritual role as guarantor of well-being and protector of fertility than in his role as military protector of his people, or as arbitrator of intercommunal disputes, or as administrator whose commands ensured the necessary co-operation in practical matters between the communities of his realm. The lords claimed to be the embodiment of their ruling ancestors.[121] As such they established the calendar for most activities. Not only did they control the timing and the amount of rainfall on which all life depended, but they also initiated all the seasonal rituals concerning sowing, first fruit, herding, hunting, long-distance trade, or war, as well as the puberty rituals for boys and girls.[122]

Both the extent of the reach of central government and its limitations through its control of timetables are perhaps best illustrated by the conduct of the rituals of the initiations into adulthood which affected every individual in the polity. They were both sponsored and initiated by lords or local headmen once every few years but the authorities neither stage-managed nor otherwise interfered with their conduct at all. Still, because

119. See Nogueira, *Raça*, pp. 124–35, for three different cases.

120. On internal structures, Siiskonen, *Trade*, pp. 46–49; Loeb, *In Feudal*, pp. 56–61; Estermann, *Ambos*, pp. 157–66; Estermann, *Nhaneca-Humbe*, pp. 162–70; Lang and Tastevin, *La tribu*, pp. 55–62; Wunenberger, "La mission et le royaume de Humbé," pp. 251–52, 261, 269, 270–72.

121. Charms played a much smaller role in their ideology than they did in the monarchies of the planalto and farther north.

122. This summary of rule rests on many descriptions. See, for instance, Estermann, *Nhaneca-Humbe*, pp. 16–70; Lang and Tastevin, *La tribu*, pp. 59–61; Nogueira, *Raça*, pp. 116, 263–69; Siiskonen, *Trade*, pp. 46–49; Estermann, *Ambos*, pp. 157–60; Tönjes, *Ovamboland*, pp. 107–12, 116–21; "Ladislaus Magyar's Schilderung," pp. 1001–3. Because of their professions and influenced by general anthropological theories, most of these authors have erroneously called this type of governance "divine kingship" (e.g., Siiskonen, *Trade*, p. 46) even if it was believed that the spirits of his ancestors resided in the king (a belief that is not well documented) as Estermann, *Nhaneca-Humbe*, p. 162, has it, the expression would still be incorrect.

they controlled the timing and supervised who was admitted to each initiation, they did exert a significant impact on the timing of marriages and of other gender relations among young adults. Elaborate initiations for girls (*ehiko* 5/6, *efiko* 5/6, *efundula* 5/6) were conducted exclusively by elder women. These were similar all over the agropastoral zone whether or not a group of girls was initiated collectively, as was most common, or not, for even collective initiations did not create any special relations of comradeship between the girls who had been initiated together.[123] In the inner Cunene basin, boys' initiations (*etanda* 5/6)[124] were always collective, dry-season affairs. In contrast to the girls' initiations, however, these ceremonies gave rise to permanent age-sets named after some special feat the boys had achieved during their seclusion. Male age-mates not only assumed new names but remained comrades for life, a tie which cut across ties of kinship and status. Although ethnographers have neglected them, these ties were clearly significant in subsequent social relationships, especially in cattle camps and as a basis for association on trading expeditions. The political authorities exercised absolutely no control over these age-sets, apart from dictating their composition by limiting the candidates inducted into the initiation which they sponsored to boys from their own domains. Thus age-sets were territorial groups.[125]

Assisted only by a few major councilors whom they chose themselves and a further handful of titleholders, in addition to the district chiefs which they appointed or at least confirmed in their position, the lords ruled from their capitals (*ombala* 9/10). In most of the inner Cunene basin, but not in the Cuvelai basin, they were located on permanent sites, many of which were fortified, at least by the eighteenth century if not long before. The royal house, the sacred fire, and at least one sacred house, were central features of every capital. The lord's officials and district chiefs (among whom were some of the royal women[126]) were chosen from the ranks of a triple nobility, namely,

123. Estermann, "La fête de puberté," pp. 128–41.

124. They were largely absent in the Cuvelai basin.

125. Nogueira, *Raça*, pp. 262, 302–3, underlines their importance; he also speaks of "confraternity or league"; for Brochado, "Descripção," pp. 190, 192, circumcision was general among the Nkhumbi in the late 1840s, while at that time only lords accompanied by two or three of their servants were circumcised among the Kwanyama; Lang and Tastevin, *La tribu*, pp. 25–28; Estermann, *Nhaneca-Humbe*, pp. 69–78. Given Brochado's testimony, the chronology in Loeb, *In Feudal*, pp. 236–39, is certainly incorrect. The mention of masks in his account points to a recent reintroduction of initiation from the Nyemba area.

126. Nogueira, *Raça*, pp. 114–15.

members of the dynasty or the children of the lord or the lord's favorite followers, including wealthy commoners, the two latter categories being restricted to the lifetime of its members. The usual activities of governance
consisted for the most part in carrying out the recurrent rituals associated
with the annual round of activities, the crisis rituals in times of calamities
(such as wars, droughts, epidemics, or epizootics), the supervision of a tribunal headed by one of their titleholders, and the management of external
relations with other principalities. Envoys of various other principalities
resided at their court so that one can view the whole of the inner Cunene
basin region or that of the Cuvelai basin as a single network of principalities
structured by both temporary mutual alliances and equally temporary hos-
tile relations.[127]

The lords derived income from fines,[128] as well as tribute (Nyaneka:
elilimu 5/6) and some corvée labor, which were channeled through their district chiefs, who also derived their own income in this manner. By the nineteenth century, the justification for these practices was that the ruler personally owned all the land in his domains. Hence every leader of homesteads
who did not belong to his matrilineage was supposed to be there on sufferance only and only for as long as it pleased the ruler. Therefore every homestead in his domains was required to pay various annual rents and corvées.
In earlier times, fines and tribute may have been perceived more as payment
for services rendered than as "rent." For instance, fines were payment for
arbitration and tribute in first-fruit offerings for the procurement of fertility.[129] No doubt, however, the practical extent of the coercive power of the
ruler determined the amount and frequency of payments made or corvée
rendered; hence, these practices certainly varied from principality to principality and from ruler to ruler as Nogueira underlined, in contrast to most

127. Ibid., p. 116. Such diplomats were called *mukwandira,* "those of the roads."
128. *Oluhito* 11/10, or *olufito* 11/10, or *efuto* 5/6. *Futa* "to pay" is an old term in Kimbundu and perhaps Umbundu that later spread widely under Portuguese colonial influence and still later was adopted in the colonial Congo. The forms used in southern
Angola bid fair to be recent loanwords.
129. Siiskonen, *Trade,* p. 46; Estermann, *Nhaneca-Humbe,* p. 166; but Nogueira, *Raça,*
pp. 265, 301, disclaims any notion of rent. It is evident though that by the nineteenth century the new market and money economy already exerted a strong influence in the
agropastoral zone and this formulation may therefore have been quite recent. It was perhaps more an interpretation by European visitors and settlers than a faithful rendering
of local opinion. One would rather expect that tribute and corvée labor were legitimized
as a return for services rendered by an ideology that stressed the ruler as the heir of the
"first ancestor-founder" and the guarantor of fertility for all on his lands.

other nineteenth-century observers who tended to revel in descriptions of despotic behavior.[130]

To abandon this sketch of the agropastoralist principalities at this point would be misleading because it would erase significant differences in governance between them, differences not merely between the polities in the two basins but even differences between the east and west sides of the inner Cunene basin. The main difference between the western and eastern principalities in the inner Cunene basin was the ritual of *ondyelwa* 9/10, an elaborate annual procession of a sacred ox around the principality lasting several weeks. This took place in July, that is, at the onset of the high dry season. On its return to the capital, this ox was presented with a specific salty treat in order to predict whether the coming year would be fruitful. If he licked it, the year would be prosperous—and he nearly always licked it. Hence every year this spectacular procession renewed and expressed the primacy of cattle over all other goods, the subjection of the various chiefdoms to the center, and the territorial extent of the principality. Clearly this was the most meaningful as well as the most spectacular ritual in all the western polities from Caluquembe in the north to the Ngambwe on the Caculovar River in the south. Yet it was absent from the Handa, Mulondo, Kamba, and Nkhumbi principalities along the Cunene River.[131] Across the Cunene, the Kwanyama held a comparable annual ritual in the beginning of August which they called the *epena* 5/6. Here all the cattle of the country were assembled at the capital before being sent out for transhumance early in August. Here too the fruitfulness of the coming year was predicted, albeit not by the ruler's ox but by four senior diviners. At the conclusion of *epena,* the cattle herds were then sent out on their transhumance far away, as were the smelters and smiths who traveled northward to the iron deposits, and the bands of warriors on

130. See Nogueira, *Raça,* pp. 117–18 (some rulers were more severe, but even so they respected "justice"), pp. 266, 300 (absolute "paternal power," limited by customary law); Siiskonen, *Trade,* p. 47 and n. 37; Estermann, *Nhaneca-Humbe,* p. 161 (absolute monarchy only among the Kwanyama), and his *Ambos,* pp. 157–58; Tönjes, *Ovamboland,* pp. 105–8, 111–13; Silva and Franco, "Annaes," p. 486; Brochado, "Descripção," pp. 191–92, and his "Noticia," p. 206; "Ladislaus Magyar's Schilderung," pp. 1001–3.

131. *Ondyelwa* is spelled *geroa* in all the sources before the 1880s, except for "Magyar." See Nogueira, *Raça,* pp. 262, 288–96; Brochado, "Descripção," p. 193; Silva and Franco, "Annaes," p. 486 ("This was their only festival"); Lang and Tastevin, *La tribu,* pp. 159–61; Almeida, *Sul,* pp. 311, 371–72; Estermann, *Nhaneca-Humbe,* pp. 190–92. "Ladislaus Magyar's Schilderung," p. 1003, writes Jeluva but refers to another cattle festival among the Kwanyama.

raiding expeditions to foreign lands. When the cattle returned, they celebrated the *Jeluva* festival.[132]

Despite the similarity between *ondyelwa* and *epena* and the use of the word *ondyelwa* in Kwanyama, the differences between the polities in the Cunene and Cuvelai basins were more pronounced than those between Nkhumbi and Nyaneka.[133] In the 1850s, the inhabitants of the Cuvelai basin differed from the former in that their rulers enjoyed more stringent powers. They appointed more of their favorites as *elenga* 5/6 district headmen and military officers, but they had fewer formal titleholders than was the case in the west and they relied less on them. These eastern lords also attributed districts to the highest bidders but removed them equally easily, surrounded themselves with sizeable bodyguards, raided more frequently, with more forces, over greater distances, claimed more tribute and corvée supposedly as rent for the fields which their subjects had received in usufruct, and controlled trade more. Apart from kingship itself, they recognized no hereditary positions at all, and most of the many officials who had personal ties to a king were dismissed by his successor.[134] All these characteristics have been linked to the special environmental features of the Cuvelai basin and, in particular, on the need to dispose of a sizeable labor force to keep water channels in order and to dig reservoirs when needed. In the manner of Karl Wittfogel's theories about oriental despotism and hydraulic civilization, it has been argued that this necessity explains the emergence of strong kingship.[135] More likely the reverse is true. As among the Herero, such operations had been conducted at first cooperatively by people within each neighborhood as needed. But once kings appeared, they assumed responsibility for such operations, which they centralized and enlarged as part of their task to set the calendar for all major activities. Indeed some groups on the western edge

132. Brochado, "Descripção," p. 193, made the comparison between *epena* (spelled *punra*) and *ondyelwa*. Later ethnographers, such as Estermann, *Ambos*, pp. 165–66, 174, 182, or Loeb, *In Feudal*, p. 191 (citing a manuscript source of 1916), p. 277 (a similar ritual in Ndonga and in Kwambi), pp. 277, 285, clearly underestimated the importance of this festival. For Jeluva, see the preceding note.

133. There were also differences in social organization, the major one of which was the significant place of collective boy's initiations (*etanda*) and hence of age-sets in the Cunene basin and their lesser role or even absence in the Cuvelai basin.

134. Siiskonen, *Trade*, pp. 44–49. Yet "Hugo Hahn's Reise," p. 290, praised the state of law and order and concluded that "overall the lords rule well."

135. William Gervase Clarence-Smith, *Slaves, Peasants and Capitalists*, p. 75; Clarence-Smith and Richard Moorsom, "Underdevelopment," pp. 98 and 110, n. 10. See also Karl Wittfogel, *Oriental Despotism*.

of the basin managed their water supplies just as well as the others without any central authority at all.

Some of the differences mentioned between the Cuvelai and Cunene basins probably resulted from environmental differences relating especially to the availability of water, but others, including nearly all the differences between the Nyaneka and the Nkhumbi ways of governance, cannot be explained away in that fashion. They are best accounted for by accepting that early principalities arose largely independently from each other in the Cuvelai basin, along the middle Cunene, and in the Chela Range to the west, albeit from a common base, that of the earlier ohámba chiefdom. The differences in the most fundamental state rituals, such as *ondyelwa* 9/10 and *epena* 5/6, especially must have evolved independently from each other. On the other hand, emerging principalities in various parts of these zones soon began to influence each other, as is evident from the transfer of words such as *omukunda* 3/4 or *elenga* 5/6 and from detailed similarities of emblems, etiquette, or dress.

The differences between the agropastoral principalities and those on the *planalto* to the north were much larger, however, than those within the agropastoral zones. They were so large in fact that they can offer no support at all for a theory of wholesale diffusion of "the principality" from the north to the south. Nogueira had already rejected such a diffusionist view for that reason. In addition to the absence of circumcision rites on the planalto, he also cited the opposition of patrilineal to matrilineal descent in political succession.[136] More important differences relate specifically to the ideology and the style of rule. They include the nearly insignificant role of charms and the absence among the agropastoralists of the important cult for the royal skulls, as opposed to polities on the planalto, the different character of all major rituals in both areas, as well as the layout of the capitals in which they were set, and finally the much more extensive system of titleholders and the greater complexity of the territorial hierarchies on the planalto. It is easy to see that no common blueprint underlay the polities in the two areas and a comparison of their basic political vocabularies confirms it. Thus not only early chiefdoms but also principalities originally developed independently on the planalto and in the south.

Yet one also finds a set of special terms common to the polities on the planalto and their southern neighbors. These include politically important words such as *ombala* 9/10 "capital," *elombe* 4/5 "nobility," *-vyala* "to become

136. See Nogueira, *Raça*, p. 262.

OF WATER, CATTLE, AND KINGS

king,"[137] and two or three of the main political titles. Once again these are due mainly to later borrowing, especially by the agropastoralists, who began to be impressed by the larger scale and the greater military power which the major principalities on the planalto had achieved from the thirteenth century onward. And, no doubt, borrowing of this kind was facilitated by the still later (sixteenth or seventeenth centuries?) immigration of new dynasties from the planalto to which the southern oral traditions refer. The most important of these borrowings was undoubtedly the model of a stable and fortified capital. All other transfers in both directions, such as the borrowing of an emblem here, a title there, a mode of address elsewhere seem to have occurred in piecemeal fashion over the centuries. But eventually these details produced a spurious air of similarity between the polities of the planalto and those of the south. Yet this very similarity in unessentials bears witness not to some static preservation of a common *ur*-model of the distant past, but to a process of continual reciprocal innovation by peer polity interaction.

Networks

Hitherto we have sketched the growth of scale of societies as a result of the advent of centralized institutions of governance. However extensive though, the reach of political control, its arena, had its limits. Nor were all other relations strictly conditioned by kinship. Parallel overarching institutions did exist and regulated stable relationships between individuals belonging to different local communities, different kinship groups, and even different polities from the earliest period of settlement. They flourished with the development of sedentary settlements and of their economies, for they seem to have functioned in an economic context involving producers and traders. These institutions consisted of networks between individuals belonging to different collectivities and were based on achieved statuses rather than dictated by birth.

Unfortunately, while most observers noticed the existence of networks, they were not interested in them so that rather little is known about most of them. This holds true especially with regard to the networks that linked professionals of the same highly specialized crafts such as diviners-healers, metalworkers, and hunters, networks which were always completely free from any outside political interference. All we know is that these professional statuses were highly rated, that they were acquired through individual initiation conducted by older members of the profession, that deceased mem-

137. And derived from that: "king" *ombyali* 1n/2 (Umbundu) *ombiai* 1n/2 (agropastoralists).

bers were buried with special ceremonial by their fellows, and that from time
to time a group of fellows convened on other occasions.[138]

Most of the authors, being missionaries, claim that professional expertise and the high status associated with it were derived from favorable religious forces. But they evidently underrate both the importance of the years
of training required in achieving full proficiency in these professions and the
nature of continuing contacts between these experts linked to the practice
of their craft. That is especially evident with regard to blacksmiths and
smelters. Smelters regularly welcomed smiths to assist them in their tasks
and to inform them about the quality of the raw metal produced, while from
time to time ordinary blacksmiths visited mastersmiths elsewhere to acquire
more expertise. This had certainly been going on ever since metal began to
be worked in the area yet we remain ignorant for lack of study of any developments relating to these associations over time.[139]

Perhaps the most significant among these networks was the one affecting traders. Trade, which took place mostly in the dry season, was nearly as
essential for survival as agriculture or cattle-keeping were. It involved a host
of products, among which cattle, other livestock, salt, iron, copper, pottery,
and shell beads were but the most crucial commodities.[140] We have seen that
trade was already flourishing at Nqoma and at Kapako by the tenth century
and that glass beads from the Angolan coast were reaching Vungu Vungu in
the seventeenth century, well before any slave traders appeared in the zone.
But apart from the fact that trading occurred, little is known at present about
its organization and especially about how the necessary condition of trust
between traders was created. Probably trade over short or medium distances
was conducted by an institution such as hxaro or epanga, in which two
unrelated but trusted partners practiced delayed exchange. Even in the
twentieth century, hxaro was apparently still practiced between Kwanyama
and San.[141]

Hxaro or epanga relationships have probably been the inspiration in the
inner Cunene basin agropastoral zone and the neighboring lands to the

138. See Loeb, *In Feudal*, pp. 121–23, 191–92; Estermann *Ambos*, pp. 181–86 (smiths)
236–50 (diviners); Lang and Tastevin, *Ethnographie*, pp. 148, 174–80 (healers and diviners), 101 (hunters); Estermann, *Nhaneca-Humbe*, pp. 194–95, 249–58 (smiths, hunters,
diviners), 259–60 (diviners).

139. For the requirements of the craft, see Kriger, *Pride of Men*, pp. 55–157.

140. Siiskonen, *Trade*, pp. 68–85 (overview centered on the Ambo); Augusto Bastos, *Traços geraes*, pp. 37–42, and *ocisoko:* 66–70; Brochado, "Noticia" and his
"Descripção."

141. Manuel Viegas Guerreiro, "Ovakwankala (Boximanes)," p. 531.

northwest for the invention of the institution known as *ocisoko* 7/8 (*olupikai* 11 in Nyaneka proper).[142] By the nineteenth century, this was found over most of the agropastoral zone, in the adjacent coastal regions, and as far northwest as Benguela and its hinterland. In principle, this was an alliance or a joking relationship between two matriclans, in which members treated each other as privileged partners. They could seize almost any object they fancied from their partner, refrained from pursuing judicial claims of whatever nature against each other, covered for each other's debts, assisted in each other's funerals, and claimed some material recognition by the partner clan on that occasion. But for any object taken, a more or less equivalent one would be claimed later on (delayed exchange), thus ensuring a flow of goods between communities. Moreover, the relationship seems to have been exercised between adult men, who usually were heads of their respective homesteads and to have been inherited by their successors. In short *ocisoko* seems to be a further development of the epanga or hxaro relationship as the range of partners was now generalized far beyond two individuals. Hence it became quite practical for conducting trade over longer distances. Because clans extended over large areas including many polities and different ethnic groups, travelers could find and trade with *ocisoko* partners nearly everywhere. Nothing is known about the historical development of this institution, but its geographic distribution in the hinterland from Benguela suggests that it developed with the arrival of Portuguese traders on the coast by or after 1600. Yet *ocisoko* may well have existed earlier in order to expedite essential local exchanges, such as those involving salt, metals, cattle, cereals, and even shell beads between different ecological zones or other resources between the coast and its hinterland.[143] Indeed, it is quite likely that the traveling ironsmiths, who are occasionally mentioned as hawking their wares around, conducted their exchanges through *ocisoko* or epanga partners.[144]

142. See Lang and Tastevin, *Ethnographie*, p. 46; Estermann, *Nhaneca-Humbe*, pp. 154–60; Bastos, *Traços*, pp. 66–70. Among the Nyaneka, see Heintze, *Besessenheits-Phänomene*, pp. 15–16. Rather than stressing the mystical nature of the ties of equality involved in these relations as the reason for their existence as Lang and Estermann do, one should interpret these mystical ties as legitimizing existing practice. Although Bastos rightly focuses on the transfer of goods and the geographic extent of the institution, he still did not clearly perceive its commercial character either. He did not realize that in order to build trust, equality and reciprocity are essential requirements for trading partners.

143. Bastos, *Traços*, p. 67, thought that it had to be many centuries old to achieve its huge extension.

144. In the nineteenth century, another form of trading was by caravan (Siiskonen, *Trade*, pp. 76–77, 80–81; "Hugo Hahn's Reise," p. 290b; also Nogueira's trading adventure in *Raça*, pp. 124–31). In the Cuvelai basin, at least during the nineteenth century, par-

History, Environment, and Collective Imagination

This chapter has shown the effects of the introduction of large herds of cattle on the growth in size and in complexity of the societies which adopted them in southern West Central Africa. Already by the onset of our era, sheepherders were obliged to introduce new basic notions of property in order to be able to manage their flocks. Individually owned property also led to the notion of wealth and may have introduced a still rudimentary divide between the haves and the have-nots and perhaps the recruiting of have-nots as labor to help take care of the flocks. But the introduction of larger herds of cattle used for their milk rather than for their meat was something different again. They had to be grazed in more restrictive environments than ovicaprids (goats or sheep) could be. The unit of worthwhile wealth, a head of cattle, was of greater intrinsic value than the previously coveted sheep or goat. The patterns of herding also became somewhat more complex. The milking herd had to be kept intact as much as possible, which required precise dispositions for its inheritance, and matrilineal succession was chosen as the means. The risks of loss by raiding dictated a dispersal of the herds just as the risk for epizootics did; that meant placing portions of a herd in the care of relatives (usually matrilineal) or of cattleless dependents. The risk of rustling also raised the necessity to protect herds at all times and especially during transhumance necessitated the commitment of rather more men to herd the cattle than would otherwise be necessary, thus adding to the labor requirements. As a result of all of these factors, the consequent social structures of descent and of class became more complex than they had been heretofore.[145]

The first cattle herders, certainly the first Njila speakers who kept cattle, were also farmers; thus, agropastoralism developed well before cattle nomadism. Agriculture imposed sedentarization on the cattle-keeping communities and added its own effects to those linked to herding. More precise claims of ownership with regard to territory were one of these effects while, at the same time, the possession of large cattle herds produced the familiar social stratification. The combination of these factors then led to the assumption of formal chieftainship by the wealthiest cattleowners. Later prin-

---

ties were assembled as caravans to conduct long-distance trade. Local rulers strictly controlled this trade and, on the arrival of a caravan at their capitals, they designated a person to supervise the dealings of each trader in the caravan. Is it significant in this context to note that the Ambo did not practice either *ocisoko* or epanga.

145. Given these factors (especially epizootics and cattle rustling), it seems that, on the whole, more people lost their herds and dropped to the bottom layer of society than the reverse.

cipalities grew out of chiefdoms in much of the agropastoral zone but not everywhere. In contrast to the principalities and kingdoms farther north, it strikes one that the ruler of each polity in the agropastoral lands kept a much tighter control over the local units, especially in the Cuvelai basin. Yet paradoxically the organization of the central courts was much less elaborate among agropastoralists and their polities seem to have been more prone to instability and secession than was the case on the planalto.

Contrary to received opinion, we found that the agropastoral system of governance seems to have developed independently at several points within the Cuvelai and the inner Cunene basins[146] and was certainly not borrowed lock, stock, and barrel from farther north. But once they existed and were growing, all the principalities began to influence each other, even while they were still developing new differences between themselves and even though they did maintain old ones. This probably occurred first among principalities in the agropastoral zones but later also between the polities of the planalto and of the agropastoral zones. What was borrowed were small features such as individual titles, less important emblems, a bit of royal etiquette, so that each transfer scarcely affected the institutions overall. Yet as this process of borrowing continued for perhaps a half-millennium between the planalto and the south, and centuries longer within the agropastoral zone itself, its cumulative result was to create a family resemblance between all of these polities. That family resemblance is not the result of a common legacy from a common proto-Njila past, and even less the legacy of some mystical blueprint labeled divine kingship that would have been inherited from East Africa, Egypt, or the Mediterranean,[147] nor is it an ineluctable outcome of a uniform and automatic evolutionary process. The resemblance is simply the outcome of what anthropologists call a process of "peer polity interaction." Each of these polities first grew in a specific way out of specific local conditions so that at first the exigencies of local contingencies actually increased the divergence between them. But later on, constant mutual intercommunication between them over a very long period of time led to greater convergence and finally crafted the familiar face or rather a familiar makeup on fundamentally different faces.

146. For instance, the Ambo term *omukanilwa* 1/2 "king," alongside the usual *hamba* 1n/2, as well as the more frequent use of *elenga* 5/6 for the class of commoner chiefs than in the Cunene basin, along with differences in governance noted above could be adduced as arguments for a separate development in the beginning but they are not conclusive. The whole issue requires more in-depth research.

147. Romantic theories to which, unfortunately, Loeb, *In Feudal*, pp. 10–21, 315–18, still subscribes.

The societies of cattle nomads started around 1300 as agropastoral ones at a time when chiefdoms had hardly developed. Faced with the lack of water, the need to move around, and the fact that milk was even more the mainstay of their diet than was the case farther north, they reorganized their societies in consequence. The result was the creation of autonomous yet interrelated local units articulated into a far-flung network of clans in which the richest persons were the most influential. In addition, the geographic distribution and the requirements of various environments and resources fostered the production of specialized goods by some groups, which then led to trade flows between cattle nomads and others around them by means of delayed exchanges between pairs of hereditary partners. Thus a single large-scale system arose and came to encompass most of northern Namibia and the coastal lands of southern Angola. Thus pastoral nomadic society grew in scale and became internally more complex than it had been in earlier times; yet, in sharp contrast to the agropastoralists, it remained just as decentralized.

The main collective emotional involvement of pastoral nomads and the stuff of their dreams was cattle. Not just because cattle were so important as food, for so had sheep been earlier, yet sheep never evoked the same response. Cattle were the stuff of all important rituals both expressing and creating power and governance. Farther north, however, agropastoralists were not as single-minded about cattle as their nomadic brethren. Here political theater also included major annual agricultural rituals at sowing and harvest times along with the one for cattle and there was a heavy focus as well on a crucial sequence of rites to install new lords and to celebrate the polity they incarnated. Yet, on closer examination, it becomes clear that here too people identified with cattle and celebrated them above all else, even though farming was actually much more important for subsistence. Both the annual ceremonies for cattle and the installation ritual for lords were the reference points and the climax for all others in their symbolic play about government. Leader and cattle vied with each other for attention. If one digs deeper, it then appears that collective imaginations here were, in the last resort, not as fascinated with power as with cattle. For the expressions of governance in such fields as titles, emblems, etiquette, or spatial disposition of the courts remained far less luxuriant than they were on the planalto, while the vocabulary to describe the colors and shape of cattle or to praise them was more exuberant by far than the vocabulary devoted to governance. After all, power among agropastoralists still rested on control over cattle and cattle still created power. Thus both cattle nomads and agropastoralists show that despite their obvious importance, environmental factors did not dictate the focus of collective imagination. That focus remained as unpredictable in advance as that of a dream experience can be.

One should not forget that beyond the overarching institutions of of governance there still existed a rich fabric of other institutions. In this region, one should remember the formalized friendships crucial to trading and for nearly continuous intercommunication between communities and societies to the point that any kind of innovation anywhere quickly came to be known all around. Indeed some information could then provide a stimulus for either a local imitation of the foreign example or for its studious avoidance.[148] Neither should one forget the ties of comradeship forged during the initiations of teenagers. Among girls they merely led to more- or less-enduring friendships between two or, at best, a handful of girls, but among boys collective ties between coevals became long-lasting, especially in the inner Cunene basin, where each graduating promotion formed an age-set. Furthermore, privileged relationships between certain professionals exerted considerable social influence. Together, all of these relationships embroidered a dense pattern of social relationships beyond the framework of institutions regulating kinship, wealth, and governance. Despite their importance, these other social relationships have not been the stuff that has intrigued and fascinated collective imaginations. Why not? Who can really say—but may we think perhaps that collective imaginations are only truly enthralled by features linked to institutions essential for the survival and maintenance of common governance and society?

148. See Nogueira, *Raça,* p. 269, and Wunenberger, "La mission," p. 269, about the means for, rapidity of, and extent of the dissemination of news and information.

4

OF COURTS AND TITLEHOLDERS

EVEN A CURSORY GLANCE AT MAPS OF PRESENT population density in West Central Africa discloses a striking contrast between two nearly adjacent large areas of higher population density inland from the coast in western middle Angola, on the one hand, and all the surrounding regions on the other (map 16). In addition, there exists a set of smaller population clusters strung from east to west around latitude 5° to 7° S and another one in the floodplains of the upper Zambezi.

The two nearly adjacent large population clusters are located on the Benguela planalto, now inhabited by Umbundu speakers, and in the middle Cuanza basin and its environs, now settled by Kimbundu speakers. Neither of these clusters are the product of recent colonial situations. The one in the Cuanza region was already noted around 1580 while the existence of the other was reported by the later eighteenth century and documented in more detail around 1850.[1] It could be argued that these clusters resulted from population movements caused by refugees fleeing Portuguese wars of conquest and slave raiding in the seventeenth and eighteenth centuries. Indeed, considerable population transfers did occur in the Cuanza Valley, especially between ca. 1620 and 1650 when the lands between Massangano and the coast were partly depopulated, while those north of Ambaca saw an influx of refugees.[2] Yet in the wider context even such sizeable movements only slightly displaced the center of gravity of an earlier cluster of high population density just as that center would later gravitate to the lands around Malange after 1856.

1. Filippo Pigafetta and Duarte Lopes, *Description du Royaume*, p. 46, concerning the Kingdom of Ndongo between Cuanza and Lucala, comments, "very dense population, more than one would believe," and p. 36 speaks of "a dense population" in the lands of the middle Kwilu basin. For the planalto, see Heywood and Thornton, "African Fiscal Systems," pp. 213–228 (map of reconstructed population density: p. 221). Data from the Cuanza basin from ca. 1845 to ca. 1855 allow population densities to be reconstructed there, but this has not yet been done.

2. Beatrix Heintze, "Gefährdetes Asyl," pp. 321–41.

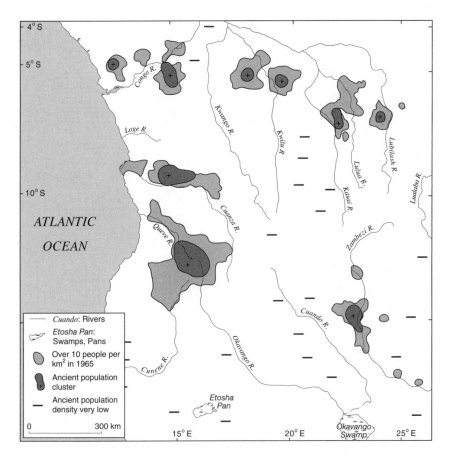

MAP 16. Population Clusters (1000–1500)

Given this case, it is reasonable to assume that something similar occurred on the planalto. Joseph Miller has argued that many people fled from the Cuanza Valley and the Portuguese dominions to the northern and western rims of the planalto starting in the later seventeenth century.[3] But was this displacement substantial enough to produce a dense population over the entire planalto? Quite substantial numbers of undated and mostly unexplored stone ruins of walls and tombs everywhere on planalto seem to attest to the existence of a population cluster, but then again some have

3. Joseph Calder Miller, *Way of Death*, pp. 22, 37–38, summarizes many sources, including Cavazzi. Oral traditions about the dynastic origins of most of the western and northwestern Ovimbundu kingdoms, especially Bailundu, but also some of the kingdoms on the southwestern planalto refer to late–seventeenth-century origins in the Cuanza basin.

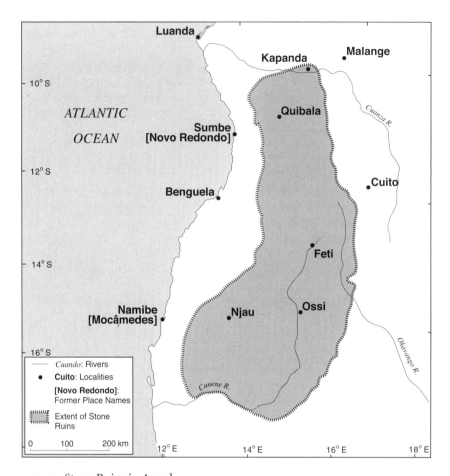

MAP 17. Stone Ruins in Angola

claimed that all of these ruins also date only from the late seventeenth century onward (map 17).[4] Although these claims are certainly exaggerated, only
further archaeological research can settle the chronological issues. Meanwhile the population density map still suggests that clustering first took place
somewhere north of the middle Cuanza basin and also somewhere on the

4. See Mesquitela de Lima, 88–136, but he himself believes that most walls belong
to sites dating before the fifteenth century. Most graves and cemeteries may well date
to the eighteenth and nineteenth centuries, but some definitely existed in the seventeenth century (Manuel Gutierrez, *Archéologie*) and an illustration in Cavazzi (António
de Montecúccolo Cavazzi, *Descrição,* 1:book 1, par. 266, 127). Others may well be older.
Beatrix Heintze gave a state of the question in "Bestattung in Angola," pp. 184–93, up-
dated by a personal communication in April 2002 entitled "Die Steinnekropolen von
Quibala."

planalto. Until further notice then, and taking the known data after ca. 1600 into account, it looks as if significant population clusters did exist before 1500 both on the planalto and in the wider Cuanza basin.[5]

A high density of population leads to more repetitive interactions between communities living in neighboring villages, a situation which favors the emergence of overarching common institutions to regulate or channel such interactions, followed by the recognition of belonging to a common society. One choice for such an overarching common institution can be a monocephalic chiefdom as happened among the agropastoralists of the south. This was also the choice made in the regions of middle Angola, where we now find the highest population densities. The earliest written records already describe the vast majority of the inhabitants there as organized into principalities, themselves composed of partly autonomous chiefdoms, which implies that chiefdoms preceded the creation of principalities or kingdoms. Chiefdoms were formed when a single leader succeeded in obtaining the allegiance of several villages. The development of the new political status and role of chief, superior to and different from those of a village or lineage leader, was a crucial innovation, and when this new status appeared, a new word, a term of reference rather than of address, was coined to designate it (map 18). In middle Angola, this was *soba* 1n/2n,[6] from *-sompá*, attestations of which still exists in the languages of the Moxico subblock as a verb meaning "to try, to arbitrate," which itself is probably proto-Moxico.[7]

As this etymology shows, the new status grew out of a context of formal meetings concerning the resolution of conflicts or the desirability of common action. Apparently the first chiefs gained authority thanks to their skill in resolving disputes between communities. One visualizes heated discussions taking place in the forerunners of those round sheds that later served

5. The other population clusters shown on the map probably also date for the most part from before 1500. This is certainly so for the Lower Congo and the Middle Kwilu (see Pigafetta and Lopes and other written data) and probably so for the Zambezi floodplain and in the present Kasai Province (oral traditions). Archaeological surveys and excavations are sorely needed to elucidate the whole matter.

6. *Soba* in Kimbundu, *swa* in southern Yaka, *sòmá* in Umbundu [tones after Thilo Schadeberg, *Sketch of Umbundu*, p. 55], *hompha* in Kwangari and *hómpa* in Dciriku. All these attest to an original form *-sompá* and not *-còmpá*, for by the end of the first millennium *-c* had long since become *-s* in the whole area.

7. Lwena, *-sòpa* "to try a case, to palaver"; Cokwe, "to enquire into, to judge, to try, to plead a case"; Lwena and Ndembu *sompa*, "to argue, to try a case"; Lucazi, "to discuss, to try" and also *cisompo* "matter under discussion"; Nyemba, "to discuss, to upbraid, to censure" and also *cyisompo* "a question"; proto-Moxico: *-compa*.

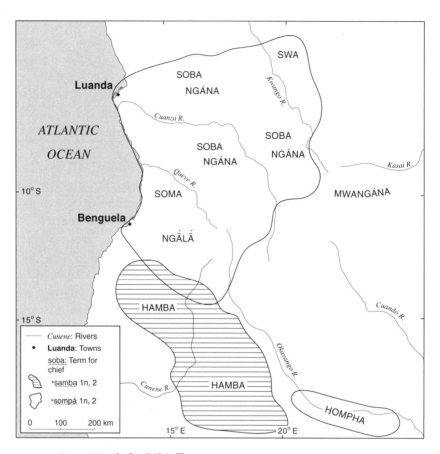

MAP 18. Some Words for "Chief"

as assembly halls throughout the planalto as well as in the lands farther east.[8] Whether such individuals rose to prominence because of their especially wise counsel, or because they had a special talent for summarizing arguments in settling conflicts, or whether they already claimed precedence, perhaps as lineage heads of the first occupants of the soil, we cannot know. Nor do we know whether in the beginning only a single person played this role in a community or whether several "elders" did. Still, by the end of the palaver a single person summed up the consensus reached; once that role became a routine, that person gained a status that could be used to claim territorial control over those villages which were most frequently involved with each

8. They were called *onjango* 9/10 "dance floor" (Umbundu, Nyemba, Ngangela, Lwena, Ndembu from *-jáng- [CS 1936] "to dance about") and *cota* 7/8 (Cokwe) from "to warm oneself."

other and hence between which conflicts were the most frequent. Indeed the very existence of such conflicts and their resolution indicated that these village communities were beginning to coalesce into a single society. The formal acknowledgment of a single chief merely recognized that fact.

Once the status of chief became routine, the chiefdom was born. At first the role of chief may have been bestowed more or less temporarily on a person by the consensus of local leaders, but eventually that role came to be permanently vested in a single person. Once that occurred, succession to this new office became an issue. The ethnographic data suggest that the succession to chieftaincy in these regions became both hereditary and elective because the local village and kingroup leaders chose one individual among the potential heirs. Now, given the disharmony between matrilineal descent and virilocal residence, it was just as likely that succession would occur in the male as in the female line, and in recent centuries both situations have been documented. Nonetheless, where succession was matrilineal, it seems to have rested on the claim that the chief was first in line among the descendants of the founder of the group. That could mean either that he or she was the most appropriate descendant of the first lineage to settle on the territory of the chiefdom or that he or she was the most appropriate descendant of the person who had been chosen as the first chief of the chiefdom.

Given the distribution of the languages in which it occurs, the *-sompá word for chief was probably coined in or near the region where the southern Moxico, Umbundu, and Kimbundu languages met at that time, and, given the link with conflict resolution, probably within an early population cluster. These indications point to a region somewhere not far from the Cuanza River, near or on the northeastern rim of the planalto. As to a date for the emergence of chiefdoms, all one can say is that chieftaincies were created between the time when the first clusters of sedentary villages were being formed and the time that Feti became the capital of a far more complex polity. That, in the present state of knowledge, makes a date in the tenth or eleventh centuries more plausible than any other.

A second term, *ngána* 1/2 "lord, sir, master," also concerns chiefs but as a term of address. It has nearly the same distribution as *-sompa*. However, the word is also applied to any person of distinction who exercises authority over others. It is found in the languages of the Kimbundu and Moxico groups as well as in Umbundu where the form is *ngālā*.[9] *Ngána* 1/2 is derived from

9. *Ngána* in Kimbundu, Cokwe, Lwena, Lucazi, Nyemba (Nyemba also *ñgālā*). Note that *n* in second consonant position between vowels in Kimbundu corresponds to *l* in Umbundu with nasalization of both preceding and following vowels. E.g., *mwene* "owner" (Kimbundu) becomes *mw~el~e* (Umbundu).

ngána 9/6 "wisdom, wit, meaning" in Cokwe and Lwena and hence can be translated as "Wise one."[10] Obviously the term arose in the same palaver context that gave rise to *-sompá. Ngána* 1/2 probably also was first coined in a northern Moxico language because only these languages also invented *ngána* "wisdom" 9/6. Moreover, the reference term for paramount chief there is *mwangána* and *mwanangána.*[11] It is therefore likely that *ngána* 1/2 arose near or in the same place that saw the emergence of *-sompá* 1n/2n as the term of address corresponding to the term of reference.

Once the chiefdom existed, this institution gradually and probably quite slowly spread over a vast region from the upper Cuanza River to the ocean and from Kongo to the southern limits of the planalto, that is over nearly the entire area with higher population densities. Yet chiefdoms did not take root everywhere. Thus by the sixteenth and even nineteenth centuries, there still were some regions between the great bend of the Cuanza River and the Kwango River labeled *Malemba,* a word which implies that territorial rule there was still decentralized and in the hands of a collective body of *lémba* 5/6 leaders.[12] *Lémba* is a word that originated in the Kwango-Kwilu region to designate the leader in charge of a corporate matrilineage, and we will consider its historical significance when the past of the Middle Kwilu region is discussed, for the term was only of marginal importance in middle Angola since it was unknown in this region except for Kimbundu (especially eastern Kimbundu).[13]

10. Ultimately from *-gána* "to tell a story." See Meeussen and CS 772, 773, 775, 776 (but Guthrie gives a low tone). See also the verb form as *-ana* "to swear" in Nyemba. The abbreviated form of the word: *ngáá* + substantive as in Kimbundu seems to be identical with the same form in Kongo, Tio, and languages related to Tio, with the meaning "expert."

11. *Mwanangána* (3/4!) is to be construed as *mwàna* + *ngána* and *Mwangána* (3/4!) as an abbreviation. The *mwàna* 1/2 element occurs as an honorific prefix to names in the form *mwàà.*

12. Pigafetta and Lopes, *Description,* p. 36, is the earliest mention. Later *Malemba* recurs in many documents but does not always refer to the same place. See Heintze, *Fontes,* 1:212, n. 79, and index 413. See also Magyar, *Reisen,* map (*Malemba*) and p. 387 (". . . Mulemba with about 120 settlements administered by just as many headmen [*sekulu*].") Evidently Mulemba is a misspelling of Malemba.

13. The Kimbundu dictionaries include only the well-known cognate verb *-lemba* "to make a gift, to give bridewealth," from which Angola Portuguese *lembamento* "bridewealth" is derived. But *lémba* "leader of matrilineage" is mentioned only in the dictionary that focuses on eastern Kimbundu and Imbangala (Missionários do Espiritu Santo, *Vocabulario,* p. 256, under "*tio*"). Yet Carneiro did give the definition "main person of a family, uncle" for *lemba* or *rilemba* in his "Observações," p. 177. *Lemba* was also the name of the two oldest kinswomen of a bride in the region of Pungo aNdongo according to the report of Diniz, "Observações," p. 144, dated to 1 August 1847.

As time passed, the role of chiefs became more permanent and their authority grew far beyond the mere arbitration of disputes. Soon the local inhabitants of each chiefdom began to speculate about the wellsprings of that authority and to explain it within the framework of existing local beliefs. That, in turn, strengthened the transformation of what had once been a novel status into a "natural" state of affairs, which gave individual chiefs plenty of authority—as long as they were successful. For a chief's authority was attributed to supernatural powers, especially to those which they supposedly derived from their ancestors, that is, their predecessors in the office. Moreover, in some places, and especially so in the northern regions, their legitimacy was also thought to derive from nature spirits who themselves could or could not be considered as ancestors, according to local belief. Indeed, in many places, the chief was perceived as the first occupant of the land, which, among the central Ambundu at least, implied that he or she stood in a special relationship to the local nature spirits, especially those of the rivers. In addition to this, it also came to be generally believed that much of a chief's power was provided by his or her detention of charms, that is, objects with mysterious supernatural properties somehow connected to spirits. Shrines to ancestors or other spirits, tended by the chief himself or by his delegate, began to appear in their residences. Furthermore, everyone believed that chiefs controlled rainfall, and hence the fertility of their lands, because of their supernatural powers. For that reason, they presided over first sowing and/or first-fruit rituals. Over time, the supernatural powers attributed to the chief became more and more exuberant, to the point that it also became more and more evident that newly chosen chiefs could not just start to rule without more ado but had to undergo a special initiation to induct them into what had become a sacralized office.

Despite this accumulation of supernatural support, chiefs were far from monopolizing all authority. Here, too, certain professionals whose spectacular achievements were thought to derive from special relations with supernatural powers had independent powerbases and could sometimes rival the chiefs. Three professions especially were involved, namely, master hunters, masters of metalworking, and diviners. Until very recent times, professionals from these three callings formed associations that met to initiate and to bury each other.[14] The most spectacular professionals were the male or fe-

14. In general Heintze, *Besessenheits-Phänomene*, pp. 103–7 (diviners), 129–31 (hunters), 131–32 (smiths). Most standard ethnographies mention such associations, for instance, for the planalto, see Merran Mc Culloch, *The Ovimbundu*, pp. 12, 14, 38, and Hauenstein, *Hanya*, pp. 154, 156–58 (hunters), 326–38 (female diviners); Read, "Iron-

male diviners, who operated by spirit possession.[15] Once in a trance, they directly relayed the wishes and observations of the spirits who entered into them, which gave them an unchallengeable authority.[16] Eventually such persons came to be thought of as the wives of the spirit which possessed them and hence were called *kimbàndà* (in Kimbundu) or *ocimbàndà* (in Umbundu).[17] The presence of *-bàndà* 7/8 in eastern Central Africa with the meaning "spirit, ghost" is an intriguing but perhaps misleading parallel.[18] *Mbàndà* 7/8 "diviner" seems to be a derivation of *-mbàndà* 1/2 "(favorite) concubine,"[19]

---

smelting and Native Blacksmithing," pp. 44–5. For the Ambundu, see Diniz, *Populações,* pp. 8 (hunters), 53.

15. The use of trance in divining and in healing (combined with sucking objects out of the body of the patient) is very common in southwestern Central Africa as well as among all San and Khoe farther south in contrast to the situation farther east or north. See Beatrix Heintze, *Besessenheits-Phänomene* and Oscar Ribas, *Ilundo.*

16. Divination by spirit possession is not nearly as widespread outside of the area now as within it. It is also very common among contemporary Khoe and San so that spirit possession among Njila speakers in southwestern Central Africa may well have been taken over from autochthonous foragers.

17. CS 51 gives an incomplete distribution of *-mbàndà* 7, 8 "healer" to which all the languages of the Moxico group should be added, as well as Nyaneka, Nkhumbi, and Kuvale, but not Kwanyama, Ndonga, or Herero. No useful chronology can be proposed at this time for the emergence of the term.

18. See CS 50 for an incomplete distribution. One should add at least Valley Tonga, Kimbundu (the form there is *kianda*), and the passive forms current in Nyoro, Rwanda, and Rundi. This is an Eastern Bantu form. Were it not for Kimbundu *kianda* and given the distribution of *-mbàndà* 7/8 "diviner" in a single block, one would explain this as a transfer accompanied by a change in form from the eastern word for "ghost." As CS 50/51 states, the relationship, if any, between the two forms remains obscure. Everything considered, I think that the similarity between the forms is accidental and that the form for "diviner" probably derives from southwestern Angola from that for "(favorite) concubine" and later spread throughout Angola. Such diviners were certainly present in the region of the Ndongo kingdom well before 1500 since the kings of Ndongo chose a number of official diviners or *shingila* from among them.

19. In Herero, Ndonga, Kwanyama, and Nyaneka as "queen, (favorite?) concubine" and in Rund and Mbunda as "wife." In Kongo, *mumbanda* "queen" (1652), and now: *mumbànda* "sister or wife of a *lémba* priest activating a *nkisi* or assistant of a medicine man" and in the southern dialects "queen." See also Mbala *mbáánda* "friend." Given its present discontinuous distribution, this word for concubine seems to be quite old in contrast to the word for diviner. Lacerda "Noticia da Cidade," p. 641, defines *mumbanda* among the Ovimbundu as wife of any man but the king. Rund *mbánd* and Mbunda *mbanda* (Johnston) "wife," but *mumbanda* "grown girl" in Lucazi. One notes that *mbanda* 1/2 does not occur in the languages that have *-mbanda* 7, 8 "diviner," except for Umbundu, Nyaneka, and Kuvale, which may therefore indicate that the latter innovation was coined in that region.

which explains why male diviners dressed as women and often were passive homosexuals.[20] The -*mbàndà* diviners enjoyed considerable authority, independently of and parallel to that of the chiefs, an authority to which chiefs could not remain indifferent for long and which many of them eventually attempted to co-opt.

All the elaborations on the status of chief did not arise in the same chiefdom nor even necessarily in adjacent chiefdoms. Rather the innovations enumerated here appeared one by one and in different places, each one as a new consequence or inference drawn from previously held local worldviews. Given their political efficiency, many of these were then later adopted in neighboring chiefdoms. Later still, when polities were of much larger scale than the chiefdom, this mutual piecemeal borrowing of the most attractive local ideas, practices, and interpretations concerning authority would lead to a widespread homogeneity of political culture over large regions.

Once chiefdoms had become well entrenched, the incidence of quarrels between neighboring chiefdoms over the allegiance of individual border settlements tended to increase and could easily lead to fighting, especially in more densely populated regions.[21] Various ways were followed to cope with such situations. Thus two chiefdoms might form a permanent alliance for mutual assistance against outsiders. This was called *ocisoko* in Umbundu just like the trading alliances between matriclans in southern Angola, even though matriclans did not develop on the planalto.[22] Sometimes a number of chiefs would form a temporary alliance in order to resist more powerful neighbors as happened, for instance, in the early 1630s when five chiefs formed a "republic" to resist the Portuguese.[23] In such circumstances, such

---

Kimbundu also has *ki-anda* 7, 8 "Nature spirit (spirits of lakes, rivers, springs, mountains and caves)," which reconstructs as *-*banda* and hence could well be the source for the form with the initial nasal—which may have first appeared to place the word in either class 1a, 9, or 10.

20. Heintze, *Besessenheits-Phänomene*, pp. 95–99; Hermann Baumann, *Das Doppelte Geschlecht*. What happened when the diviner's spirit was supposed to be female remains unclear. In the known cases, female spirits were married to other spirits and the diviner may have been a co-wife.

21. All available land was probably occupied as population densities rose to four persons per square kilometer. See Vansina, "Le régime foncier," pp. 899–926, for a landscape that is roughly comparable to central Angola except for the rainfall, which was much higher and more reliable.

22. Edwards, *The Ovimbundu*, pp. 13–14, *contra* Childs, *Umbundu*, pp. 114–15. Moreover the abstract *usoko* 14 is "royal power" in Umbundu.

23. Corrêa, *História de Angola*, 1:242–43.

allies often accepted the temporary military leadership of one among them.[24] Such an arrangement could become permanent and the chosen leader could turn into the overlord of the others and fuse them into a single larger polity, a principality. But sometimes also a chief managed to subjugate another or others by force and was then recognized as paramount.

If the emergence of principalities seems often to have been prompted by a desire for greater security, this, nonetheless, was rarely achieved. For once ignited, the process of territorial enlargement continued on and on, as larger polities were tempted to raid and to subdue smaller and weaker ones around them until a regional balance of equal forces came into being. In such a climate of insecurity and war, it made sense to fortify capital sites. Some of the stone walls and other defenses on many fortified hilltops in central Angola may well belong to this period.[25] Yet, this pattern of a slow increase in scale was not a foreordained conclusion. Sometimes one very successful polity managed to overrun an unusually large number of others within a few years and suddenly turn itself into a large kingdom, out of all proportion in size with the surrounding polities. This seems to have occurred more than once, the earliest known case being that of Feti, a site which, in its later stages, is best explained as the capital of a very large kingdom.[26]

Feti: An Angolan Zimbabwe?

Feti is one of the largest known ancient sites anywhere in West Central Africa.[27] Its destruction first by a fortune seeker, Júlio Diamantino de Moura

24. For instance, the alliance led by Ngola aNjimbu in 1637 or the "Giraulo" alliance in Quilengues led by Kiambela against the Portuguese in 1722. See Ralph Delgado, *O Reino,* pp. 133, 256–60.

25. See note 4 and C. Ervedosa, *Arqueologia,* pp. 395–413; Rodrigues, "Construções bantas," pp. 169–89 and endmap; Lima, *Os Kiaka,* 1:90–136; Gutierrez, *L'Art,* pp. 30–32. The bells found at Feti may well be another indication of the importance of war. In recent times, a bell (double and clapperless) *lunga* 5/6 came to be synonymous of army since the dictionary uses the term to designate an army chief (*verbo* "chefe da guerillha").

26. Possibly one or several of the other large undated sites enclosed by stone walls elsewhere on or near the planalto may well prove to be as ancient as Feti and to have been early capitals of other kingdoms. But Feti is the only one claimed by Ovimbundu traditions as the cradle of their kingdoms. Obviously, also the Ndongo and Matamba kingdoms farther north arose independently from each other, as well as from Feti and from Kongo.

27. Already in 1893, Lecomte said it was "at least as large as Lisbon." B. Heintze, *Alfred Schachtzabel,* pp. 52–53 (quote from n. 1). The site was soon famous. It was visited both by Schachtzabel and de Lima Vidal in 1913 and later by Keiling, Moura, and Childs.

in 1945 and 1947, and later by the construction of a hydroelectric dam, is a grand disaster for the history of Angola. Despite the brutal and disorderly manner in which Moura uncovered the finds from the site, they simply cannot be ignored.[28] It presented itself as a plateau near the confluence of the Cunene and Cunhangâma Rivers, three kilometers away from the latter, in which the stone pillars of an ancient bridge still stood in 1913.[29] On the plateau arose a stone "pyramid," 5 meters high and 15 meters on each side. A circular ditch 6 meters wide and 5 meters deep surrounded it at a distance of some 80 meters and was itself surrounded by another circular ditch also 6 by 5 meters with a radius of 150 meters. Unlike the first one, this one was not centered on the pyramid. Farther away to the north followed another ditch about 500 meters long according to Moura, but according to Ernest Lecomte it ran from one river to the other, cutting the promontory off and it was 6 meters deep and 10 to 12 kilometers long. Tangent to that ditch was a mound some 150 meters long, 4 to 5 meters high, and 6 to 10 meters wide.[30] This was constituted by ashes covered by a layer of earth 70 centimeters thick, which Moura thought had been brought up from the river valleys. These ashes also contained ceramics, many animal bones from cattle and wild ruminants, as well as human remains, including skulls and jawbones. Farther north still and a little higher than this mound, one encountered several (9?) round mounds each with a radius of 3 to 5 meters and 1.50 meters high, all flanked by rockslabs, of which some weighed more than 100 kilograms. These mounds consisted of red earth taken from the ditches. Additionally, the pyramid was separated from this mound by about 1 hectare of dark soil under which lay a network of empty galleries that are probably best interpreted as evidence of mining. Finally in 1913, Alfred Schachtzabel still saw the remnants of standing walls that were unreported by Moura.[31] From Moura's description, one can calculate that the site's surface must have been at least 75,000 meters square (7.5 hectares), while according to Lecomte it was many times larger.[32]

Typically enough, both Lecomte and Schachtzabel thought it was the work of white men. Among other similar sites, Ossi was perhaps equally large.

28. Moura, "Uma história," pp. 55–75, and Ervedosa, *Arqueologia*, pp. 210–20 and ill. LIX A B; Ervedosa transcribes part of the preceding.

29. Heintze, *Alfred Schachtzabel*, p. 53.

30. The estimate of 5 meters high and 10 wide was made by G. M. Childs.

31. Heintze, *Alfred Schachtzabel*, p. 53.

32. Probably the size was much larger than Moura's estimate because he found no living quarters, some of which were probably located outside of the 150-meter radius ditch; 75,000 square meters is four times larger than Nqoma or two and one-half times larger than Toutswe.

The extent of the disaster becomes apparent from the description of the excavations near and under the pyramid. Apparently, at ground level and posed on flagstones, the pyramid covered a large standing rock, 1.75 meters high and flanked by two large (75 centimeters long) and many small iron arrows. Under this level, Moura encountered at least two occupation layers, of which the uppermost one contained graves and some 400 hoes (75 in one spot, apparently a tomb with two occupants). In the underlying layer various pits had been dug, one of which may have been the tomb of a blacksmith as it contained twelve hoes, one smith's hammer, and one iron chisel located half a meter above four skulls. Among many other small finds that are not described, this layer also contained a frame made of iron rods, which, in his reconstruction, looks like a bedstead. Many pits containing ashes, stones, and iron implements, including knives, hoes ("of three now unknown types"), and arrows were also located. Although most objects found at the site, including all the ceramics, were discarded, a number of iron implements were taken away and housed at the museum of Huambo. A clapperless bell, two cowbells with clapper, four hoes, one anvil, one hammer, two tusks (warthog or hippo?), many arrowheads, two knives, and at least one ornamental spearhead can be seen on the photographs included in Ervedosa's work. Moreover, already in 1893, Lecomte, who himself took a single souvenir, was told that wonderful objects such as arrows in iron, copper bows, and the metal statue of a dog had been found and removed from the site. The bells recall the three cowbells "in brass" and the ancestral bow which were among the most revered emblems of kingship in Bailundu.[33] This, more than Moura's imprecise report about the graves found, has convinced us that Feti was indeed a kingdom.

Later, Gladwyn Childs took two samples for carbon dating from the 150 meter long mound or "kitchen midden." The bottom one was dated to 722±100 ad and one from a high middle level to 1262±65 ad.[34] The site was

33. Hastings, "Ovimbundu," pp. 39–40, 42–43.
34. Childs, "The Kingdom of Wambu (Huambo)," p. 368 n. 2, and letter of 23 October 1962: Charcoal from the bottom of a shaft at the south side of the kitchen midden at 2.5 meters depth with animal bones, pottery and iron implements in associated burials. Dated to 1240±100 = 722±100 ad. Another sample from the same shaft at about 1.5 meters depth yielded 700± 65 = 1262±65 ad. One remembers that the top 70 centimeters consisted of barren soil. Thus the distance between the top of the occupation levels and this sample was 80 centimeters and the distance between the level of this sample and the bottom 100 centimeters. This means that the occupation continued for some centuries after the second level. Many more dates from many more features and levels in association with specific remains would be needed to obtain a solid chronology. Meanwhile there seems to be no reason to dismiss the two we have. These two dates

then first occupied in the ninth or even tenth centuries and, given the place of the second sample, lasted apparently for several centuries after the late thirteenth or fourteenth centuries.[35]

Despite all the deficiencies of the Moura report, one can at least state that Feti is characterized by its size, its extensive defensive works (especially the outer ditch), and stone structures, including walls, all of which suggest a considerable input of labor. Moreover, the galleries suggest mining—perhaps for iron given the number of iron objects of all sorts—while the hoards of new hoes suggest both their use as objects of wealth and indicate that some inhabitants were quite wealthy. So does the apparent consumption of large numbers of cattle as well as of game. It should be noted as well that Feti lay on an ecotone near the southern edge of the planalto in a spot from where one could easily travel from this land of farmers into the agropastoral lands to the south while the abundance of hoes as well as the mining activities may well indicate that it also was a flourishing emporium of trade. Be that as it may, Feti was obviously the central settlement of a complex society, and, given the existence of large kingdoms on the planalto later on and the presence of royal emblems on the site, it was probably the capital of a kingdom. The chronology for the site, however, spans more than five centuries. By 800, the site may well have been occupied by a modest settlement of iron-using farmers. It developed later into a large kingdom, but the prosperity of its inhabitants may well have declined well before the end of all occupation on the site. All one can say on present evidence is that its heyday as a large kingdom may have lasted several centuries. If and until further research yields better dating, we have to accept that the Feti kingdom probably emerged during the thirteenth century. It lasted "for another 80 centimeters of accumulated deposits," which I interpret to correspond to between two and three centuries.[36] The heyday of the kingdom occurred then during the fourteenth,

---

are uncalibrated and a Southern Hemisphere calibration is likely to yield calendar dates about a century later.

35. Taking the numbers at face value, it took 540 years to deposit 1 meter of remains, so if the rate of deposition in the mound remained constant, the top 80 centimeters would take 432 more years to 1694! But the top layer of 70 centimeters (if natural deposit) militates against accepting this result, for that would yield a date of 2072.

36. The rate of deposit was certainly faster than the earlier rate of accumulation between 722 and 1262 because one presumes that the site contained more people, producing more detritus (e.g., pottery, animal bones) and, for the elite at least, also probably more per person. The earlier rate was 540 years (around 20 generations of 27 years each) for 100 centimeters or 0.18 centimeters per year or 4.86 per generation. At double that rate post-1262 for 80 centimeters, we obtain an end date of 1484 AD and between 8 and 9 generations.

fifteenth, and perhaps early sixteenth centuries. The very fact that Feti, un-like some other major old sites such as Ossi,[37] is well remembered in Ovim-bundu oral traditions, gives some support to the idea that its demise oc-curred later rather than earlier, perhaps around 1500. Only further archaeological research of other ruins can establish whether Feti really was the first large kingdom, as Ovimbundu traditions seem to imply, or indeed even the only one.

Principalities on the Planalto

It is evident from ethnographic data gathered during the last two centuries that Umbundu speakers developed the political organizations of their para-mount chiefdoms and kingdoms for the most part by elaborating continu-ally on already-existing political institutions and practices.[38] Thus as chiefs became kings and kings became even more powerful, they acquired an ever more sacralized status: i.e., rituals of kingship became more elaborate, em-blems more numerous and more revered, the royal household larger and larger, and the controls over the legitimacy of succession more precise. The process of development is well illustrated by the change of meaning by which *elombe* 5/6 came to mean "palace" or "residential quarter of the king within the capital." Its original meaning was "shrine for a royal ancestor" and each chief's residence contained several such shrines.[39] But as royal power grew,

37. Ervedosa, *Arqueologia*, pp. 409–13. Here the inhabitants knew only that the site was older than anyone could remember and probably a creation of God.

38. Most of the early ethnographic evidence stems from Viye (Magyar) and Bailundu (Hastings). Yet we can use these data to reconstruct the underlying basic structural fea-tures attested to for all these kingdoms, but at the unavoidable price of foregoing much concrete detail. Despite the enlargement of scale, no new term for king arose and *soma* remained the designation for all leaders at all levels. Still, a new word was introduced from the south, namely, *ocisambo* 7/8 for "principal chief."

39. Valente and Le Guennec have *elombe* 5/6 "palace [*paço*]"; Sanders "house of the chief"; but Valente and Le Guennec, as well as Hastings, have *eyemba* 5/6 for the pre-cise meaning "sleeping house of the king." See also Hastings, "Ovimbundu," pp. 34, 35, for *velombe* "of the palace." Dignitaries or courtesans came then to be called *vakwelombe* (= *vakwa* +), or as Magyar, *Reisen*, p. 237, has it in shorthand (also Umbundu 247) 237, *erombe*. The belief that kings embodied supernatural spirits is not unique. Thus the Kuba king was deemed to become a nature spirit, after he died—and was from time to time possessed by the spirits of his predecessors. In Kimbundu generally, *rilombe* 5/6 means "shrine" and in Libolo "shrines in the residence of a chief containing a tooth and a bone of the deceased chief" (Vidal, *Por Terras,* p. 112). All these are derived from CS 653 *-dómb* "to ask for," which occurs in all the languages for the region except in modern Kim-bundu. In Umbundu, ancestral chiefly shrines are now called *etambo* 5/6 (Hastings,

it eventually came to be believed, as in Bailundu around 1900, that all the ruling ancestors of the chief were supposed to reside in his body. Hence his palace became their residence and *elombe* became the palace. That happened well before the seventeenth century.[40] A direct link between Feti and recent evidence from Bailundu concerns royal emblems. The three cowbells and one bow in brass (copper?) that were major recent emblems of kingship with magical power in Bailundu irresistibly recall the bells found at Feti; the story about the copper bow that had been taken from Feti reminds one that Bailundu's most sacred emblem was the bow of its founder.[41]

Similarly royal tribunals were but the old chiefly tribunal writ large, formal military institutions developed out of the preceding occasional calls to arms, and more formal fiscal institutions grew out of the occasional gifts to or corvée for elders or chiefs.[42] Older chiefdoms survived as territorial units within the new kingdoms and even the larger paramount chiefdoms survived as such as parts of a larger kingdom, although such units were now designated by a new word, *etumbu* 5/6 "portion" or "province."[43]

"Ovimbundu," p. 39), which is used from the seventeenth century onward to designate the funerary ritual in Kimbundu as well as a tomb for the Jaga of Cassange. (Cavazzi, *Descrição*, p. 2: "*tambi*") *-tamb* is widespread in the area. The word stems from CS 1659, *-támbí* "footprint," itself derived from one of CS 1654, 1655, 1656, 1657, *-támb* "to call, to offer, to receive, to travel." The relationship between *elombe* and *ocilombo* 7/8 "camp, camping ground," a term derived from the same root, remains unclear. *Ocilombo* is not to be confused with *olumbo* "fence, palissade" in Umbundu and Nyaneka or with Kongo and Kimbundu *lumbu*. Hastings, "Ovimbundu," p. 278, erroneously translated it as such to describe a funeral festival for medicine men.

40. Hastings, "Ovimbundu," pp. 44, 47 (situation observed around 1920).

41. Ibid., pp. 39, 42–43. The bells were called *olongunga*, sing. *ongunga* 9 (*ongonge* in Valente and Le Guennec). The three "white balls" (pp. 40, 46), which were the other essential emblem of kingship, probably contained kaolin or *pembe* (as well as medicines), a substance well known from all over West Central Africa as an essential element in the installment of chiefs and kings. A bow was also an essential emblem in the Ndongo kingdom while clapperless bells were insignia of note there.

42. "To pay tribute" is *-lambula* and "tribute" *ulambu* 3/4 or *ocivanda* 7/8, which also means a "share" or a "duty tax." The form *-dàmbú* 3/4 occurs also in Kimbundu and Kongo as well as over large parts of the savanna woodlands area of central Africa (CS 484, 489 for partial distribution) and seems old. It is cognate to and may be derived from CS 487 *-dàmbá* 7/8 "raffia cloth," itself from CS 483 *-dàmb* "to sprawl" (Vansina, *Paths*, p. 293). This indicates that Umbundu *ulambu* is a late transfer from Kimbundu. Magyar still cites it as *mulambo*, a Portuguese rendering of the Kimbundu form (Magyar, *Reisen*, pp. 204, 248) and Umbundu (Fodor, pp. 214, 252).

43. Child, *Umbundu*, pp. 23–24, from *-tumbulula* "to transplant." Compare with Lweta *-tumbu* 1/2 "supreme leader."

The major institutional transformation within the kingdoms occurred at their capitals. These now contained not only more inhabitants than the earlier settlements of chiefs did, but grouped different categories of people in different quarters according to their status and role. Thus there were quarters for the royal household, for the major groups of courtiers, and for the ordinary population of farmers who cultivated the surrounding land. Hence, a royal capital was designated by a new word, *ombala,* while the residence of a subordinate chief was *ocikanzu* 7/8.[44] As more complex government required specialized officials, a new word, *ocinduri* 7/8, came to designate such officials. These officials "are the oldest slaves of the state and hence they are the electors [of the kings]."[45] Eventually the number of titles would multiply to the extent that by 1916 no less than 107 of them are enumerated at the Bailundu court.[46] This luxurious proliferation marvelously illustrates the workings of the collective imagination here. In some ways, politics and the political establishment are a theater, a make-believe world in which real power can derive from imagined majesty. The proliferation also tells us that the court and its appearance were of utmost interest to these societies. This plethora of titles irresistibly recalls a similar abundance of terms to describe the appearance of cattle in the south and, as we shall later see, the cornucopia of masks found in eastern Angola and southern Congo, where the recognition of dozens of social positions became the cynosure of collective imagination.

As the polities and especially their capitals grew in size, their societies also became more and more diversified and intricate, as the situation in the nineteenth century shows.[47] Hierarchical categories emerged, which eventually developed into a complex network of statuses that went far beyond

44. *Ombala* 9, etymology not traced. The form is not related to *-bádí* "open space" (CS 28) as in Kongo *mbazi* 9 or Tio *mbali* 9, both meaning "court." Lacerda "noticia," p. 642, dated 10 November 1797, defines *Quicanzo* as "the suffragan towns or places which have their *macotas* [elders] or captains." Le Guennec and Valente have *ocikanjo* 7/8 as "suburban town (aldeia suburbana)" and Childs, *Umbundu,* p. 24, remarks that Magyar used this term for "province," the original meaning being "branch" (*okanja*). He claims that *ocikanjo* was coined for "province" under European influence. Still, see also Siiskonen, *Trade,* p. 48, *oshikanjo* "provincial chief" in the Ambo languages.

45. Citation from Lacerda, "Noticia," p. 641. He calls them *quindares* and *quindures.* *Ocinduli* 7/8 is derived from *enduli* 5, 6, a species of small bees. According to Hauenstein, *Hanya,* p. 244, the titleholders swarm around the king just as these bees like to swarm around their nest. At the court they represented the people as opposed to both the royals and the nobility.

46. Hastings, "Ovimbundu," pp. 54–73, lists all of them.

47. Unfortunately there is no evidence at all to trace even the rudiments of a history of social change after the emergence of kingdoms for lack of adequate linguistic data. As Umbundu became standardized over the centuries, as the necessary detailed dialect

the cliche of a threefold social stratification into nobles by birth, free persons, and slaves. The title system crossed those categories since titles came to be bestowed on persons in all three categories and especially on slaves.[48] Matrilinearity coupled with virilocality created several groups of kin. In most cases, the village headman was a "big man" related to most men in his settlement by patrilineal descent, or at least by a chain of father-son relationships, and his patrilineal ancestral ghosts protected their descendants. In most other matters, however, matrilineal descent prevailed. Thus property, such as cattle, trade goods, or slaves, was inherited matrilineally; witchcraft only operated within matrilineages, and in contrast to protective patrilineal ancestors, matrilineal ancestral ghosts were held responsible for disease and even death. Yet these descent groups operated only locally. Neither patriclans or matriclans existed. Beyond the village, only territorial political relationships prevailed and political succession seems to have been bilateral: any close descendant of a chief or a king, whether by a slave mother (often preferred!) or by a free mother could be chosen by the titleholders as a successor.[49] Slaves did not form a homogeneous social class either since both the most powerful titleholders and the most overworked menials were slaves.[50]

---

studies do not exist, and as it becomes impossible in most cases to establish even a relative chronology between words, the method of "words and things" is of little assistance here. Hence we have to rely on the ultimate outcome of social change as described mostly by nineteenth-century ethnographic evidence, while keeping the powerful social effects of the Atlantic slave trade and of Portuguese occupation constantly in mind. This explains why only a generalized overview can be presented here rather than a detailed description that is certain to be anachronistic.

48. Bastos, *Traços*, pp. 22–24, and Hastings, "Ovimbundu," pp. 51, 54.

49. Hastings, "Ovimbundu," (basically matrilineal except for some patrilineal) pp. 17–19, 84–85, 88–90, 94–95; Bastos, *Traços*, pp. 33–34; Childs, *Umbundu*, pp. 202–15; McCulloch, *Ovimbundu*, pp. 17–20 (double descent), 24; Edwards, *Ovimbundu*, pp. 14–17, 17–19, 12 (political succession), 13–14 (*Ocisoko* as alliance).

50. A class of hereditary servants or slaves certainly emerged centuries before the Portuguese arrived on the coast. The appearance of the term *ngãlã* "master" implies the notion of subordinate persons, but these need not have been slaves, i.e., persons without kin. Still slavery developed out of that kind of background even though we do not know precisely how (as pawns, as prisoners, as criminals?). Slaves, having no kin, were entirely dependent on their masters, a situation nineteenth-century (and earlier?) kings seem to have soon exploited when they began to choose most of their *ocinduli* 7/8 among their slaves. Eventually this even reached the point in Bailundu that royal sons by a slave woman came to be preferred as successors to the throne, for thus a king would be succeeded by a son despite the general rule of matrilineal descent since the "matrilineage" of the son and his slave mother was deemed to be the king's own! (see Bastos, *Traços*, p. 26, and Hastings, "Ovimbundu," pp. 51–52; the queen was always a slave).

Moreover, even the menials came to be divided into two groups: household slaves, i.e., born within a household, and people newly enslaved as the results of wars or fines. People were perhaps already enslaved in these times, as happened in later times, to atone for proven witchcraft by one of their relatives. Nor were all menials slaves either. Some were bondspeople or pawns, that is, persons who worked and were treated like slaves but who could still be redeemed by their kinsfolk if these were able to pay off the original debt.[51] Finally many diviners, great hunters, and renowned metalworkers were believed to enjoy the protection of powerful spirits, were grouped in their own respective associations, and enjoyed as much power and as elevated a status as any political authority barring only the king—and then not always.[52]

The elaboration of such an intricate and sometimes far-flung socio-political structure was possible only because it rested on sturdy environmental foundations. Much of the planalto was free of malaria and tsetse, which may help to explain the rise in population densities. True, from time to time the lack or irregularity of rainfall led to crop failures and food scarcity, and when a drought lasted over several years, there erupted severe famines that could not always be mitigated by exchange, by the gathering of famine foods, or by the use of riverside irrigation.[53] People were well aware that farming was the bedrock that made everything else possible. Whenever the rains failed, they begged for rain at the graves or settlements of former kings.[54] The farming system itself did not change much during the centuries that saw the growth of principalities and kingdoms but there were improvements: some subsidiary crops, such as plantain, sugarcane, eggplant, water yams, and perhaps taro, were introduced, while eventually people also began to establish irrigated riverside gardens (*onaka* 9/10). Whether the invention of the double-handed hoe, which could be dragged through wet soil, was related to these irrigated gardens is unknown.

Meanwhile cattle were certainly appreciated, but in the region of Feti and on most of the planalto, they were kept in small herds and raised only for beef. Agropastoralism did not develop and milk was not consumed. Hence there was a constant need to import cattle and hides from the south or west

51. Bastos, *Traços,* p. 34 (mentions also pawns).

52. See Edwards, *Ovimbundu,* p. 14 and n. 18; Rodrigues, "Construções," p. 184, for a twentieth-century case of the ousting of a royal line by a diviner in Quibala.

53. See Miller, "The Significance of Drought," pp. 17–61; Keiling, *Quarenta anos,* pp. 17–18 (famine in 1916 around Caconda and how the population attempted to cope with it).

54. For instance, Rodrigues, "Construções," pp. 170, 175, 179–80; Moura, *Uma historia,* pp. 56, 59, 63.

in return for other products, such as mats, baskets, or hoes. Strings of beads made on the northwestern portion of the plateau from the shells of the large snail *ondongo* 9/10 that lived primarily in the misty forests of the western escarpments occupied by the Mbui and Sele were probably already then another major commodity for export.[55] Ecological factors certainly fed other trade links, especially to the west where several major ecotones lay close to each other. Goats thrived on the escarpments, sheep and sheepskins abounded in the steppes to the southwest, and the coast produced fish, shells, and vast amounts of salt.[56] Specialized industrial products fashioned in places blessed with special resources and special know-how were also exported. Iron or copper products were the most precious, but less valuable products such as mats or furs were traded as well.[57] The result was to throw a dense net (in which various capitals were the knots) of interlocal social relationships over the planalto and thus to raise the standards of living all across the highlands.

One might think that the elaboration of the complex political structure and "divine kingship" just sketched occurred at Feti and was inherited by all the kingdoms which succeeded it on the planalto since the site is famous in Ovimbundu oral traditions as the supposed cradle of origin for all Ovimbundu in general (map 19). It is also the place from where the rulers of Ngalangi and Wambu, two of the largest Ovimbundu kingdoms, were said to have come. This claim is most plausible for Ngalangi because everyone outside that kingdom also recognized its derivation from Feti.[58] Later emi-

55. See Rodrigues, "Construções," p. 176. Imported from Amboim and Seles (still today!), fashioned by northwestern groups of the Bailundu area in Pambangala, Cela, and Bailundu, and traded south to Kwanyama for cattle, recently at the price of four strings for one beast.

56. See Bastos, *Traços,* pp. 37–41, for a rich description of this interenvironmental trade as he saw it ca. 1900 facilitated by *ocisoko* relationship between clans in the western and southern regions. Note that -*landa* "to buy" in Umbundu was also used throughout the south but differed from Kimbundu –*somba*, which must have been the case before the arrival of the Portuguese as well. Hence trade relations beyond the planalto to the north were much weaker than to the south.

57. Ibid., pp. 41–42, lists specialized products such as hoes, knives, bush knives, spears, bracelets, rings, mats, baskets, hampers, leather, and even brooms.

58. It is clear from Childs, "Kingdom," pp. 368–70, that, according to oral tradition, Cimbili, an early king of Wambu, was of local origin and was associated with the site Nganda (hence the "Vanganda"). The claimed link with Feti there is not acknowledged elsewhere on the planalto. Ervedosa, *Arqueologia,* pp. 219–20, summarizes the relevant literature for Ngalangi. A claimed secondary link to Viye (Bihe) disagrees with the traditions of origin, for the first dynasty there and the tradition proposed by Childs and Hauenstein for the origin of the dynasty of the Ngola of Pungo aNdongo seems to be a late fabrication unsupported by the more detailed oral traditions that follow both for

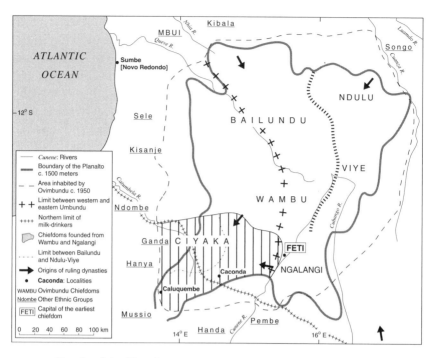

MAP 19. People of the Planalto

grants from Ngalangi are said to have founded the smaller kingdoms on the southern edge of the plateau while Ciyaka is said to derive from Wambu.[59] But none of the other kingdoms were founded from either Wambu or Ngalangi.

According to its oral traditions, the Bailundu kingdom which became the most powerful of all from the eighteenth century onward was founded by an emigrant from a small kingdom in Kibala, a Kimbundu-speaking area, and the rulers of Kibala themselves are said to have immigrated from the region of Pungu aNdongo to the northeast. Later emigrants from Bailundu are said to have then founded Sambu and other smaller kingdoms on the northwestern parts of the planalto.[60] Farther to the northeast, the Kingdom of Viye

---

Wambu and Hanya. See Childs, "Kingdom," pp. 368, 370; Hauenstein, *Hanya*, pp. 11–12; but note also that *Feti* means "beginning." On the link between Feti, Ngalangi, and Wambu, see Keiling, *Quarenta anos*, pp. 90–91, 108–10.

59. For Ciyaka: see Lima, *Os Kiaka*, 1:217–22, and Childs, "Kingdom," pp. 176–78; for Ngalangi: see Childs, "Kingdom," pp. 174–76, and Hauenstein, "L'ombala," who also discusses the foundation of Ngola, Kalukembe, and Ganda.

60. Childs, "Kingdom," pp. 171–72 (Bailundu) and 178–79 (Sambu); Rodrigues, "Construções," pp. 182–84 (Kibala, Bailundu); Keiling, *Quarenta anos*, pp. 100–102 (Sambu).

seems to have first emerged as part of a larger kingdom, which included territory now occupied by Songo (Kimbundu) speakers to its northeast, well beyond the Cuanza River.[61] Later this kingdom broke into two parts, of which Viye was one. Ndulu's first ruler also was said to have come from the same northeastern region.[62]

The earliest written source about kingdoms on the planalto dates from the 1630s and mentions the large realm of Muzumbu aKalunga vaguely located somewhere inland, east or perhaps northeast of the Cunene River.[63] Later, but well before 1680, this same kingdom is said to have fought a war with the Kingdom of Cassange. It was still famous in 1755 and then located way upstream along the Cuanza River; it was still there and still significant in 1797. But then it suddenly disappeared between 1797 and 1805![64] We think that this is the kingdom mentioned in the Viye traditions and that Viye broke free from it in the late seventeenth or early eighteenth century. Perhaps the Kingdom of Ndulu was also one of its offshoots.

Thus Ngalangi and Wambu, the heirs of Feti, were responsible only for a small portion of the later kingdoms on the planalto. For that reason alone it would be unwise to think that the "typical Ovimbundu kingdom" was a legacy of Feti, even though these two kingdoms could have succeeded to Feti.[65] First, one should remember that any social organization always undergoes change, so that a "typical kingdom" can at best be a snapshot of a

61. Magyar, *Reisen*, pp. 265–69, is the oldest and most reliable of the reported versions. If one disregards the then recent additions relating to the Rund Kingdom and the Jaga of Cassange, its gist is that Viye and a good deal of Songo land were once part of the same kingdom, which I am tempted to identify with that of Muzumbu aKalunga. For Keiling, *Quarenta anos,* pp. 19–20, the first kingdom was supposedly Nkhumbi, while the interpretation of Childs, *Umbundu,* pp. 172–74, is obviously forced.

62. For Ndulu, Childs (*Umbundu,* pp. 170–71) mentions the elephant hunter cliche and has these travel from the nearby confluence of Cuanza and Luando.

63. R. Delgado, *O Reino,* pp. 123–4, 131, according to Cadornega, *História,* 3:175–76. He was encountered between 1629 and 1637. The title *Muzumbu aKalunga* is Kimbundu and means "Interpreter of the great lord." Hence one expects the center of the kingdom to have been rather far northward in a Kimbundu-speaking area such as Songo and not just opposite the upper Cunene River, but the text is far too vague to establish where contact was made with this lord.

64. See Cadornega, *História,* 3:175–78, 218; Sebestyén and Vansina, "Angola's Eastern Hinterland," pp. 317, 322, 340, 346, 356–57, and references there; Honorato da Costa's letter of 1804 in "Documentos," pp. 238–39. A localization somewhere in present Songo country near the headwaters of the Kwango and near the upper Cuanza Rivers is indicated by all sources except for the first one.

65. Wambu seems to have existed by or before 1600 and Ngalangi perhaps even in the sixteenth century, even though the first known written mention to it dates only from

moment in time. Second, we should not forget that the "typical Ovimbundu kingdom" of the late nineteenth century is mainly a product of eighteenth- and nineteenth-century developments, when the realms of Bailundu and Viye reached their apogee. The political structures of these kingdoms then contained features that had originated from all over the planalto and its sur- roundings, while the two realms in turn disseminated all sorts of other fea- tures to polities around them, in the same way that Bailundu's dialect disseminated far and wide to become the standard Umbundu language. Moreover, neither Bailundu nor Viye's political organization was wholly novel. These polities inherited basic patterns from earlier ones, perhaps mostly from Kibala or Muzumbu aKalunga's realm, although some also probably stemmed from Ngalangi or Wambu, who, in their turn, had in- herited basic patterns not only from Feti but from other places as well. Hence one must reject the idea of a single blueprint invented at Feti and later pho- tocopied in all the later kingdoms of the planalto. But one may date the first elaboration of an original large-scale structure capped by a central court with a king at its apex to the time of Feti and to the central and southeast- ern parts of the planalto in general.

An Inner African Frontier

In the nineteenth century, four chiefdoms, whose inhabitants all spoke the closely related Kavango languages, were strung along the lower Okavango River west to east from the point where the river bends eastward to just be- yond its confluence with the Cuito River (map 20).[66] Their situation can be compared to that of an oasis. It was possible to farm along the banks of the river despite the rather low and irregular rainfall (534 to 621 millimeters) while that could not be done farther away.[67] Cereal farming procured the main food, although, fishing, gathering, and cattle herding also contributed significantly

---

1718 because the Ngola Njimbu, one of the kingdoms that was founded by a dynasty from there, was already flourishing by ca. 1620 (Cadornega, *História*, 1:65 and 3:172). Wambu was a major kingdom by 1725 at the latest (Delgado, *Reino*, p. 270, n. 2). Heintze, *Schachtzabel*, pp. 85–6, nn. 1, 2, summarizes the known data. The earliest written men- tion of Ngalangi is 1718 (Childs, *Umbundu*, p. 224) followed by others for 1739, 1755–1756, 1764 (Delgado, *Reino*, pp. 267–68, 272, 288–89). Unfortunately, the king lists recorded from oral tradition by Childs, *Umbundu*, pp. 224–31, and Keiling, *Quarenta anos*, pp. 108–10) cite no rulers earlier than the eighteenth century.

66. For an ethnographic survey, see Gibson et al., *Kavango*. Oral traditions there: pp. 22–23, 38–41, 83–84, 99–100, 163–64.

67. See Gibson, "General Features," p. 12.

to the diet, while, at least in recent times, cattle were much less valued than was the case farther west. All around this "oasis," the bush was inhabited by San foragers who contributed game and honey mainly in return for cereals. These settlements and their economy were clearly quite old in the region, as two known archaeological sites show. The riverbank had been inhabited at least since the ninth century and the Kapako site clearly formed part of the Nqoma system. The early seventeenth-century (1630± 45 ad) site of Vungu Vungu contained remnants of fishing and herding activities as well glass beads of Atlantic origin and some copper beads, probably from Namibia.[68] The beads and the wealth they presuppose tell us that the settlement was then of some importance locally and linked by trade to distant places far to its west. Recent oral tradition associated the site with a former capital of the Sambyu chiefdom.[69]

The present inhabitants of the region are not linguistically related to others in the vicinity but to populations farther north. Their languages are closest to Umbundu, but they contain transfers from surrounding Khoe and San languages, as well as many loanwords from Kwanyama or Ndonga and some from Nyemba, but rather few from their eastern neighbors, despite the claim of most recorded oral traditions that the inhabitants migrated from the Cuando and the Zambezi Valleys. On the other hand, ethnographic comparison shows that the Kavango speakers shared a series of minor features with other small communities of fishing and farming peoples to their east as far as the Zambezi River above the Victoria Falls. Kwangari chiefly traditions point to specific origins among the Nyemba and Handa farther north along the river even though those languages are unrelated to Kwangari itself. As to the Dciriku, they even lay a vague claim to the Tsodilo Hills as a place of origin. Moreover, despite linguistic evidence and traditions, several major features and loanwords of the main sociopolitical institutions recall those of the neighboring Ambo but on a reduced and simplified scale and without the emphasis on cattle, which suggests that the region was subjected to continual impulses from their more mobile and perhaps more aggressive western neighbors.

68. See Sandelowsky, "Kapako." Kapako contained ceramics, stone artifacts (indicating close relations with San hunters) metal fragments and bone, most of which are in layers later than the carbon date of 840± 50 ad obtained for the site. These include most of the identified bone fragments of bovines (but domestic?) and fish, while hippo is associated with the carbon date. Vungu Vungu contained pottery, including fragments of clay pipes; bones, mainly of hippo, domestic bovines, fish, birds; shells; and beads in ostrich shell, glass, bone, and metal (copper and iron). As no stone tools at all were found here, no San foragers seem to have lived on the site.

69. McGurk, "The Sambyu," p. 99.

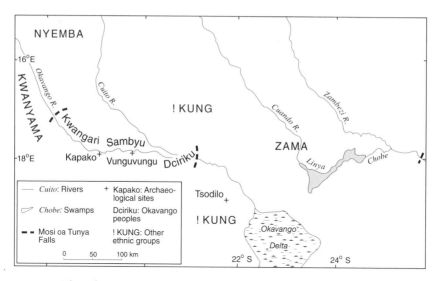

MAP 20. The Okavango Peoples

The known record of the recent histories of the area leaves the impression that the lower Okavango was a refuge area. The forebears of its inhabitants entered the region at different times from many directions, most probably as refugees. Thus in 1961 it was found in the Sambyu chiefdom that only 30 percent of the heads of all the 364 local settlements or compounds were of Sambyu origin.[70] Or, again, around 1900 all the adult Dciriku men, barring only their chief, were exterminated in a war. They were replaced by male immigrants from surrounding groups, among them many Kwangari.[71] Admittedly such recent processes should not be extended uncritically into the distant past; still when one deals with fairly small populations strung out over 300 kilometers, similar occurrences probably have happened in earlier times as well. All things considered, one reaches the conclusion that at an unknown but early time (given the language link to Umbundu), some Kavango-speaking groups led by chiefs called *hompa* (*-*sompa*!) moved into this region from farther upstream to found the first chiefdoms. Such chiefdoms then provided a social framework that allowed for the later absorption of individuals or small groups, including San, from places all around the Okavango oases, a process that lasted for many centuries. But as these im-

70. Ibid., p. 128.
71. Möhlig, *Dciriku*, pp. xxiii–iv, 52–4. Dciriku is still becoming more and more like Kwangari. Möhlig shows the severity of the impact of this event on the old Dciriku language.

migrants were absorbed, they in turn also influenced the social institutions of their hosts with the result that the sociocultural makeup of the region went, so to speak, from compromise to compromise, rather than developing into a new direction of its own.

What is particularly striking about the sociocultural profile of the Kavango people is that their collective imaginations remained so unfocused. Yes, they kept cattle and drank milk, but they were not fascinated by cattle and there was no "cattle culture." Yes, they had chiefs, but their standing was so unremarkable that even their initiations and burials were rather modest. These chiefs were not involved as central figures in intricate ceremonials except to request rain from the chiefly ancestors. They were not surrounded by any titleholders, let alone a plethora of them, nor was there anything remarkable about their dwellings or their settlements. The Kavango simply did not have any special fascination with the means or paraphernalia of power. Nor did one find a series of interlocked initiations accompanied by the exuberant masquerades that were so typical for eastern Angola. In fact, all of the main rituals were also found among one or the other of their Njila-speaking neighbors, perhaps especially among the Ambo. There was very little original input into any of these manifestations, with the partial exception of the harvest rituals, which were the central event of the annual Kwangari round of activities.[72] Thus the disconcerted observer keeps finding what could be called a cultural esperanto: a mix of impoverished reminiscences of rich features that are typical for one or another of the surrounding regions but nothing original to the region itself, no new vistas along which the collective imagination could have developed into greater luxuriance. And yet, is this not what one would expect in a refuge, a mixing bowl of immigrants of such diverse origins?

The region was and still is an outstanding exemplar of an inner African frontier. Yet it does not conform to the typical trajectory for such frontiers laid out by Igor Kopytoff.[73] That trajectory described only relatively empty places that came to be settled by pioneers who were later largely left alone to reproduce the societies from where they came. But this scenario did not foresee much interference by immigrants from elsewhere later on. Yet the Okavango oasis seems to have been first and foremost a refuge area of great an-

---

72. Gibson and McGurk, "Kwangari," pp. 45–46, 72–74.
73. Kopytoff, "African Frontier," pp. 3–80. The main weakness of his hypothesis is its static character even though it appears to be a dynamic process model. For Kopytoff, the same sequence repeated itself over and over again during several millennia, which is clearly unrealistic and the result of divorcing the development of institutions of governance from all other contexts and from all contingent effects.

tiquity, which attracted new immigrants from nearly every direction during many centuries. Hence the original planalto type of chiefdom from which the earliest influential communities came was not faithfully reproduced here. Rather, the original simple chiefdoms developed into a society that was constantly making compromises with the customs of new immigrants to make them acceptable to all its inhabitants so that their social institutions came to be vested in the lowest common denominator of all the societies of origin of those who sought refuge there, barring perhaps only the San. Rather than being insulated from others, then, this region was constantly influenced by the influx of people from many origins. Under these circumstances, one should not expect original forms of social institutions to develop and, indeed, that did not happen. These societies always remained marginal.

In and Around the Lower Cuanza Basin

In the sixteenth century, the main population cluster in the Cuanza basin lay in the Kingdom of Ndongo, which was roughly upstream of the confluence of the Cuanza and Lucala and mostly between those two rivers (map 21). Smaller secondary clusters also arose both in the northern highlands in favorable places along the valleys of the Bengo-Zenza, upper Dande, and even upper Loge Rivers as well as in the Quibala region to the south where some of the thousands of stone tumuli for which this region is famous may be considerably older than the sixteenth- to eighteenth-century ones that have been dated.[74] The rise of the overall population clusters and the location of the ancillary ones has certainly been strongly influenced by the ecological conditions of the area. Settlers were attracted by the fairly rich well-watered soils in the main valleys and by the lightly wooded savannas with *Cochlospermum* and thickets between the much drier lands of the coast and the higher elevations inland. At the same time, they also appreciated easy access via the Cuanza and the Bengo Rivers to the resources along the coast, especially those of the Luanda lagoons. A further variety of ecotones facilitated ex-

74. Rodrigues, "Construções," pp. 179–87 (some 3,000 tumuli, 200 cemeteries); Baumann, "Die Frage," pp. 132–37, and "Steingräber"; Rudner, "Archaeological Reconnaissance," pp. 99–111; Heintze, "Bestattung in Angola," pp. 145–205, her "Beiträge," pp. 178–80, and her manuscript update "Die Steinnekropole von Kibala" from 2002. Most tombs are thought to be quite recent, but very few have actually been dated. In Pungo aNdongo, a few atypical ones excavated by Gutierrez, *Archéologie,* date to the 1600s. The beads on top of one tomb at Ebo near Quibala date from the 1500s (Saitowitz et al., "Chevron Beads," pp. 135–42) and a sizeable number of other tombs there may be as old or older. See also n. 4.

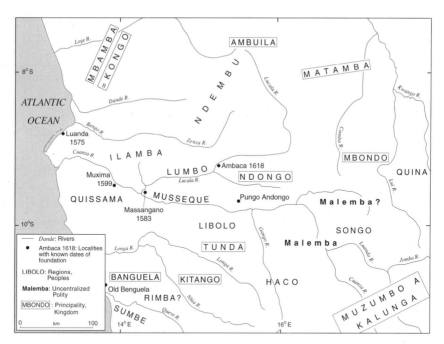

MAP 21. The Cuanza Basin, ca. 1575–1600

changes of regional products within the region as well as beyond it. In the centuries following the initial adoption of cereal agriculture and the herding of cattle (tenth century), agriculture was further enriched by the adoption of a number of secondary crops with higher yields per acre. Among these, plantains and water yams were the most significant.[75] Just as important was the use made of the annual riverfloods to irrigate the floodplains of the lower courses of the main rivers (Cuanza, Bengo, Dande, Longa), which

75. We follow the chronology proposed by Rossel, *Taxonomic-Linguistic Study,* pp. 188–95, which points to a fourth to sixth century CE arrival in Africa and perhaps three centuries later in the northern Njila-speaking regions. This dating stands, despite claims for a ca. 1000 BCE date of introduction based on a phytolith found in Cameroon indirectly dated to ca. 500 BCE (Christophe Mbida Mindzie et al., "First Archaeological Evidence," pp. 1–6). The identification of the phytolith as *musa* and not *ensete* seems doubtful and the chronology by association of the find are both too tentative to carry the day in the face of massive negative written evidence in northeast Africa and the Middle East and from Red Sea on sites with excellent preservation of macroplant remains. For more detail, see Vansina, "Bananas." Bananas are of a later introduction, although probably still pre-1500. For water yams (still *kidingu* in Kimbundu of Malange), see Gossweiler, *Os nomes,* pp. 37, 484. Water yams were probably introduced on the east coast by the eighth century at the earliest and cannot be expected to have reached eastern Angola long before the turn of the millennium.

helped to mitigate the effects of the thin and uncertain rainfall in the coastal lands. Thus, over time, agriculture became more efficient and could easily support substantial population growth.

Commerce and industry grew apace with population growth and trade thrived on its uneven distribution as much as it was fueled by the uneven distribution of natural resources. Salt, fish, palm oil, foodstuffs, hoes, and other iron products, copper rings, raffia cloth, ivory, and cattle were only the main commodities from a very long list of goods on offer, ranging from baskets and brooms to mats and unguents. Salt from the mine of Ndemba in Kisama or from the saltpans of the Lui in the basin of Cassange[76] was so important that it had become the main currency throughout the region well before 1500. Still the actual buying and selling remained a barterlike exchange of goods and all trade was retail. There were no professional traders, and no one rose to great wealth by trading.[77] The most important places where commercial exchanges took place were located in the settlements of chiefs and princes but no formalized markets arose: no periodicity for the market, no market supervisors, no special means to settle differences, and no taxation.[78]

The reader recalls that beginning around or a little before the turn of the millennium chiefdoms had begun to appear in this region. Later, at an undeterminate time, several chiefdoms grew into principalities and did so independently in different places. All one knows is that Ambundu principalities north of the Dande River were in place well before the late fourteenth century when the Kingdom of Kongo was formed. Perhaps the first ones arose around 1200, also the estimated date for the creation of the first principalities in the Lower Congo Region.[79] Later on, a set of such principalities

76. See Grandvaux Barbosa, *Carta,* pp. 238, 243: (*salgados*) 14 kilometers south of the market of Quibau, on the Quionga river, an affluent of the Luanda and saltpans (*salicornia*) just East of Mbondo. For the unit of salt here, see Vidal, *Por Terras,* p. 65 (*mucha* package and unit). For the salt and the saltbricks of Ndemba, see Heintze, "Beiträge," p. 165, and Lacerda, "Noticias," p. 122 (observed 1783).

77. As in Kongo "to buy" was -*sumba* and "to sell" *sumbisa,* i.e., "to cause to buy." Traders were "travelers," "business" was rendered by an abstract form of "travel" and specific notions of "price" and "profit" do not seem to have existed.

78. *Kitanda* 7/8 meant first "wooden platform" with "market" as a secondary meaning. This term was not used for "market" in Kongo and, unlike the practice there, the notion of a week and a weekly sequence of periodic markets did not exist. The *kitanda* was a daily market, mainly for food, in which salt was used as currency. See Brásio, *MMA,* 2:511 [1563]. It underwent a substantial development from the sixteenth century onward to serve the Atlantic slave trade. Thus, by 1563 a periodic market (once every five days) called by its Kongo name *sona* operated at the capital (Brásio, *MMA,* 2:509 [1563]).

79. See Vansina, *Paths,* pp. 149–52. A principality at Feti probably appeared first by the late thirteenth century. For Kongo, see Thornton, "Origins," pp. 119–20.

succeeded sometimes in controlling unbridled violent rivalries by forming a more or less stable confederation, as attested to in the seventeenth and eighteenth centuries among the Ndembu and in the "seven kingdoms of Kongo."[80] But in some other cases a principality rapidly overran a series of others and a kingdom came into being. The large Kingdom of Ndongo in the Cuanza basin was definitely constituted by conquest during the later fifteenth century and the contemporary Kingdom of Matamba may also have grown in a similar manner.[81] The magnitude of the transformation which this process of growth from early chiefdom to late kingdom entailed is astonishing and its impact on economic, social, and cultural life must have been equally great. By that point, most large polities were at least twenty or thirty times larger in population than the small chiefdoms of yore. By 1564 Kabasa, the capital of Ndongo, contained 5,000 to 6,000 houses for a population between 12,500 and 24,000 compared to perhaps 500 for the residence of a chief, while the whole kingdom certainly included well over 100,000 people and perhaps double that number compared to a 1,000 or so for a small early chiefdom.[82]

By the middle of the sixteenth century, Ndongo was still expanding and provoking wars all across the region, but it was not the only kingdom in the Cuanza basin and its environs.[83] Large Ndembu principalities were centered mainly on the higher reaches of the Dande and Bengo Rivers. Matamba lay to the northeast of Ndongo next to Mbondo, which overlooked the major saltpans of the Quionga to its east. While most of the Songo people to the southeast of Ndongo lacked principalities and even chiefdoms, as the name Malemba suggests, farther to the southeast, astride the upper Cuanza River,

80. Thornton, "Origins," pp. 110–12 (also on the growth of Kongo by voluntary federation).

81. Heintze, *Studien*, pp. 64–67, summarizes the sources for Ndongo. No traditions were recorded concerning the foundation of Matamba, which suddenly appears in the record as an autonomous agent on 28 January 1530 (Brásio, *MMA*, 1:540).

82. See Brásio, *MMA*, 10:233 [dated 1 November 1564] for an estimate of houses in Kabasa. The population estimate I derive from this counts 2.5 to 4 inhabitants per house, which seems more credible than the 100,000 for the city estimated by Francisco de Gouveia. If the capital contained some 10 percent of the total population, the latter would amount to between 125,000 and 240,000.

83. In 1563, António Mendes tells us "for it contains many other kings on its borders who continually wage war on him, like the king of Quitango, the king of Banguela, and many other important lords who unite to wage war on him [the king of Ndongo]" and goes on to tell how the king of Ndongo defeated the king of Banguela, divided the realm and installed his own "sons" as his tributaries and how the sons then rebelled against him (Brásio, *MMA*, 2:509).

lay the kingdom of Muzumbu aKalunga, which was flourishing by or before 1600. Southward, Ndongo extended beyond the Cuanza River to include the local rulers of Haco, Libolo (Tunda), and Kisama all the way to the Longa River. But in the far southwest, the "Kingdom of Banguela," an enemy of Ndongo, consisted of the coastal lands between the lower Longa and Queve Rivers while a set of several principalities or perhaps a single kingdom flourished in the Quibala region. Maybe Quibala was the localization of the Kingdom of Kitanga, another bitter enemy of Ndongo in the 1560s.[84] Little is known about the political situation of the peoples who then lived in the western corridor between the sea and the escarpments south of the Cuanza basin, although according to early reports the land around the newly founded Benguela was occupied in 1617–20 by a mix of polities ranging from small chiefdoms to bigger and aggressive principalities. Yet in 1600 Andrew Battell reported only that they "have no government among themselves."[85]

Because lords arose so far above ordinary chiefs, their spiritual credentials also needed to surpass those of ordinary chiefs. While the latter were believed to be supported by both their ancestors and by the nature spirits of their lands, the lords' greater success, power, and authority was attributed not merely to their ancestors and spirits but even more and especially so to their detention of a mysterious object or objects, a charm of office that granted political power to whomever held it.[86] Even though many believed that the efficacy of such an object ultimately derived from ancestors or nature spirits, still as an embodiment of pure power for its holder it was a potent new tool of legitimacy.[87] So important were such objects that the designation for a lord or king was often the same as and derived from the word for his or her charms of power. Thus among the Ndembu, *ndembu* 9/10 was

84. Heintze, *Studien*, pp. 61 (map), 69–70.

85. Battell, *Strange*, p. 17. The list of battles fought by the first governor, as described by Delgado, *O Reino*, pp. 66–72, shows the changed situation in 1617–20. For the original documents from 1618, see Brásio, *MMA*, 6:298–99, 315–19.

86. A late example of the importance of holding these charms is the fact that the Portuguese in 1850 could not install a new King of Kasanji until the charms (including a *lunga*), which were kept in the royal *manuma* 6 shrine, of that Imbangala kingdom fell into their hands (Neves, *Memoria*, pp. 64, 115, 117–18).

87. Despite the great number of references to and descriptions of religious objects and beliefs from the 1560s onward, the practice to call all objects "fetishes" or "idols" and all shrines "houses of fetish" obscures the record. The most one can conclude is that boxes and/or houses of objects of power, as well as some emblems, such as armrings or warbells with ritual power were associated only with powerful lords, whereas single statues, however much venerated, and lumps of consecrated white kaolin were linked to chiefs as well as to lords.

both the title for a lord as distinct from mere chief or *soba* and meant "remedy, medicine."[88] *Kalunga* 1/2 was the title of address for most lords and *lunga* 5/6 was their object of power, while *ngola* 9/10 was the title of the king of Angola and also the name of his or her charm of office.

The first and most general term accompanying the rise of principalities to designate a lord was *kalùngà* 12,[89] used both as a term of address for such a person and as a metaphor in reference.[90] It derives once again from a root meaning "intelligent" or "wise" so that the parallel with the meaning of *ngána* is striking.[91] In the nineteenth century it was most common with this meaning in and around the upper Kwango Valley and, given its prefix, may have been coined there.[92]

88. Given the absence of tonal data, one can suggest that the form *ndembu* 9/10 "lord" is probably identical with *ndembu* 9/10 "medicine" despite a diacritic differentiation made in the dictionaries. In Kongo, *ndembu* referred to "something which destroys a sortilege," that is a charm any ruler would need to protect himself or herself against the envy of rivals. For a nineteenth-century case, see Sarmento, *Os sertões d'Africa*, p. 91 (the "fetish box" of Nambuangongo). This is strikingly similar to the object of power called *bwene* 14 or *wene* 14 common in Kongo and in the middle Kwango regions. That word is derived from the old *mwene* 1/2 "owner, leader."

89. This is the tone in Lwena. In Umbundu, Schadeberg (*Sketch*, p. 58) has *Kalùngá*.

90. Part of the distribution area of this word overlaps that of the distribution of *ngána* and its meaning almost duplicates that of *ngána*. This confirms that it was introduced at a later time, most likely as a derivation from *lunga* 5/6 "charm of power."

91. From proto-Bantu *-*dùnga* (CS 711) "to become fitting," from which "become straight" (but also "be round"!) and the latter derived (CS 715) *-*dùngù* 1? "God" [East]. See Mbala: -*lùung* "to be complete," "to have everything that is needed," -*luungisa* "to complete," *ndùùngì* 10 "intelligence, cleverness"; Pende: *lunga* "to suit, to fit," -*lungila* "to be able to, to suit," *lungisa* "to enable, to complete" and the adjective -*lunga* "to be just, to be suitable, to be adapted"; Holo: -*lúúng* (tone?) "to be complete," *kalúúnga* 13 "the underground" and *káluunga!* "yes, sir!"; Kongo: -*lunga* "to triumph," -*lungidika* "to accomplish, to make perfect," *malunga* 6 "perfection" (also the name of a power charm); Kimbundu: -*lunga*, "to triumph," -*lungisa* "to judge, to decide, to deliberate, to resolve," *ndunge* "intelligence," –*lunga*, "to be right, to triumph"; Homburger, pp. 95, 109: -*dungu* "intelligent" and Umbundu, *lunguka* "to be intelligent," Nyaneka *ondungi* "expert," Nkhumbi *onondunge* "intelligence" and Ndonga *uukulungu*, Nyemba *ku-lunga* "intelligent, expert." Over time, *kalunga* acquired a whole array of additional meanings, including "great spirit or ancestor," "ocean" and, after the introduction of Christianity, both "supreme being" and "the netherworld." The same basic form also produced *lunga*, *malunga* 5/6 "charm of power." Given the etymologies, it is likely that *lunga* produced *kalunga* and not the reverse.

92. The prefix *ka*- is a diminutive, except in the Moxico languages, where it can denote importance. But *kalunga* 12 was not common in these languages, except for Nyemba and Lwimbi.

As to the -*lunga* 5/6 objects, their introduction accompanied the rise of the first major principalities according to oral traditions gathered by Miller.[93] These traditions remember nothing definite about the shape of the earliest *lunga* or about the material from which they were made beyond the suggestion that they probably were wooden statues. But among the central Ambundu in the sixteenth and seventeenth centuries, such objects were a single (*dilunga, lunga*) or double clapperless metal bell (*malunga* 6), or *malunga* 6 metal rings, worn by the ruler and inhabited by protective ancestors.[94] These bells, rings, or another *lunga* object of power apparently were kept in a special shrine, presumably one created when principalities came into being, a shrine that was different from the *rilombo* 5/6 shrines that were dedicated to the forebears of the prince.[95]

Some time after the *lunga* charm had been introduced, a new object of power called *ngola* 9/10 was invented. Its name is a straightforward derivation from *-*kóda* "to become strong."[96] Local oral traditions associate it with the rise of the Kingdom of Ndongo and imply that it is as old as that kingdom was, i.e., the late fifteenth century. The kings of Ndongo were called *ngola,* after the charm, and the Portuguese derived Angola from the title. The *ngola* 9/10 was a piece of iron, in the shape of a hammer, a bell, a hoe, or a knife, kept in a shrine with a guardian, as is still the case among the Holo.[97]

93. Miller, *Kings,* pp. 55–63. According to his informants from Malange, the *lunga* was a wooden figure or figures (p. 59). The term occurs very often in the plural *malunga* all over the Kimbundu region and north of it in Kongo and along the Kwango as far as the Malebo Pool, as well as in the middle Kwilu region (even Bushong has a related item) to designate either the armrings "of power," or/and the double bell, the major emblem of power and war. Also in Vansina, "Antécédents," p. 23.

94. Among many more general declarations, Cadornega, *História,* 2:169 is especially striking. Queen Njinga consulted her *malunga* armrings in which her familiars resided. They reacted to her questions by giving her a true/false sign. See also Cavazzi, *Descrição,* 2:147. On bells, see Vansina, "Bells of Kings," pp. 187–97. *Lunga, malunga* was a very common term in West Central Africa for either the single or the double bell. In Umbundu, a military commander was distinguished from other chiefs by the specification "of the *lunga.*"

95. Some or many of the "fetish houses" or "temples" mentioned by early foreign observers were such shrines. In the recent ethnographic record, they are famous among the Pende and Holo. Among the latter, one of the two shrines of power was called *muuya* 3/4 ("armring, belt") and its keeper *Holo dya lunga* or *Holo dya Khula* (Niangi, *Sculpture,* pp. 102, 109, 421–23, 443).

96. See *ngola* 9/10 from CS 1104 *-*kód* "to become strong." See also the derivation in CS 840 *-*gòdò* "strength" 9/10. Unlike the case of Kongo, a nasal followed by *k* becomes *g* in Kimbundu and many other languages in the area.

97. According to the informants cited by Miller, *Kings,* pp. 58–59, 63–70, it was a small piece of iron. This description reminds one of rather similar counters for a *ngombo*

Once invented, this charm was adopted not just in Ndongo but spread far into the western corridor southwest of the Cuanza basin, as well as on the planalto, and even as far as Huila.[98]

Here, as on the planalto, the essential glue holding principalities or kingdoms together was the notion of a common ruler rendered concrete in the shape of a person. The existence of a ruler created the consciousness among the subjects of belonging to a common realm.[99] The larger the realm, the more exalted the king had to be. Thus the Portuguese considered the ruler of Ndongo to be a divine king, for did not the inhabitants of the realm declare that what God was to the Portuguese, their king was to them?[100] And the idea that their king was imbued with the highest supernatural spirit remained common even after a century of Christianization. It was the ruler who was held responsible for the very life of his subjects through his or her power over rain and all forms of fertility, and government consisted in managing the supernatural in such a way that prosperity reigned. Rulers rarely appeared in public, but when they did, it usually was to be shown to promote fertility and prosperity. They solemnly presided over sowing and first-fruit rituals, they initiated the rituals to obtain rain, to end an epidemic, and they declared war.

In these essentially spiritual tasks, the most exalted rulers, such as those of Ndongo, were assisted by a special group of diviners, the *shingila* 1n/2. Each of these was believed to be the earthly vessel of a royal ancestor or of an equally powerful deceased ruler from another kingdom and whenever the

---

divining basket. Among the Holo, *ngola* 9/10 still is a shrine of power objects such as *muuya* 3/4, and it always contains a small iron statuette of a dog (Niangi, *Sculpture,* pp. 109, 113–14, 423–26).

98. For example, Cadornega, *História,* 3:249–50, mentions Angola Cabangi, Angola Quitumba in Libolo, Angola Ulenga in Sumbi, Angola Amginbo (known already by 1620) on the planalto and Angolo in Huila. In Umbundu, *ngola* means "royal power." These occurrences should not be interpreted as evidence of dynasties emigrating from the Kingdom of Ndongo from the late seventeenth century onward. In any case, Ngola aNjimbu was already known by 1620. Rather, these attestations are evidence for the diffusion of a charm and a title, the names of which are so obviously derived from the older verbal form found in all the languages of the area.

99. For the following section, see Heintze, *Studien,* pp. 60–92, and her "Unbekanntes Angola," pp. 749–805.

100. The most telling among the early Jesuit letters concerning this topic is the one of 1 November 1564 by Francisco de Gouveia (Brásio, *MMA,* 15:230–31), in which he states that they hold their gods to be their lords and do not imagine a single God, lord of everyone. Even in the 1660s, Gaeta in *Maravigliosa,* pp. 136, 163, 187, 385, 415, concluded that although the Ambundu venerated Njinga like a goddess, they were essentially "atheist."

ruler needed advice these spirits were consulted. Moreover, thanks to her or his *malunga* 6 rings, the ruler herself or himself could communicate directly with his or her ancestors. While it is easy to recognize that every element in this complex of "divine kingship" had its more humble precedents in various practices of less-exalted leadership, even in the most modest dance for fertility at the new moon, or in the ordinary lineage headman's mysterious power over the fertility of women, still the whole became so elaborate and so surrounded by etiquette, prescription, avoidance, and calendar, so majestic and theatrical in public appearance, so exuberant in its display of esoteric symbols, that to the ordinary person it was self-evident that no one else's ritual was even comparable to this and that the ruler was a supreme being. In the end, it was that conviction held by nearly everyone that turned the principalities and the kingdoms into a genuine reality. Hence the ruler's majesty also required that he or she live relatively isolated from his or her subjects in quarters that also housed the shrines for ancestors, spirits, and national charms. Located at the heart of their capitals, these palaces were surrounded and protected by tall fences in such a way that visitors had to cross a labyrinth of passages and gates before finally gaining access to the august presence.

If the prince or king was the main embodiment of the realm, the capital (*mbanza* 9/10) was its heart. The whole country was ruled from there and the main titleholders lived there. In 1564, Kabasa, the capital of Ndongo, was said to be as large as the city of Evora, clearly much larger than the district capitals (*sanzala* 9/10, *sanza* 9/10) in which the subordinate chiefs lived.[101] At Kabasa the ruler presided over a court of titleholders or *makota* 6 ("elders"), and from there he or she sent orders to the territorial chiefs. It was to the capital that newly subjugated or installed chiefs traveled to swear fealty (*-unda*)[102] and to pay homage (*-bakula*) to their overlord and later to bring tribute (*luanda* 11) and to receive countergifts of considerable value. It was there too that diplomatic envoys (*makunji* 6) and their gifts arrived from the courts of other kings or powers while one's own envoys set out from the capital for other courts, on a voyage during which they were honored and

101. Gouveia in Brásio, *MMA,* 15:232–33. For *mbanza,* see Vansina, *Paths,* pp. 271–72. The word is a transfer from Kongo. Before this loan, capitals were called *sanzala* 5 or *sanza* 5 from a root *-sanza,* as in *sanzeka* "to extend," *-sanzuka* "to extend itself," *-kusanzumuna* "to enlarge, to extend," *sanzamuka* "to be enlarged." In the Ndembu dialects, *musanzu* 3/4 meant "extension" and the well-known *ndala* 9/10 is given as its equivalent.

102. The terms cited in the next paragraphs are local Kimbundu innovations with obvious etymologies.

showered with gifts as if they were the ruler herself or himself. There, too, was the square that was the usual venue for the royal assembly and tribunal, which reminded everyone of the ruler's power over life and death. In that square, sentence was sometimes passed to undergo the *nduua* 9/10 poison ordeal, the most dreaded of all judicial ordeals, and one which seems to have been directly linked mystically to the royal power itself.[103] Moreover a large number of people unconnected to the court also lived in various quarters of the capital under their own headmen and leaders of kingroups, just as if each quarter was a village.

The foremost titleholders at court were the *"mani" ndongo,* the foremost ritual authority at the capital, the viceroy or *tandala,* who acted as magistrate as well as a general and the *ngolambole,* a general in charge of war in the countryside and probably in charge of all territorial affairs. The duties of most of the other senior titleholders at court, whether men or women, were only related to the running of the royal household so that even in the capital there was no single central administration. Whenever the king and his advisors required anything from anyone or from any community, they would dispatch a messenger. The only action the subordinate chiefdoms and principalities were expected to take on their own initiative was to pay an annual tribute.

A formal territorial organization, let alone administration, did not exist. Nearly every chiefdom and former principality continued to exist as before the conquest and to settle its own internal affairs. However, many of these entities were directly linked to the court by a woman, daughter of their chief and wife of the ruler. For the rulers married women related to chiefs all over the realm, who then informed their husbands of what happened at their homes of origin and probably also served as conduits for messages and news to the chiefs. In addition kings also placed some of their close relatives at the head of small chiefdoms, either by ousting the ruling line there or by carving out new chiefdoms out of larger ones, so that with the passage of time an increasing number of chiefdoms came to be more closely linked to the court in this way. In addition, some of the ruler's agents were settled on domains interspersed among those of the local chiefs. Such a person was a *kilamba* 7/8, a special representative of the court whose task was to enforce the

---

103. *Nduua* 9/10 designates both the night-jar or a related bird and their long trailing feathers. After the fall of Ndongo and despite repeated Portuguese attempts to eliminate the practice, Ambundu still resorted to it well into the nineteenth century but at a spot beyond the colony in the Imbangala Kingdom of Cassange. *Nduua* feathers and their terrible immanent powers were also known along the Kwango as far as the Tio kingdom.

execution of orders from the capital, to supervise the payment of tribute, and to keep the court (presumably the *ngolambole*) informed.[104]

By 1610 an observer recorded four social classes in Ndongo: the *makota* 6 elders, the people in free villages (*murinda* 3/4), inalienable communal slaves (*kijiku* 7/8), and slaves who could be sold (*mubika* 1/2).[105] Once again this was certainly an oversimplification that did not take other statuses or roles into account. It did not recognize the existence of nobles by birth (*mumvale* 1/2) or allow for low-status people in high-status offices, such as that of *tandala,* which always seems to have been held by a slave. Or again while *makota* at court carried great political weight, humble lineage leaders in small villages were also *makota.* In addition, the frequent wars certainly engendered considerable social mobility as high-status persons sometimes became captives and slaves sometimes became chiefs or even lords. Finally, here too, religious experts, expert hunters and expert metalworkers enjoyed a much higher status than other "ordinary people."

Jaga Marauders and Their Government

In December 1590, the Portuguese lost a major battle against the combined forces of the kings of Matamba, Kongo, Ndongo, "and of the Guinda and the Yagua who are kings adjacent to the kingdom of Angola."[106] A decade later

104. By the time of Cadornega (*História,* 3:236–39), the *kilamba* 7/8 was clearly (a) directly subordinate to the Portuguese and (b) a foreigner to the locality where he was posted. For the 1620s, see Heintze, *Fontes,* 1:126, where he is "an African official in the *guerra preta* [auxiliaries of the Portuguese]." Presumably the *kilamba* performed the same tasks for a local ruler in earlier times. But the earliest mention I found dates to 1580–82 and merely says "in the lands of a nobleman they call Quelamba" (Brásio, *MMA,* 15:365). The term is related or even derived from -*laamba* "to watch out for, to keep an eye on." But the word is also certainly related to the widespread terms *kalamba* 12/13 "a sort of chief" and *mulambo* 3/4 "tribute," which are discussed in the next chapter.

105. See Heintze, *Studien,* p. 77, for a full citation from Iarric (1610). Also her *Fontes,* 1:120, 123, 127.

106. Brásio, *MMA,* 4:533 (1591 account by Domingos de Abreu e Brito). This was not the first mention to armed marauders in the country. Some of these, called Soaso, are already mentioned in December 1585 (Brásio, *MMA,* 3:332–35). In his *Um Inquérito à vida adminstrativa e económica de Angola e do Brasil...* (p. 15), Domingos de Abreu e Brito claims that he himself spoke to "soaso slaves" who were bandits and "lived from traveling." They clearly were not Jaga, however, whom he also mentioned. Moreover these Jaga in Angola are not to be confused with the earlier ones in Kongo. Abreu e Brito makes it clear that they were two different groups, Battell's Iagges being his Guinda. It is barely possible that the "king of the Bangela," known from the 1560s onward, was a king of the Imbangala and hence that these migrants were already active in the old Benguela area by that date.

the English sailor Battell speaks of the "Gagas, Giagas, Iagges or Gindes" and goes on to describe their predatory way of life.[107] These are the first mentions of those marauding armies whom the Portuguese would henceforth call Jaga and who were locally known as Imbangala. Their sudden appearance on the scene has attracted much scholarly comment, while their later exploits exerted a considerable impact on Angolan history.[108] They arrived in the Cuanza basin at the end of a mass migration that had carried them northward from southern Angola along the corridor which runs between the coast and the steep escarpments inland from the Catumbela River to old Benguela and the lower reaches of the Longa River between the coast and the escarpments of the planalto (map 22).

The migrants started from the cattle-keeping regions in the south and attracted more and more followers as they went northward.[109] Their numbers snowballed so much that, after fifty-odd years of wandering there, well over 10,000 or 20,000 of them settled near old Benguela where their first

107. Battell, our only early source about these Jaga, lived with them for well over a year (ca. 1600–1601) and left two accounts about their way of life, both of which were edited by S. Purchas. The first account was actually written by Purchas on the basis of conversations with Battell, who later supposedly penned the other one himself, but in editing it, Purchas obviously also altered that text as well. Battell's testimony is therefore far more difficult to evaluate than has been taken for granted in the past. The standard edition of Purchas still is Ravenstein, *Strange Adventures*. For the Jaga, see pp. 19–35 and 83–87.

108. See state of the question in a set of contributions to *CEA*, namely, Miller, "Requiem," pp. 121–49, and his "Thanatopsis," pp. 229–31, as well as Thornton, "Resurrection," pp. 223–27.

109. The two main clues about their origin are the ethnic name Imbangala and *nguri* "lion," from which derives Kinguri, the name of one of their early leaders. In the Nkhumbi vocabulary gathered by Nogueira in the 1850s, "vagabond," "vagrant" is translated as *Chimbangala* (Brito's *Soaso* were also vagrants!) and notes that this term was not used in Umbundu. The word also occurs in Nyaneka with the meaning "robber" (*salteador*) and was used in Kwanyama to designate Nkhumbi and Nyaneka (see Estermann, *Nhaneca-Humbe*, pp. 13–15). In the 1790s, Lacerda, "Noticia," p. 461, claimed that "Quimbangala" was the name given to those Ovimbundu (lords?) who were cannibals— but that does not mean that the term or the Imbangala themselves originated from there. For Cavazzi (*Descrição*, 1:190 (book 2, para. 31), *nguri* meant "lion" in the Jaga language, and *nguri* does mean "lion" in Nyaneka and in Hanya (Hauenstein, *Hanya*, p. 248) but not in Nkhumbi or in standard Umbundu. My inclination is to place the origins of the earliest migrants somewhere in the Quilengues region, which was famous by the late eighteenth century as a refuge for defeated lords from elsewhere. But most of those who joined the Jaga camps along the way stemmed from the region of the escarpments now known as Seles. Finally the toponym Benguela and the ethnonym Banguela are probably both derived from Imbangala.

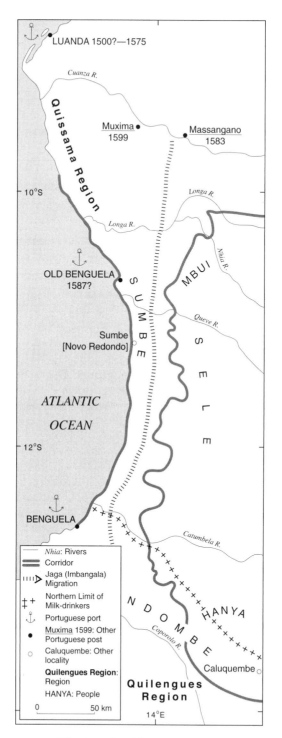

LUANDA 1500?—1575

Cuanza R.

Muxima •
1599

Massangano •
1583

Quissama Region

— 10°S

Longa R.

Longa R.

OLD BENGUELA
1587?

S
U
M
B
E

MBUI

Nhia R.

Queve R.

S
E
L
E

Sumbe
[Novo Redondo]

ATLANTIC

OCEAN

— 12°S

BENGUELA

Catumbela R.

N
D
O
M
B
E

HANYA

Coporolo R.

Caluquembe

Quilengues
Region

14°E

Nhia: Rivers
Corridor
Jaga (Imbangala)
Migration
Northern Limit of
Milk-drinkers
Portuguese port
Muxima 1599: Other
Portuguese post
Caluquembe: Other
locality
Quilengues Region:
Region
HANYA: People

0   50 km

MAP 22. The Jaga Corridor

leader Elembe had settled. But Kalandula, "sometime his page," accompanied by large numbers of Elembe's people soon resumed the plundering life.[110] Those who arrived in the Cuanza basin before 1600 seem to have allied themselves at first to the king of Ndongo. Soon, though, most of their war bands became Portuguese allies and it is not much of an exaggeration to claim that it was largely due to Jaga support that the Portuguese managed to defeat the Ndongo king by 1620. From the 1620s onward, Jaga lords then began to create polities in competition with older lords in many parts of the Ambundu lands and on the planalto. But in doing so, they gradually lost their mobility, their distinct ideology, and the warring customs that distinguished them from all others.[111] This was the fate of even the largest of their creations, the Kingdom of Cassange founded in 1629/1630 in the basin of the upper middle Kwango Valley.

Jaga society was devoted entirely to war. The Jaga lived in war camps and were organized in army units headed by captains under the command of a single leader, the "great Gaga." He was a charismatic leader whose appeal stemmed from his courage and his success in battle, a success that was attributed to his extraordinary supernatural powers as a diviner of the future and as the recipient of the unquestioned support of his deceased predecessors, the ancestors. This society had fully adopted a roving way of life, as is strikingly shown by their use of boxes to transport the hallowed bones of their leading ancestors rather than to venerate their gravesites. So ruthless was this adaptation that the wanderers refused to shoulder the burden of caring for their own children, perhaps because these would have slowed them down and hampered their military operations. These children were killed at birth, while the reproduction of their society was ensured by raiding teenagers as slaves who were then indoctrinated in their military life.[112] The internal regulation of their communities rested on both a set of stringent rules and on unquestioned obedience to their leaders. No doubt the strict ruthlessness of their internal organization was responsible for the survival for more than a century of a society based on such extreme predatory principles.

110. Battell, *Strange Adventures,* p. 33 (more than fifty years since they left the "lion mountains" and eighty-five for Elembe).

111. Both Cavazzi, *Descrição,* 1:book 2, 173–260, and Gaeta, *Maravigliosa,* pp. 392–449, described the specific ways in which they saw the Jaga as different from the Ambundu.

112. The recruiting of teenagers was not unique, but infanticide was. In the nineteenth century, Herero families would give some of their children to others (just as they did with cattle as a precaution against disease) and adopt foreign teenagers as their own. See Vedder, "Herero," p. 177, and compare with the practice for cattle in Vedder, *South West Africa,* p. 47.

For the Jaga economy was totally predatory: other societies produced, they consumed. They only produced slaves for sale to the Portuguese in return for luxuries. They obviously strove to imitate the amenities of life enjoyed by the great and the rich in other societies, carousing and feasting without any regard for the preservation of resources for the future: they killed the palm trees from which they drew wine, they consumed the herds they acquired rather than manage them, they reaped the crops of others, and they knew nothing about granaries.[113] They obviously utterly rejected the particular attraction to and affection for cattle that was so common in the agropastoral milking zones of the south (they craved palm wine, not milk!) just as much as they rejected the pleasures of a settled life and the splendors of well-organized courts. In that sense, they were anarchists.

No one knows how or why exactly the Jaga migration occurred. One may suspect that the first Jaga were refugees from drought, or epizootics, or wars between principalities. Be that as it may, one must never forget that this migration behind the coast took place shortly after the first slave traders with their attractive wares began to arrive on the coasts of central Angola. Nor do we know anything about the particular social institutions which served as a starting point for this extraordinary Jaga way of life. The original model may well have been the organization of life in the cattle posts during transhumance, or in that of the dry-season camps for circumcised boys, or most likely in military camps set up during wars or raids between principalities.[114] Whatever the model, one thing is certain. From the first moment that enthusiastic followers began to swell their numbers, if not perhaps from the outset, the Jaga bands became the expression of a revolt of the have-nots against the haves. They were born as a consequence of the chasm between rich and poor. The rich controlled the means of making a living, from

113. The data about the Jaga are very incomplete because Purchas (a pious man) and later Cavazzi or Gaeta (ardent missionaries) aim to describe the horrors of what was to them an inhuman life of pure evil. In consequence, they mention only the destructive aspects of Jaga behavior and omit not only references to such aspects of social life as could be considered virtuous but even those that seemed banal or "normal" and hence all too human.

114. The Jaga camp was called *kilombo* 7/8. The same word meaning "war camp" is also found in Kimbundu and Umbundu, Nkhumbi, and Nyaneka. But this proves little as the term in any of these languages, except for Nyaneka, may well have been borrowed from the Jaga word because Jaga rulers seem to have popped up everywhere except among the Nyaneka proper. Still the term did originate somewhere in the area and I suspect it was in the Nyaneka principalities. As to the practice of building temporary fortified camps, Portuguese traders did exactly the same thing (Battell, *Strange Adventures*, p. 16).

cattle to agricultural surpluses and the most-needed tools, such as hoes, while the poor "hangers-on" survived only as servants by the grace of the rich and the powerful. When Portuguese slave traders appeared on the coast, these poor people were precisely those most at risk of being sold as slaves. Once they turned into Jaga, however, it was they who sold their betters into slavery. Once they had shaken off their servitude, they dreamed of revenge and of leading the life of the rich themselves. Battell tells us that when they overran the principality of old Benguela, they killed not just the ruler who lived there but over a hundred of his lords—rather than sell them as slaves.[115] As to good living, they succeeded in equalling or surpassing the rich both in their sumptuous banquets and in their display of finery while also equalling them in the utter contempt in which they now also held all those wretches who produced rather than looted.[116]

Despite its unique features, Jaga society became nearly totally identical with that of the local Ambundu or Ovimbundu principalities and kingdoms by the late seventeenth century, to the point that even their own largest polity, the Kingdom of Cassange, founded in 1629–30, had by then become but a mere variant of an Ambundu kingdom. This was not surprising for by then, too, the vast majority of Jaga followers, and even leaders, were of Ambundu stock and naturally reverted to a Kimbundu view of the world.[117] All in all, then, it is not an exaggeration to claim that the specific Jaga raiding way of life and their institutions of governance appeared as a product of the arrival of slave traders on the coasts and vanished by absorption once wars were no longer economical as the major means to procure slaves.

Ladders of Power and the Dynamics of Centralization

It would be a mistake to imagine that political centralization occurred only once in the regions where higher densities of population emerged in middle Angola and that the practice then spread automatically all over those regions, like an oil spill on the sea. That was not so. Our own relentless focus in this chapter on a story of ever-growing centralization glossed over the effects of

115. Ibid., p. 21.

116. The context of the earlier "Jaga" invasion of the Kongo kingdom also involves the slave trade and differentials of wealth between rich and poor even though that divide was probably less extreme there than in agropastoral or pastoral Angola.

117. The linguistic data show this preponderance of Ambundu, for most of the terms cited even by an observer as early as Battell turn out to be Kimbundu. For the founding of the Kingdom of Cassange by Kasanji, in general, see Miller, *Kings*, pp. 151–264. Cassange seems to have been founded in 1629–30.

a countervailing force, the continuing universal hankering to preserve local autonomy. Thus, even at the outset, chiefdoms were not adopted by every community since they were absent in Malemba lands, while later many principalities escaped incorporation into larger kingdoms by creating mutual alliances. Everywhere and at all times central power had to compete with this hankering for autonomy and could succeed only by providing some attractions for local leaders.

Still, given the evidence of *-sómpa and ngána, one could argue that all chiefdoms in this region derive from a single first one, at least by imitation (stimulus diffusion), although the clustering of populations by itself seemed to facilitate the independent formation of at least neighborhood societies in many different places at once. Principalities developed more rarely, although they appeared at several different points. While the emergence of larger kingdoms was even rarer, several of them did emerge independently from each other. The earliest one may well have arisen on the planalto in the thirteenth or fourteenth centuries and the latest ones in the Cuanza and Kwango basins in the fifteenth century, or in the case of Muzumbu aKalunga, perhaps even in the sixteenth century. Yet as the political vocabularies of the various kingdoms make quite clear, the more recent ones were not directly inspired by the earliest ones. Thus the Kimbundu-speaking kingdoms innovated their own political vocabularies rather than copying those of the Ovimbundu. Nor did the Ambundu kingdoms borrow most of the relevant terminology from the Kingdom of Kongo. Thus most major centralized polities in these regions arose independently from each other, and their institutions of governance were elaborated in each case from humble local institutions. It is therefore not only implausible to invoke long-distance diffusions of whole political models from other parts of Africa, but there is not a shred of evidence by which to do so.[118]

Moreover, even the picture obtained from such comparisons of terminologies is skewed because it creates the impression that all the principalities and kingdoms *within* the Kimbundu- or Umbundu-speaking lands severally derived from a single model, a first principality or kingdom in each of the two cases. But that impression is only a spurious effect of the fairly recent standardization of Kimbundu and Umbundu. While considerable linguistic diversity existed within each region as late as the nineteenth century, all our data stem, unfortunately, from standardized dictionaries in which

---

118. Hence culture historical claims about the input of various "layers of culture" (e.g., Zimbabwean) or from northern Katanga (Luba) or even legacies of "divine kingship" from as far afield as pharaonic Egypt can all be dismissed out of hand.

nearly all local variations have been erased.[119] Moreover, from the seventeenth century onward, Portuguese authorities began to standardize a political vocabulary for their own use, which later spread to wherever they governed. Thus the image of a single Ovimbundu or Ambundu model of polity or political traditions is an illusion. Yet, a certain standardization of the local Kimbundu and Umbundu dialects did occur as each large principality or kingdom took shape because its subjects began to imitate the forms of speech current at the capitals. Hence the extent of the Kimbundu and Umbundu speech communities by 1900 also documents the cumulative effect of the major kingdoms and chiefdoms over several centuries and over large regions. These language distributions indicate that once successful, large and enduring polities had taken root, a certain homogenization of political ideologies and practices followed within their territories. And not only that. Known fifteenth- or sixteenth-century loans of several Kongo terms in Ndongo (e.g., *mbanza* or *bakula*) show that prestigious kingdoms influenced the terminology of their neighbors. Hence ideas and practices also came to be borrowed *between* large, well-established polities and not just *within* the territory of each. Even though such loans were limited to marginal features, still their long-term effect was to enrich the political culture within each of these kingdoms. Therefore some of the intricacies of the governing institutions in kingdoms must be ascribed to the effects of what anthropologists call "peer polity interaction." But why was there such an enthusiasm for the elaboration of these centralized polities, why were so many local people inspired to contribute further independent inventions for this purpose when they all so staunchly desired to preserve their local autonomy?

Because many of these people stood to gain from it. Casting a look backward at this chapter, we have seen that the specific Jaga way of life appeared around 1550, already under Portuguese impact. A century earlier warlike Ngola lords began to rise in the northeastern Cuanza basin and to disperse southwestward from there. Earlier on *kalunga* 12 lords had begun to create principalities in the same basin and on the planalto. Before that, perhaps from the late tenth century onward, the first *soba* had organized their chiefdoms. Gains in population density, in agricultural efficiency, in trade, and presumably in industrial production, seem to have paralleled and accom-

119. For Kimbundu, some of the diversity can still be observed in Koelle. For Umbundu, we only know that the dictionaries are based primarily on the dialects of Bailundu and Viye, that a major distinction existed between the speech of Ovimbundu north and east of the Queve and that of people west of that river and, finally, that other Umbundu-related languages were spoken west of the planalto as in Hanya or Ganda.

panied the gains of polities in terms both of scale and of centralization.[120] But the congruence of these developments does not mean that governance was simply a result of agricultural or demographic history, nor the converse. The latter two histories were not just effects of larger scale centralized governance either. The congruence merely means that all these developments supported each other mutually. Polities of larger scale protected more people from strife in a context of rising populations, while more intensive farming allowed population growth and was itself fostered by an enlargement of political scale. The favorable soils and rainfall of middle Angola encouraged agricultural development, demographic growth, and an enlargement of the scale of governance. But the environment had nothing to do with monocephalic rule. That was only one sort of governance among other possible ones. It was a choice though that could be made to fit smoothly with environmental realities by proclaiming the ruler to be the guarantor of security and fertility since she or he controlled rainfall, fostered the birth of children, and defended everyone against foreign raiding. In return for such eminent services, ordinary farmers expected to be exploited to some extent and may consistently have produced a little more than they otherwise intended to do.

But it was not a necessary choice. It became the preferred choice because the collective imagination came to be fascinated by the notions of power, fame, and centralization around a celebrated ruler. A glorious court was one way to realize this dream in the concrete world. The long roll calls of titles and the frequent, often spectacular ceremonial performances at courts are proof that the inhabitants of these regions focused their collective imaginations on the splendors and the theater of centralized rule even though they also cherished their local autonomy.[121] But such a common fascination was only possible insofar as it was collective. Collective means that there had to be something in it for everyone. In practice that meant something for every family head. The essential something in this dream was what can be called a ladder of power, a ladder consisting of an ever-growing number of rungs, a body of more or less ranked titles centered on the capital and the court, crowned by the title of the ruler himself or herself. Most family heads could hope to obtain at least a minor title in their careers and saw such an achievement as a thing of glory just as the *légion d'honneur* is perceived by the average Frenchman. For obtaining a title made one an actor in the whole mag-

---

120. Again, future archaeology will be able to determine the extent to which these developments did occur and were congruent with each other.

121. Just as in Bali. See Geertz, *Negara*. But Geertz underestimated how much profane power actually flows from dreaming and role-playing in such a theater.

nificent theater of power. When we discussed the fascination of pastoralists or agropastoralists with cattle in the south, we showed that the substance of any collective imagination about governance need not necessarily focus on notions of a pyramidal centralized government. What was essential in their vision as much as in the vision of middle Angolans was its collective character, including the possibility for every local community leader to participate in it. Just as here every local leader could hope for a title, every local leader in the south could hope to accumulate more power and fame by amassing more cattle. The next chapter shall show yet another focus for collective imagination as it developed in the east, where it consequently provided a forum for the achievement of the aspirations of every local family head.

5

OF MASKS AND GOVERNANCE

A THICK LAYER OF POOR GRAY OR WHITE INFERTILE sands, dubbed Kalahari Sands after their geological origin, covers the subsoils that stretch over the entire interior of West Central Africa. These are wholly unsuited for growing crops except where major river valleys have carved deep gullies to give access to more fertile red soils and alluvia.[1] Still these soils supported mostly dry forests in the north where the rainfall was well over 1,000 millimeters per year while farther south park and grasslands dominated the landscape. Game, especially ruminants, abounded in these environments and provided a good living for foragers.[2]

The earliest farmers emerged at the northern border of these lands and settled there along the major rivers to clear fields for their root crops in the forest galleries that filled most of their lower valleys, thus leaving the vast uplands wholly to the aboriginal foragers. Over time, this pattern of agricultural settlement gradually spread south and southeastward as far as yams and palm trees could be grown profitably. Later, with the advent of cereal cultivation, sorghum, which is well adapted to the soil and rainfall conditions of the region, soon became the main crop, for it could also be cultivated on the infertile uplands, albeit at a high cost of additional labor.[3] Nevertheless, farming remained difficult, villages remained small and ephemeral, sedentary settlements remained confined to patches along the major river valleys, and the overall population density remained very low. Still, the

---

1. Achim Von Oppen, *Terms,* pp. 121–24 and map 2. Hence, access to red soils was of great importance and is stressed in traditions from the Kwango to the margins of the upper Zambezi Valley.

2. For Stone Age sites, see Ervedosa, *Arqueologia,* pp. 55–77, 107–9, 112–13, 128, 149–53, 242–43, and Lanfranchi and Clist, *Aux origines,* pp. 83–86, 123–26.

3. Sorghum could be tilled on the infertile gray sands by cutting and burning the bush over a considerable surface and then concentrating the resulting ash unto a small plot, a system called *citimene.*

scanty archaeological record, which begins only in the eighth or ninth centuries, shows that farmers settled in various parts of the region.[4] The time depth involved in the separation between the Kwilu and Eastern blocks of Njila languages suggests that their speakers settled in the region many centuries earlier than that.

According to oral traditions, which describe a time that cannot have been much earlier than ca. 1600, only San-speaking foragers occupied all the lands south of the upper Lungue-Bungo River and everywhere between the edges of the Zambezi and upper Cuanza Valleys, while numerous foragers of a different appearance, speaking unknown languages, still roamed northward of the upper Kasai River.[5] A network of settled Njila-speaking villages existed only north and west of the Lungue-Bungo River, not far beyond the 1,200 millimeter isohyet and near the southern limit where domesticated yams would grow. By the 1800s, however, that network had expanded as far as the upper Cuito and Cuando Valleys, even though some !Kung bands could still be found in these latitudes. Farther south, farming villages remained quite sparse and were then still expanding southward along the major rivers in !Kung territory.

When the first indications regarding population density became available in the eighteenth century, they provided a picture of a region where small groups of people settled in patches here and there along the larger river valleys surrounded by unoccupied wilderness. Somewhat larger and more

4. So far, very few sites have been found, in part because so little research has been done, but also in part because where more intensive research has been conducted, as in Lunda Province, very few sites actually turned up. The relevant excavated sites are the ceramic-age sites of Ricoco I (undated) and Dundo (ca. 760) plus a single pot at Mussolegi, the Iron Age site of Ricoco II (ca. 940), all in the Lunda province of Angola, then Lukolwe (ca. 1500) in Zambia near the Angolan border near the Zambezi, and the very late site of Mashita Mbanza (ca. 1700) south of Kikwit in Congo. To this must be added the chance find of a mask at Liavela (ca. 750–850) near the headwaters of the Cuanza, some rock engravings east of the uppermost Zambezi in Angola, a Janus-faced pole sculpture in wood on the banks of the Kwango at Tumbica (ca. 1000) in Angola not far from the border with Congo, a few undated pots near Tshikapa in Congo, and many iron weapons of unknown date in the rivers of the Lunda Province in Angola. See Ervedosa, *Arqueologia*, pp. 197–202, 220, 244–53; Lanfranchi and Clist, *Aux origins*, pp. 220, 222; Derricourt and Papstein, "Lukolwe," pp. 169–76; Pierot, *Étude Ethnoarchéologique*; Van Noten, "La plus ancienne"; Martins, "Arqueologia," pp. 10–12; de Maret, "Les trop fameux pots," pp. 4–11. I thank Constantijn Petridis and Nuno Porto for the Diamang reference about the find at Tumbica 1.

5. For such traditions, see Von Oppen, *Terms*, p. 104; Cheke Cultural Writers, *History*, pp. 9, 10, 23; Sangambo, *History of the Luvale*, p. 2; De Sousberghe, "Noms donnés aux pygmées," pp. 84–86; and Sebestyén and Vansina, "Angola's," pp. 319–20; 343, 355–56.

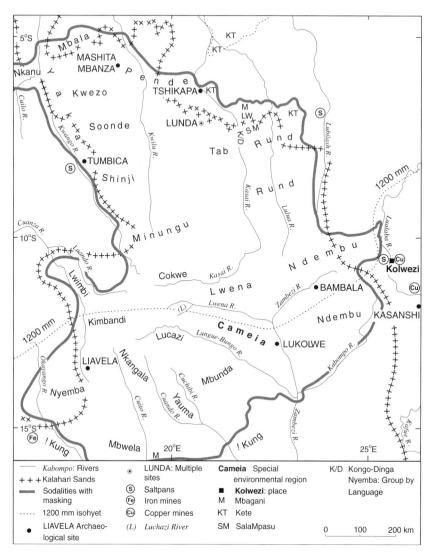

MAP 23. The Eastern Region

continuous concentrations of population were found only northward of the latitude 7° S and in or near the flooded plains of the upper Zambezi Valley. There was also a very restricted concentration of population in the region itself, on the ridge running eastward from the headwaters of the Kwango and Kasai Rivers.[6] This low population density and its distribution are obviously correlated with the quality of the soils (map 23).

6. Vansina, "Du nouveau," p. 57, for the north.

Given this situation, it is not surprising that, relative to the better endowed neighboring lands to the west, north, or east near the middle upper Zambezi, the whole sparsely settled region of the Kalahari Sands appears as a huge backwater, marginal to developments elsewhere. The peoples who inhabited it in the eighteenth century shared closely related languages mostly belonging to the Kwilu and Eastern blocks of Njila, were organized in apparently similar polities, and seemed to participate in a homogeneous culture. Yet one soon discovers that this region was not just a periphery with better peopled lands around it; its inhabitants had developed a strikingly original form of social organization characterized by sodalities (fraternities or sororities) based on gender and age that celebrated great masking festivals that dominated all social life.

Further probing discloses that the overall history of governance of the region constitutes a sequence of three periods before 1600. First villages, inhabited by aggregates of kinsfolk emerged. They were grouped into small clusters of adjacent settlements or vicinages (a specific type of neighborhood). Then, throughout the region there developed two sets of institutions, namely, corporate matrilineages within villages and common sodalities based on age and gender within each vicinage and perhaps also linking several of these. These sodalities and their spectacular masquerades have remained the hallmark of all the societies in the region.

Not much seems to have changed since then in the southernmost quadrant of the region. But elsewhere, further refinements on the existing institutions of governance occurred during the first half of the second millennium. Such elaborations varied in different parts of the region; hence, one must discuss each of these cases separately. People in the northeast quadrant of the region elaborated on the existing sodalities to create a form of truly collective governance. Meanwhile, people in the northwest quadrant and in the central portions of the region chose instead to bolster the authority of the leaders who represented each vicinage and turned them into chiefs. But they did so in two different ways.

From 1600 onward, a considerable upheaval of the older patterns of governance began to occur as the result of the invention and the meteoric rise of a Rund Kingdom in the far northeastern corner of the region, which was followed soon thereafter by the irruption of the transatlantic slave trade in the same region.[7] The expansion of the slave trade then interacted with a century-long (from before 1680 to ca. 1770) Rund expansion that resulted in the emergence of a Lunda Commonwealth, which included the whole region

7. Miller, *Way of Death,* describes and analyzes this trade.

north of the valley of the uppermost Kasai River from the headwaters of the Zambezi to the very banks of the Kwango.[8]

Villages, Vicinages, and Sodalities

As horticulturalists spread into the region, they chose to settle in or on the outer ridges of major rivers where they found adequate soils. This created a pattern of settlement in which villages were established in a more or less linear fashion along stretches of such rivers. This was still the pattern by the mid-nineteenth century when villages were strung out along rivers, espe-cially along the smaller affluents of the main rivers, and were located on the edges of the valleys, leaving large unsettled expanses of wilderness between them. Thus, however low the overall population density might be, they still formed stretched-out patches of settlement separated from each other by the uplands except for similar patches upstream and downstream of the rivers. Each patch formed a well-defined particular human-shaped landscape cor-responding to a "natural" vicinage.[9] The pattern of settlement was so pro-nounced that many of the first known ethnonyms are names of rivers, such as the large Lwena River or smaller affluents such as the Luchazi River.[10] In the nineteenth century, most villages were built on higher ground along the

8. Unfortunately, a satisfactory detailed analysis of the creation of the Rund King-dom and of the Lunda Commonwealth remains to be written. Even the latest general overviews contain a number of errors because of the misevaluation of various tradi-tions. Meanwhile, the least unsatisfactory summary to date remains Ndaywel e Nziem, "The Political System of the Luba and Lunda," 5:601–7.

9. "Vicinage" was first used in this context by Turner, *Schism and Continuity,* pp. xx, 44–48. The term is used here to render the flavor of the combination of human and natu-ral features found in such territorial entities. Its usage corresponds to the implications of Italian *paese,* French *terroir,* or even the German *Landschaft.* For a particularly good nineteenth-century example, see Serpa Pinto, *How I Crossed Africa,* pp. 1, 316 map 8 (the small tributary of the Cubangui near Chaobango), and, in general, p. 237 map 3, p. 273 map 5, p. 279 map 6 (but exception!: a concentration of villages near the headwaters of the Cuanavale). The concept of "vicinage" or "country" was rendered by a new term *-fuci* 5/6, 7/8 attested to in Kimbundu, Pende, Mbala, the Ngangela cluster, Cokwe, and Lwena. In Sala Mpasu, *ifuci* 5/6 means "foreign country." But in Kimbundu, the term also came to mean "crowd." The form can be reconstructed to *-kμ + cí* "to the coun-try," in which CS 331 *-cí* is the proto-Bantu form for "country."

10. These names are attested to by the late eighteenth century and were probably a nomenclature developed at the latest at the time when slave traders arrived here or well before 1750 (Von Oppen, *Terms,* p. 133.) Other ethnonyms refer to soils (Mbunda "red soil") or landscapes (Nkangala), downstream location (Ngangela) or special activities (Minungu "iron smelting furnace," Kimbandi "pottery land.")

river valleys, not far from the lowlands with their fertile red soils, while only a few built at river's edge.[11] This pattern seems to go back to the time of the earliest settlements in the region. Ever since, these vicinages have remained the main arena for the construction of a wider society and its institutions of governance. Before addressing those issues, however, further sketching of how villagers exploited these environments will establish the economic context in which these societies flourished.

By the time iron-using settlements appeared and once cereals had been adopted, sorghum had become the main crop in most of the area, although villagers continued to plant root and tree crops (oil palms, raffia, *Canarium schweinfurthii* Engl.) in suitable places such as the forests near the northern fringe of the Kalahari or the valley of the uppermost Kasai River. There agriculture intensified further, beginning from around the turn of the millennium onward, with the adoption of the water yam (*Dioscorea alata* L.) and some other subsidiary crops of Asiatic origin.[12] Nevertheless, in all the Kalahari Sands environments, agriculture still remained a precarious source of food so that both gathering and hunting remained exceptionally important to the food supply. After all, the region was exceptionally rich in game. All the men would have been expected to be thoroughly familiar with what the bush had to offer and they were all hunters to some degree. But only some became professional hunters. The latter practiced year-round, formed their own association, and initiated apprentices into the supernatural forces linked to their art. They enjoyed a very high status and their communities considered them to be creatures of legendary skill and the most illustrious of men.[13]

11. Indeed, this was the case in the shelter of Ricoco II around 1000 (Lanfranchi and Clist, *Aux origines*, p. 220). Such was the sensitivity to the importance of the precise place of settlement that, according to Kubik, "Masks of the Mbwela," p. 4, the ethnic difference between the Nkangela/Nkangala and the Mbwela was that the first built their villages some 500 to 800 meters from the floodplains of the rivers while the Mbwela settled on the very edge of these plains. Also see Kubik, "Introduction," in Chikota cha Luchazi Association, *Luchazi*, pp. 14–15, and Von Oppen, *Terms*, pp. 123–24.

12. Water yams (*Dioscorea alata* L.) and perhaps taro were introduced from the east in the lands near the headwaters of the Kasai River, probably between 800 and 1200. Water yams and taro are very well suited to inundated river valleys, have a high yield, and seem to have been eagerly adopted there. But other plants of the Asiatic complex, such as plantain, eggplant, and sugarcane remained ancillary crops.

13. The professional hunter and his status were of considerable antiquity as shown by *-yanga* or *-nyanga* 5/6, 7/8 "initiated specialist hunter," and in class 14 "state of being such a hunter," attested to in the Lweta group and in the whole Eastern block of languages, except for Rund and Sala Mpasu, which express the same notion by *-binda* 7/8—as in all the Luba languages farther east. Although some of these extensive distri-

In contrast, even though the contribution to the daily food supply of gathering was probably quite as significant as that of game, gathering was not celebrated at all, perhaps because everyone did it. Nevertheless, seasonal foraging for honey, fruits, caterpillars, or termites yielded crucial contributions to the diet.[14] Gathering was pursued both by men and by women (honey by men, caterpillars and leaves by women, fruits by everyone). Moreover, wherever San foragers lived in the neighborhood, they probably provided villagers, as they still did in recent times, with a good deal of honey, game, fruits, and other products of the bush in return for cereals, some metal goods (arrowheads and knives), and some *Cannabis*. Fishing was apparently practiced to some extent nearly everywhere as well, but in favorable locales, it was particularly intensive. This was the case during the proper season in such seasonally inundated landscapes as the Cameia, which was between the Kasai and Lwena Rivers, the marshy lands off the Cuchibi River, or the flatlands along other rivers. It was also the paramount activity year-round for some villages on the banks of major rivers such as the Luando, Cuanza, Kasai, and Lulua.

Brisk trading in basic commodities between different parts of the region must have closely followed on the settlement of villages and certainly grew over time. Iron ore or potting clays could be found only in rare places not covered by the nearly ubiquitous sands. The few districts that were rich in iron ore were those near Cassinga and in the land of the headwaters of the Kasai, Kwango, Cuanza, and Lungue-Bungo Rivers. Metal goods produced there, especially hoes, were in demand over long distances. Then at some time in the early second millennium, smelting specialists near the headwaters of the Kasai invented a particularly efficient furnace, the *lutengu* 11, which greatly enhanced productivity.[15] As to ceramics, in many places people made

---

butions came about because of borrowing, still the variation in form and classes points to an older ancestral source. Nothing expressed the prestige of the expert hunter better than the myth of Cibinda Ilunga (Ilunga the hunter) and the nineteenth-century Cokwe statues that represent him. See Bastin, *Chibinda Ilunga*.

14. For gathering and fishing, see Von Oppen, *Terms*, pp. 131–33, and Vellut, "Diversification," pp. 93–112.

15. For the terminology in general, see Kriger, *Pride*, pp. 75, 78–79. The term -*lungu* 5/6 is more widespread and came here from the east. It is found in practically all the Luba languages; in Tabwa, Bemba, and Fipa, as well as in Lwena. In Zambia, the ethnonym Lungu derives from it, as does "Nnungu" (Minungu in the plural), an ethnonym given before 1755 to people on the upper Kwango who were reputed for their production of iron. This -*lungu* 5/6 is an innovation of unknown date from the verb -*lúnga*, "to mix, to mingle." In the east, but not in Angola, it usually refers to a tall, induced-draft shaft furnace. As to -*tengu* 11, this term occurs in Ndembu, Rund, Lwena, Cokwe, and

do as best they could with gourds or wooden vessels. Still, potmaking became a considerable industry for export in the rare places where good clay
soils could be found, such as the Lwimbi or Kimbandi country[16] or at some
locations near the uppermost Zambezi. This circumstance is probably responsible for turning potting, usually a female craft, into a male one in this
latter region.[17] Little is known about the development of trade in other goods
such as mineral salt,[18] fish, mats, baskets, unguents (redwood, red earth?),
and even locally produced cotton or raffia cloth.[19] Apart from such basic
commodities, some luxury goods, such as a few head of cattle from the
agropastoral southwest and copper ornaments from the south or west were
also in demand, probably from early times onward. But substantial imports
of copper from the copperbelt near Kolwezi or farther away in Zambia only
began after ca. 1000.[20] As archaeological research progresses, much more will

---

Lucazi. It refers primarily to a lower furnace from which the slag could be tapped (see
J. Bebiano, *Notas sobre a siderurgia*, pp. 36–54, 65–70, and Chikota cha Luchazi, *Luchazi*, pp. 46–48. - *Tengu* 11 is derived from *-tenga* "to fabricate in clay, to mold" in Cokwe,
Lwena, and Ndembu and "to make something conical" in Rund. Both the term and the
type of furnace it refers to are clearly younger than *-lungu* 5/6 and the type of furnaces
that this designates. Still, *contra* Kriger, its diffusion is probably older than the Cokwe
expansion (starts ca. 1850) and could well be older than the onset of the Lunda Commonwealth ca. 1700. So far, none of the furnaces in the region have been dated. For an
early trade in hoes from the headwaters of the Cuanza, see Sebestyén and Vansina, "Angola's," pp. 322, 346.

16. Kimbandi actually means "land of potters." See "Ladislaus Magyar's Erforschung," p. 227, n. 4.

17. Derricourt and Papstein, "Lukolwe," p. 175. Pottery is a male-only craft among
the Lwena and Mbunda and one practiced by both men and women among the Cokwe
and Lucazi.

18. Most of it seems to have stemmed from the saltpans of the Lui River, from
Matamba (Koelle: 15/4) in southern Kasai, from the Lualaba downstream from modern
Kolwezi, from northern Namibia by way of Kwanyama speakers, and from Kaimbwe in
Zambia (Roberts, *History*, pp. 88–89, 103, 104).

19. For raffia, see Vansina, "Raffia Cloth," pp. 263–81. Its fabrication just beyond the
northern fringe of the Kalahari Sands region was probably much earlier than that of
woven cotton cloth, which dates at the earliest to the thirteenth or fourteenth centuries.
In recent times, the Kimbandi and Nyemba regions were known for their cotton cloth
production (Heintze, *Schachtzabel*, pp. 218–19, especially n. 126) but cotton weaving was
probably introduced from the Victoria Falls region and Zimbabwe where the technique
is only first attested to around 1200 (Vogel, "Eastern and South-Central African Iron
Age," p. 444).

20. Sizeable amounts of copper (in the form of crosses) were imported in the last
few centuries to the headwaters of the Zambezi and beyond as far as the Kwango River,
but we do not know when this trade began. An indirect clue may be the attempt to

eventually be known about this subject. Trading probably took place on a very small scale from vicinage to vicinage and by informal means such as mutual exchange between friends and affines since no trace of a special institution associated with trading has been detected.

From first settlement until the nineteenth century and in most parts of the region, most villages seem to have been quite small, although a few may have grown, even then, to several times larger than the average. In any case, their size varied both over time with the growth and then scission of each village, as well as in space at any given time. Until we have more archaeological data, we can only guess at their size by comparison with data from the nineteenth century and colonial times.[21] Moreover, most settlements seem to have been both remarkably mobile and quite ephemeral. Yet it is also true that in the more recent past a few villages remained rooted in the same spot for periods of a century or even more.[22] But these are exceptions which prove the rule for these villages were the residence of major chiefs—and no such chiefs existed in earlier times.

Nearly all ordinary settlements were highly mobile, mostly for economic and environmental reasons. First, some or many may have moved between their main emplacement and the bottom of the valley according to the season because they relied as much on other foods as on crops. This was still the case by the mid-1800s for settlements in the Cuito basin (but not in the

---

render a guilloche design on undated rock engravings near the headwaters of the Zambezi (Ervedosa, *Arqueologia*, pp. 244–27, especially at the Bambala site), which could well be an imitation of Kansanshi pottery. There a guilloche design was created during the seventh century and became ubiquitous in the ninth (Robertson, "A New," pp. 59–64). Archaeological data are sorely needed to document the trade in luxury goods such as copper, conus shells, cowries, beads, and perhaps others.

21. Before the changes wrought by the slave trade, their size seems to have varied between 5 and perhaps up to 40 adults. Among the Lwena in colonial times, they then became very small and their average size dropped to 15–30 people, that is, between 5 and 15 adults. See White, *An Outline*, pp. 4–11. That is a size comparable to that reported among the Ndembu and one that is not higher than that of many foraging communities according to Pritchett, *Lunda-Ndembu*, p. 91. In contrast, 4 to 20 houses, that is from less than 8 to 40 adults, was the average size of villages in the northern Cuito basin during the 1840s as estimated by Porto, "Uma viagem," p. 275, for the "Ngangela," in this case mostly Nyemba.

22. For cases of great stability of settlement, see White, *An Outline*, p. 3 (some Lwena villages were stable for thirty years or more); Porto, *Viagens*, pp. 324–25, and his "Uma viagem," p. 277, for the village of the major Lucazi chief, called *mwatiamvu*, which remained stable from ca. 1800 to at least 1850; Heintze, *Schachtzabel*, pp. 171–74 for villages of chiefs with an implied stability of a century or more.

Kimbandi region). During the rainy season, a community would have settled in on what was, presumably, its main site, which had a well-built village well outside the floodplain, and during the dry season, the community
moved to a camp on the plain or close to it. In sharp contrast to this pattern,
the Lwena abandoned their main settlement for seasonal camps in the dry
season to go fishing.[23] Second, most villages seem to have moved their main
emplacement every three years or so and sometimes settled many miles away
from their original settlement.[24] Presumably such villages would move most
of the time alongside the valley of a single main river, but some of them followed affluents upstream and eventually crossed over to other major river
valleys. This practice, as well as the annual seasonal shifts every year and the
high intersettlement mobility of individuals (men as well as women), explains why the populations of the region seem to have been exceptionally
mobile at all times.[25]

With such highly mobile settlements, these populations could expand
over great distances. Oral traditions of Ngangela-speaking farmers regarding their southward advance during recent centuries illustrate this and, in
the telling, also account for the spatial distribution of various ethnicities
there.[26] This high mobility also explains how a single language, with minor
dialectical differences (the Ngangela cluster) came to be spoken over a distance of nearly 1,000 kilometers distance from west of the Okavango to the
upper Zambezi. Such a situation requires a high intensity of continuing
communication throughout the entire region, a requirement that was met,
most likely, by a continuously high level of internal population mobility.[27]

23. Porto, "Uma viagem," p. 276 (they left the main villages from November to July
for farming purposes). For the Lwena, see Cabrita, *Em Terras,* pp. 161–62).

24. The frequency of these moves was usually dictated by the requirements of shifting cultivation (especially before the introduction of cassava ca. 1700). They are reported
from all parts of the region—for example, Porto, *Viagens,* p. 325 (Lucazi).

25. Many vocabulary transfers in all domains of social and cultural life indirectly attest to a very high and long-lasting rate of mobility. Pritchett, *Lunda-Ndembu,* pp. 91–92,
emphasizes individual mobility and movements over smaller distances.

26. That advance took place from about 1600 onward between the upper Cuanza
and Okavango basins on the one side and the Cuando-Zambezi basins on the other. For
the traditions in question, see Cheke writers, *History,* pp. 8–13, 23–49, and Chikota cha
Luchazi, *Luchazi,* pp. 29–31, 39–42, 72–74, 77–78, 94–95, 107–9, 121–40. The most spectacular example of mobility is the expansion of the Cokwe after 1850 (Miller, *Cokwe Expansion*). Eastern Angola is famous for the fluidity of ethnic designations for populations who speak practically the same language and follow a common way of life, yet
most of these ethnonyms were known by the 1790s and all of them by the 1840s.

27. Ngangela differs from both Lwena and Cokwe (forming themselves a single congeries of dialects) who are its closest relatives. To provide a satisfactory label for this

Residence in a village was, at first, based primarily on ties of kinship. The local kin group, still called *-coko 7/8 "kinsfolk" as in proto-Njila was bilateral, probably rather like the organization of the local foraging communities living around these horticulturalists.[28] Elder persons, designated by the word -kota 5/6, were the first leaders of their families.[29] Later, after the separation of the main linguistic blocks, a new term, -anta 3/4, "leader" appeared.[30]

Beginning in the last centuries of the first millennium, however, this overall social organization began to be transformed by the effects of two nearly simultaneous occurrences: the invention of sodalities to administer rites of passage to new age and gender statuses and the adoption of small local matrilineages. The sodalities were of greater importance in structuring societies than were lineages; nonetheless, a brief discussion of matrilineages is in order before one turns to the associations.

Corporate matrilineages were established everywhere in the region of the Kalahari Sands and came from the outside. The only semantic clue available

---

single language may not be possible because so many competing ethnonyms are used to designate it. It has been labeled Lucazi, Mbunda, Mashaka, Nkangala, Nyemba, Mbwela, and Ngangela. Unfortunately, every single one among these labels implies the adoption of a particular political stance and to coin a new one (such as the tempting Nyembunda from Nyemba at one end to Mbunda at the other) would merely compound the confusion. Hence, we are resigned to use Ngangela, its official Angolan name, and we talk of the Ngangela cluster.

28. When the residential composition of the settlement was stressed, the same term was used but in classes 3/4.

29. Thus *-kota 5/6 "person older in status" already in proto-Njila from CS 1158 *-kot- "become aged" attested as "adult" in Pende and Sala Mpasu, as "leader" in Holo, Mbala (godá 5/6 and godá "to rule" or probably derived from it) and in the Kwanza Block of languages. In Nyemba, the verb -kota means "to be important." In Lwena, Cokwe, and Ndembu -kota 5/6, 7/8 became "stem, stock, progenitor of family, clan, lineage."

30. Mwata, or mwanta, are reflexes of *-anta 3/4. It is attested in Rund, Ndembu, Kaonde, Lwena, Cokwe, Lwimbi, Kimbande, Lucazi, Mbunda, Nyemba, Mbwela, Pende, and Holo. It is absent from Sala Mpasu and Kete Ipila. (See also Hoover, "The Seduction," 2:527, 534 where his "proto-Lunda//Moxico" is our "proto-Eastern.") The term was borrowed much more recently in Kimbundu, Songo, Tshiluba, Sanga, and Kaonde. With the exception of Rund, the meaning never refers to the paramount level of chieftaincy, and as Rund actually uses the vocabulary of kinship to designate its political relations, this exception proves the rule. The fullest range of meaning occurs in Lwena mwata 3/2+4 and is glossed as "elder or important man, head of family, master, lord" and used as an honorific. Also in Cokwe "chief, patron, oldest or worthiest person of a village or of a family" and in Ndembu "chief, master, senior member of kinship group, slave owner." In the Ngangela cluster, the meaning is restricted to "headman, subchief, spokesmen for chief." In Nyemba, the form is only an honorific preceding a title. Unfortunately, the etymology of *-anta 3/4 remains unknown.

tells us that the concept probably diffused from a single point of origin into territory inhabited by the southern Moxico speakers and then farther north as far as the present limits of the matrilineal belt north of the lower Kasai and the Congo Rivers.[31] But whereas agropastoralists had used matrilinearity to regulate the management and inheritance of cattle herds, in the Moxico-speaking regions, cattle herds were absent or unimportant as a means of livelihood. Yet the same matrilineal principle was used as an ideal to establish local residential matrilineages.[32] The idea was for an enterprising man, accompanied by his brothers of the same mother, by their wives and their children, and by some of their sisters, to found his own settlement and residential matrilineage despite the centrifugal effects of virilocal marriage which continually dispersed the women and the children of that matrilineage into different villages. To achieve the desired goal, children had to be separated from their mothers when they were "six years" of age and sent to live with their mother's brothers.[33] At the same time, different sorts of preferential marriages were practiced to counteract the centrifugal effects of virilocality.[34] It is clear that the ethnographic reports all describe idealized situations that could never have corresponded to actual practice, if only because of demographic accident. In practice, the ideal setup resulted in high residential mobility for men as well as for women, in high rates of divorce, and often in the formation of very small and ephemeral settlements.

In reality, matrilineages had to accommodate themselves to pre-existing

31. *Contra* Vansina, *Paths,* p. 152, where I argued for an independent innovation in Mayombe. While the relationship between the adoption of corporate matrilineages and the availability of wealth in the form of material goods (metals, raffia) certainly holds true, this only establishes a context for this adoption and does not necessarily mean that matrilineages were invented independently in this region.

32. In this regard, the adoption of the ancient form -*soko* 14 "bilateral group" to refer to matrilineage among Moxico speakers is significant. Baumann, *Lunda,* pp. 122, 124–25, and index has *usoko* "matrilineage." In Nyemba and Ndembu, one finds *vusoko,* "family, lineage."

33. For an example of such reports, see ibid.

34. Most of these involved direct or classificatory cross-cousins. Marriage with a father's sister's daughter made certain that grandsons occupied exactly the same position as their maternal grandfathers and were therefore preferred nearly everywhere. They also created a stable alternating alliance between pairs of clans. But some groups preferred marriage with a mother's brother's daughter even more because it kept a son's children in the village of their matrilineage. If this was systematically practiced from generation to generation, the men of the matrilineage always did remain in the same village as desired, but at the price of linking each clan successively to all the others in turn (ibid., p. 125).

situations. In some cases, they came to exist beside bilateral groups; in others, they were the main principle of social classification but had to acknowledge the special link that tied a father to his children, who, it was believed, inherited his talents. In other cases, a founding matrilineage was the undisputed core of local social organization but was surrounded by dependent matrilineages issued from the children of its own men. As a result, different sorts of local village organizations developed in the three main parts of the region, ranging from a small set of brothers and sisters with their matrilineal relatives among Moxico speakers to a matrilineage as a subsidiary grouping in villages (which continued to be dominated by a bilateral organization) in the northeast to the emergence of somewhat larger lineages surrounded by subsidiary ones in the Kwilu area.[35] The terminology used for the matrilineage reflected these different trajectories. They came to be designated by a variety of different metaphors, such as "belly," "umbilical cord," a term derived from "to be born," "progenitor," or "base of treetrunk."[36]

The invention of sodalities organizing the various rites of passage owes much to environmental conditions. In these poor lands, horticulturalists and farmers soon found that they could not subsist on agricultural foods alone and that they had to pursue foraging as well. In fact, the main male occupation in these societies was to forage and, specifically, to hunt. Proto-Njila horticulturalists may have known the collective rites of passage to turn boys into adults with or without circumcision even before they entered the area,

35. For recent social organizations in the matrilineal belt, see Vuyck, *Children,* esp. pp. 11–36 (general), 37–71 (kinship), and 73–104 (marriage). For contrasting structures, see, for instance, Von Oppen, *Terms,* pp. 250–57 (generalized: northeast Angola and northwest Zambia); de Sousberghe, "Les Pende," pp. 17–48; Ceyssens, *Pouvoir* (Lweta group); Crine, "Thèmes de la culture lunda," pp. 44–87 (Rund).

36. "Belly" (as in Mbala, Pende, Holo *vúmu,* and *jimo* in Cokwe and Lwena and also family in Cokwe) is a common metaphor. Nyemba has -*vembo* 5/6 derived from -*vemba* "to procreate, to give birth." The older form -*kota* 5/6, 7/8 now came to mean "stem, stock, progenitor of family, clan, lineage" in Ndembu, Lwena, Cokwe, Lucazi, and Mbunda. Is this related to the notion of -*koto* 5/6 "root person" in Kongo-Ndinga (Ceyssens, *Pouvoir,* pp. 317–18, 432), which designates the oldest woman founder of a matrilineage and also "old woman" (*ohonkoto* 1/2) in Umbundu? Ceyssens sees these as attestations from CS 1114 and partial series 306 *-*kódo* 5/6 "base of tree trunk." While these forms actually differ from the Moxico ones, the imagery remains the same. "Hearth" -*jiku* 7/8 was the metaphor in Mbala and Pende. "Umbilical cord" as a metaphor is quite unusual. It occurs in Lucazi and Mbunda, Nyaneka, Nkhumbi -*kova* 7/8, which suggests a historical link, most likely that corporate matrilineages spread from the agropastoralists of the Cunene basin to the northeast. (But see also Lwena, -*kowa* 9/10 "umbilical cord" and Ndembu -*kovu* 5/6 "navel.")

but similar collective rites for girls and young mothers, the main gatherers and the persons who reproduced society, may well have been practiced by the Late–Stone Age foragers since they are still common among foragers and pastoralists alike in the entire southern part of West Central Africa.[37] Be this as it may, the development of sodalities to administer collective rites of passage must be set in an economic and environmental context and not just taken as a gratuitous symbolic ritual. The collective initiation for boys started at the outset of a long dry season, the ideal season for hunting and living in the bush. Their main training was aimed at rendering them proficient in hunting and gathering. Their initiation required a year or sometimes more because it takes a long time to become thoroughly familiar with the offerings of the different seasons in the bush and with the techniques required to exploit them. Moreover, a certain overall maturity had to be instilled in the youths to prepare them to be ready to cope with the unexpected as well as with familiar routines.

Gradually, the initiations for boys and girls spawned a further series of rites of passage to mark passage into the status of mature adult and, in some cases, even a later one to acquire the status of initiator. Thus, rites of passage for female puberty were followed by rites for young mothers, while the initiating mistresses may themselves have undergone a further stage in a second rite of passage. Initiated boys underwent a second initiation as young married adults and the master initiators underwent a second stage in this second rite of passage. Consequently, the rites of passage became the backbone of the social structure because they divided the population of each gender into a series of age-sets within each of which common experience bred solidarity.[38] The rites of passage, especially those for entry into the sets of nubile adolescents and the sets of mature adults, were accompanied by masked dances and sometimes by spectacular displays, such as the so-called nocturnal fire dance during the initiation ritual organized by the women's sodality for entry into the adult women class.[39] Among the main effects of the initiation rite for boys was the formation of strong bonds of friendship be-

37. See, for instance, Estermann, "La fête," pp. 128–41, and his three ethnographies as well as Hirschberg, "Khoisan," p. 392; Baumann, "Die Südwest Bantu Provinz," pp. 496–97, and his "Die Sambesi-Angola Provinz," map 596, pp. 601–2. Recent ethnographic distributions cannot by themselves prove great antiquity, but they can still be quite suggestive.

38. G. Kubik, *Makisi*, pp. 89–90. Members of the age-set of initiated young men were called *-kwenzi* 1/2 (Gangela, Ndembu), *-kwézi/e* 1/2 (Cokwe, Lwena), *-kwenje* 1/2 (Mbunda), and *-kwendji* 5/6 (Nkhumbi).

39. Kubik, *Makisi*, pp. 90, 170–71.

tween male cohorts of the same promotion of adolescents.[40] Because female adolescents underwent their initiation severally, such group friendships did not easily develop among them. Just as important, however, was the creation of a clear separation between the different gender and age statuses among members of the older sets, a separation that was rekindled whenever they initiated new members into their ranks. In general, these ties of solidarity resulted in an implicit alliance between alternating generations and enveloped all residents of a vicinage into a common web of relationships, whatever their affiliation with separate corporate descent groups.

Among all these initiations, the one that provoked everyone's greatest enthusiasm, be it in terms of numbers of adult participants, duration, effort, or lavish public display, was that of young boys into adulthood. In the recent past, only the installation ritual for a new ruler could compete with it in importance, if not in frequency. The boys' initiation was the main regularly recurring event in every village and vicinage and was the occasion for most exuberant displays, especially masquerades, in which all the various social roles and statuses recognized by society were acted out.[41] While pastoralists developed a wealth of descriptive names for cattle, and a cornucopia of titles developed in middle Angola, the people of the Kalahari Sands created a plethora of masks.[42]

Because masks in recent times have been linked above all else with boys' initiations, it is tempting to think that it has always been so and to claim, for instance, that the mask found near the headwaters of the Cuanza at Liavela, which dates to 750–850 proves that Liavelans already initiated adolescent boys. That may well be so, but it does not necessarily follow at all. Even in recent times, masks appeared not just during these initiations but also on a wide range of other occasions, ranging from other rites of passage (initiations, funerals) to a means for maintaining order. Hence, a thousand years ago they could well have been used in a context that had not yet anything

40. Pritchett, *Ubwambu,* shows its considerable importance among the Ndembu in the twentieth century. *Ubwambu* in Ndembu corresponds to *kasendo* in Lwena and in Cokwe where Baumann (*Lunda,* pp. 96, 124, 132–33) reports it as an astonishingly strong relationship. Also see Von Oppen, *Terms,* pp. 331–33, and 394–95 (in relation to trade).

41. These initiations and especially the masks have also fascinated many scholars. Book-length monographs about them now exist for almost every single ethnic group in which they occur. Even though their historical conclusions should be rejected, the reader will find the comparative works of both Kubik's *Makisi* and Felix's and Jordan's *Makishi* very useful as an introduction to the question. The best single study of masks and the most sensitive to their history remains Strother, *Inventing Masks.*

42. Kubik, "Masks of the Mbwela," pp. 4–5, recorded forty-one of them in one Cuito district but there were many more, probably over fifty.

to do with boys' initiations.[43] Moreover, a genuine age-set organization for both genders does not arise all at once, nor does that automatically grow out of the practice to initiate adolescent boys and girls. After all, initiations for boys and girls are very widespread in Central Africa, but the division of all the members of society into age-sets existed only in this region. It follows that the system of age-sets as a whole appeared only once the voluntary *mungonge/i* 3/4 and *ciwila* 7/8 initiations for mature adults had developed out of the older rites of puberty. Therefore, the whole system did not appear fully formed at any particular date but slowly developed from the very beginning of settlement in the region.

Nor was the system invented in one locale only. It has long been known that a large number of common words linked to initiations and masks occur throughout the area.[44] This situation clearly resulted from a vast amount of

43. E.g., Felix and Jordan, *Makishi*, p. 47, "Masks are also used as instruments of divination and healing, and on such occasions as circumcisions, enthronements, title nominations, funerals, conflicts, trials, sacrifices, inaugurations, important meetings, and agrarian and hunting rituals." Both this work and Kubik's *Makisi* show many instances of their use in other age-set related initiations.

44. Especially with regard to the more intensively studied boys' initiation, which is also the most complex. But the initiations for adults remain practically underreported or unreported and may well share a large number of words as well. Everywhere the boys' initiation is now *mukanda*, the common initiation for adult men *mungonge/mungongi*, and that for mature women *ciwila*. Lest one be inclined to deduce from this that all these forms are at least proto-Eastern and of hoary antiquity, one must remember how sensitive all these initiations are to current fashions and events and how easily various groups borrowed new features from each other. Given the parallel of known patterns of historical communication in the region from ca. 1700 onward, it is much more likely that each of these terms, once invented, spread from the language that coined it, into all the others. Thus Horton tells us that before Lunda chiefs arrived in the area that is now called *mukanda*, it was called *mungongi* in Lwena—and *mukanda* seems indeed to be an older term in Suku, Mbala, Pende, and in the Lweta languages than is the case farther south. For *mungongi/e*, see Bastin, "Mungonge," pp. 361–403. *Ciwila* is common to all languages between Yaka or Pende to Ndembu and may have been developed anywhere in the northern half of the area, since the term does not exist in Ngangela where the adult women's initiations are *makisi avampwevo* ("women's masks") and *tuwema* ("the flames"). Similarly, words for the novices (*kandanji, kandanda*) and initiator (*cilombola*) among others (including whole sets of names for masks) are found near and far, suggesting a common elaboration from a whole variety of sources. See, for instance, Baumann, "Mannbarkeitsfeiern," pp. 1–54, and especially 40–48. In contrast, note the absence of a common term for the girl's puberty initiation. It is *Cikula* or *litunga lyamwali* in Ngangela, *kukula* in Lwena (*cikula* is also a term used everywhere for a phase in the *mukanda* ritual), *nkanga* in Ndembu, *chilunga* in Cokwe, *ngidi* in Holo, and *Cisungu* in Luba and Bemba, which suggests multiple parallel developments and especially greater resistance to borrowing.

mutual borrowing. When it comes to details such as the names or even the shapes of specific masks, recent borrowing certainly plays a role since each initiation strives to be up to date and to flaunt the latest fashions. Could then not the whole complex also be of rather recent origin? Perhaps it was ve-hiculated by the Cokwe expansion after 1850? Perhaps it was due to the in-tensification of contacts during the era of slave trade? Perhaps the spread of the Lunda Commonwealth during the eighteenth century was responsible? Perhaps the system was brought—if one takes oral traditions literally—by the first chiefs?[45] While any and all of these events, as well as others, proba-bly furthered the diffusion of particular details, they are most unlikely to have propagated the entire system of age-sets or even major rites of passage themselves. The Cokwe expansion is too late, the Rund political system did not spread them easily because its establishment was rather opposed to ini-tiations, which strengthened local autonomy, nor does the slave trade appear to be a very plausible candidate for the diffusion of such major institutions.

The elaboration of initiations within the entire region and even beyond it as far as the Nkanu and eastern Kongo is probably much older. Indeed, the earliest reference to one of these comes from Kongo and dates to the mid-seventeenth century.[46] One suspects that the various parts of the whole com-plex must be old because they all correlate so well with the area over which a number of other unrelated loans, including a number of kinship terms, have also spread over time.[47] This sort of situation only occurs as the result of intensive intercommunications over many centuries. Thus the complex of age-sets did not arrive ready-made from anywhere at all. It was innovated within the region and was slowly constituted by the accumulation and jux-

45. The last two views are held by Papstein, "Upper Zambezi," pp. 137, 174; White, "Notes," p. 115; and Von Oppen, *Terms,* p. 303. Yet this argument rests on the supposed absence of these rites among the "ancestral" Mbwela of yore. That is not acceptable be-cause Mbwela is not a homogeneous category and especially because the main point of these oral traditions was to portray the Mbwela as savage. See also the definition of *ngongo* 3/4 in Horton's Lwena dictionary.

46. Cavazzi, *Descrição,* 1:99 (and vol. 2 index *quimpaxi,* i.e., *chimpasso, chimpassi*). Other sources include Thornton, *The Kongolese Saint Anthony,* p. 58, n. 16.

47. Nearly all the kinship terms are reflexes of the same forms in the whole region of the Kalahari Sands, not just the Eastern Block languages, but also in the Kwilu Block (except for Mbala) and even within the Lweta unit and also among Suku and Yaka. These include, e.g., *mujikulu/muzukulu* 1/2 "grandchild," *nantu/matu/nanato* 1n/2 "mother's brother," *mwip(h)wa* 1/2 "sister's son," *musonyi* 1/2 "cross-cousin," *mpangi* 1n/2 "sibling of the other sex." Some of these are ancestral to Njila or even older and more widespread, others have diffused into the region from central Eastern Bantu languages and a few originated somewhere within the region. See also n. 86.

taposition of many local ideas, practices, and institutions, each of which may well have stemmed from a different location, and passed along from one place to another, until everyone in the region shared them. Instead of a single inventor then, a multitude of dispersed local actors is responsible for the elaboration of this complex. It is therefore useless to search for a single cradle and date of invention. That process of construction had already begun by the time the Liavela mask was fashioned in the eighth or ninth century (if the mask was used for an age-set ritual), and ever since people have been building, amplifying, and embroidering on age-sets for over a thousand years.

As the reader may well have suspected all along, most early villages were too small to be mostly self-sufficient. They lacked a sufficient number of people for several essential communal efforts, such as, for instance, the great annual dry-season hunt.[48] They lacked a sufficient range of specialists, be they diviners or healers or even circumcisers, smiths, or other professionals, including even specialized hunters. There would also be far too few children in the community to perform rituals at regular intervals, such as the collective initiations of adolescent boys. Moreover, in a small village inhabited by less than a dozen adult men and women, every debilitating illness, every death, provoked a labor crisis. Such villages could flourish only if they could frequently call on others in the neighborhood to help as needed.

Even the rare large villages with as many as forty adults could not be self-sufficient.[49] They would be better able to rely mostly on their own resources as far as labor or know-how was concerned, they would be less easily disrupted by disease or death, and they could—if necessary—carry out most common collective rituals of passage, including the initiations of young teenage boys, by themselves, but, at best, they could do so only once every five years or so. Such a village would not yet be too large for the annual transhumance between wet and dry season locations. Yet, however large it was, no single village was large enough to contain the whole complex web that formed its social foundation in its own community. Not only did people often have to marry outside the village, not only was the collective involvement of several villages necessary for some activities, such as burning the open grasslands at the onset of the dry season for communal hunts, but the very ability to maintain a satisfactory frequency for the celebration of the various rites of passage required a demographic mass larger than the size of any one village. Hence even large villages still had to rely on their neighborhood for assistance. While nearly everyone in such a village was kin, it was

48. Pearson, *People*, p. 127.
49. For the variability of village size in the nineteenth century, see n. 21.

too large for everyone to be a member of a single two- or three-generations deep local matrilineage or the spouse of one. There had to be several competing matrilineages; hence, a large village could no longer be governed by the head of the single resident matrilineage. The larger villages were, of necessity, governed by a council of the heads of the several resident matrilineages meeting in a men's clubhouse. There they debated, decided about common activities, and resolved (-sompa) whatever conflicts arose among themselves.[50]

Whether large or small, villages required a helpful neighborhood and the obvious arena for wider interaction was the vicinage, that natural aggregate of settlement along the rivers. Being mutually interdependent, the villages of a vicinage needed common overarching institutions. This role was fulfilled by the organization of the various rites of passage that created sodalities, brought initiates from the constituent villages together, fostered their feelings of solidarity, and created *ubwambu* or *kasendo* friendship between their inhabitants. A vicinage could easily be ruled informally by convening a council of their *mwa(n)ta* when necessary, and such a procedure was common in at least one corner of the region.[51] Nothing more was needed. Yet eventually most vicinages came to be represented by a single individual, a person chosen because of his or her perceived wisdom in palaver debates, since as was the case farther west, here too such people were referred to as *ngána* 1/2 "wise ones." Their relationship as representatives of the whole within the vicinage was well expressed by the title *mwene*, with its connotation of identity, followed by a proper name or the name of a vicinage.[52] Having a common representative then helped to cement a feeling of solidarity among the villages of the vicinity. It was also quite practical whenever disputes between different vicinages had to be settled. A mid–nineteenth-century example concerning the Yauma of the Cuchibi River shows us how the choice of such a representative could have come about. There, Mwene

50. Palaver houses were found everywhere except in Kwilu. They were called *coota* (in Cokwe and Rund while in Ngangela, *cota* now means "courtyard of chief") or *ndzango* (in Ngangela, Lwena, Umbundu). Ndembu borrowed *ndzangu* from Lwena. Recent Ndembu villages seem to have been too small to have had men's clubhouses. See Pearson, *People*, pp. 67–69, and further *Kusompa mulonga:* "to complain, to arbitrate," pp. 105–8). The reader remembers that in Middle Angola *soba* "chief" was coined from this -*sompa*.

51. Pearson, *People*, pp. 49–50.

52. From *-yene* "self" and derived meaning "owner as extension of self." Von Oppen, *Terms*, pp. 246–47, rightly stresses the fairly equal relationship and the personal links involved and the tie between "ownership" and "union." *Mwene X* is a "representative of *X*."

Gambo, a sixty-year-old woman, ruled the district in 1847. Having founded a settlement there herself, she then had thirteen children, most of whom established villages of their own around hers and thus created a vicinage.[53]

The oral traditions of the ruling dynasties who entered the lands of the upper Zambezi in the seventeenth century lumped all the agriculturalists they found there together under the label Mbwela or "autochthon" and described all of them as boorish simpletons, naturally in contrast to their own position as highly civilized immigrants.[54] Although all the features of this portrait are very slanted, two recurring cliches about them may well have had some foundation in reality. One pertains to their great numbers scattered all over the land, the other to the fact that they did not pay any tribute to their *mwene*. The first cliche can be understood to refer to a multitude of small political entities, probably of vicinage size rather than to absolute numbers, and the lack of tribute stresses the character of a *mwene* as a representative—just as Mwene Gambo still was in the mid-nineteenth century.[55]

Common institutionalized links between inhabitants of different vicinages were rare and always took the form of networks. The best known of these was the matriclan. In theory, this resulted from the dispersal of new residential matrilineages issued from older ones through the operation of virilocal marriage, usually whenever sister's sons stayed with their fathers rather than rejoin their mothers. Hence, matriclans supposedly arose automatically a few generations after corporate matrilineages had been adopted. In practice, however, local matrilineages often seem to have chosen themselves which clan they wanted to affiliate with. Recently, there were only a dozen of these clans in the Moxico-speaking region and they were common to all the peoples of the region, including Lunda-Ndembu speakers, barring only the Rund and their neighbors in the northeast. The formal links between members of the same clan were rather weak, yet each clan had its own

53. Porto, *Viagens*, pp. 328–29. Note that formerly this district had once been tributary to the Lozi king. This woman is not to be confused with the 24-year-old woman Mwene Mutembe who headed the district of Cuti (Outi is a misprint and Cuti is Cuchibi!). She was found to rule there in 1853 and may well have been a daughter of Mwene Gambo and still subservient to her or her successor (Porto, "Uma viagem," p. 280). This was not a unique case.

54. Well noted by Papstein "Upper Zambezi," pp. 77–79; Von Oppen, *Terms*, p. 103. Yet both forget elsewhere that the term refers to a congeries of autochthons, not to a distinct collectivity.

55. I fully concur with Von Oppen's interpretation of "multitude" in his *Terms*, p. 103. For a summary of views about the Mbwela, see Schecter, *History*, pp. 264–69; Papstein, "The Upper Zambezi," pp. 77–84.

name,[56] each clan was exogamous,[57] and each clan boasted of a formula, which included some names of its progenitors and alluded to their deeds, but, unlike clans elsewhere, these clans did not observe any common food prohibition. Beyond this, lineages belonging to a common clan were supposed to be allies, especially in feuds, while visiting members from other lineages of the same clan were granted hospitality.[58] The main effect of this network of clans was to provide a rudimentary framework for social classification beyond the vicinage, to allow for safe travel between villages, and to provide additional protection for matrilineages in local conflicts.

Collective Government

Once the peoples in the region were well established and had developed the basic social and territorial organization just described, they began to elaborate on their systems of governance, although they did so in different ways in the three main parts of the region (map 24). Long before 1600, a highly original mode of government was invented by the peoples living in the northeast of the area.[59] This type of government was still common in recent times among the Lweta- and Rund-speaking populations who live between the Kasai and Lulua Rivers along latitude 7° S. But before 1600 it was also

56. Formed as was the case among the agropastoral Ambo by *vaka* + name but, contrary to the Ambo, only some of the names used were those of animals. Others referred to a legendary progenitor (McCulloch, *Southern,* p. 21). With the exception of Mbala, where *gáanda* 5/6 "clan, tribe" also meant "association in general" and Pende, where *giputa/gifuta* 7/8 also referred to notions of association, fellowship, friendship, and to a clique, the word "clan" was the word used to designate all natural species: Cokwe, *munyaci* "lineage, progeniture, race, tribe, clan, family"; Lwena *muyaci* "tribe, clan, species, class"; Lucazi *muyati*, "clan, tribe, race, nation"; Ndembu *muchidi* "tribe, kind, species, clan"; Ngangela also *musovo, muxovo, vungu* "tribe, stock race, nation"; and Mbunda "species, kind, breed."

57. McCulloch, *Southern,* pp. 21, 40, 63, but Heintze, *Schachtzabel,* p. 213; yet among the Pende, only local matrilineages were exogamous. See de Sousberghe, "Pende," p. 24; Muzong Wanda Kodi, "Pre-Colonial," 1:222.

58. McCulloch, *Southern,* pp. 19–21, 40, 63. The clan formula included the names of early progenitors and some of their deeds.

59. Dating is obtained both from the estimated date for the rise of the first Rund Kingdom (Hoover, "Seduction," pp. 614–28) and from that of the mature Kingdom of Kuba (dated to ca. 1625), two developments which occurred when collective governance was flourishing in the region. As shall be seen later, its connection with the spread of the word *kalamba* 12/13 "big man" also supports a date far earlier than 1600, as does the mention of *kilamba* in Kimbundu by the 1620s.

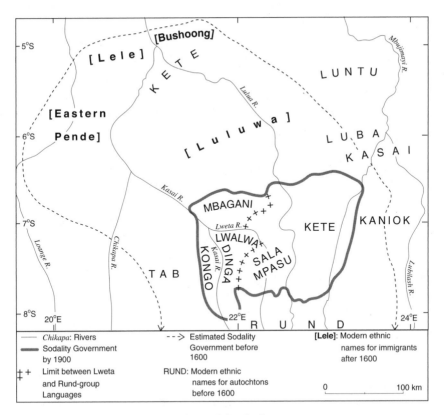

MAP 24. Collective Government by Sodality before 1600

practiced over a much larger region.[60] This system of governance first developed in the lands that straddle the major ecotone formed by the boundary between the Kalahari Sands and the regions with better lateritic soils to
the north that also straddle the border between languages belonging to the
Lweta unit and the Rund subgroup of the Njila unit.

Environmental conditions in the northeast were much more favorable
than in the south as most of this region enjoyed good soils, greater rainfall,
and a longer rainy season. Staple crops of West African origin, such as palm
trees (both oil palms and raffia) and yams, grew well here, while the land also
provided good hunting and fishing. Moreover, the horticultural farming way
of life was more ancient and sedentary villages probably also arose some cen-

60. Unless indicated elsewhere, this section follows Vansina, "Government," pp. 1–22.
This system of government can only be reconstructed from ethnographic data relating
to the Lweta people and some of their neighbors. Hence, the crucial significance of
Ceyssens's *Pouvoir* despite the recent date of his fieldwork.

turies earlier here than was the case to the south. At first, horticulture in this area was more intensive than on the Kalahari Sands to the south, and after the introduction of cereal crops it came to be based, in the northern parts of the region at least, on a system of two fields worked at the same time. The first one, cleared by men in the richer soils of the rainforests was planted mainly with root crops while a second one cleared by women in the savanna was sown with cereals. The resource basis for developing industries was good. One could make pottery nearly everywhere, reasonably good sources of iron ore and salt were scattered here and there, cultivated raffia trees were abundant, and raffia cloth was woven. Although the villages were still settled along river valleys, the resulting dendritic pattern of settlement was far less pronounced than it was farther south because the rivers flowed much closer to each other. Hence, especially in the northern parts of the region, a regular network of settlements tended to occupy the entire landscape and resulted in a strikingly higher concentration of population than was usual farther south.[61] In such a situation, contacts between settlements on all sides were more numerous but disputes over land or marriages were also inevitably more frequent. Quarrels over land could become all the more intractable because, ideally, after the introduction of cereals, each village strove to include in its domain a stretch of lower lying forestland near a river as well as a large stretch of higher lying savanna or *mpata* 9/10.[62] The latter, which was used at least as much for hunting and foraging as for farming, was considered as essential as the first.[63] Given such circumstances, increased friction was bound to occur and one might well expect the rise of a form of centralized governance to cope with it. But that did not happen.

The villagers were organized in several local matrilineages per village called *édzungú* 5/6, "cooking pot," each of which was subdivided into households or tiny sublineages called *edjiku* 5/6, "hearth." In turn, the *édzungú* themselves were equal members of a wider network of dispersed matriclans.[64]

61. For a reasonably early map, see Forminière, "Congo Belge" supplementary maps to *Bulletin de la Société royale de géographie belge de Bruxelles,* 1923, sheet D4S; for the human ecology, see Jules Wilmet, "Essai," pp. 307–63 (habitat types: 354–59, esp. 358–59; agriculture on red soils: 330–49; population densities: 321, that is densities of 10–15 people per square kilometer in both Luiza and the adjacent Kazumba Territory to the north in stark contrast to 1–3 per square kilometer generally farther south).

62. Unless otherwise indicated, all the terms cited in this section stem from Kongo-Dinga.

63. The Lweta languages used *bulá* 14 "village" in the sense of "home" and *mpata* 9/10 in the sense of "plains" but also with the connotation of "home."

64. For -*jiko* 5/6 or *cooto/a* 7/8 as used elsewhere to designate coresidential social groups, see Vansina "Government," pp. 14–16. In Cokwe, *coota* designates the

Beyond this, the whole village also formed a "House," called *shoóto* 7/8, "fire-place." Such a House consisted of a single group composed of a set of related extended bilateral families whose "fathers" recognized a single overall "father" or big man. Well after these institutions had matured, the local languages then borrowed the word *kalamba* 12/13 from the adjacent region to the south to designate such big men.[65] The "hearth" and the "cooking pot" complemented each other. To knit the community together, alternating generations were allied with each other. Such an alliance was encouraged by preferential marriages between grandparent and grandchild as well as between cross-cousins. Grouping by age was thus at least as important as grouping by descent. Age-sets were structured by at least two different rites of passage accompanied by masked dances for each gender, one into young adulthood and one into full maturity. While everyone underwent the first one of these, participation in the second one was facultative. The second rite of passage for men, but not of women, then gave access to a further set of ranked initiations and grades, called *ngongo munene*.[66] Social age was so important that the spatial layout of the village directly reflected its age-sets. The older married people, including all the notable persons, lived at the prestigious downstream end of the village while the younger age-sets were settled in the chronological order of successive initiations at the plebeian end upstream. Clients (*shiloolo* 7/8), that is, followers of a big man who were not related to him by kinship, were settled on the sides. This pattern of settlement remained the practice in Kongo-Dinga villages well into the colonial period.

---

communal men's house only, but in Tshiluba it is a patrilineal group. Kongo-Dinga speakers do not seem to have known a dispersed matriclan, but Mbagani and Lwalwa did and called it *bulungu* 14, a form related to those found farther north as far as the Sankuru. In the south, the Sala Mpasu and the neighboring Mbal and Kete had only six matriclans and called them *mupanga* 3/4 (Pruitt, "Independent," pp. 109–14).

65. For a discussion of *kalamba*, see n. 121. Today its precise meaning in these languages is the following: Ceyssens, *Pouvoir*, p. 483, -*lamba* 12/13 [*kalamba, tulamba*] (a) "head of an extended family"; (b) "father"; -*lamba* 14 [*bulamba*] "authority of a chief" (tones not indicated); also p. 71, *kalamba* "chief," and p. 407, n. 368, *bilamba* "age set, generation." Compare with Pruitt, "Independent," pp. 115, 132, for whom *kalamba* was "the oldest warrior" or the "big man" who was head of his own settlement, subservient to none but vulnerable to conquest.

66. The word for initiation in general and not just for boys specifically is *mukandá*, which derives from a verb "to mandate, to order about." The word was invented in this region or in the adjacent one. The second initiation for men was the *ngongo munene*, which included several ranked levels and appropriate masks for each level. The use of copper on a mask and the presence of the number of peaks on it expressed this hierarchy (Ceyssens, "Sens du 'grand masque,'" pp. 355–81).

Each settlement was thus structured around a House and the big man who was its lynchpin because he was the only common reference point by kinship or by clientage that tied everyone else together within the House and the village. He was therefore the *de facto* leader of the village, or at least a *primus inter pares*. He had direct control over all the marriages of the girls of his settlement, which is an indication of the fierce competition for members between big men and their respective Houses or villages. Indeed that competition was all the more fierce because the power and relative well-being of everyone in each settlement depended first and foremost on the number of their followers. It is possible in this context that slavery may well have existed even before the era of the slave trade.[67] A man could be a big man only if he attracted and retained followers, and he could do that only by having *budiyi* 14, or wealth—literally "the essence of food."[68] Wealth consisted in "fresh goods," such as goats, or "dry goods," hoardable manufactured products of any kind, including standardized items such as locally made raffia squares and perhaps iron hoes, or exotic items such as copper ingots. Such items were given to settle social payments, such as the transfer of women in marriage, the payment of fines, and perhaps the acquisition of slaves. Objects of this sort could also be loaned to someone who was unable to pay the fines he, she, or an older person in his House or lineage had incurred. In return, that individual became a bondsperson or a pawn. Moreover, all sorts of objects could be given away to attract clients to the village.[69] Although this description refers to recent times and these practices have certainly been shaped in part by the financial and commercial practices that developed after the arrival of the slave trade by or before 1750, still, the particular way commodities were inserted into social life and the perception of a House leader as one "with things to eat" are more ancient.

Several individual settlements constituted a vicinage, which was identified by a name and a slogan. Its territory or *ngongo* 9/6 consisted of a number of *mpata* 9/10 "plains," one or more per House. The vicinage was ruled collectively from a designated special place by representatives of those matrilineages thought to have first settled on the land and to which the leaders of each House in the vicinage belonged. Both the grouping of such founding lineages and the place of their meeting were called *ekuluwandá* 5/6, an expression which contains the notion of *ngandá* 9/10, a notion that designated all the inhabitants of the vicinage and is best translated as "society."

67. Vansina, "Government," p. 8.
68. *Budiyi* 14 from *-dia* "to eat." In this context, one recalls the relative richness of the environment in contrast to territories farther south.
69. Vansina, "Government," p. 9.

Ekuluwandá, then, is the "place of the elders of the society." This collective government was exercised on behalf of all the constituent settlements and of all age-related initiation groups. It was expressed through the performances of the sodality called *ngongo munene* or "great territory." This sodality included three or four ranked levels complete with a hierarchy of masks marked in different ways to indicate their rank. Induction into the initial rank of the association was voluntary, collective, and open to all adult men. Accession to higher ranks was, in part, hereditary in that it had to be patrifilial but descent was not enough. Candidates had to have the approval of the members of the rank they wanted to join, and they had to pay a hefty entrance fee.[70]

Government was exercised by members of the highest rank of the *ngongo munene.* These were the *mutúmbú* 3/4[71] who decreed[72] the necessary measures for all collective endeavors from organizing collective hunts to initiations, war, and the adjudication of all court cases. Wars and especially headhunting were endemic in these parts, at least in recent centuries when the slave trade and the expansion of the Lunda Commonwealth created a great deal of turbulence in the region. Given the density of population and the consequent high potential for clashes between villages, wars and headhunting were probably a hallmark of the system long before then. War was conducted by the braves (*mban(d)jí*) 1n/2, that is, the initial age-set of younger men in the *ngongo munene.* But *bumbandji* 14 also meant "sovereign authority" and, in this sense, the word was applied to the whole *ngongo munene* and its leaders. In the final analysis, the authority of this council was not based on coercion. Rather, it rested first and foremost on the status of its members as first occupants in control over the well-being and the fertility of their lands, a status backed by their ties to ancestral and nature spirits. It also rested on the wealth its members extracted through entrance fees and fines from the rest of the community and on their collective ability to defend the vicinage against outside aggression. Hence, while one recognizes that the slave trade brought a great increase in collective violence to the region, one should not attribute the whole martial ethos to that circumstance. Organization by age-sets clearly predates the slave-trading era, headhunting defeats the goal of slave raiding, and a similar martial ethos prevailed over

70. Ibid., p. 19. Note the contrast between the matrilineal rule for inheritance of goods and the patrifilial one for the inheritance of these rights, a contrast that favored cross-cousin marriage.

71. The term is related to **-túmbá* 5/6 "war" (both from CS 1870, 1871, 1872) **-tùmb-* "burn." See Vansina, *Paths,* pp. 281–82.

72. See *-kandá* "to decree" and hence *mukandá* 3/4, the generic term for any initiation.

a larger region that included even the distant Lele of the lower Kasai, a population never affected by slave trading or raiding.[73] The female equivalent of the *ngongo munene* exercised authority over women with regard to issues concerning them, but data are sorely lacking concerning their ruling organization.[74]

Relations between neighboring vicinages were structured by alliances. Two or three of them supported each other to form an aggregate in opposition to a rival aggregate and also perhaps to exchange women so as to strengthen their alliance. Such aggregates were named and had a common praise name. At the next higher territorial level, several adjacent aggregates formed a larger named ensemble that seems to have corresponded to a specific landscape. But the aggregates within such an ensemble do not seem to have collaborated with each other at all. They were only juxtaposed to each other as part of an attempt to create an overall taxonomy that described the geographic distribution of all the known settlements in the country. The names of such ensembles, often the names of rivers, were then perceived as complementary to each other. This then allowed the bundling of these groupings into two or more larger ones until the level of a single ultimate ethnic unit was reached, however ephemeral that unit might prove to be. Thus, in the nineteenth century, the Kongo-Dinga were divided into five major groups while the Sala Mpasu had then recently been bundled into only two very large complementary groups, namely, "those of the fire" and "those of the water."[75]

Finally, outside the whole framework of community and vicinage groups and initiations there also existed an illustrious association (*buyanga* 14) for professional hunters marked by their own initiation.[76] Besides initiations,

73. See Vansina, "Government," p. 14, for the set of meanings of *mbandji* in the wider region. The practice of publicly exhibiting the skulls of deceased enemies was also common in the Kwango-Kwilu area. See Sebestyén and Vansina, "Angola's," pp. 319, 343, for a mention from 1755.

74. The advanced women's association is barely mentioned. Ceyssens, *Pouvoir,* pp. 196–97, 288–89, 399 n. 288, only says that the members were called *bilumbu* and that they were led by a single leader, the *kayendi.*

75. For the Sala Mpasu, see Pruitt, "Independent," pp. 83–85.

76. For Kasai, see Ceyssens, *Pouvoir,* pp. 166–71, 413 n. 436, 490; Vancoillie, "Grepen," pp. 95–97; *- Yanga* 14 (*-nyanga*) refers both to a specialized hunter with a charm and to the associated initiation. It is one of several words related to hunting and is not restricted to Lweta languages. It has a wide but compact distribution suggesting diffusion from a single center somewhere in middle or eastern Angola. It is attested to in Pende, Holo, Yaka, Mbagani, Kongo-Dinga, Rund, Ndembu, Umbundu, Hanya, Mbui, Sele, Kimbundu, Imbangala, Cokwe, and Lwena. In Ndembu and in Lucazi, the verb *hanga*

this association also practiced other rituals, including special funeral rites for members, which, unfortunately, have not been described well. This association certainly extended beyond individual communities and probably well beyond the vicinage so that they formed their own networks within the wider world. The very existence of these associations highlights the high regard in which such hunters were held, as well as the economic importance of hunting in the entire region.

Before considering the extent of the social organization just outlined beyond the smaller Lweta-Lulua-Kasai region, it must be emphasized that in the late nineteenth century and undoubtedly also in earlier times, details of its institutions differed from district to district. In some places, there were four ranks of the governing association and in others only three; in some places, such as among the Sala Mpasu, individual big men held more power than the ruling sodality, while in other places the balance of power tilted in favor of the sodality, as among the Kongo-Dinga. The exact layout of villages differed somewhat in the region and the terminologies used were not uniform. Still, in essence, it remained the same system: everywhere society was structured by a hierarchy of age-sets and governed collectively by an oligarchy.

This system of governance had been more widespread than it was at the close of the nineteenth century. Around 1600, Lweta speakers occupied the whole of central West Kasai Province as far north as the southern parts of the later Kuba kingdom.[77] The system of governance seems to have been even more widespread than this, for collective governance also prevailed then in what later became the core lands of the Rund Kingdom while there are some indications in the Cokwe and Lwena languages and in their traditions that at one time the system was practiced as far as the upper Kasai to the south.[78]

---

signifies "to chase, to pursue" and in Nyemba, -*nyanga* is "to be expert." The only detailed description and interpretation of a *buyanga* ritual stems from outside of the region, namely, from the Aluund (western Lunda). See De Boeck, "From Knots," pp. 341–52. But it is likely that they brought it with them since they immigrated (ca. 1750) there from the Rund heartland, which lies within this region.

77. See Vansina, "Government," pp. 5, 12. Tshiluba speakers began to immigrate from ca. 1600 onward and Tshiluba contains many loans from Mbagani, sometimes with innovations in meaning such as *cooto* 7/8, which no longer meant "bilateral House" but "patrilineage"; and this probably is also true for *musoko* 3/4 "village."

78. All the Moxico-speaking peoples as well as Lunda speakers recently had two successive male initiations called *mukanda* and *mungonge* but no collective government. With regard to the latter, the term *ngongo* is crucial. In Kimbundu, *ngongo* means: "suffering, danger, world" and in the Ngangela cluster, "woods." In Cokwe and Lwena, *ngòngo* 3/4 means "a rough bush shelter," and in Lwena, it also means "initiation" before

Additionally, the legacy of collective government can still be discerned in other lands now occupied by Lele and eastern Pende speakers. Thus, the social organization of Lele villages in recent times may seem extraordinary when seen in isolation but it was also based on age-sets and government was also exercised by members of the highest rank in a hierarchy of initiations.[79] Age-sets were particularly important among the eastern Pende between Loange and Kasai and among all Pende an association of orators regulated common affairs between their polities. The system was not unique to this region since an original form of republican government called *lwaba* was practiced in the lands occupied by Tshiluba speakers to its northeast. There, a big man was elected by his peers as a temporary leader to whom he paid a vast amount of wealth for the privilege of being in charge during a stipulated two to three years.[80]

Local Leaders, Chiefs, and Palavers

While people in the northeast of the region developed collective governance, their neighbors to the west took a slightly different path by choosing to strengthen the authority of individual leaders in villages and vicinages without enlarging the scale of governance much beyond that of a vicinage. This northwestern quadrant of the region consisted mainly of the Kwilu basin, that is, a territory stretching from the northern edge of the Kalahari Sands at around latitude 5° S to the latitude of the headwaters of the Kwilu, and

---

mukanda was later introduced from Rund (Horton, *verbo ngongo*). In Cokwe, *ngóngo* 9/10 means: "large deserted stretch of land," "place of terror or fear," "wild beast" [mask?]. In a Cokwe text, "people without chiefs" lived in their country before chiefs arrived. This is rendered as *mathungu angongo*, "country without kings or chiefs" in a manuscript text by Kanyungulu edited by Papstein, "The Early History," pp. 41–42. I thank Papstein for this information. In Lwena traditions, a *Mwene Matunga ngongo* was also a famous autochthonous chief (Papstein, "Upper Zambezi," pp. 133–36). Sangambo, *History*, p. 23, also cites *Matunga ngongo* and glosses *matunga* as "countries" but leaves *ngongo* unexplained. Given the other meanings in Lwena and Cokwe of *ngongo*, the whole title means either "wilderness" or Kanyungulu's "land without chiefs."

79. Douglas, *The Lele*. Some terms—such as *ilunji* 5/6 (Bushong *iloonc* 5/6) "clan," *mukanda* 3/4 (Bushoong *nkaan* 3/4) "initiation," *mbanj* 9 (Bushong *ibaanc* 5/6) "authority," "place of authority"—are related to those in Mbagani or Kongo-Dinga. So perhaps is *nghongo* 1n?, a term designating a ritual to avenge. But note that *ngóng* in the Bushoong expression *ngóng ambaang* refers to commoners, not to nobles.

80. Verbeken, "Accession," pp. 653–75; Vansina, *Paths*, pp. 182–83, 355 n. 51. The system was called *lwaba* 11. Farther east, the *eata* 7/8 variant of this system was in use among Songye speakers.

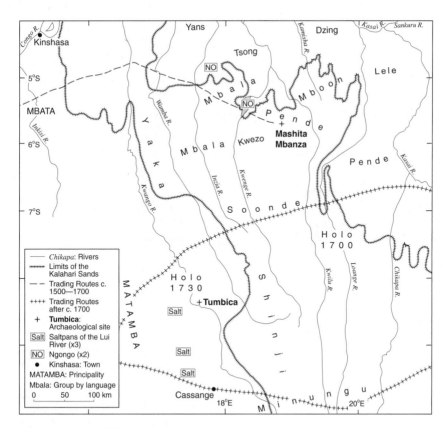

MAP 25. The Middle Kwilu

from the Inzia Valley in the west to the Loange Valley in the east (map 25).[81]
Readers will recall that it was here that proto-Njila emerged and that horticulture was first practiced during the last centuries BCE in or near the sizeable gallery forests of the main rivers while foragers continued to occupy
all the uplands. Among the horticulturalists, a few households agglomerated
into a small village with its own domain but without an overall leader. As
such communities then spread farther south along the Kwango, Kwilu, and
other major rivers, they founded the typical dendritic aggregates of settlements that became vicinages.[82] These early settlers fused with the surrounding foragers and in doing so adopted not only a good deal of their basic

81. For a description of the sharp contrast between Kalahari Sands on the uplands
and the lower more fertile land to the north, see Torday, *Camp*, pp. 118–19.
82. "Vicinage" is rendered as -*fuci*, -*fuji*, -*futi*, all 7/8 from *-*puta* or *-*kuta*. The distribution of this term includes all blocks of Njila except the Kunene one, which suggests
that the term was proto-Njila but later lost in Kunene.

economy but some of their initiation practices as well. It certainly looks as if the first *mukanda* 3/4 initiation for boys was created as the fusion of two other rites of passage into adulthood and into the ways of the bush, one from the foragers' side and one from the villagers' side that included circumcision.

The cultivation of sorghum only reached the region many centuries after the adoption of horticulture, perhaps as late as the ninth or even the tenth centuries. This increased the output of agricultural food and allowed the settlement pattern to become a little less restrictive since additional fields could be sown on the open savanna as well. From approximately the ninth century onward, additional available supplementary crops, such as plantain, taro or water yams, eggplant, and sugarcane, also began to arrive in the region, mostly from the north, and that further helped to ease constraints on the food supply.[83] At about the same time, the overall economy began to intensify as well. Trade across the northern ecotones developed with increased exports to the south of northern products such as palm oil, raffia cloth, and redwood, but we do not know exactly what was given in return. In addition, mineral salt from the Lui River pans was certainly traded over a good portion of the region, while a commerce in iron goods also flourished since they were often hoarded as wealth to be disbursed for social payments such as bridewealth.[84] Wealth probably included goats and iron hoes from the beginning, to which raffia cloth was added later on.[85]

Parallel to or not long after the adoption of sorghum, a first set of internal changes began to occur both in the structure of the village and in patterns of governance. Within the village, rights of residence, which had been open to any relative, now came to be determined primarily by matrilineal descent, even though patrifilial descent continued to be recognized as well since children were believed to inherit talents and spiritual protection from their fathers. Only members of the matrilineage of the founder of a settlement were considered "owners" of the village, that is, fully qualified residents, while all others became residents on sufferance. Preferential marriages with

83. Plantains (*-*kondo* 5/6; Pende -*khondo* 5/6, Mbala *goóndu* 5/6) and water yams (*-*diingu* 7/8; Mbala *gídiingu* 7/8 "yam"), and perhaps taro, sugarcane (Mbala *musungu* 3/4; Pende *mukhukhu* 3/4) were all introduced from the north, along the forest galleries. Eggplant *-*jilu* 11/10 (Mbala *lunjilu* 11/10 and Pende *njilo* 9/10), a savanna crop, arrived either from the east or from the north. Bananas (genomes AA, AAA) and finger millet were introduced only many centuries later.

84. Although iron smelting is now very rare within the region, it was common in some parts a few centuries ago. Production may well have ceased for lack of adequate fuel. See Roelandts, "Die Bevölkerung," pp. 4, 5.

85. Today the known words for wealth or money in the local Njila languages are of Kongo origin, but Pende *ikumba* 8 "goods, wealth" may still represent the older term.

cross-cousins to achieve some residential stability within the core matri-lineage of each village were introduced from the southeast. For it is from the southeast as well that the new kinship terms for cross-cousins, nephews, and grandchildren, terms which accompanied matrilineal succession and the de-velopment of preferential marriages, were introduced.[86] While all this was happening, we believe that, wholly independently from any matrilineal dis-pensation, two new layers of initiations into sodalities for more mature adults were added to the basic rites of passage from adolescence to adult-hood. The first layer was the *mungonge/i* 3/4 for men and *giwila* 7/8 for women, while *kela* 5 for men was the second.[87]

Frictions between villages, especially within the same vicinage, were set-tled by arbitration through common palavers in a thoroughly decentralized manner. In these assemblies, "speakers" (*ngambi* 9/10) for each matrilineage set out their positions, and decisions were reached by a consensus of the whole audience. *Ngambi* were "big men." They were chosen within each line-age for their wealth plus oratory talent and they enjoyed a status marked by special privileges and customs.[88] They also formed a sort of club or guild that transcended individual vicinages. The institutions of the palaver and the *ngambi* were the main overarching institutions that tied the villages of a vici-nage together and which settled serious conflicts between neighboring vici-nages. They would remain so later, even after the vicinages themselves mu-tated into small chiefdoms.[89]

86. The most obvious ones are *-jikulu* 1/2 (Pende, Holo; not Mbala) for "grand-child," *-nanu* 1n/2 for "mother's brother" (Pende; Holo is unknown; Mbala has another term derived from Kongo), *-sonyi* 1/2 (Pende, Mbala; Holo unknown) for "cross-cousin," and *-éehu* /2 [from *-jip(ú)á* 1/2] for "sister's son" (Pende, Holo, Mbala?). They all stem directly from Moxico languages and indirectly from much farther to the south-east well outside the Njila area.

87. See de Sousberghe, *Les danses rituelles;* Plancquaert, *Les sociétés secrètes,* pp. 14–54 (*ngongi* and *iwila*). Also see De Boeck, "From Knots," pp. 270–337. Despite the fact that all Pende, Yaka, and Suku traditions cited attribute the origin of these rituals to Rund overrule and that other evidence adduced by de Sousberghe (pp. 8–14 and *passim*) seems to support this, de Boeck (pp. 270–72), who studied these initiations most in depth among the westernmost Lunda, still could not confirm a Rund origin. These claims and situations are similar to the ones made about *mukanda* itself, and the Lweta data show that despite strong Rund influence, these rituals were not recent diffusions. These so-dalities themselves once formed part of a single hierarchy.

88. See de Sousberghe, "Pende," pp. 54, 57 n. 93.

89. The palaver as an institution is best described in Torday, *Camp,* pp. 69–73. For *ngambi,* see Kodi, "Pre-colonial," 1:235, and de Sousberghe, "Pende," p. 54. *Ngambi* 1n/2 is derived from CS 770 *-gamb-* "to speak." In Mbala, these orators were called *nngéenzi* 1n/2n "messenger, advocate," a widespread term in the lower Kwilu area and farther east

After that, there was a period between about 1200 and 1500 during which further changes transformed governance at both the local and the territorial levels. These were linked to political and economic developments that occurred from ca. 1200 onward in the adjacent areas to the northwest and north. There long-distance trade, centered on the Congo River, appeared first shortly after 1000. It increased in scale and extent over the following centuries. All over Lower Congo and as far as the lower Kasai, principalities then emerged, perhaps by 1200. Some of these, such as Mbata on the lower Inkisi, grew considerably in size during the following centuries and ultimately led to the formation of the Tio kingdom and the Kingdom of Kongo in the later fourteenth century.[90] Their capitals attracted trade, especially in luxury items, among which the earliest written documents (1491–1505) mention raffia velvet and embroidered raffia cloth. These mentions are particularly interesting because some of these were made in producing centers located well east of the Kwango River and in the immediate vicinity of the region considered here.[91] Beginning in the early sixteenth century, trade further intensified when the existing network was integrated into the overall transatlantic slave trade.[92] As a result of these trading contacts, strong social and cultural influences from Kongo and from the lower Kwilu basin began to affect the middle Kwilu region and were to remain the dominant foreign influences there until at least ca. 1700.[93] Not only were all the commercial institutions or activities and their relevant vocabulary borrowed from Kikongo, but the inhabitants also began to turn their vicinages into small chiefdoms in imitation of the institutions of their northern neighbors and those of the eastern Kongo. The increased availability of wealth in goods and in slaves, acquired in war or by trade, also triggered a further transformation to the local lineage organization at the village level.

---

as far as the Bushong with a connotation of "message" or "rule" and derived from CS 806/807; 1975/1976 *-gend-, "to go, to walk."

90. See Pinçon, "L'archéologie," p. 248; Thornton, "Origins"; Vansina, *Paths,* pp. 149–52, 155–58, 162–65, and his "Antécédents."

91. Vansina, "Raffia Cloth," pp. 263–65. The nearest center of velvet cloth ca. 1900 was located at the mouth of the Kwenge River. See Torday, *Camp,* p. 253.

92. The disruption caused by the slave trade was such that it provoked the celebrated Yaka/Jaga invasion of Kongo in 1568. These Yaka came from the Kwango basin in the immediate vicinity of the region studied here. See Hilton, *The Kingdom of Kongo,* pp. 69–71.

93. Cadornega, *História,* 3:273–80, and also 186–88, 194, 195, 198–99. The large site of Mashita Mbanza of 1680–1700 with its glass bead and imported brass bracelet was probably a central place in this network (Pierot, *Étude, passim,* and esp. pp. 151–52, 157, 196). In later times, it became a mythical place of origin for those chiefs who adopted the ethnonym Pende (Kodi, "Pre-colonial," 1:182–88).

At the local level, a new sort of residential matrilineage was created at the core of each village. While the earlier matrilineage had consisted of an unstable set of brothers and nephews with their spouses, joined by some of their widowed or divorced sisters, the new matrilineage now also included smaller satellite and dependent matrilineages founded by the wives of sons who continued to live with their fathers as well as segments of the original matrilineage founded by slave women captured in war and used as a transfer to pay a fine or a debt, or bought, and then married to a member of the original lineage.[94] The result was a much larger residential group and a much more stable one than had existed before, one better suited to remain the core of an enduring village community. To flourish, such an ensemble required careful management of its wealth in order to buy slaves and to attract sons. In turn, that required leadership by a single manager. The emergence of just such a leadership was signaled by the invention of a special new word, a term which was no longer an ordinary kinship term, namely, *lémbà* 5/6. The word alludes directly to the sort of wealth that could be used to attract followers and hence to increase a leader's power, for *lémbà* 5/6 is derived from a verb the general meaning of which is "to placate, to make a gift" but which particularly means "to pay bridewealth."[95] Note that even though in Pende, and probably elsewhere too, a species of fig tree called *mulemba* 3/4 was considered to be an the ancestral tree, that has nothing to do with *lémbà* 5/6 for its root is –*lèmbà* 3/4.[96]

Lémbà 5/6 was thus the eldest of all the resident mother's brothers as the one who always negotiated and received the main gift or bridewealth in return for giving away a girl in marriage. He was also the manager of the common estate of his matrilineage, even though he usually did not assume the

94. See de Sousberghe, *Structures,* pp. 19–20, and his "Pende," pp. 23–24, 26–33, 41–48; Kodi, "Pre-colonial," 1:222–30.

95. *Lémba* 5/6, "local lineage leader, mother's brother" is attested to in Mbala, Ngong, Tsong (*lim* 5/6), some southern Yans (*lim* 5/6), Yaka, Suku, Hungaan (*leme* 5/6), Pende, Holo, Kweso, Imbangala, Kimbundu. Note also Angolan Portuguese *alembamento* "bridewealth"; *lémba* "to appease, to placate by a gift, to give bridewealth" or some of its verbal derivations in all these languages, and also in Kongo, Yombe, Tshiluba, Rund, Sala Mpasu, Kongo-Dinga, Lwena, Ndembu, Lucazi, Nyemba, and Umbundu.

96. Gossweiler, *Os nomes,* pp. 66, 96, 454, attests to this: -*lèmbà* 3/4 in Kimbundu, Umbundu, and Nyaneka. Found also in Pende, Rund (*muléèmb* 3/4), Cokwe, Lwena, Ndembu, Lucazi, Nyemba. The name of the tree seems to be derived from -*lèmbà* 4 "birdlime glue" since that product is obtained from it. But it is ultimately linked to -*lèmbà* "to be in the shadow, to be cool." Cf. Lwena *lemba* 4 "cool, shady place." Finally in Cokwe, the contrast between -*lémbà* 7/8, "prayer, request, supplication" and -*lèmbà* 4 "ancestor, grandparent, elder," in which the first one belongs to the set that elsewhere includes "mother's brother" while the second one relates to the tree, the coolness, and the birdlime!

role of *ngambi* for his matrilineage.[97] That such a *lémbà* was the leader of all the members of the matrilineage was shown by a rough offering table or *kwyi* 5/6 installed outside the door of his house on which his juniors put all the game they caught for distribution by him, their senior leader. They did so because it was believed that all game was caught thanks to the powers of the ancestors who also maintained all sorts of fertility in the village domain. These "ancestors" were in fact the *lémbà*'s forebears, to whom he rendered a cult, so he controlled it all. Despite this spiritual link, the *lémbà* was perceived above all as an economic manager of the lineage's estate, while fathers and their ancestors remained the protectors of their descendants in most other spiritual matters.[98]

The word itself was coined somewhere between Kwango and Kwilu on the very edge of the region, in a landscape that was well endowed with natural resources and most favorably situated to trade with the outside. Because *lémbà* 5/6 "lineage leader" presupposed the availability of wealth in goods that could be used for social payments such as bridewealth, its invention can have occurred only once trade with the principalities of the eastern Kongo and of the lower Kwilu was flourishing, that is, from the thirteenth century onward. It existed by the sixteenth century when Duarte Lopes mentions governance by *malemba,* that is, by a collection of village leaders.[99] It was the introduction of bridewealth that made the emergence of the larger stable residential matrilineal complex possible. Bridewealth had not been required for preferential marriages in which adolescent children were supposed to settle at their mother's brother's place. Bridewealth made it possible to initiate another type of marriage in which the wife was not a preferential partner. In return for the wealth given to her guardians, her children were supposed to reside at their father's residence until his death and some of his sons would stay on there permanently, thus founding ancillary matrilineages. In the same vein, payment for slave wives, which were both incorporated into and

97. See de Sousberghe, "Pende," p. 38, which seems to confirm that the status of *ngambi* was older than that of *lémbà*.

98. Ibid., p. 37. Along the lower Kwilu, Tsong clan chiefs had a similar table called *kitala* (de Beaucorps, *Basongo,* p. 72). Although a *mulèmbà* tree was planted in every settlement of most of the peoples in the region as an "ancestral tree," this was not related to the *lémbà*'s cult for "the ancestors." But among the Ambundu, the unquestioned power of *lémbà* over female fertility explains his role during the rituals of bridal seclusion when he unlocked the fertility potential of the future bride and then protected it from malevolent interference. Elsewhere, however, such a direct link between *lémbà* and human fertility has not been reported.

99. Pigafetta and Lopes, *Description,* p. 36. He also noted the unusually high density of population in the region.

married within the matrilineage, was seen as a sort of bridewealth as well. It all amounts to the possibility for wealthy big men to create much larger matrilineages and villages than any one else could.[100]

The creation of chiefdoms occurred in parallel with the emergence of *lémbà* or a little later. This was marked by the introduction of the word *fumu* 1n/2n "chief," a term that was most probably borrowed from the chiefdoms of the lower Kwilu, where it had persisted from proto-Bantu times to designate the leader of a territorial district.[101] Its introduction in the middle Kwilu basin also occurred probably in the thirteenth or fourteenth centuries after principalities and chiefdoms had emerged to its north and west. At first the adoption of this term merely indicated the pretensions of some more successful and wealthy leaders of vicinages who had become big men, and it does not seem to have led to an enlargement of most polities, which until quite recently remained rather small chiefdoms for the most part—not bigger than the earlier vicinages. Moreover the creation of chiefs did not lead to the emergence of developed courts and a set of titleholders.[102] The small size of the chiefdoms and the absence of a developed court explains why interpolity relations still continued to be mediated by palavers and by *ngambi*. Despite their small size, these chiefdoms eventually acquired a structure and some institutions of their own, several of which were copied from their northern and western neighbors. The most important one among these was

100. Torday, *Camp*, pp. 94–95, offers the clearest exposition of the situation as it existed around 1905.

101. For *-kúmú*, see Vansina, *Paths*, pp. 274–75. In my view, the term and the position were dropped by proto-Njila speakers to be readopted later on because it is not attested to anywhere in any Njila language that is not adjacent to Kongo or Lower Kwilu languages. Still, one might argue instead that *-kúmú* survived in proto-Njila and was later lost everywhere by all the other Njila languages when they split from the Kwilu Block. But the related earlier words for "village" and "district/territory" were also dropped in proto-Njila, which makes the second interpretation less convincing than the first one.

102. Nearly all the outside sources extant confirm this situation whether they refer to those they label Mbala, Pende, Holo, or Shinji. In the only available source that describes a situation before the Lunda conquest, all the polities with one exception consisted of a single main settlement and a few outlying villages. The exception was Malundu (a Shinji chiefdom), which obviously was a powerful polity. See Sebestyén and Vansina, "Angola's," pp. 314, 318, 336, 341, 353–58. Later documents of the 1760s concerning Holo chiefs confirm this situation. See Torday, *Camp*, for the situation in those parts of the middle Kwilu not under Lunda lords around 1905. Most chiefdoms were just "villages" but three or four southern Pende polities were sizeable. He mentions three major ones (pp. 220–21) and reckons that yet another one could field up to 2,500 warriors (p. 255).

the notion that a chief's authority and legitimacy was vested more in the possession of a power object or charm of office than in supposed support by his ancestors.[103] Hence whoever captured the charms of office became a legitimate chief, and indeed many chieftaincies in the middle Kwilu region seem to have experienced numerous dynastic changes.[104] These charms of office (Mbala: *wééni* 3/6; Pende: *gifumu* 7/8) were kept in a special house, chamber, or shrine in the charge of a keeper who in the recent past often was a slave of the chief.[105]

In general chieftainship was apparently merely *lémbà* leadership writ large. Its ideology was founded on the claim that the matrilineages of persons who were *fumu* had been the first settlers on their territory just as the *lémbà*'s lineage was the founding lineage of the village. That set chiefly lineages apart from others as "nobles" from commoners, just as only full members of the *lémbà*'s lineage were "owners" of the village. The role of the chief in rituals of fertility at his capital or *mbanza* 9/10 was also the same as that of the *lémbà* in his settlement.[106] The main sign of a chief's power was a forked post or a line of posts or *mbanjí* 9/10 planted near his house. On this were placed the portions of game which were offered there to him by his subordinates, which recalls the *kwyi* table of the *lémbà*.[107] Nevertheless, the *mbanjí*, like the shrine for the charm of office, was a place which also underlined the main difference between *lémbà* and *fumu* for it was only here that one found the severed heads of enemies killed in war just as skulls were also kept in the shrine of office. In this way the *mbanjí* was a reminder of the

103. See de Sousberghe, "Régime foncier," p. 1346. The main charm always included kaolin and some bodily remnants of all the deceased chiefs who had ruled over the chiefdom—hence the charm did include "ancestors" after all. Also his "Pende," p. 53; Kodi, "A Pre-colonial," 1:231.

104. Kodi, "A Pre-colonial," 1:192, 231.

105. See de Beaucorps, *Basongo*, pp. 65–67, 69–71, (*muwa-wen*) among Yans, Tsong, Mbala, and Ngongo; de Pierpont, "Les Bambala," p. 191 (Mbala and Kwese); de Sousberghe, "Pende," p. 57; Kodi, "A Pre-colonial," 1:232 (Pende); Niangi: *La sculpture*, pp. 102–10, 109, 420–26.

106. See de Sousberghe, "Les Pende," pp. 55–59. *Mbanza* was a word borrowed in Kwilu from Kongo. But among Holo speakers, however, and their neighbors, the Imbangala, the word came to mean "chief."

107. Ibid., p. 53. The posts of the *gínini* 7/8 enclosure around a cemetery among the Mbala, Ngongo, and even Yans replaced the Pende *mbanjí* 9/10 (see de Beaucorps, *Basongo*, pp. 71–72). Vansina, "Government," p. 14, gives its distribution (to which Ndembu must be added) and concludes that *mbanjí* originated in Pende and spread from there northeast as far as Lele country, southeast to Ndembu land, and south as far as the Cokwe villages. Just possibly the Pende word is related to Kongo *-bàndzi* 11/10 "small tree species," "club."

special and awesome power of the chief and underlined his role in leading his people in war.[108]

Internally, these small chiefdoms were not very stable. After all, mere possession of the charms of office legitimized a chief's rule and his "ancestors" were only the previous holders of the chieftaincy. Hence many chiefdoms were plagued by numerous attempts to obtain power. Sometimes such attempts led to mutual agreements between claimants. Some claimants were recognized as subchiefs (*fumu akhota*) in their own territory and formed an unstable confederation with the main *fumu ambandji;* sometimes the parties might agree to a rotation of the main office between the lineages of the several contestants. In that case, such lineages were then conveniently considered to belong to the same clan.[109] War between chiefdoms was endemic even before the era of slave raiding because quarrels between the many small and separate chiefdoms who lived cheek by jowl in the densely settled parts of the region frequently erupted into violence. Confrontations usually were first settled by a prearranged and supervised fight on a specified plot of land but frequently they then degenerated into full-fledged war. Still, there were cases in which neighboring chiefs formed a compact never to resort to bloodshed, even to redress acts of violence; rather, they submitted the dispute to arbitration.[110] Nonetheless, by the eighteenth century, wars had not led to any enlargement in scale nor to any further increase in the powers of chiefs. When immigrants used to larger scale polities then invaded the region, they dismissed the locals as uncouth simpletons without kings.[111]

108. Just as the local age-sets of young men in the northeastern region were headhunters who brought their spoils to their chiefs; hence the term *mbanji* by then acquired the additional meaning of "awesome power." As to *ngunza* 1n/2 in Yaka, *ngúúndzá*, "prophet," "40-year-old man"; in Kimbundu according to Assiz: "messenger, envoy, subaltern, helper, hero, lord of armies, half god, object with great power, godhead, warrior"; and according to da Matta: "Providence" and "omnipotent." For Battell, *Strange Adventures*, p. 33, *Gonso:* "soldier." In South Kongo, *ngunza* 1n/2 is "herald, prophet, hero," but in Pende, *ngunza* 9/10 is "executioner," although de Sousberghe, "Pende," p. 55, claims that the word designates the killer of any noble animal or of any person. For Kodi, "Pre-colonial," pp. 1, 241, however, *ngunza* 9/10 was a "war leader." In Mbala *ngúunza* 1n/2n merely means a "young man."

109. Kodi, "Pre-colonial," 1:201–6, 212–14, 216–17, 235, 236, 242; de Sousberghe, "Pende," pp. 51–52.

110. Torday, *Camp*, p. 101 (two kinds of war) and pp. 73–74 (a peace coalition). For wars in the 1750s not far from the major trading emporium of Cassange, see Sebestyén and Vansina, "Angola's," pp. 318–19, 340–43 (frequent wars, duels between nobles, contingents always led by old people [*lémbà*], fortresses).

111. For example, an immigrant Suku song taunting the neighboring Mbala whom they had ousted "[They] are *bahika* [slaves] because they have no king"; in Kopytoff and Meiers, "African slavery," p. 17.

Until the early 1700s, the raffia and slave trade in the region continued to follow the old routes to the Kingdom of Kongo but then the main route shifted decisively to Matamba and to the great market of Cassange in the southwest. By mid-century, Imbangala and Ambaquista traders had pioneered a major route through the more densely peopled lands north of latitude 8° S from the Kwango toward the middle Kasai. By the nineteenth century, many of these traders had settled in the country and some even established small chiefdoms of their own.[112] Meanwhile, the Lunda Commonwealth was taking shape by violent means. Rund warriors overran the whole region from ca. 1720 to 1770 and wrought havoc on its small chiefdoms. They subjugated many chiefs and established several larger polities of their own between the Kwango and the middle Kasai. The Yaka kingdom of the Kiamfu was but the largest among these. The new Lunda chiefdoms incorporated nearly all the earlier ones except for most of the Mbala speakers, who tended to emigrate rather than to submit. From then on, Lunda overrule deeply influenced local government, an influence that is well attested to both in oral tradition and by numerous semantic transfers, including that of titles, such as *kilolo* 7/8 "overseer" or even the partial replacement of *fumu* by the Lunda terms *mwata* 3/4 "local leader," *kalamba* 12/13 "chief of the land, subordinate chief," and *mulambu* 3/4 "tribute."[113]

From Vicinage to Dynastic Web

By the time the first written report reaches us in 1794, the picture we have painted of villages loosely grouped into vicinages had ceased to be valid, for that text succinctly stated, "This land of Lovar [Lwena River] . . . is governed by eighteen male and female Souvas [chiefs], the most powerful among them being Quinhama whom the others obey."[114] Clearly by then a wider political organization had arisen in the central eastern region comprising the basins of the upper Kasai and of the Lwena and vicinages were no longer the largest social arena. As the oral traditions of the region portray it, this shift in scale of polity is attributed to the arrival of conquering lords from the north and

112. Vansina, "Du nouveau," pp. 45–58; de Sousberghe, "Pende," pp. 3, 41–42, 76; Torday, *Camp:* photo opposite 230 ("Enterprising traders"). Thus Haveaux, *La tradition historique* refers to the clan traditions of Imbangala who had founded or taken over a chiefdom near the Kasai as de Sousberghe disclosed in a review of this book in *Zaïre* 9 (1955): 79–83.

113. Vansina, "Du nouveau"; Kodi, "Pre-colonial," 1:268–353; de Sousberghe, "Pende," pp. 6–9, 69–75.

114. Felner, *Angola,* 1:237 (document #21) and *Arquivos de Angola* 1, no. 4 (1933).

to the introduction of proper tribute, which they portray as the hallmark of a proper polity.[115]

There is more than meets the eye in this reference to tribute because *mulambu* 3/4 "tribute" should actually be translated as "offering"[116] and the concept has ritual overtones. The underlying view was that while rulers ritually ensured the fertility of their land and their people, their subjects recognized this and claimed the protection of their lords by offering them a portion of the bounty that flowed from that fertility. Hence the essence of tribute consisted in giving a prescribed portion of large game animals to the ruler. For hunting was the fertility of men and the ruler ensured it (map 26).[117] The notion of *mulambu* is extremely widespread in Central Africa between the Kwango River and Lake Tanganyika and from the Kuba kingdom in the north to the Lozi realm in the south.[118] Although the existing evidence does not indicate where the word was originally coined, it certainly was in a chiefdom and, given its total geographic distribution, somewhere in East Central Africa. The most likely place of origin is a chiefdom in the Upemba depression, where Kisalian chiefdoms began to flourish from ca. 750 onward.[119]

As this conception of chieftaincy spread from polity to polity, so did the associated practice of tribute offerings, which eventually reached the easternmost vicinages of West Central Africa in lands that probably were already speaking Rund, Ndembu, or Lwena.[120] To stress the new conception of a covenant between leaders and followers vested in the reproduction of fertility,

115. Schecter, "History," pp. 267 (Mbwela lacked tribute), 178, 300–301 (tribute as recognition of suzerainty).

116. *Mulambu* is derived from a now unattested underlying verbal form [-*lamba*] meaning "to be made an offering to" and thus it signifies "offering." The verb is widely attested to in its regressive transitive form -*lambula*: "to make an offering to."

117. See von Oppen, *Terms*, pp. 351–54; Schecter, "History," p. 202; De Boeck, "From Knots," pp. 339–66 (hunting and fertility).

118. CS 489 *-*dambú* 3/4 is attested to in all the Luba languages, Yao, Lamba-Lala, Bemba-Bisa, Lui, and related tongues, all Lunda group languages, the Lweta languages, the Kwilu languages, Suku, Yaka, Tsong, and Yans, Umbundu, and the Moxico languages. The colonial appropriation of the word to designate "poll tax" certainly helped to spread it, e.g., in Bushong and Tetela. However, the related verbal form CS 484 *-*dambúd-* "to make an offering" is nearly equally widespread in Central Africa as the verb is absent only in Yans and perhaps Tsong.

119. See de Maret, "L'archéologie du royaume Luba," pp. 236–37.

120. In this context, it may be relevant to recall that prestigious guilloche designs on ninth-century elite ceramics at Kasanshi in the copperbelt and on rock engravings of unknown date near the headwaters of the Zambezi prove contact between these sites, contacts that also may have involved chieftainship. See Robertson, "A New Early Iron Age," pp. 59–64; Ervedosa, *Arqueología*, pp. 244–53.

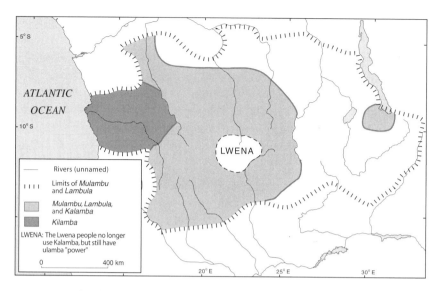

MAP 26. *Mulambu* and *Kalamba*

the speakers in one of these languages then coined the new word *kalamba* 12/13 to supplement the older *mwene*,[121] and then derived *ulamba* 14 from this to express the notion of "authority, majesty."[122] We do not know precisely when this happened. One can only say that the two words were coined well after 750 and had achieved a very wide distribution long before 1600.[123] The

121. *Kalamba* 12/13 means etymologically "the one to whom an offering is made." The word originated in an Eastern Block language because these are the only ones in which classes 12/13 denote fame or greatness. The term is attested to in all the Eastern Block languages with the meaning "chief" or "big man" (Sala Mpasu) and also in Kongo-Dinga ("family head"). For further distribution, see Hoover, "Seduction," 2:527, 534. Although he believed the word to be proto-Lunda, it certainly arose at a much later time. Farther west, *kalamba* dropped its prefixes to become *kilamba* 7/8 with the prefixes appropriate to denote greatness in the languages of the Kwanza Block as well as in Pende and Holo.

122. Hence in Lwena "the wars of *ulamba*" referred to their attempted conquest in the eighteenth and early nineteenth century of adjacent Ndembu lands. See Papstein, "Upper Zambezi," pp. 179–85.

123. *Kalamb* was in use in the northeast well before the rise of the Rund Kingdom ca. 1600, while at the other end of the distribution of the word, writings mention *kilamba* in Kimbundu as early as 1626. See Heintze, *Fontes*, 1:126. Here *Quilamba* referred at first to local overseers in the provinces for the kings and later to trusted military of the Portuguese. By 1850, *kilamba* was also said to be the title of the leaders of the original inhabitants of the basin of Cassange before Kasanji's invasion in 1629–30. See Neves, *Memoria*, pp. 102–5. For the specific meaning of *kilamba*, see Cadornega, *História*, 1:247, 3:236–38.

introduction of this concept of tribute did not alter the scale of the older vicinage but it added tribute giving as yet another overarching institution and, just as happened in the northwest, turned the vicinage into a chiefdom. Above all, the introduction of tribute elaborated the status of leadership and legitimized it in a new way. This, in turn, increased the authority of these leaders so that they began to exert some control over the various initiation sodalities by setting dates for most of the initiations and by keeping some of the required paraphernalia under their control.[124] Their newly exalted status was also enhanced by its integration into the panoply of masks linked to the initiations. New masks representing chiefs were created, decked out with attributes referring to their control over fertility and given a leading role in the interplay of masked dances. Thus were abstract notions of chieftaincy rendered concrete.

Although their leaders had become *kalamba* chiefs and the older vicinages were now chiefdoms, their scale and interrelations did not change much during the following centuries. Lwimbi speakers living on the edge of the planalto did innovate further. Despite having major principalities on the planalto as neighbors, they did not find it necessary to organize themselves into larger polities. Indeed, they valued local autonomy to the point that they eventually even rejected permanent chiefs despite the fact that they borrowed all the paraphernalia of rulership on the planalto, complex initiation, titleholders, ancestral cults, sacred fire and all. They adopted the pomp but they rejected the centralization. They decided to appoint their chiefs for a limited period of time only. Chiefs were installed first for two years and could then be reconfirmed for a total of six or maximum of eight years. One suspects that this periodicity was probably associated with that of initiations into the set of male mature adults.[125]

The Lwimbi form of governance remained unique and a very different tendency appeared in the upper Kasai and Lwena Valleys during the seventeenth or early eighteenth centuries. There, an enlargement of scale from the

124. For instance, Schachtzabel in Heintze, *Schachtzabel*, pp. 223–24 n. 150, 252 n. 139, noted that in between initiations Nyemba chiefs kept the sacred trumpets and some of the masks in their care. Also Van Koolwijk, "Entronização," p. 199, reveals how much all the initiations had come under the chief's control. For an extreme case of chiefly control among the Mbunda, see Fernandes, "Breve notícia," pp. 35–37.

125. Baumann, *Lunda*, p. 146; Heintze, *Ethnographische Zeichnungen*, pp. 20–21. It is worth remembering that part of the adjacent Songo lands were ruled by *malemba*, i.e., village headmen in council. Just such a council decided on the election and length of term of a chief among the Lwimbi. Moreover, the Lwimbi case is particularly suggestive because their solution to the issue of leadership was identical to that of *lwaba* system practiced by the Luba Kasai.

chiefdom/vicinage into larger polities was accompanied by a further strengthening of monocephalic leadership. This seems to have been prompted by the need for a common defense in a climate of general insecurity generated by the aggressive expansion of the newly formed adjacent Rund Kingdom and its creation of a Lunda Commonwealth. These new polities were formed by the bundling of a number of vicinages into a single federation through the fiction that the leader of each of the participating entities belonged to a single matriclan, or better a single matrilineal dynastic web, and should hence recognize a single paramount leader for the whole web. This paramount lord was to be the representative of the supposedly oldest genealogical branch of the web. In practice, the resulting federations were still thought of as vicinages writ large, for at least two of three or four, namely, those of the Lwena and the Lucazi, were still based on river basins, while some Cokwe speculated that this also was true of their own.[126] Although they were so weakly centralized, these alliances still fostered such an *esprit de corps* among its participants that they turned into ethnic groups such as, for example, the Lwena before 1794.

Oral traditions of Genesis pertaining to the rulers of the populations living in the upper Kasai and Lwena basins, that is Lwena, Cokwe, and Lucazi, all claim a single origin for they all hold that they are descendants of a common ancestress Nama. They further hold that Nama herself descended from the founders of the Rund Kingdom, but this belief is demonstrably a later addition, probably of early nineteenth century vintage.[127] The most common assertion is that the first clan to form a web was Nama Kungu and we can take it that its first ruler, male or female, lived near or in the eastern portion of the valley of the upper Kasai.[128] Although many of the claims for Nama

126. Lwena and Luchazi are the names of rivers. One Cokwe tradition of ca. 1935 could not resist the claim that their ethnic name was also derived from a river, an affluent of the Kasai—but no such affluent could be found. See Roelandt, "Die Bevölkerung," p. 8 (Cokwe an affluent of the Kasai) versus p. 16 (they came to Kahemba from the "sources of the rivers," which is correct).

127. For summaries and compendia of these traditions of Genesis, see Bastin, *Art décoratif,* pp. 30–33, 42–45; Baumann, *Lunda,* pp. 139–41; Cardoso, "Em Terras de Moxico," pp. 14–18 (data gathered in 1903); Papstein, "Upper Zambezi," pp. 97–109, 116–62; Sangambo, *History;* Chikota cha Luchazi, *Luchazi;* Cheke Cultural Writers, *History.* Neves, *Memoria,* pp. 96, 99, heard in 1850 of Nama (Nhâma) as the origin from where Cokwe, Minungu, and Imbangala chiefs emigrated to the upper Kwango. For the spurious character of the link to the Rund, see Vansina, "It Never Happened," pp. 390–403.

128. Bastin, *Art décoratif,* pp. 30, 42–45, (Nakapamba musopa Nama was the ancestress of all Cokwe); Papstein, "Upper Zambezi," pp. 129–62. Sangambo, *History,* pp. 8–9, 22–32 (Nyakapamba Musopa Nama was a female chief of the Cokwe); Chikota cha

Kungu descent now made by various other than Lwena rulers may be of recent vintage, still a single Lwena polity grouping eighteen vicinage *mwene* existed in 1794 and had probably taken shape long before then.[129] It emerged, at the latest, in the earlier part of the eighteenth century and perhaps well before that.[130] But Lwena may not have been the first aggregate of this kind. The first one known may well have been a Minungu federation that existed before 1680 when Cadornega heard about the Ndonji, "a people" who thrice had defeated the Lunda armies—which implies that they were much more powerful than any single vicinage could have been. They formed at least a temporary federation perhaps cemented by a common dynastic web. This Ndonji seems to refer to the paramount ruler of the Minungu ethnic group, then settled near Quimbundo not far from the upper Tshikapa Valley, a ruler also referred to in the oral traditions about the creation of dynastic aggregates.[131] The Cadornega text informs us that people in the region banded together to resist the Rund onslaughts and it is very likely that this explains why dynastic webs were formed in the first place. Various Holo leaders near the Loange River also banded together into a single coalition to stem Lunda advances in

---

Luchazi, *Luchazi,* pp. 54–61, 181. (Nama refers to "Nyakapamba musompa musompa Nama," the first female ruler in the land of origin); the Mbunda made *Nkungu* a male ruler and *Nama* his daughter. See Cheke Cultural Writers, *History,* p. 1 (first ruler Mwene Nkuungu, second one his daughter Vamwene Naama . . .). Lucazi and Mbunda traditions are evidently constructed from parts of the Cokwe and Lwena ones. One may think that only the Lwena body of traditions can be relied upon, as recorded Cokwe traditions are rather fragmentary, yet the shadowy common Cokwe ancestor Nama was already widely known in 1850.

129. From a comparison of the existing data, one concludes that a single set of oral traditions about the origin of a dynastic web and hence of a "federal kingdom" existed well before 1794 without specific reference to Lwena (Kinyama) or to Cokwe (Nyakapamba usompa Nama) ethnic groups. One can accept the validity of this tradition when it tells us that a dynastic web was created in or near the upper Kasai Valley without having to accept that historical personages called Cinyama or Nama created it and called it Nama Kungu.

130. Unfortunately the Lwena lists of rulers cannot be used to date this development. In "Upper Zambezi," pp. 118–28, Papstein's chronology is far too long in that he confuses reign length and generations, because a 30–year "normal" average for a matrilineal generation is too long, and because the advent of a strong chieftaincy of Kakenge cannot be dated before ca. 1800. In the absence of genealogical data, an initial date can hardly be calculated even if one accepts the historicity of the last seven Cinyama titleholders before the first Kakenge.

131. Cadornega, *História,* 3:220. For mentions in traditions, see Bastin, *Art décoratif,* pp. 33, 43, 44; Papstein, "Upper Zambezi," pp. 101, 109; Sangambo, *History,* pp. 9, 26.

the eighteenth century; although their coalition was cemented by common kinship, it does not seem to have recognized a single paramount.[132]

All the oral traditions pertaining to the rulers of the area describe their settlement in the lands they now occupy as a legitimate conquest of the uncouth autochthonous Mbwela by more civilized immigrants. According to these stories, Nama lived somewhere around the bend of the upper Kasai River. When she died, her children divided the country among themselves, one for each later ethnic group. The name of each child was then assumed by its successor as an official title. Furthermore, each child began to move southward to occupy the lands between the Kasai and the Lungue-Bungo Rivers. In succeeding generations, further splits occurred within each group and the names of seceding chiefs also became titles. These seceding chiefs continued to migrate, mainly southwest and southeast as far as the Luanguinga River. Within each ethnic group, the seceding chiefs nonetheless still recognized the one who bore the most senior title, that of a child of Nama, as their paramount. In this fashion, a differentiation between ethnic groups and a clustering of chiefdoms within each group occurred without genuine centralization. These stories are obviously structured to explain how their present situation ca. 1900 came about and are not an account of what actually happened. It is likely that dynastic webs developed without much migration at all and that the details of the migration stories recall in fact how each dynastic web took shape during the eighteenth century when various Mbwela *mwene* were coerced to pay tribute or did so voluntarily and when members of the paramount's entourage carved out new vicinages in those places where they managed to chase other Mbwela *mwene* away.

The first developments of the internal organization as well as the functioning of dynastic federations in the first decades after their emergence cannot be separated from elaborations that took place after the early 1700s when the region became engulfed in the Atlantic slave trade, which exerted its own strong impact on local institutions of governance. It is also no longer always

---

132. Holo was either a common clan name or the title of a set of at least four and perhaps seven interrelated chiefs in the 1750s whose alliance later also forged a single ethnicity. See Sebestyén and Vansina, "Angola's," pp. 314, 336. Like the Minungu, they also fought the Lunda with varying success. They were defeated near the Loange in or before the 1720s, then they defeated the Lunda of Nzovu in turn near the Wamba some time later, then they lost the next round to Nzovu, but then they decisively blocked further Lunda advances toward the Kwango in the 1760s. See Vansina, "Du nouveau," pp. 47, 48, 52–53, 56; Roelandts, "Die Bevölkerung," pp. 5, 18.

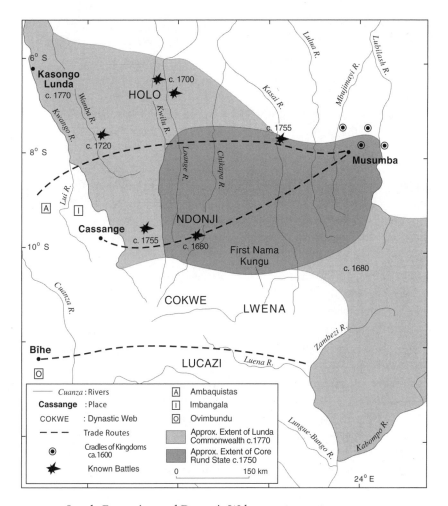

MAP 27. Lunda Expansion and Dynastic Webs, ca. 1600–1760s

possible to disentangle what was earlier and what came later in the descriptive evidence at our disposal, most of which dates from the nineteenth and even from the early twentieth centuries. All that can be said is that the significance of a dynastic web or "federated kingdom" lay in the enlargement of scale of the largest unit of governance from the start. The very existence of this claim itself enlarged the scale of society, even in the absence of other changes, even if every chief remained just as autonomous as before, and even if the claimed dynastic links were fictional, for henceforth society at large was no longer coterminous with a vicinage-chiefdom but with an aggregate of chiefdoms. Hence, to the Lwena, for example, that meant a fusion of 18 societies into one and the creation of a single ethnicity (map 27). Moreover, from the very time of its formulation, a dynastic web consisted in making preexisting ephemeral and occasional alliances permanent through the invocation of supposedly common ancestors in the dynastic web.[133]

By the 1750s, the Atlantic trading network laid its own grid of communications over the lands of the upper Kasai and Lwena basins nearly as far as the banks of the uppermost Zambezi River. Trade followed routes that were easy to travel and went through a countryside sufficiently populated so that caravans could readily obtain the necessary food supplies. The settlements of friendly chiefs along these routes became way stations where food, slaves, ivory, and wax could be bought in return for cloth, beads, guns, and other imported goods. Soon such chiefs became wealthy and their settlements began to attract ambitious young folk from far and wide around them.[134] Thus by the 1850s each of the capitals of the four main Cokwe chiefs counted over a thousand inhabitants.[135] Such leaders turned into big men and their power was recognized by moving their name or title up the genealogy of the dynastic web to a position as close to that of a child of Nama as their power seemed to warrant it.[136] The Atlantic trade subverted the other institutions of governance as well. Offerings became a tribute in significant goods, rendering justice became a means to extort fines and to acquire pawns or slaves, wars were fought to capture slaves, and in internal affairs powerful chiefs centralized governance in their own hands and turned into despots who displayed skulls on their fences as a means of cowing their own subjects.[137]

One can draw a valid portrait of the main outlines of society and governance for the first half of the nineteenth century from ethnographic descriptions derived from oral tradition or from later observations.[138] The para-

133. "Mutual conferences" of *mwene* after an invocation of the ancestral spirits of the host were quite common among the southeastern Ngangela. See Pearson, *People,* pp. 49–50.

134. See Von Oppen, *Terms,* for a study of the Atlantic trade, its institutions, and its main effects.

135. See "Ladislaus Magyar's Erforschung," p. 229. The population of these core Cokwe lands was by then "extraordinarily great."

136. Thus while Cinyama was still the undisputed overlord in Lwena land during the 1790s, he was soon thereafter ousted by Kakenge, who was better placed on the main trading route Teixeira, "Relação," p. 237; de Vasconcellos, "Anno de 1799," p. 160 (Kakenge the first chief on the route to Lwena in 1795); for 1806 "Ladislaus Magyar's Erforschung," p. 233.

137. See Von Oppen, *Terms,* pp. 345–77.

138. Besides accounts by travelers such as Silva Porto, Livingstone, or Magyar, and studies by Papstein, Von Oppen, and White, the main ethnographic sources used for this

mount leader was designated by a newly coined title *mwanangána* 3/4 or *mwangána* 3/4.[139] The legitimacy of each ruler was based on his membership in a dynastic clan. His selection and initiation by the *mwata* 3/4 of the realm was guaranteed by the ancestors of the clan, for his very success in being elected was a sign of their backing. This legitimacy was acknowledged by the lighting of a new fire in every village of the realm whenever a new ruler was elected and by the payment of offerings, especially those of the prescribed portions of game. The lord ruled from a capital, *ngandá* 9/10,[140] where he received his offerings and presided over a court of justice as well as over the organization of various age-set related initiations in which the mask that represented him came to preside over all.[141] But the court remained modest in size and comprised only a handful of officials. Several of the titles mentioned are of later vintage and clearly derived from Ovimbundu or Rund titles, the splendid Cokwe thrones were inspired by those of the Ovimbundu, and the main features of the rituals of royal burials are copied from the Ovimbundu as well.[142] The paramount lord also proclaimed war and peace.

---

sketch are Baumann, *Lunda;* Cabrita, *Em Terras;* Fonseca Cardoso, "Em Terras de Moxico," Chikota cha Luchazi, *Luchazi;* Cheke Cultural Writers, *History;* Heintze, *Schachtzabel;* Pearson, *People;* Van Koolwijk, "Entronização."

139. *Mwangána* 1+3/2+4 is probably a contraction of *mwànangána* 1+3/2+4, which is a compound of *ngána* 9/10 (Lwena; Cokwe only in the plural *mána*) and *mwà*. This first element is also an honorific commonly prefixed to the names of chiefs and probably an abbreviation of *mwàna* (not *mwána* "child"!), a term ignored in most dictionaries but that is widespread as such or as the interjection *mwànè* "sir, madam" (Cokwe, Lwena, Luba-Katanga). *Mwàna* "chief, leader" recurs in Rund titles (*mòna*), in Tshiluba, Kanyok, Luba-Katanga, Songye (residual), Bushoong (residual), and perhaps elsewhere (e.g., Swahili *bwana*?). Its etymology and origins require further study. The compound is a local invention in the Moxico languages.

140. *Ngandá* 9/10, CS 780, comes from *-gandá* 5/6 "House" (Vansina, *Paths,* pp. 268–69). It designated a village in Herero, a large village in Kongo, Bushoong, Luba Katanga near the Lualaba, and Lwena among other languages, and a chief's compound and capital in the Moxico languages, Ndembu, the Lamba-Lala, and Bemba-Bisa groups of languages and also in Vili or Tetela. Its meaning expanded to "territory" in Rund and Ndembu.

141. All the oral traditions in the region claim that initiations were introduced some time after paramount chieftaincy had been established and hence claim preeminence for the latter—even though in reality the contrary was true. Thus Papstein, "Upper Zambezi," pp. 174–79.

142. The adoption of the title *mwatiamvu* reported ca. 1810 among the Lucazi and Cokwe is an obvious loan from the Rund royal title *mwant yaav.* See Porto, *Viagens,* p. 324. The Lucazi chief he knew since 1840, was 70 years old in 1847 and the founder of

Thus the main Lwena lords coordinated their forces during the eighteenth and nineteenth centuries during the wars they fought against the Ndembu and the Lozi of the Zambezi floodplain.[143] Nevertheless, except in the realms of significant big men enriched by the slave trade, major decisions were still collective and still reached in consultation with the various *mwata*. It is telling that these federations were still small enough so that the lord knew all his *mwata* personally and everyone knew everyone else in the vicinage.[144]

The matrilineal dynastic framework of the polity maintained and reinforced the older distinctions between nobles and commoners. All the members of a ruler's matrilineage were *mwangána* 3/4 just like the ruler, while the male consorts of women of that lineage were designated by the new title of *mukwatunga* 1/2 and received lifelong consideration.[145] The sons of male rulers or *mwanauta* 1/2, although not *mwangána* themselves, were nevertheless privileged during the reign of their father. They often founded new settlements and in the Lucazi polity they even ousted the headmen of established settlements and took their place.[146] But everyone who did not belong to the dynastic matrilineage was demoted in status. Commoners were considered to be merely immigrants on sufferance and came to be labeled *ndungo* 1n/2 "pawn," a word that was coined in Cokwe or Lwena.[147] Thus the

---

his chiefdom, perhaps even ca. 1800. See also Baumann, *Lunda*, pp. 139, 143, for a Cokwe chief with this title. The Ovimbundu influence is obvious in the adoption of the titles *kesongo* and *kalei*, and in the custom of wrenching the head off the deceased ruler reported in Baumann, *Lunda*, p. 136, and Chikota cha Luchazi, *Luchazi*, p. 61. Some other insignia, such as the *nduua* feathers, were probably introduced by Ambaquistas.

143. See Papstein, "Upper Zambezi," pp. 166–73, 179–96.

144. Chikota cha Luchazi, *Luchazi*, p. 75. Nineteenth-century travelers found that the territory of a chiefdom did not extend to more than two or three days travel (perhaps 15 to 20 kilometers per day as the crow flies).

145. Note that -*tunga* in this compound name comes from -*túnga* "to build" (CS 1847, 1848, 1877) and not from -*túnga* 5/6 "country," a term foreign to the area but common among the Lozi and in the Luba-speaking world.

146. Chikota cha Luchazi, *Luchazi*, p. 161, claims that this supposedly occurred on request by villagers. But this taking over of older chiefdoms or villages is not confirmed anywhere else.

147. *Ndùngo* 1n/2 "slave, bondsman" (all Moxico languages) coined from -*lùnga* "mix, mingle" (Lwena, Cokwe), which also formed -*lungama* "to settle, as a solid in a liquid" (Lwena, Cokwe). Later, by or even before 1800, *ndùngo* 1n/2 also came to designate a slave. The use of the term indicates that wealth for social payments such as fines was already available before the Atlantic slave trade since the relevant Umbundu, Kimbundu, and Imbangala words were not borrowed. Archaeologists may well discover one day that trade in copper and perhaps other luxuries already flourished in earlier times

establishment of dynastic webs increased social differentiation and class even before the Atlantic slave trade further exacerbated class distinctions by producing large numbers of slaves.

The Rund Kingdom and the Lunda Commonwealth

Meanwhile, around 1600, the populations of the settlements in the far northeast along the Nkalaany River and its eastern affluents, which were to become the core of the later Rund Kingdom, were still organized in vicinages, each of which was governed collectively by the members of the highest rank of the sodality of adult men. To the east and northeast, these people bordered on patrilineal Luba-Katanga speakers along the Lubilash, with whom they had been in close contact for many centuries and whose polities were of about the same size as those of the Rund. But from the late sixteenth century onward, these Luban polities began to be raided frequently by warriors from a newly emerging Luba kingdom to their east. This kingdom had grown out of a long series of earlier centralized polities from the well-populated Upemba depression, the last of which apparently declined from the sixteenth century onward.[148] Yet it is not known what prompted the rise and the expansion of the main Luba kingdom.[149]

In order to defend themselves more efficiently against this new threat, the inhabitants of the Lubilash Valley rallied around three large localized patrilineages that then federated with each other to create a kingdom of their own. But this development now threatened their western neighbors whether they were Kaniok or Rund speakers. This threat induced local Rund vicinages to federate into two somewhat larger entities, in both of which government was entrusted to a single common new council superior to the *mungongo* of each vicinage. The members of this new council co-opted each other in the usual fashion among the members of the hitherto highest rank of each of these *mungongo*. They were all big men or *kalamb*, each one

---

along a route running from the copperbelt over the headwaters of the Zambezi to the upper Kasai.

148. For a summary of the archaeology, see de Maret, *L'archéologie*.

149. Reefe, *The Rainbow and the Kings*, pp. 200–207, stressed a symbiotic relationship between intensifying trade in local commodities, such as salt and iron, and the growth of political power starting in a nucleus of high population density surrounded by large tracts of hinterland. The main Luba Kingdom appeared when the center of the political system shifted northward from the Upemba Valley to the plateau and began to incorporate larger and larger areas of "hinterland." Still a fully satisfactory explanation for that move and at that time continues to elude us.

backed by a prosperous bilateral House. In Rund oral traditions, these members of the new supreme council are known as the first chiefs of the land or *kabung* 12/13. The word actually means "gourd" and the council members were probably called "gourds" because they adopted gourd masks as their insignia and elevated these to the apex of the hierarchy of masks.[150]

During the next generation, more of these *kabung* came to be more closely related to each other as the result of marriages by their predecessors and eventually one of them claimed supremacy over all the others on the grounds that they were all related to him and hence part of his House, so that he was their *mwant*. From then onward, the other *kabung* became the ritual investors of the kings.[151] As soon as the *kabung* recognized a single *mwant* as their leader, however, their collective government was suddenly transformed into a centralized monarchy, albeit a monarchy structured like a House. There remained one major problem. The composition of a House depends on the exact kinship relationship in which every member stands with regard to its head; hence, a House is by definition an unstable group, since after the death of its head all the relationships of the members with his or her successor are necessarily different from what they had been before.

When the Rund formed a monarchy, they remedied this weakness by a stroke of genius. It came to be accepted that each successor to the leadership of a House legally became the very same person his or her predecessor had been, a practice called positional succession. In assuming the social identity of that predecessor, the successor also inherited that person's exact kinship relations to every single member of the House. Thus kinship relations became permanent and perpetual. From then on, the royal House was a stable group with an everlasting inner structure that could and did serve as the framework for the internal organization of the whole Rund Kingdom and the Lunda Commonwealth that grew out of it. All the political relationships within it continued to be expressed by specific kinship terms and were regulated by the behavior associated with those specific terms.[152] Yet the Rund

150. Hoover, "Seduction," 1:103–4, 111, 183–86 n. 3; 2:527, 536. In the Lwimbi/Kimbandi and Lucazi *mungonge* farther south, the gourd mask was the highest in the hierarchy. Serpa Pinto, *How I Crossed Africa,* 1:237–38 and figure 36, reports the Kimbandi chief Mavanda dancing with a gourd mask while Felix and Jordan, *Makishi,* p. 42, provide an illustration of a gourd mask with the legend "senior masked character of the Luchazi *mungonge* secret association for adult males."

151. Hoover, "Seduction," 2:534 n. 2.

152. Ibid., 1:111–21. Hence in his monograph, Crine, "Thèmes," discusses the political organization immediately after the presentation of the kinship terminology and the behavior associated with each term.

also became fascinated by the expressions of political power through the ceremonial at court and through titleholding, just as their Luba neighbors had been. They invented a set of titles of their own and borrowed others from the adjacent Luba kingdoms, while the latter borrowed some of theirs.[153] At the same time, their hierarchy of age-set related initiations lost their original meaning. Henceforth the court became just as much a cynosure for everyone as courts were in middle Angola. Yet most of the sodalities and initiations survived by turning into healing cults.[154]

Both the Rund-speaking coalitions of vicinages, that of the Kanincin and that of the Rund proper, underwent this process and turned into small centralized kingdoms. But the Kanincin would always remain a small polity while the Rund were destined to become a major power.[155] Rund oral traditions present this outcome as the result of the takeover of the small adjacent Rund federation by a Luba leader from Mutombo Mukulu across the Lubilash.[156] We may never know if such a takeover actually occurred but it is evident that the Mutombo Mukulu, Rund, Kanincin, and Kanyok polities (and perhaps others) all interacted with each other and developed simultaneously. Still, that does not explain why only the Rund polity then began to expand so rapidly and why it became so powerful while the others did not. The expansion occurred in part through the voluntary adhesion of most of the immediate neighbors of the nascent Rund Kingdom to its pattern of perpetual kinship and positional succession. At the same time, or perhaps somewhat later, ambitious individuals situated at the top of the hierarchy of male sodalities were able to rally substantial numbers of young warriors from their sodality and set forth to conquer new lands located on major trading routes to the southeast and the west. In the latter direction, the first indirect tentacles of the Atlantic slave trade seem to have reached the middle Kasai around 1650. Whatever the exact circumstances and well before 1680, these military

153. Hoover, "Seduction," 1:195–96, 202–5; 2:527–29, 534–52. For detail, Crine, "Thèmes," pp. 97–104.

154. See de Boeck, "From Knots," pp. 269–428, 453–457; Crine, "Un aspect du symbolisme luunda," pp. 79–108.

155. On the Kanincin, see Musasa Samal-Mwinkatim Dizez, "Comment les Kanintshin" and his "États lunda."

156. According to the well-known tale, based on the widespread cliche of the foreign hunter Cibinda Ilunga, a Luba hunter, married Ruwej, the Rund *mwant* and took over from her. Hoover, "Seduction," 1:227–36, 243, remarks that the story originated among the Rund and spread from them to the Luba and not the reverse (despite other indications on pp. 197, 206–8). He concludes (pp. 239–43) that the historical reality of a Ruwej and a Cibind Yirung seems probable.

leaders then set out to conquer lands and to found their own principalities to the west and the south of the original cradle of the kingdom. In the next generations, other ambitious leaders followed this example and continued to travel farther and farther in search of new realms. Thus was the Lunda Commonwealth born.

In the Rund Kingdom itself, the first remembered ruler after the Luban hunter episode was Yav, hence the royal title Mwant Yav. Already during his reign, war parties set forth to raid vast tracts of land to the west and the south. They were evidently in the nearly empty lands between the middle Kasai and the Kwilu well before 1680 and by then they also occupied Katukan-gonyi, a territory lying just east of the bend of the upper Kasai River.[157] Cal-culations backward from the known date by or just before 1680 place the fed-eration of *kabung* and the first germ of the Rund Kingdom around 1600.[158]

This is not the place to pursue the later history of the Rund Kingdom and of the Lunda Commonwealth which issued from it and which, from the eighteenth century onward, affected most of the northern part of our study area to the west and most of southern Katanga to the east.[159] Let us conclude nonetheless with a remark about the growth of centralization in the region. A genuinely centralized government, bolstered by a set of territorial offic-ers and a hierarchy of titles, developed in the Rund Kingdom proper. Parts of this model were imitated by the various kingdoms and principalities in the Lunda Commonwealth. Yet the arrival of Lunda rulers did not always lead to the creation of fully centralized polities. Every kingdom or princi-pality developed its own formula. At one extreme, the large Yaka kingdom on the Kwango developed a fully centralized regime while at the other ex-treme no genuine centralization at all occurred in the Kanongesha "king-dom" among Ndembu speakers of what is now northwest Zambia. Here titles were inherited in puny matrilineages, titleholders did not reside at court and were rarely seen there, no ranking was established between them, nor did any lateral relationships between them develop, for every titleholder sepa-rately continued to derive ritual protection and prestige from the ruler alone in return for a light tribute as a recognition of his authority.[160] In this case, the earlier society was enlarged but without any centralization. This time that feat

157. Direct evidence by Cadornega, *História*, 3:219–20, for the west. For the south, a credible chronology has been established by Schecter, "History," p. 161.

158. On this chronology, see Hoover, "Seduction," 2:614–31, esp. 628 ("around 1600").

159. A careful synthesis of these topics could require a book-length study.

160. Schecter, "History," pp. 199–226, esp. 214 (no state at all), 216 (largely a ritual kingdom only) and 222 (tiny matrilineages and truly decentralized).

was achieved by the fiction of the paramount as a common reference point for all titles rather than by the fiction of a common dynastic genealogy as was the case among the Lwena, Lucazi, and Cokwe to their west.

Environment and Collective Imagination

The most striking aspect of the history in the lands of inner West Central Africa is the persistence of small political units in which governance remained essentially collective. Societies there came to be structured by sodalities, successive initiations, and a celebration of all social statuses through the display of the panoply of masked dances which represented them. In this way everyone, women as well as men, youths as well as elders, participated in it. Over time, this collective bend of government turned into a government by big men in the northeast, but it remained collective and the political units remained small. Elsewhere small units also persisted despite the elaboration of a chiefly status at their apex, a status inspired by examples from the outside, well beyond the borders of the Kalahari Sands. While the luster attached to these chiefs enhanced their roles as representatives and managers of their societies, it did not affect the autonomy of individual settlements, nor did it corrode existing patterns of collective decision making or lead to increases in territorial scale. Essentially the vicinage continued to remain the basic political unit. This pattern began only to be truly altered both by the rise of the Rund Kingdom, itself part of a process of change which began in Katanga, and by the irruption of the Atlantic slave trade into the region.

This persistence of such small-scale societies obviously can be linked to their infertile environment with its sparse populations clustered around the main rivers, a milieu that encouraged the rise of "natural" vicinages yet discouraged the elaboration of larger scale social units, for it easily induced local collaboration while discouraging strong monocephalic government because it was all too easy for the discontented to strike out on their own and settle somewhere else. One appreciates that such an environment would encourage the formation of bush schools to prepare adolescents for a life in which foraging remained just as crucial as farming.

Even so, the environment did not actually dictate how communities or societies were to be organized. The incentive to create a society around palavers, sodalities, age-sets, initiations, dances, and masks came from elsewhere. All of these were the fruits of a collective imagination that envisioned society as an ever-changing interplay of statuses and roles and expressed this in the choreographies of masked dancers. In this imagination, governance was not just a collective collaboration between communities for survival more or less imposed by the environment; governance was imagined as a structure or a play in which everyone could achieve individual distinction with advancing age and recognition of one's special talents. Once this vision took hold, it was never abandoned. Rather, generation after generation continued to elaborate on it.

6

A COMING TOGETHER

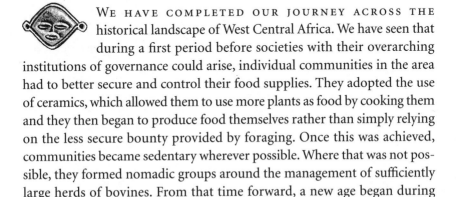 WE HAVE COMPLETED OUR JOURNEY ACROSS THE historical landscape of West Central Africa. We have seen that during a first period before societies with their overarching institutions of governance could arise, individual communities in the area had to better secure and control their food supplies. They adopted the use of ceramics, which allowed them to use more plants as food by cooking them and they then began to produce food themselves rather than simply relying on the less secure bounty provided by foraging. Once this was achieved, communities became sedentary wherever possible. Where that was not possible, they formed nomadic groups around the management of sufficiently large herds of bovines. From that time forward, a new age began during which communities came together as societies under a common governance and later elaborated on their common institutions.

Not so long ago, scholars still understood the underlying dynamic of the first period as one in which Bantu-speaking immigrants introduced the whole package of technologies as they colonized the area. Gradually it became evident that there was neither a single package nor any large-scale immigration. As demonstrated in Part I of this book, the dynamics were different. First of all, the adoption of new technologies proceeded slowly, and the technologies were adopted in a piecemeal fashion rather than as a package. Starting with the acquisition of ceramics and pursuing this with all the acquisitions which followed, autochthons first experimented with a novelty because they foresaw, that is, they imagined ahead of time, that it would help either to increase their food supply or to render it more secure. Over time, they became familiar with less desirable side effects and learned to cope with them while they also learned how to insert the new technology into the overall economic management of their lives and to better fit it to the needs of the moment. After all this trial and error, the innovation was then internalized and community after community made the final choice to adopt or to reject it. Rejection transpired when an innovation could not be adopted or be sustained: for example, there was no suitable clay to make pots, the environment did not allow the introduction of the main crops around which horticulture was practiced so that only cowpeas and cucurbits continued to be planted, game and vegetal food was so abundant that there was not much incentive to adopt food production, and so on.

Moreover, each new technology brought about social change as well. To make ceramics enhanced the status of women potters, horticulture required a new sort of coordination of male and female labor to prepare fields and it could lead to a seasonal separation of women and men as the women stayed put to plant while the men roamed about for game. The smelting and the forging of metals widened gender distinction and created new prestigious careers, and some of its products became highly prized valuables that gave a new sort of power to those who detained them. Indeed once metal hoes became the preferred tool for cereal cultivation, women farmers became dependent on men in a way they never had been before and a gender hierarchy developed. As argued earlier, keeping large herds had to be preceded by the acceptance of delayed returns on labor, yet that provoked new divisions of labor (by gender, and age), fostered social inequality, created new notions of wealth and inheritance, and thus seems to have led to the invention of unilinear matrilineal descent and its consequences.

No wonder then that the adoption of new technologies had to be piecemeal and stretched out over half a millennium or more, even if one excludes earlier, more modest innovations such as the introduction of ground stone tools. The entire process was complete everywhere only by the ninth or even tenth centuries with the full spread of cereal farming and with an intensified production of metals. Compared to other parts of Africa, this is remarkably late, centuries later than anywhere else except for arid southwestern Africa.

Obviously, these technologies—from making ceramics to adopting new crops, planting fields, tending domestic animals, and creating metal from stone—diffused into the area from elsewhere; they were not introduced by immigration on any large scale. Yet there was immigration of a sort. Proto-Njila speakers living in villages and practicing horticulture entered the area, but only drop by drop, as one community at a time shifted every few years perhaps a dozen kilometers or so from one site to another. Although they spoke proto-Njila, most of the villagers were locals who had married or settled there and brought their own habits and customs with them. Even those immigrants did not come from far away since they, too, were descendants of earlier local people, very likely from not even 150 kilometers or so away. Many centuries later, Njila languages also began to spread in another way, namely through language shift among whole foraging communities in a process of general acculturation.

As the proto-Njila language and its descendants diffused along with the spread of farming, so did social and cultural features that were especially linked to a sedentary lifestyle. These fused in each case with the local practices and beliefs of the surrounding foragers. Thus the later ways of life associated with Njila, as well as with other Bantu languages, are not the heritage of a pristine proto-Bantu tradition as some ideologues seem to believe today. It was, instead, a compound in which the ancient legacy of the various groups of Stone Age foragers who had roamed the area for millennia predominated. While the absence of aboriginal languages makes it nearly impossible to document this point, this absence does not disprove it.[1] Rather than think about a single sociocultural tradition that was inherited intact from proto-Njila times onward, we should interpret the commonalities in the later West Central African ways of life as a tradition that first began to take shape out of the fusion of various earlier traditions of foragers with a number of sociocultural features related to sedentarity and agriculture among Bantu-speaking villagers. Later a single whole emerged as the result of centuries of convergence among the inhabitants of the area. Once cereal farming had spread to the north from the south, the two original regional cultures which belonged, respectively, to southern and central Africa, two hitherto completely different historical parts of Africa, were unified from the eighth century onward into a single new area, namely, West Central Africa. Hence, if one absolutely must credit some forebears rather than others with the ancestry of one's own cultural makeup, one should credit this legacy to those unspectacular Late–Stone Age foragers and not to some very distant proto-Bantu–speaking yam farmers somewhere on the present border between Nigeria and Cameroon.

Once the foundations for a sedentary life or at least a nomadic life primarily grounded on food production had been laid, overarching institutions of governance and hence societies also appeared. These developed during the second period and in three strikingly different ways. In middle Angola, which was blessed with fertile soils and sufficient rainfall, life became easier and population density began to increase. This, in turn, increased the frequency of contacts between neighbors and hence created a greater need for some common institutions of governance. At first consultation through palavers became routine; this eventually fostered the appearance of chiefdoms whose leaders were then held to be the guardians and managers of local fertility, which thus gained the allegiance of their subjects. Later, sev-

---

1. In the absence of aboriginal languages, one could only show that innovations cannot be traced to proto-Bantu or proto-Njila etymologies and show highly unusual formal features for Bantu words.

eral chiefdoms agglomerated into principalities or even kingdoms with central courts and a loose set of political titles arranged in a more or less hierarchical whole. The lords took over the conduct of the essential rituals of fertility for the entire territory and thus acquired the allegiance of their subjects in their turn. The concomitant growth of a panoply of titles was crucial because it ensured active participation in the system by local leaders who hoped to eventually acquire such a title and thus increase their prestige among their peers as well as among their subjects. At the same time, this moderate centralization was helped by the fact that within the cradles of denser populations it was no longer practical for dissatisfied or ambitious leaders to emigrate into empty lands and to set up new chiefdoms of their own.

In the arid south where rainfed or even irrigated farming was not possible, cattle herds became crucial to the survival of local communities. Only nomads could thrive under such conditions, so that even groups which had first formed under the better climatic conditions of the thirteenth century in southwestern Angola were forced to abandon sedentarization when the climate became drier. They had to become just as nomadic as the foragers, sheepherders, and even some cattle herders farther to the south. In these conditions, significant population densities could not appear, and any ambitious cattleowner could nonetheless leave his community of origin and strike out on his own whenever he wished. At the same time, local cattle herds required a single responsible manager in order to prosper and to remain sufficiently large. The result was the rise of strong patriarchal and almost despotic leadership within each community and the creation of overarching institutions to cope with the requirements of transhumance and the dispersal of cattle. Also, given these conditions, the seamless web of an undifferentiated society could not be maintained and a hierarchy of strongly differentiated social classes appeared, namely those of owners, "tenants," and servants in which control over cattle was the crucial factor.

Yet another pattern arose in the lands of the infertile Kalahari Sands to the east. Keeping large herds of cattle there seems to have been impossible, probably because of tsetse fly infestation, but there was sufficient rainfall for farming. However, one could only farm on a very small proportion of those lands and even then the food supply had to be more heavily supplemented by foraging than elsewhere. The availability of good farmland in the main valleys led to the emergence of dendritic clusters of settlements separated from each other by vast tracts of land suited only for foraging and in which foraging communities did survive for many centuries before they were eventually assimilated. These circumstances meant that initiations into adulthood for boys became crucial since they included extensive and prolonged training in bushcraft. These also drew increased attention to the differences in tasks and roles between men and women as well as between different age-sets. This then led to the emergence of a hierarchical series of initiations managed by sodalities. As such, initiations required groups larger than a single community, they were organized collectively within each population cluster, which thus turned into a vicinage. Decisions within the vicinage continued to be made collectively, especially by the members of the most senior age-sets, but the representation of a vicinage in its relations to other vicinages facilitated the emergence of a single representative, the *mwene*. Over time and in some parts of the region, vicinages turned into chiefdoms when their representatives began to assume new ideologies that, once again, stressed their role in the collective management of fertility. In the northeastern quarter of the area, however, these representatives fell by the wayside and governance within vicinages became fully collective as it was assumed by the "big men" who composed the most senior male set. This set then also conducted relations with the neighboring vicinages.

At the time they first emerged, the scale of societies was modest as each society encompassed only four or five communities inhabited perhaps by 500 people, at the most, per society. Thereafter that scale increased in the densely populated parts of middle Angola until it came to encompass perhaps up to 200,000 inhabitants distributed over hundreds of villages in the Kingdom of Ndongo. Elsewhere in both the southern and the eastern regions, the scale of society did not grow at all. By the sixteenth century, it remained unchanged. One can attribute this lack of growth to restrictions imposed by environmental conditions, but it makes more sense to attribute it to a lack of desire or vision, however preposterous that proposition may seem at first sight. The collective imaginations in these societies were simply not interested in enlarging the scale of their societies.

Collective Imagination, Tradition, and the Dynamics of History

Just as the three modes of governance just sketched developed along three different lines, so did a fascination, powerful enough to be called an obsession, with three different visions of governance, each of which is perfectly correlated with a particular mode of government. Each of these visions captured the imagination not just of leaders but of the general population as well. Every person participated to some degree in them because they were collective; hence, every person was also concerned to some extent with the actual mode of governance of their particular society. We have seen that the three modes of governance correlate well with the patterns of rainfall and soil fertility prevailing in each of the three regions, although the correlation is not perfect. Clearly environmental conditions played a major role in the constitution and development of these different modes of governance and hence with their collective imaginations as well. Yet these visions were not inspired after all only by the prevailing physical environment.

In the south where cattle were crucial, a cornucopia of words sprang up to describe every variation in the physical appearance of particular beasts, the most central theme in poetry praised the beauty and relative strength of cattle, living cattle commemorated the deceased, cattle played the central sacrificial role in most rituals, and every man developed a special bond of affection and identification with a particular animal. That cattle nomads would be obsessed by animals so essential to their lives is understandable, yet this interest is not directly dictated by their environmental conditions. Sheepherders, for instance, were equally dependent on their flocks but they did not develop a similar obsession with sheep. In middle Angola, meanwhile, the pageantry of the courts with their frequent rituals of fertility and especially their titleholding attracted everyone's attention. Titles proliferated over time until the major polities boasted of having over a hundred of them, each of which linked to different emblems, etiquette, privileges, and a special relationship to the ruler or the court. While the political role played by such titles is obvious, their proliferation and the imagery associated with them still was not directly inspired by environmental conditions. Finally, in the east everyone was mesmerized by initiations, especially by the masked dances that accompanied them, to the point that over time several dozen masks were invented, each with its own costume and its own dance, each acting out a different role and status within society. Indirectly, one can trace a link between masking and the sands of the Kalahari, but once again there is no necessary link between the environment and this plethora of masks. Hence, in each of the three cases these fascinations of the imagination developed according to dynamics of their own; since in the final analysis they are an expression of modes of governance, these modes were not merely dictated by the requirements of their natural environments.

This is particularly evident in the eastern region, where the situation began to change dramatically from around 1600 onward with the sudden rise of the Rund Kingdom under the influence of East Central African influences. Then, around a half-century later, the transatlantic slave trade irrupted into the entire region and began to interact with the continuing Rund expansion. To resist conquest, sudden ad hoc coalitions of a set of chiefdoms united by a single dynastic web sprang up and soon turned into permanently federated principalities, of which the largest known included perhaps as many as 8,000 to 10,000 people belonging to eighteen or so of the older small chiefdoms. But this opposition by coalition to Rund expansion was only partly successful, and by 1770 the whole northern part of the region as well as the Ndembu-speaking lands to the east had become part of a single Lunda Commonwealth, a political entity that was then many times larger in territory (but perhaps not in population) than any previous polity Central Africa had known, including, by then, the Portuguese colony of Angola.

Ostensibly, this story merely tells us how outside agents can rather suddenly transform a political landscape. Yet neither the environment nor outside agents can fully account for what occurred. Thus, the prevalence everywhere in this region of societies based on matrilineages, age-sets, multiple rites of passage, and masking was not imposed by the natural environment, nor was the highly original form of collective government in the Lweta-Kasai region. The rise of the Rund Kingdom occurred in a totally unexpected way and led to a totally unexpected structure, even if the urge to unite may have been a reaction to an increased threat from beyond the Lubilash River. But even this is insufficient explanation, for—faced by the same threats—the Kanincin still remained a toy-sized kingdom while the Sala Mpasu and Kongo-Dinga successfully resisted everyone, including the later Rund Kingdom, without any known institutional change at all. To fully account, then, for the history of this region, one must accept that something else played a leading role. That something else was the collective imagination of the societies involved. In each case, a single person first imagined an effective response to a new challenge from the outside, and everyone else in a community then accepted it.

When confronted with the need to meet new challenges from the outside, people tended to perceive, think, and react to them in the familiar terms of local institutions. Thus, the creation of a dynastic web merely invented something like a vicinage but did so on a larger scale while still preserving the cherished age-set sodalities. Faced by wholly new circumstances on their borders, the Rund had to imagine something well beyond the earlier structures of initiations, intricate small-scale societies, and masquerades. Still thinking in terms of familiar institutions, they rose to the challenge by inventing a novel and truly grandiose fiction in which scores of powerholders in a huge arena were arrayed around a single focal person as if they were still members of a single household led by a single senior relative. Thus they inflated the old practice of a small community to nearly cosmic proportions and turned it into a wholly new vision of a centralized state.

One may be tempted to conclude from all of this that members in the older small-scale polities in the region of the Kalahari Sands could at any time have imagined the kinds of enlargements of social scale that actually took place. They did not do so before the seventeenth century; hence one cannot simply attribute the earlier absence of a drive to increase the scale of polities to a supposedly permanent physical constraint since their physical environment did not change during that century. Their human environment did change, however, since they then responded to human challenges originating outside the area. If the changes did not happen earlier, the reason was that there was no incentive for them. Earlier on, the people of the area had felt comfortable with the small scale of the vicinages in which they lived. They had been so little interested in any enlargement for enlargement's sake that their collective imaginations, although always active, did not bother to speculate about this kind of issue. This leads us to probe somewhat further into the nature of collective imagination and how it relates to the flow of history.

Collective imagination is a set of representations of perceived realities and values that are accepted without question by most, perhaps even by all, members of a given community. Because it is collective, it focuses on objects of interest to all and usually on more than just one topic. For example, a famous object of collective imagination common to all farmers and herders of West Central Africa, but not to foragers, is pure witchcraft. The notion of witchcraft is accompanied by an extended imagined lore about the evils of witches, their customs and their meetings, the ways in which they can cause disease or death, their activity, their motivations, and the ways to identify and fight them. The often lurid details varied from community to community and changed over time but the basic beliefs were held firmly by all. Everyone believed, for example, that witches always killed out of envy, that they could only harm relatives by blood or by marriage, or perhaps only people within the local community, or that witchcraft always occurred between certain sets of persons of unequal status. Thus, accusations of witchcraft were always linked to overwhelming social tensions, although the specific tensions and their causes varied greatly from case to case as well as over time. Actual accusations and trials "proved" that witchcraft was a real and ever present danger. At the same time, people did not consciously realize that the ultimate effect of this set of beliefs was to provide the very foundation of their celebrated solidarity within kingroups and/or local community groups, without which the existence of such groups could not have been sustained for very long. Indeed both the fear of being accused and the need to stick together to guard against the attacks of witches created this solidarity and kept it alive. Consequently, belief in witchcraft actually undergirded the social basis of kinship and community.

The objects of collective imagination encountered in this work all deal with the realm of governance. Although people knew they were obsessed by objects such as cattle, courts, and titleholders, or masked dances, in this case, as in the case of witchcraft, they probably did not fully realize that the effect of their fascination was the very foundation of their overarching institutions of governance and hence of society at large.

All imagination occurs, of course, in the minds of individuals—not collectivities. People think about events, dream, and sometimes have visions, which they communicate to others in conversations with family or friends when they think that these persons will be interested. These communications then often lead to speculation. The same happened when travelers came to the settlement with "news" about events, practices, or beliefs from elsewhere. Thus innovations spread by gossip, and the information, whether of internal or external origin, tended to be accepted as valid as long as the tenor of each bit of news or each story fitted in well with current ideas, stereotypes, or prejudices and reinforced them. More particularly in the case of discussions about governance, someone's dream, idea, or even a vision in a trance, as well as a bit of news from foreign parts tended to suggest a new twist to be added to an existing practice, or a slight change in existing bits of cognition. To communicate any innovation, however, one needed to put it in words, often as a clumsy paraphrase at first, but eventually by coining a new word and with it a new concept.

While many novel speculations or propositions were regarded as idiosyncrasies and were rejected by others as uninteresting or even weird, some were adopted by all and became collective because they fitted in well with existing preconceptions and because of the special authority of the person who offered them. The views of respected, experienced elderly people, who were halfway ancestors already, those of renowned arbitrators, reputed diviners, persons speaking in trance (irrespective of gender), or recognized experts on the point discussed were far more persuasive than those of ordinary folk. Thus an expert dancer would propose a new masked dance, an expert manager of cattle a new classification of animals, or a diviner a new ritual at court. In the realm of governance, assemblies probably played a special role, albeit perhaps less so during formal palavers than in the course of informal discussions surrounding such occasions. Regardless of the avenue by which it reached the public, once an innovation had been adopted by a local community, it was put in practice there. Neighboring communities soon heard the news and if the innovation impressed them, they too borrowed it.

Thus masks, political titles, names for cattle colors, and the like actually diffused in the manner of all fashions.

Since collective imaginations were fed by intercommunication, the frequency and the spatial range of that intercommunication could be expected to strongly influence or even determine the rate of innovations proposed by the collective imaginations. One might even think that the larger the scale of a society, that is, the more people who interacted in a common social pool, the faster the rate of innovation should be. If so, every increase in the scale of society should lead to an "acceleration of history." By that rule the small-scale societies of the eastern and of the southern portions of West Central Africa would innovate much more slowly than the larger scale ones in middle Angola. This seems to hold true at first: overarching institutions developed faster and further in middle Angola than elsewhere, especially in the last few centuries before 1500, and public life at the major political courts there was far more intricate and sophisticated than elsewhere. But the proposition is only partly true at best. Consider the entire eastern region with its small vicinages before 1600. While the individual societies were quite small, the region as a whole shows massive evidence for large-scale convergence and hence also for far-flung and enduring communications. The situation in the southern region is much the same. The communications in these regions resulted both from a high overall demographic mobility and from commercial networks, including special networks for metalworkers, diviners, and hunters.

Hence the scale or size of a given society is not essential to an acceleration of history, and such an acceleration might not have any connection to the scale of polities at all but would merely consist in a faster rate of invention of instruments of governance, such as new words for cattle colors, new titles, or new masks. Yet soon after 1600 the Atlantic slave-trading network established more intensive and more extensive communications throughout the area than had existed earlier on even in regions still remote from direct Portuguese control. A flood of new inputs, mostly from far away, now flooded the collective imaginations, which then produced innovation after innovation inspired by the confrontations between homegrown truths and hitherto exotic features. Innovations occurred irrespective of their necessity. Those that were essential to meet new macropolitical circumstances were perhaps rather less frequent than less momentous or even frivolous ones. The result was a genuine historical acceleration in ways of life and thinking. Thus the slave-trading network fostered not only the general rise of monarchical polities far and wide, it also provided these with the elaborate trappings of what anthropologists know as divine kingship, trappings that were cobbled together from older Ambundu and Ovimbundu practices.[2] The result was the onset of an acceleration of history that has continued ever since.

While the raw materials of the imagination, be they individual dreams, visions, inspirations, or gossip, can deal with any subject matter at all, that is not true for collective imaginations. A person will only communicate such items to others when he or she thinks that the subject matter interests his or her audience. Sociocultural relevance becomes the filter to turn the chaos of raw imagination into useable inspiration. Everyone was certainly interested in pesky practical problems crying our for a solution, questions that related to such matters, for example, as the distribution of cattle, how to burn the bush more safely, how to cope with an epidemic or a drought, and so on. Many of these issues concerned challenges or opportunities presented by the physical environment; hence it is only predictable that collective imaginations often drew inspiration from their environmental conditions. But everyone was just as intensely interested in questions concerning governance, since these directly affected everyone's individual security, their personal lives, and their individual ambitions. That explains why everyone, and not just those who had the right to be heard, attended palavers. People wanted to learn about the outcome but they wanted even more to listen to the arguments presented during the discussions, because these arguments closely impinged on the conduct of everyone's lives. Such assemblies decreed common cooperation, resolved conflicts, and laid down precedents in social matters such as marriage or debts. While collective imaginations seized on these points, they did not inspire them particularly. What fascinated them above all were issues that involved individual career aspirations in relation to common governance. Whether such aspirations actually concerned cattle, titles, or masked dances was of little importance. What mattered was that by entertaining them people participated in the governance of their societies and sustained these by doing so. Indeed, since most of the existing modes of governance lacked any effective means to exert sustained coercion on the population, societies survived mainly through the dreams and the participation of their members.

Once created, the fundamental features and practices of the overarching institutions that maintained the wider society were never put into question again. Rather, they were continually enriched by the ceaseless activity of collective imaginations about governance. This activity continually added new facets to their meaning, their expression, and their functioning so that these institutions became ever more intricate and ever more fascinating. The

2. The same dynamic holds true for the Lunda Commonwealth with its creation of small monarchies and ritual trappings copied from the Rund heartland.

result of these continuous small additions was to continually reinforce the existing institutions as fundamental, unquestionable cognitive realities. It became unimaginable to dismiss them out of hand or to replace them by something quite different. In this way, choices, once made, tended to become irreversible—even when new circumstances required new adaptations. The Rund case is a striking example of this. Here is a fundamental transformation to cope with a new context yet it is but an elaboration on the foundation of existing institutions. Their validity was never questioned and there was no repeal of choices made long ago. It is this dynamic property of building on existing frameworks rather than of replacing them that explains how traditions could take shape and continue to exist over time.

The reader can now better understand why this book focuses so much on collective imaginations as the underlying dynamics that explain continuity and change rather than dwelling on the concept of a tradition as I did in my earlier work on Equatorial Africa.[3] The reason is that whereas the concept of political tradition to understand continuity and change is just as central here as in Equatorial Africa, the link between tradition and the ideas, aspirations, and activities of individuals was not explored in that case, even though individuals are the only actors in history. The operation of those individual imaginations that were accepted by their collectivities now establishes that link. Collective imaginations are the underlying dynamic processes that account for the gradual crystallization of traditions and for their maintenance over considerable periods of time. Additionally, we now also better understand why it is both right and wrong to speak of a "single ancestral western Bantu tradition."[4] It is wrong because so many inputs of all sorts into the later societies and cultures of West Central Africa stemmed from the original communities of foragers who were the majority of those who created sedentary villages, yet it is right in that, initially, these people accepted a framework of governance that first entered the area with the earliest horticulturalists. One can say that the result was the crystallization of a novel overall tradition fusing aboriginal and imported elements out of the older western Bantu one. Yet one can also say that that new tradition was an innovative continuation of the older one. To my mind, it is far more important to better understand the dynamics of history than to quarrel over a genealogy of traditions. Hence the stress I have laid in this book on collective imaginations as the process that creates and sustains those long-term yet ever-changing continuities called traditions.

3. Vansina, *Paths*, pp. 249, 251–60.
4. Ibid., p. 251.

APPENDIX: THE NJILA GROUP OF LANGUAGES

I. The Njila Group of Languages[1]

The existence of a single large genetic set of Bantu languages in southern West Central Africa comprising some sixty tongues was first recognized in the 1970s on the basis of a lexicostatistical calculations by Robert Papstein.[2] Its full extent within Bantu has only recently been established on the basis of a range of lexicostatistic calculations carried out on a very large number of languages. Nevertheless, even this very large body of data still lacked Kimbundu or any other language closely related to it. To include these, I carried out some elementary additional calculations, which confirm the earlier findings of Papstein on this point.[3]

But lexicostatistics, the calculation of the portion of basic vocabulary that is retained between two languages, is only one avenue for establishing a genetic relationship. Some linguists put more trust in common innovations, that is, features that do not exist outside the posited larger genetic unit but are present in a majority of its main subdivisions. Such innovations must have occurred in the common ancestral language and therefore prove its existence.[4]

1. Njila, meaning "bird," is a common innovation to the languages of this group—hence this label. Hitherto, this unit was known as "proto-Western-Savanna-Bantu," as in Papstein, "The Upper Zambezi," pp. 68–74, and Ehret, *African,* p. 45, or "Southwest (Bantu)" for Vansina, "New Linguistic Evidence," pp. 182–85.

2. The group first clearly appeared in Y. Bastin et al., "Statistique lexicale et grammaticale," p. 380 (lexicon group-average). Heine, "Zur Genetischen Gliederung," pp. 164–84, has three subgroups in his subdivision 11, namely, 11.6 Rund, 11.7 Luchazi-Lwena, 11.8. Kimbundu-Imbangala-Ovimbundu (with all the most southwestern languages).

3. The elementary new calculations were done two-by-two on Kimbundu in relation to Holo, Pende, Kongo, Cokwe, and Umbundu. Kimbundu is clearly closest to Holo and Pende. It is hoped that Michael Mann will soon be able to include Kimbundu in the overall corpus of lexicostatistics.

4. Still the use of innovations also has drawbacks. The first one is that one cannot easily distinguish ancient loans from common origin, especially when the geographic

TABLE 1. Innovations in the Njila Group of Languages

Modern reflex	Proto-Njila form	Meaning
-jila 9/10	(*-jịda 9)	"bird": replaced *-(j)unjị 9
-binga 9/10, 11/10		"horn" (separated from the head)
-wa, -waba, verb	(?*-ba(pa)	"to be beautiful, good"
-imbo 5/6	(? *gịmbo 5)	
	and the compound	
	*-gumbo 5/6	"residence/village":
	replaced *-gị 3 as well	
	as *-da 14/6 "home"	
-njamba 9/2, 9/10	(*-jamba 9)	"elephant": replaced *-jogụ 9

TERMS RELATING TO SOCIAL ROLES OF GROUPS

-coko 7/8		"kinsfolk or other persons of equal rank"; -coko 14, kinsfolk; -coko 3/4 "settlement of kinsfolk"
-pánga 1/2		"sibling of other sex"

In the case of Njila, the five innovations shown in table 1 have been identified, of which the first three belong to the basic vocabulary.

In addition, one is tempted to posit a weakening of the initial phoneme *b- (but not mb-) to a bilabial fricative or affricate as an innovation found only in this genetic unit and in the whole unit. Still, it is possible that this feature resulted from transfer (borrowing) at a later time, not unlike the general upheaval in the phonetic inventory linked to spirantization and the shift from seven to five vowels, which also spread by transfer.[5] Only further study can clarify the situation.

The evidence from lexicostatistics as well as from innovations is sufficient to prove the existence of the genetic group, which I have labeled Njila.

---

distribution of the item is continuous. Second, to avoid the use of negative evidence, the argument needs to indicate which other feature existed before the innovation occurred and which alternative feature is found in languages outside the group. Given the vast number of Bantu languages and the lacunae in their documentation, uncertainties in some cases remain. On the whole issue, see Colette Piron, "Classification interne," 3:539–42.

5. By ca. 500, Eastern African "five-vowel" Bantu languages still were "seven-vowel" languages, as an examination of the phonological characteristics for "chicken" indicates.

II. Composition and Internal Structure

The composition and the internal structure of the group are ascertained by the following data. A comparison of the seven lexicostatistical trees, excluding the most extreme presuppositions, shows that five stable blocks are involved. These are labeled as follows: *Eastern* (eastern Angola-Lunda languages); *Kunene* (western Angola-Namibia); *Middle Kwilu* (Mbala, Pende, and related)[6]; to which we add *Kwanza* (Kimbundu and related)[7]; and perhaps *Lweta* (Mbagani, Lwalwa). In all the trees, Eastern and Kunene join to form a single southern unit opposed to Middle Kwilu, Kwanza, and/or Lweta. A common innovation, namely, the loss of the form *-cádá* 11/10 "feather" confirms this southern unit. The structure suggested is shown in figure 1.

FIGURE 1. Internal Structure of Njila

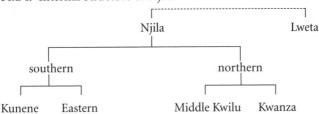

In six of the seven trees, Middle Kwilu is part of the northern unit whereas Lweta appears only once in this position (Tree Vn 33). Lweta is the closest block to the whole group in two trees (Tree VN 67, Tree BrAv), but it belongs to a different group in one (Tree VN 83). It obviously is the most peripheral member of the group and probably does not belong to it at all. In this context, it is relevant to note that Mbagani has only one of the Njila set of innovations ("people of" but "horn" is unreported) and that Lwalwa has only two ("bird" and "people of" but "horn" is unreported), which could well be a transfer from another language in the group.[8] The Lweta Block probably was coordinate with the whole of Njila rather than a part of it. At this point, one should stress that, contrary to the impressions of Mukumbuta Lisimba and Christopher Ehret, this genetic group excludes the Upper Zambezi Block, which comprises the Luyi and related languages. Such a group-

6. This unit is less stable than the others for in Tree VN 33 the Mbala and Pende subgroups are separated from each other, although they are still close.

7. In Bastin et al., *Continuity,* pp. 216–18: Described as K1–2 enlarged (Eastern), R1–3 enlarged (Kunene), K5 enlarged, (Middle Kwilu) L22, (Lweta). They do not have Kwanza.

8. Only one of the words considered is reported in Kongo-Dinga vocabulary of Ceyssens, *Pouvoir.*

ing appears nowhere in the lexicostatistical evidence and the common innovations do not occur there either.[9]

In contrast, the innovations are present everywhere in the Kwanza Block. In the Kwilu Block, the Pende subunit has all of them but Mbala only has two ("bird," "village"). This may well be an effect of its geographic position on the very edge of the area because within the Lunda subgroup, which obviously does belong to the Eastern branch of the southern unit, Rund and Lunda have three innovations ("bird," "elephant," "to be beautiful") while Sala Mpasu and Kete Ipila on the edge have only one ("bird"), but three items are unreported in Kete Ipila. All the forms that are not the expected common innovations are also found in neighboring languages outside the group and should be considered to be later transfers from them.[10]

On this basis, one concludes that the group consisted of two units: a southern unit consisting of the Kunene and Eastern Blocks and a northern one consisting of the Kwilu and Kwanza Blocks.

Within the southern unit, the validity of the Kunene Block on the basis of the class 5 prefix has been demonstrated by David Crabb and is supported by internal innovation.[11] Jeffrey Hoover established the validity of the Eastern Block, which is also supported by internal innovation.[12] Both authors detail the genetic subdivisions of their respective groups down to the level of obvious dialect continua and these correspond to the lexicostatistical evidence. The only remaining issue here is the exact position of the nearly undocumented Ndombe.[13]

In the northern unit, the unity of the Middle Kwilu Block is not (yet) evident from data other than lexicostatistics. It is obviously composed of Mbala and Pende subunits, of which Mbala consists of a single dialect continuum. The Pende subunit comprises seven languages, of which four remain almost undocumented. This subunit is characterized by a residual augment *o* in all classes except in class 9, where it is *e*. It is *o* in all classes in the whole Kwanza

9. Mukumbuta Lisimba, "A Luyana Dialectology," p. 25; Ehret, *African*, p. 45.

10. Under similar circumstances, Herero, Dciriku, and Kwangari in the far south lost the innovation for "elephant" and adopted the form used by their neighbors outside the Njila unit.

11. D. W. Crabb, "Nasal and Nasalized Roots." See also Homburger, *Le groupe sudouest.* One common innovation is *-inya/-enya* 6 "feather."

12. J. Hoover, "Seduction." One innovation is the fusion of the notions of body hair and feathers into a single word (with the exception of Sala Mpasu) and a separate form for the feather used in an arrow.

13. Ndombe could belong to the Umbundu, Nyaneka, or Herero subunits or form a subunit of its own equal to Nyaneka or Herero.

TABLE 2. Genetic Classification of the Njila Languages

Block	Subblock
NORTHERN UNIT	
1. *Kwilu*	Mbala
	Pende, Sonde, Holo, Kwezo, Shinji, Minungu, Taba, Kosa?
2. *Kwanza*	Kimbundu, Libolo, Kisama, Ndembu, Hungu
	Songo
	Mbui
SOUTHERN UNIT	
3. *Eastern*	Lunda
	(i) Rund, Sala Mpasu, Mbal, Kete-Ipila
	(ii) Southern Lunda (Ndembu)
	Moxico
	(i) northern: Lwena, Cokwe
	(ii) southern: Lucazi, Mbunda, Nyemba,
	Lwimbi, Mbwela, Ngangela
4. *Kunene*	Subblock:
	(i) Umbundu:
	Umbundu, Hanya-Ganda, Sele
	(ii) Okavango:
	Kwangari, Dciriku
	Subblock Cimbebasia:
	(i) Nyaneka, Nkhumbi
	(ii) Kwanyama, Kwambi, Ndonga, Mbalanhu
	(iii) Herero (and Mbanderu), Cimba, Dimba, Kuvale,
	Kwisi?
Unclassified	Ndombe

Note. The Lweta group consists of Mbagani, Lwalwa, and Kongo-Dinga. It is coordinate with Njila as a whole.

Block. This suggests that the Pende subunit and the Kwanza Block form a single subunit opposed to Mbala.

The internal unity of the Kwanza Block is supported by innovations, among which -*nama* 7,8 ("leg") is particularly convincing. Moreover, the tongues that belong to the block form a dialect continuum with the possible exception of Songo and perhaps Mbui.

The Lweta group consists of Mbagani, Lwalwa, and Kongo-Dinga, all of which are obviously closely related to each other.

The results are as shown in table 2.

III. Links to Other Units and Points of Origin

As a major subdivision within Bantu, Njila should be linked to other major units, but to which ones? Should it be linked to units in the savanna to its east or to units mainly in the rainforests to its north? On nearly all the lexico-statistical trees, Njila is linked to a group now labeled "West Coastal," which includes the Kongo and Kasai-Mfimi (lower Kwa-Kasai and Mfimi Valleys) units.[14] Only the two trees, which grant the most weight to the "nearest neighbor," link Njila to the east.[15] One can also adduce a large vocabulary of words common to Njila and the languages to its north but absent in the east.[16] In this context, the innovation -*kwa* 1/2 + noun "people of + noun," which indicates a group of people or a characteristic of people and replaces *-cí* 1/2 + noun is quite significant for it is found in Njila as well as in Kongo.

Yet for Ehret, Njila is part of a "Savanna" supergroup that includes "Mashariki," "Sabi-Botatwe," and "Central Savanna." In support of his view, he cites nine innovations, of which eight refer to wild animals and one to gallery forest.[17] All of these are transfers. Six only occur in one or a pair of Njila languages near its eastern border but are widespread east of that border. These are completely different from the proto-Njila forms they ousted, at least in the three cases for which a proto-Njila form is attested to.[18] One item, ("eland, large deer") is attested to in Ndembu, Lwena, Cokwe, and the Nga-gela cluster, i.e., in nearly the whole of the Moxico Subblock. Yet the distribution is continuous and also abuts on East Central Africa, where the item is nearly ubiquitous.[19] Two other words ("pig" and "leopard") are more widespread in the Kunene Block and on the margins of the Eastern Block but do not occur in the northern unit of Njila. These two are deviations from proto-Njila: *-gudube* (CS 888) versus *-gudú:* "pig" (CS 887) and *-gue* (CS 866) versus -*go* (CS 834) "leopard"). Hence they are also late transfers, more easily accepted because of the similarity of form between the older word and the innovation. Ultimately, all the evidence points to a closer relationship with

14. Vansina, "New Linguistic," pp. 183, 185. Note that the term "Kwilu" was used there for what is now dubbed the Kasai-Mfimi unit.

15. Y. Bastin et al., *Continuity,* pp. 126–27.

16. Many, if not most, of those labeled as PB-A in Guthrie, *Comparative Bantu* (Farnsworth 1967–71, vols. 2 and 3) could be adduced as evidence here.

17. Ehret, *African,* p. 42, table 3a, and p. 38, table 2b.

18. They are *-cumbu:* 9/10 "wild pig"; *-mbungú* 7/8 "hyena" (*Crocuta crocuta*), CS 206; *gudungu* 1n/2 or 9/10 "bushbuck."

19. *Sefu* 1n/2n occurs in Mbala but designates a species of "warthog" and hence is irrelevant here. The "C" in Cú stands for k/p/t. See CS 316. The form occurs in classes 1n/2 or 9/10. Guthrie adds a skewed form in Duala. If this is really derived from CS 316, that would make the form even proto-Bantu!

the "West Coastal" group and none supports the view that the Njila unit is more closely related to the other "savanna" groups mentioned by Ehret.

Everyone accepts that the origins of the Njila unit lay to the north of the area it now occupies somewhere between the lower Kwilu River and the mouth of the Sankuru River, south of the lower Kasai River. Its area of origin probably lies west of the Kamtsha River, while the origins of the Lweta Block are best placed east of the Loange River. We interpret the data as follows. After Bantu-speaking settlements had been established along the lower Kasai River, some speakers began to gradually move inland to occupy the lands of the middle Kwilu and middle Loange Valleys, perhaps as far eastward as the great bend of the middle Kasai River. As the distances from the lower Kasai River became too great for all its speakers to maintain sufficiently frequent intercommunication between themselves, their original language began to differentiate, giving rise to proto-Njila around the middle Kwilu River, probably between latitudes 5° and 7° S while proto-Lweta arose farther east, perhaps on the Kasai River upstream of Tshikapa near latitude 7° S. There are no clues as to why the expansion occurred, how many people were involved, nor how they interacted with the previous occupants.

IV. Later Language History

To this day, the later histories of Njila or any of its subgroups or even languages remain essentially unstudied.[20] The few known indications about internal linguistic change derive from general studies in comparative Bantu, e.g., that there has been a passage from a seven-vowel to a five-vowel system accompanied by spirantization and other changes affecting consonants. Yet, after their emergence, neighboring languages continued to influence each other, sometimes over a sizeable area, and underwent considerable internal changes. So far, not even the expansion and the standardization of languages such as Kongo and Kimbundu, and, later, Umbundu and Rund, and later still Nyaneka and Cokwe have attracted any attention, although written documents from the later 1500s onward allow one to at least realize that these languages have exerted major impacts on others and on each other.

V. Chronology

To establish an absolute chronology for the expansion of the Njila languages is quite difficult. In the past, many, myself included, have used glotto-

---

20. With the exception of Hoover's "Seduction," 1:30–76, and tables and maps in volume 2.

chronology, a technique derived from lexicostatistics and still defended by Ehret and his school.[21] Glottochronology makes the assumption that over long periods of time the basic vocabulary of all languages is subject to a similar rate of replacement, even if over short periods there may be either bursts of sudden change or retention without any change. Most linguists, however, reject the validity of glottochronology altogether. They stress that the rates of change in different languages vary and do not necessarily even out even over long time periods. They are also wary of dates derived from lexicostatistical percentages because these vary according to different calculations and differences in basic wordlists.

However reluctantly, I finally had to accept their arguments in the face of the following considerations. The variability of lexicostatistical percentages for various trees in the case of proto-Njila is significant. In Kimbundu, the rate of change since the 1600s is too slow. Ehret may well be right to attribute this to the influence of written documents (a catechism in this case) that retarded the evolution of the vocabulary. Yet, even if this was so, this unique circumstance would distort the lexicostatistical percentages and, hence, the dates of separation calculated for Kimbundu and its neighbors. In the case of Dciriku, several basic words, each of which is worth more than one percent of the whole are suddenly lost ca. 1900, when the older language form known as Rumanyu was abandoned.[22] The defenders of the technique no doubt consider this last case as a burst of change preceded by a long period of retention. Still, even if this was true (and why would it be?), the effect is to bring Dciriku several percentage points closer to Kwangari and to produce a much more recent date of separation between those two languages than would have obtained before 1900.

Finally, one must remember that usually language separation is a gradual process by which dialects differentiate more and more to eventually reach the point at which they are no longer mutually understandable. It simply may not be sensible to propose any given date, or perhaps even a particular century, for such a process.[23] In the end, one is forced to conclude that glottochronological dating is not to be trusted.

To use archaeology for dating the presence of languages or linguistic groups is also fraught with danger. Recently, this has been often done by correlating a language with a certain style of ceramic decor, on the assumption that stylistic conventions of decoration vary according to the language of the

21. Ehret, "Language," pp. 287–89.

22. Möhlig, Dciriku, pp. xxiii–xxiv, 52–54.

23. Between Dutch and Low German, for instance, such a process could be dated as early as the first half of the first millennium or as late as ca. 1200.

makers or users of pottery.[24] This is unacceptable both because language is not necessarily linked to a stylistic expression or to a pattern of settlement and because one can adduce many documented historical cases where the proposed correlations simply do not obtain. Moreover, in this case such a correlation cannot be proposed anyway for lack of sufficient archaeological research, including systematic comparisons of the ceramics found.

But archaeology can be helpful in other ways. The reader recalls from chapter 1 that proto-Njila arose after horticulture and ceramics came to be practiced but before metalworking was adopted. Given present evidence, this yields a time span between 300 BCE and 400 CE. In the future, significantly older dates may well be found, especially for ceramics, as further sites are excavated in and around the middle Kwilu, but as of now this chronology must be accepted.

The evidence also allows one to date a later moment in the dispersion of the Njila linguistic group. As we have seen, domestic sheep, a Middle Eastern domesticate, are first reported in southern Africa on sites with Bambata ceramics, dated to ca. 200 BCE in Zimbabwe. From there, sheepherding spread westward, probably along the belts of *mopane* grasslands, which are an excellent environment for these animals, to reach sites in northern Namibia and nearby Botswana dated to or before 1 CE. Because the words for sheep in the southernmost Bantu languages of the Njila group are transfers from one or more San languages, the animal also must have been borrowed from San herders. One can conclude from this that Bantu speakers arrived in the lower Cunene and Cuvelai regions only after the dispersal of sheep, hence some time after 1 CE.

Moreover, the diffusion of sheepherding also helps to date some of the major language splits in the Njila group. For this, one must examine what happened to the term for "goat." In western Angola, the terms for sheep are direct loans from San everywhere as far north as the border of Umbundu. There Umbundu and the whole Kimbundu Block applied *mbudi,* the old term for goat,[25] to sheep. They therefore had to invent a new word for goat, namely, *kombo/hombo* and that was then adopted by people farther to the north of them, such as Kongo speakers. But speakers of Eastern Block languages adopted the term *-pembe* for goat[26] and called sheep by the ideophone

24. Huffman, *Iron Age Migrations,* pp. 9, 113 (supposed correlation between language, worldview, and settlement pattern, itself linked to ceramic style). For actual practice, see Ehret, *African.*

25. In proto-Bantu and proto-Njila: *-búdì* 9/10.

26. Earlier *-pembe* seems to have designated a species of antelopes in Lucazi and still does so today.

meme. Therefore, at the time of this diffusion, which in this area probably occurred during the first century or two CE, the Kunene and Eastern Blocks had already separated from each other. Moreover, within Kunene, the Umbundu Subblock had also separated, but within the Eastern Block the Lunda Subblock had not yet done so. Thus by about 250 CE differentiation into subblocks was going on and the period during which the units of the group split into blocks was clearly over, while the primary split of the Njila into its two units was by then ancient history. Thus the period during which proto-Njila was spoken and the first split into its two constituent units must have occurred well back in the first millennium BCE, even if one supposes that the later split into blocks occurred only just before the diffusion of sheep.[27]

The later history of the Njila languages includes their adoption through language shift by speakers of non-Bantu languages, the further extension of the area in which Njila languages were spoken, and language shifts by which Njila speakers abandoned their language for others. Very little is known about any of this. We have argued that most speakers of other languages within most of the Njila area, at least north of latitudes 12° or 14° S abandoned their languages during the first five centuries of the second millennium as the result of acculturation to Njila-speaking centers of sedentary populations. Farther south, this process of "Bantuization" was much slower, so that even now pockets of non-Bantu speakers exist in southern Angola as far north as latitude 14° S.

As to the further extension of the Njila-speaking area, it is unlikely that any speakers of Njila languages penetrated anywhere southward of the lower Cunene River and of the Cuvelai basin before the rise of nomadic pastoralism ca. 1300. If they did, such Njila speakers later lost their tongues to adopt Khoisan languages and the same may well have happened to the first nomadic pastoralists who ventured this far south. The last successful expansion here was that of the Herero, who left Kaokoland in the sixteenth or seventeenth centuries. Farther east, Njila speakers may not have begun to settle southward of the Lungue-Bungo River before 1600 or so.

Njila languages also seem to have lost some of their territory to other Bantu languages. In the northwest, some speakers shifted to Kongo and re-

27. The distribution of different terms for sheep farther north (Moxico) and east (Zambezi floodplain) exhibits the barriers between Kunene and Eastern as well as between Eastern and Luyi mapped by Mann in Bastin et al., *Continuity*, pp. 75, 91. As sheep moved north, the Luyi languages (K31) adopted new words for them but kept *mbudi* for goat and so did languages farther north where sheep became *meme, mukoko,* and so on. All of this is best explained by assuming that empty tracts of land formed buffers between regions where Kunene, Eastern, and Luyi languages were spoken.

lated languages, at least after the foundation of the Kingdom of Kongo in the thirteenth century. Farther east, the Lweta languages lost most of their territory to Tshiluba after 1600 as did some of the southern Kete groups, while a few vague indications suggest that other Luba languages may well have made gains at the expense of Ndembu in the very sparsely settled lands east of the present border between the Ndembu, Luba Samba, and Kaonde languages.

REFERENCES

I. List of Abbreviations to Standard Works

A	*Anthropos*
AA	*American Anthropologist*
AAR	*African Archaeological Review*
AEH	*African Economic History*
Annaes	*Annaes do Conselho Ultramarino. Parte não official.* In some years, *Annaes maritimos e coloniaes.*
ARSOM	*Académie royale des Sciences d'Outre-Mer,* Brussels. Unless otherwise indicated, the primary series title for books cited is Memoirs, Division of Moral and Political Sciences. The secondary specific series designation is given with each title in the reference list. From 1955 to 1960, the institution was called *Académie royale des sciences coloniales* and, before 1955, *Institut royal colonial belge.* A new numbering of memoirs began in 1955.
AT	*Africa-Tervuren*
BA	*Baessler Archiv,* Neue Folge
BNR	*Botswana Notes and Records*
BSNG	*Bulletin de la société neuchâteloise de géographie*
CA	*Current Anthropology*
CEA	*Cahiers d'études africaines*
CS	Guthrie, Malcolm. *Comparative Bantu: An Introduction to the Comparative Linguistics and Prehistory of the Bantu Languages.* 4 vols. Farnborough, 1967–71.
HA	*History in Africa*
IJAHS	*International Journal of African Historical Studies*
JAH	*Journal of African History*
MMA	Brásio, António, ed. *Monumenta Missionaria Africana. Africa Ocidental.* 15 vols. Lisbon, 1952–88.
MRAC	*Musée royal de l'Afrique centrale* (Royal Museum of Central Africa), Tervuren, Belgium. Unless otherwise noted, the primary series title for works cited is *Annales, Sciences humaines.*

NA	*Nyame Akuma*
PM	*Petermann's Geographische Mitteilungen*
SAAB	*South African Achaeological Bulletin*
SAJS	*South African Journal of Science*

II. Lexical Sources

This section contains the full lexical sources for all the words cited in the notes which stem from Njila and Lweta languages and for a number of those stemming from surrounding languages. The latter are indicated by asterisks. The essential references to the common Bantu lexicon are listed in subsection C below ("Common Bantu Lexical Forms"). For more information on linguistic materials, see the now older but still handy bibliography by Yvonne Bastin in *Bibliographie bantoue sélective* (Tervuren 1975).

A. INDIVIDUAL LANGUAGES IN ALPHABETICAL ORDER BY LANGUAGE

*Bemba
White Fathers. *Bemba-English Dictionary.* London, 1954.

*Bushong
Brown Edmiston, Althea. *Grammar and Dictionary of the Bushonga or Bukuba Language . . .* Luebo, n.d. [1929?].
Vansina, Jan. *Esquisse de grammaire Bushong. MRAC,,* Linguistique 23. Tervuren, 1959.

Cokwe
Barbosa, Adriano. *Dicionário Cokwe-Português.* Coimbra, 1989.
McJannet, Malcolm Brooks. *Chokwe-English Dictionary and Grammar Lessons.* Vila Luso, 1949.

Dciriku
Möhlig, Wilhelm J. G. *Die Sprache der Dciriku: Phonologie, Prosodologie und Morphologie.* Cologne, 1967.

Hanya
Hauenstein, Alfred. *Les Hanya: description d'un groupe ethnique bantou de l'Angola.* Wiesbaden, 1967.

*Hemba
Vandermeiren, J. *Vocabulaire kiluba hemba-français et Vocabulaire français-Kiluba hemba.* Brussels, 1912.

Herero
Brincker, Peter Heinrich. *Wörterbuch und Kurzgefässte Grammatik des Otji-Herero mit Beifügung verwandter Ausdrücke und Formen des Oshi-Ndonga-Otj-Ambo.* Leipzig, 1886.

Kolbe, Frederick William. *An English-Herero Dictionary with an Introduction to the Study of Herero and Bantu in General.* Cape Town, 1883.

Holo

Daeleman, Jan. *Kiholu, notes provisoires.* Heverlee, 1961.

Imbangala

Chatelain, Heli. "Bemerkungen über die Sammlung von Mbamba-Wörtern und über das Mbamba-Volk," in *Zeitschrift für Afrikanische Sprachen,* pp. 138–46. 1888/1889.

Diniz, José de Oliveira Ferreira. *Populações indígenas de Angola.* Coimbra, 1918, esp. pp. 108–12.

See Chatelain, Heli, under "Multiple Languages."

See Missiónarios do Espiritu Santo under Kimbundu.

See Koelle, Sigismund Wilhelm, under "Multiple Languages."

*Kaonde

Woods, R. E. Broughall. *A Short Introductory Dictionary of the Kaonde Language.* London, 1924.

Kete Ipila

Kamba Muzenga. *Esquisse de grammaire kete.* Tervuren, 1980, esp. pp. 251–58.

Mbuyi-Kabandanyi. "Eléments de grammaire kete." Mémoire de licence de l'université de Lubumbashi. Lubumbashi, 1972.

See Maes, Joseph, under "Multiple Languages."

Kimbundu

Assis Junior, António de. *Diccionário Kimbundu-Português.* Luanda, 1948.

Matta, J. D. Cordeiro da. *Ensaio de diccionario Kimbúndu-Portuguez.* Lisbon, 1893.

Missionários do Espiritu Santo. *Vocabulario de Português-Kimbundu.* Mimeograph. Malange, n.d. [1980].

Nascimento, José Pereira de. *Diccionario Portuguez-Kimbundu.* Huilla, 1903.

Kisama

See Koelle, Sigismund Wilhelm, under "Multiple Languages."

*Kongo

Laman, Karl E. *Dictionnaire Kikongo-Français* . . . . Brussels, 1936.

Kongo-Dinga

Ceyssens, J. H. C. *Pouvoir et parenté chez les Kongo-Dinga du Zaire,* esp. pp. 477–90. Meppel, 1984.

Kwambi

See Homburger, Lilyas, *Le groupe sud-ouest des langues bantoues.* Paris, 1925. (Mission Rohan-Chabot, tome 3. *Linguistique,* pp. 21–31). Also under "Multiple Languages."

Kwangari

Bredell, A. W. *Bukenkango: Rukwangali-English English-Rukwangali Dictionary.* Windhoek, 1994.

Damman, Ernst. *Studien zum Kwangali: Grammatik, Texte, Glossar.* Hamburg, 1957.

Westphal, Ernest Oswald Johannes. *Kwangari: An Index of Lexical Types.* London, 1958.

Kwanyama

Tobias, George Wolfe Robert, and B. H. C. Turvey. *English-Kwanyama Dictionary.* Johannesburg, 1954.

Kwezo

Forges, Germaine. *Phonologie et morphologie du Kwezo. MRAC,* 113. Tervuren, 1983.

Lamba

Doke, Clement M. *English-Lamba Vocabulary.* Johannesburg, 1963.

*Lenje

Madan, Arthur Corwallis. *Lenje Handbook.* Oxford, 1908.

Ryohei, Kagaya. *A Classified Vocabulary of the Lenje Language.* Tokyo, 1987.

See Torrend, Julius, under "Multiple Languages."

Libolo

See Koelle, Sigismund Wilhelm, under "Multiple Languages."

*Luba Katanga

Van Avermaet, E., and Mbuya Benoît. *Dictionnaire Kiluba-Français.* Tervuren, 1954.

Lucazi

Pearson, Emil. *Ngangela English Dictionary.* Cuernavaca, 1970.

————. *English-Ngangela Dictionary.* Cuernavaca, 1973.

See Jaspert, Friedrich, and Wilhelm Jaspert under "Multiple Languages."

*Luyi

Jaccotet, E. "Troisième partie. Textes Louyi," in his *Études sur les langues du Haut-Zambèze,* pp. 220–34. Paris, 1901.

See Mukumbuta, Lisimba, under "Multiple Languages."

See Stirke, Douglas E. C., and A. W. Thomas under "Multiple Languages."

*Lwalwa

Ndembe Nsasi. "Esquisse phonologique et morphologique de la langue lwalwa." Mémoire de licence de l'université de Lubumbashi. Lubumbashi, 1972.

Lwimbi

Heintze, Beatrix. *Ethnographische Zeichnungen der Lwimbi/Ngangela-Zentral-Angola.* Wiesbaden, 1988.

See Jaspert, Fritz, and Willem Jaspert under "Multiple Languages."

Lwena

Horton, A. E. *A Dictionary of Luvale.* El Monte, 1953.

White, Charles Matthew Newton. *A Lwena-English Vocabulary.* Balovale, 1944.

Mbagani

Vancoillie, G. "Grepen uit de Mbagani-traditie." *Aequatoria* 10 (1947): 89–101, 122–29.

See Maes, Joseph, under "Multiple Languages."

Mbala

Lumbwe Mundindaambi. *Dictionnaire Mbala-Français*. Bandundu, 1977–81.

Ndolo, Pius, and Malasi Florence. *Vocabulaire Mbala*. Tervuren, 1972.

Mbui

Maia, António da Silva. *Lições de Gramática de Quimbundo (Português e Banto): Dialecto Omumbuim*. Cucujães, 1957.

*Mbukushu

Wynne, R. C. *English-Mbukushu Dictionary*. Trowbridge, 1980.

Mbunda

Pearson, Emil. *Ngangela English Dictionary*. Cuernavaca, 1970.

———. *English-Ngangela Dictionary*. Cuernavaca, 1973.

See Stirke, Douglas E. C., and A. W. Thomas under "Multiple Languages."

*Mwenyi

Yasutoshi, Yukawa. *A Classified Vocabulary of the Nkoya Language*. Tokyo, 1987.

See Mukumbuta, Lisimba, under "Multiple Languages."

Ndembu-Kimbundu

Missionários do Espiritu Santo. *Vocabulario de Português-Kimbundu*. Mimeograph. Malange, n.d. [1980].

Ndembu-Lunda

Fisher, M. K. *Lunda-Ndembu Handbook*. Lusaka, 1963.

White, Charles Matthew Newton. *A Lunda-English Vocabulary*. 2d ed. Lusaka, 1957.

Ndonga

Brincker, Peter Heinrich. *Wörterbuch und Kurzgefässte Grammatik des Otji-Herero mit Beifügung verwandter Ausdrücke und Formen des Oshi-Ndonga-Otj-Ambo*. Leipzig, 1886.

Tirronen, T. E. *Praktiese Ndonga*. Ovamboland, 1960.

Ngangela

Pearson, Emil. *Ngangela English Dictionary*. Cuernavaca, 1970.

———. *English-Ngangela Dictionary*. Cuernavaca, 1973.

Nkhumbi

Nogueira, António F. "O Lu'N Kunbi." *Boletim da Sociedade de Geographia de Lisboa* 5, no. 188: 212–55.

Westphal, Ernest Oswald Johannes. "Olunkhumbi Vocabulary." *African Language Studies* 2 (1961): 49–63.

*Nkoya
Yasutoshi, Yukawa. *A Classified Vocabulary of the Nkoya Language.* Tokyo, 1987.

Nyaneka
Silva, António Joaquim da. *Dicionário Português-Nhaneca.* Lisbon, 1966.

Nyemba
Baião, Domingos Vieira. *Dicionario Ganguela-Português.* Lisbon, 1939.
See also references under "Ngangela."

Pende
Gusimana, Barthelemy. *Dictionnaire Pende-Français.* Bandundu, 1972.

Rund
Carvalho, Henrique Augusto Dias de. *Methodo Pratico para fallar a lingua da Lunda,* esp. pp. 339–73. Lisbon, 1890.
Hoover, Jeff. *An uRuund-English Dictionary.* Mimeograph. Rudd, 1975.
Nash, Jay. *Ruwund Vocabularies.* Champaign, 1991.

Sala Mpasu
Guillot, R. *Petite grammaire de l'usalampasu.* Mimeograph. Brussels, ca. 1955.

*Sanga
Hadelin, Roland. *Vocabulaire Français-Sanga.* St. André, 1938.
Jenniges, M. *Dictionnaire Français-Kiluba.* Brussels, 1909.

Songo
Lux, Anton. *Von Luanda nach Kimbundu,* pp. 192–215 [not very reliable]. Vienna, 1880.
See Jaspert, Fritz, and Willem Jaspert under "Multiple Languages."
See Koelle, Sigismund Wilhelm, under "Multiple Languages."

*Songye
Samain, A. *La langue Kisonge.* Brussels, n.d. [1923].

*Tshiluba Kasai
De Clercq Auguste, Willems Emile. *Dictionnaire Tshiluba-Français.* Léopoldville, 1960.
Yasutoshi, Yukawa. *A Classified Vocabulary of the Luba Language.* Tokyo, 1992.

Umbundu
Fodor, István. *Introduction to the History of Umbundu.* Budapest, 1983.
Le Guennec Grégoire, Valente José Francisco. *Dicionário Português-Umbundu.* Luanda, 1972.
Sanders, William H., and W. E. Fay. *Vocabulary of the Umbundu Language Comprising Umbundu-English and English-Umbundu.* n.l. 1885.
Schadeberg, Thilo. *Sketch of Umbundu.* Cologne, 1990.

*Yaka
Ruttenberg, P. *Lexique Yaka-Français, Français-Yaka.* Mimeograph. Kinshasa, n.d. [1970?].

*Yans/Yanzi

Swartenbroeckx, Pierre. *Dictonnaire kiyansi ou kiyei, langage des Bayanzi ou Bayey du Territoire de Banningville (District du lac Léopold II) au Congo belge*. 2 vols. Mimeograph. Brussels, 1948.

MULTIPLE LANGUAGES

Chatelain, Heli. "Bantu Notes and Vocabularies." *Journal of the American Geographical Society of New York* 26, no. 2 (1894): 212–36.

Homburger, Lilyas. *Le groupe sud-ouest des langues bantoues*. Paris, 1925. (Mission Rohan-Chabot, tome 3. *Linguistique*).

Jaspert, Fritz, and Willem Jaspert. *Die Völkerstämme Mittel-Angolas*. Frankfurt, 1930, esp. pp. 144–55 [often unreliable but still needed for Songo and Lwimbi.]

Johnston, Sir Harry. *A Comparative Study of the Bantu and Semi-Bantu Languages*. 2 vols. Oxford, 1919/1920.

Koelle, Sigismund Wilhelm. *Polyglotta Africana*. Graz, [1854] 2d ed., 1963.

Maes, Joseph. "Vocabulaire des populations de la région du Kasai-Lulua-Sankuru d'après les observations de M. Achten." *Journal de la société des africanistes* 4(1934): 209–67.

*Mukumbuta, Lisimba. "A Luyana Dialectology." Ph.D. diss., University of Wisconsin–Madison. Madison, Wisconsin, 1982.

Stirke, Douglas E. C., and A. W. Thomas. *A Comparative Vocabulary of Sikololo-Silui-Simbunda*. London, 1916.

*Torrend, Julius. *An English-vernacular Dictionary of the Bantu-Botatwe Dialects of Northern Rhodesia*. Marianhill, 1931.

C. COMMON BANTU LEXICAL FORMS

Bantu Lexical Roots II. Tervuren (electronic database).

Guthrie, Malcolm. *Comparative Bantu*. 4 vols. Farnborough, 1967–71.

Meeussen, Emiel. *Bantu Lexical Reconstructions*. Tervuren, 1980.

III. Other Works

Almeida, António de. *Bushmen and Other Non-Bantu Peoples of Angola*. Ed. Phillip Tobias and John Blacking. Johannesburg, 1965.

———. "Dos Kwadi -um povo do deserto de Moçâmedes. Angola." *Garcia de Orta* 8 (1960): 771–77.

Almeida, António de, and Franca Camarate. "Recintos mulharados de Angola." *Estudos sobre a Pré-história do Ultramar Português*. Memorias no. 16 (1960): 109–24.

Almeida, de João. *Sul de Angola. Relatório de um govêrno de distrito (1908–1910)*. Lisbon, 1936.

Argyle, John. "The Linguistic Evidence for Khoisan-Southern Bantu Livestock Exchanges: A Dissenting View." Unpublished paper, 35 pp. n.l., n.d. [ca. 1987].

Atlas geografico. Ministerio da Educação da Republica Popular de Angola. Luanda, 1982.

Bal, Willy, trans. and ed. *Description du Royaume de Congo et des contrées environnantes,* by Filippo Pigafetta and Duarte Lopes. Paris, 1965. 2d ed.

Bartram, Laurence, Jr. "Southern African Foragers." In *Encyclopaedia of Precolonial Africa,* ed. Joseph Vogel, pp. 188–94. Walnut Creek, 1997.

Bastin, Marie-Louise. *Art décoratif tshokwe.* Diamang Publicações Culturais 55, 2 vols. Lisbon, 1961.

———. *Chibinda Ilunga, héros civilisateur.* 2 vols. Mimeograph. Brussels, 1966.

———. "Mungonge: Initiation masculine des adultes chez les Tshokwe (Angola)." *BA* 32 (1984): 361–403.

Bastin, Yvonne. *Bibliographie bantoue selective. MRAC.* Archives d'anthropologie 24. Tervuren, 1975.

———. "Statistique grammaticale e classification des langues bantoues." *Linguistics in Belgium: II.* Brussels (1979): 17–37.

Bastin, Yvonne, André Coupez, and Michael Mann. *Continuity and Divergence in the Bantu Languages: Perspectives from a Lexicostatistic Study. MRAC,* 162. Tervuren, 1999.

Bastin, Yvonne, André Coupez, and B. de Halleux. "Statistiques lexicale et grammaticale pour la classification historique des langues bantoues." *Bulletin des Séances. ARSOM* 23 (1979): 375–87.

Bastos, Augusto. *Traços geraes sobre a ethnographia do Districto de Benguella.* Lisbon, 1909.

Battell, Andrew. *The Strange Adventures of Andrew Battell of Leigh, in Angola and the Adjoining Regions. Reprinted from 'Purchas his Pilgrimes'.* Ed. E. G. Ravenstein. London, 1901.

Baumann, Hermann. *Das Doppelte Geschlecht.* Berlin, 1955.

———. "Die Frage der Steinbauten und Steingräber in Angola." *Paideuma* 6 (1956): 118–51.

———. *Lunda. Bei Bauern und Jägern in Inner-Angola. Erbenisse der Angola-Expedition des Museums für Völkerkunde, Berlin.* Berlin, 1935.

———. "Die Mannbarkeitsfesten bei den Tsokwe (N. O. Angola; West Afrika) und Ihren Nachbarn." *BA* 15 (1932): 1–54.

———. "Die Sambesi-Angola Provinz." In *Die Völker Afrikas,* ed. Hermann Baumann, 1: 513–648. Wiesbaden, 1975.

———. "Die Südwest-Bantu Provinz." In *Die Völker Afrikas,* ed. Hermann Baumann, 1: 473–511. Wiesbaden, 1975.

———. "Steingräber und Steinbauten in Angola." *Beiträge zur Kolonialforschung. Tagesband.* 1: 4–56. Berlin, 1943.

———, ed. *Die Völker Afrikas und Ihre traditionellen Kulturen.* 2 vols. Wiesbaden, 1975, 1979.

Bebiano, João Bacellar. *Notas sobre a siderurgia dos indigenas de Angola e de outras regiões africanas.* Diamang Publicações Culturais 50. Lisbon, 1960.

Birmingham, David. "Society and Economy before AD 1400." In *History of Central Africa*, ed. David Birmingham and Phyllis Martin. Vol. 1: 1–29. London, 1983.

Birmingham, David, and Phyllis Martin, eds. *History of Central Africa*. 3 vols. London, 1983–98.

Bisson, Michael. "Continuity and Discontinuity in Copperbelt and Northwestern Province Ceramic Sequences." *NA* 31 (1989): 43–46.

Blench, Roger. "Linguistic Evidence for Cultivated Plants in the Bantu Borderland." *Azania* 29/30 (1994–95): 83–102.

Bohannan, Paul, and George Dalton, eds. *Markets in Africa*. Evanston, 1962.

Bouquiaux, Luc, ed. *L'expansion bantoue. Actes du Colloque International du C.N.R.S. Viviers*. 3 vols. Paris, 1980.

Bousman, C. Britt. "The Chronological Evidence for the Introduction of Domestic Stock into Southern Africa." *AAR* 15, no. 2 (1998): 133–50.

Brasio, António, ed. *Monumenta Missionaria Africana. Africa Ocidental*. 15 vols. Lisbon, 1952–88. *See MMA* in abbreviations.

Brincker, Peter Heinrich. *Wörterbuch und kurzgefasste Grammatik des Otji-Herero. . . .* Leipzig, 1886.

Brito, Domingos de Abreu e. *Um Inquérito à vida administrativa e económica de Angola et do Brasil em fins do século xvi, . . . pelo Licenciado Domingos de Abreu e Brito*, ed. Alfredo de Albuquerque Felner. Coimbra, 1931.

Brochado, Bernardo J. "Descripção das terras do Humbe, Camba, Mulondo, Quanhama e outras, contendo uma idéa da sua população, sus costumes, vestuarios etc." *Annaes* (November 1855): 187–97.

———. "Noticia de alguns territorios, e dos povos que os habitam, situados na parte meridional da provincia de Angola." *Annaes* (December 1855): 203–9.

Burmeister, Stefan. "Archaeology and Migration." *CA* 41 (2000): 539–67.

Cabrita, Carlos L. Antunes. *Em Terras de Luenas. Breve Estudo sobre os usos e costumes da Tribo Luena*. Lisbon, 1954.

Cadornega, António Oliveira de. *História das guerras Angolanas*. 3 vols. Ed. José Matias Delgado (vols. 1 and 2) and Manuela Alves da Cunha (vol. 3). Lisbon, 1940–42.

Cahen, David, and Georges Mortelmans. *Un site Tshitolien sur le plateau des Bateke (République du Zaïre)*. MRAC, 81. Tervuren, 1973.

Capello, Hermengildo, and Roberto Ivens. *De Angola á Contra-costa. Descripção de uma viagem atravez do Continente Africano . . . .* 2 vols. Lisbon, 1886.

Cardoso, Fonseca. "Em terras do Moxico. Apontamentos de ethnografia angolense." *Trabalhos de antropologia e ethnologia* 1 (1919): 11–35.

Carneiro, João Vieira. "Observações feitas em 1848 . . ." *Annaes* (January 1859 to 1861, 1867): 172–79.

Carvalho, Henrique Augusto Dias de. *Ethnographia e História Tradicional dos Povos do Lunda*. Lisbon, 1890.

Cavazzi de Montecúccolo, António. *Descrição histórica dos três reinos Congo, Matamba e Angola*. 2 vols. Trans. and ed. Graziano de Leguzzano. Lisbon, 1965.

Ceyssens, Joseph, alias Rik. *Pouvoir et parenté chez les Kongo-Dinga du Zaïre.* Meppel, 1984.

Ceyssens, Rik. "Sens du 'grand masque' dans le haut Kasayi." *BA* 41 (1993): 355–81.

Chami, Felix. "Chicken Bones from Neolithic Limestone Cave Site, Zanzibar." In *People, Contact and the Environment in the African Past,* ed. Felix Chami et al., pp. 84–97. Dar es Salaam, 2001.

———. "A Response to Christopher Ehret's 'Bantu Expansion.'" *IJAHS* 34 (2001): 647–51.

Chami, Felix, Gilbert Pwiti, and Chantal Radimilihy, eds. *People, Contact and the Environment in the African Past.* Dar es Salaam, 2001.

The Cheke Cultural Writers. *The History and Cultural Life of the Mbunda-Speaking Peoples.* Ed. Robert Papstein. Lusaka, 1994.

Chikota cha Luchazi Association, eds. *The Luchazi People: Their History and Chieftaincy. Angola, Congo, Namibia, Zambia.* Lusaka, 1998.

Childs, Murray Gladwin. "The Kingdom of Wambu (Huambo): A Tentative Chronology." *JAH* 5 (1964): 367–79.

———. *Umbundu Kingship and Character.* London, 1949.

Clarence-Smith, William Gervase. *Slaves, Peasants and Capitalists in Southern Angola, 1840–1926.* Cambridge, 1979.

Clarence-Smith, William Gervase, and Richard Moorsom. "Underdevelopment and Class Formation in Ovamboland: 1844–1917." In *The Roots of Rural Poverty in Central and Southern Africa,* ed. Robin Palmer and Neil Parsons, pp. 96–112. London, 1977.

Clifford Gonzalez, Diana. "Animal Disease Challenges to the Emergence of Pastoralism in Sub-Saharan Africa." *AAR* 17 (2000): 95–139.

Clutton Brock, Juliet. "The Spread of Domestic Animals in Africa." In *The Archaeology of Africa,* ed. Thurstan Shaw et al., pp. 61–70. London, 1993.

Corrêa, Elias Alexandre da Silva. *História de Angola.* 2 vols. Lisbon, 1937.

Crabb, David W., "Nasal and Nasalized Roots in Proto-Southwest Bantu." Ph.D. diss., University of Columbia, 1962.

Crine, Fernand. "Un aspect du symbolisme luunda. L'association funéraire des Acudyaang." In *Miscellanea etnographica,* by de Sousberghe et al., pp. 81–108. *MRAC,* 46. Tervuren, 1963.

———. "Thèmes de la culture lunda." Manuscript. n.d., n.l. [1959].

de Beaucorps, R. *Les Basongo de la Luniungu et de la Gobari. ARSOM* 10/3. Brussels, 1941.

De Boeck, Filip. "From Knots to Web: Fertility, Life-Transmission, Health, and Well-being among the Aluund of Southwest Zaire." Ph.D. diss., Katolieke Universiteit van Leuven. Louvain, 1991.

De Heusch, Luc. *Le roi de Kongo et les monstres sacrés. Mythes et Rites Bantous III.* Paris, 2000.

Delgado, José Matias, ed. of vols. 1 and 2. *História das guerras Angolanas,* by António Oliveira de Cadornega, in 3 vols. Manuela Alves da Cunha, ed. vol. 3. Lisbon, 1940–42.

Delgado, Ralph. *O Reino de Benguella: do descobrimento à criação do govêrno subalterno.* Lisbon, 1945.

———. *Ao Sul do Cuanza (ocupação e aproveitamento do antigo reino de Benguela).* 2 vols. Lisbon, 1944.

de Maret, Pierre. "L'archéologie du monde luba." In *Aux origines de l'Afrique centrale,* ed. Raymond Lanfranchi and Bernard Clist, pp. 235–42. Libreville, 1991.

———. "Ceux qui jouent avec le feu: la place du forgeron en Afrique centrale." *Africa* 50 (1980): 263–79.

———. "Le contexte archéologique de l'expansion bantu en Afrique centrale." In *Actes du colloque international 'Les peuples Bantu, migrations, expansion et identité culturelle',* 1: 118–38. 2 vols. Libreville, 1989.

———. *Fouilles archéologiques dans la vallée du Haut-Lualaba, Zaire. I Sanga et Katongo 1974.* MRAC, 120 (two parts). Tervuren, 1985.

———. "Le néolithique et l'Age du fer ancien dans le sud-ouest de l'Afrique Centrale." In *Paysages quaternaires de l'Afrique Centrale,* ed. Raymond Lanfranchi and Dominique Schwartz, pp. 447–57. Paris, 1990.

———. "The Ngovo Group: An Industry with Polished Stone Tools and Pottery in Lower-Zaïre." *AAR* 4 (1986): 103–33.

———. "Les trop fameux pots à fossette basale du Kasai." *AT* 26 (1980): 4–12.

Denbow, James R., "After the Flood: A Preliminary Account of Recent Geological, Archaeological, and Linguistic Investigations in the Okavango Region of Northern Botswana." *Contemporary Studies on Khoisan I.* Quellen zur Khoisan-Forschung 5.1. Ed. Rainer Vossen and Klaus Keuthmann, pp. 181–214. Hamburg, n.d. [1987?].

———. "Congo to Kalahari: Data and Hypotheses about the Political Economy of the Western Stream of the Early Iron Age." *AAR* 8 (1990): 139–75.

———. "Early Iron Age Remains from the Tsodilo Hills, Northwestern Botswana." *SAJS* 76 (1980): 474–75.

———. "Material Culture and Identity in the Kahahari: AD 700–1700." In *Beyond Chiefdoms,* ed. Susan Keech McIntosh, pp. 110–23. Cambridge, 1999.

———. "A New Look at the Later Prehistory of the Kalahari." *JAH* 27 (1986): 3–28.

———. "Prehistoric Herders and Foragers of the Kalahari: The Evidence of 1500 Years of Interaction." In *Past and Present in Hunter-Gatherer Studies,* ed. Carmel Schrire, pp. 175–93. New York, 1984.

Denbow, James, and Edwin Wilmsen. "Advent and Course of Pastoralism in the Kalahari." *Science* 234 (1986): 1509–15.

———. "Iron Age Pastoralists' Settlements in Botswana." *SAJS* 79 (1983): 405–8.

De Pierpont, J. "Les Bambala." *Congo* (1932/1): 23–37, 185–205.

Derricourt, Robin M., and Robert Papstein. "Lukolwe and the Mbwela of Northwestern Zambia." *Azania* 11 (1977): 169–76.

de Sousberghe, Léon. *Les danses rituelles mungonge et kela des ba-Pende (Congo Belge)*. *ARSOM*, NS 9/1, Brussels, 1956.

———. "Les Pende. Aspects des structures sociales et politiques." In *Miscellanea Ethnographica*, ed. L. de Sousberghe et al., pp. 3–78. Tervuren, 1963.

———. "Noms donnés aux pygmées et souvenirs laissés par eux chez les Pende et Lunda de la Loange." *Congo-Tervuren* 6 (1980): 84–86.

———. "Régime foncier ou tenure des terres chez les Pende." *Bulletin des séances. ARSOM*, NS 4 (1958): 1334–52.

———. *Structures de parenté et d'alliance d'après les formules Pende (ba-Pende, Congo belge)*. *ARSOM*, NS 4/1. Brussels, 1955.

de Sousberghe, Léon, Bruno Crine-Mavar, Albert Doutreloux, and Jozef De Loose. *Miscellanea Ethnographica*. *MRAC*, 46. Tervuren, 1963.

de Wet, J. M. J. "Domestication of African Cereals." *AEH* 3 (1977): 15–32.

Diamang. *Annual Reports*. Lisbon, 1967.

Diniz, António Caetano da Costa. "Observações relativas ao Presidio de Pungo-andongo . . ." *Annaes* (October 1860): 141–45.

Diniz, José de Oliveira Ferreira. *Populações indígenas de Angola*. Coimbra, 1918.

"Documentos relativos á viagem de Angola para rios de Senna." *Annaes* 3a 5/6 (1893): 162–90, 223–40, 278–97, 423–39, 493–506, 538–52.

Douglas, Mary. *The Lele of Kasai*. London, 1963.

Dupré, Marie-Claude, and Bruno Pinçon. *Métallurgie et politique en Afrique centrale. Deux mille ans de vestiges sur les plateaux batéké Gabon, Congo Zaïre.* Paris, 1997.

Edwards, Adrian C. *The Ovimbundu under Two Sovereignties: A Study of Social Control and Social Change among a People in Angola*. London, 1962.

Ehret, Christopher, *An African Classical Age: Eastern and Southern Africa in World History 1000 B.C. to A.D. 400*. Charlottesville, 1998.

———. "Language and History." In *African Languages: An Introduction*, ed. Bernd Heine and Derek Nurse, pp. 272–97. Cambridge, 2000.

———. "Agricultural History in Central and Southern Africa ca. 1000 B.C. to A.D. 500." *Transafrican Journal of History* 4 (1974): 1–25.

———. "Patterns of Bantu and Central Sudanic Settlement in Central and Southern Africa." *Transafrican Journal of History* 3 (1973): 1–71.

Ervedosa, Carlos. *Arqueologia angolana*. Luanda, 1980.

Estermann, Carlos. "La fête de la puberté dans quelques tribus de l'Angola méridional." *BSNG* 48 (1941–42): 128–41.

———. *O Grupo étnico Herero. Etnografia do sudoeste de Angola*, vol. 3. Lisbon, 1961.

———. *O Grupo étnico Nhaneca-Humbe. Etnografia do sudoeste de Angola*, vol. 2. Lisbon, 1960.

———. *Os Povos não-bantos e o grupo étnico dos Ambós. Etnografia do sudoeste de Angola*, vol. 1. Lisbon, 1960.

Fabian, Johannes. *Out of Our Minds: Reason and Madness in the Exploration of Central Africa.* Berkeley, 2000.

Felix, Marc, and Manuel Jordan. *Makishi lya Zambia. Mask Characters of the Upper Zambezi Peoples.* Munich, 1998.

Felner, Alfredo de Albuquerque. *Angola. Planaltos e Litoral do Sul de Angola.* 3 vols. Lisbon, 1940.

————, ed. *Um Inquérito à vida administrativa e económica de Angola et do Brasil em fins do século xvi, . . . pelo Licenciado Domingos de Abreu e Brito,* by Domingos de Abreu e Brito. Coimbra, 1931.

Fenton, William, N. "Ethnohistory and Its Problems." *Ethnohistory* 9 (1962): 1–23.

Fernandes, Manuel. "Breve noticia sobre as tribos Luena e Bunda no posto de Lumai." *Mensário administrativo* 11 (1948): 35–37.

Forminière. *Congo Belge.* Supplement to *Bulletin de la société royale belge de géographie de Bruxelles* 50 (1926).

Furtado, L. C. C. Pinheiro. *Carta geographica da Costa occidental de Africa . . . desenhado pelo Tenente Coronel Engeneiro o L. C. C. Pinheiro Furtado em 1790, Gravada na Pariz por Ordem do Major João Carlos Feo Cardozo de Castellobranco e Torres em 1825.* Paris, 1825.

Gaeta, Antonio da. *La maravigliosa conversione alla santa fede di Cristo della Regina Singa, e del suo regno de Matamba nell' Africa meridionale.* Ed. Francesco Maria Gioia. Naples, 1669.

Geertz, Clifford. *Negara: The Theatre State in Nineteenth-Century Bali.* Princeton, 1980.

Gibson, Gordon D. "Bridewealth and Other Forms of Exchange among the Herero. In *Markets in Africa,* ed. Paul Bohannan and George Dalton, pp. 617–39. Evanston, 1962.

————. "Double Descent and Its Correlates among the Herero of Ngamiland." *AA* 58 (1956): 109–39.

————. "General Features." In *The Kavango Peoples,* ed. Gordon D. Gibson et al., pp. 7–33. Wiesbaden, 1981.

Gibson, Gordon D., Thomas J. Larson, and Cecilia McGurk, eds. *The Kavango Peoples.* Wiesbaden, 1981.

Gibson, Gordon D., and Cecilia McGurk. "The Kwangari." In *The Kavango Peoples,* ed. Gordon D. Gibson et al., pp. 35–79. Wiesbaden, 1981.

Gifford-Gonzalez, Diane. "Animal Disease Challenges to the Emergence of Pastoralism in Sub-Saharan Africa." *AAR* 17 (2000): 95–140.

Gioia, Francesco Maria, ed. *La maravigliosa conversione alla santa fede di Cristo della Regina Singa, e del suo regno de Matamba nell' Africa meridionale,* by Antonio da Gaeta. Naples, 1669.

Gosselain, Olivier, "Sakusi: Fouille d'un premier village du Néolithique et de l'âge des métaux au Zaïre." Thesis, Free University of Brussels. Brussels, 1988.

Gossweiler, John. *Nomes indígenas de plantas de Angola.* Luanda, 1953.

Grandvaux, Barbosa. L. A. *Carta Fitogeográfica de Angola.* Luanda, 1970.

Guerreiro, Manuel Viegas. *Boximanes !Khu de Angola: Estudo Etnográfico.* Lisbon, 1968.

———. "Ovakwankala (Boximanes) e Ovakwanyama (Bantos): aspectos de seu convivio." *Garcia de Orta* 8, no. 3 (1960): 529–34.

Güldemann, Tom, and Rainer Vossen. "Khoisan." *African Languages*, ed. Bernd Heine and Derek Nurse, pp. 99–122. Cambridge, 2000.

Guthrie, Malcolm. *Comparative Bantu: An Introduction to the Comparative Linguistics and Prehistory of the Bantu Languages.* 4 vols. Farnborough, 1967–71.

Gutierrez, Manuel. *L'Art pariétal de l'Angola.* Paris, 1996.

———. *Archéologie et Anthropologie de la nécropole de Kapanda (Angola).* Paris, 1999.

Hahn, Carl Hugo L. "The Ovambo." In *The Native Tribes of South West Africa,* ed. Carl Hugo Hahn et al., pp. 1–36. London, 1966. 2d ed.

Hahn, Carl Hugo, H. Vedder, and L. Fourie. *The Native Tribes of South West Africa.* London, 1966. 2d ed.

Hahn, Josaphat. "Die Ovaherero." *Zeitschrift der Gesellschaft für Erdkunde zu Berlin* 4 (1869): 226–58.

Hall, Martin, A. Hall, and Andrew B. Smith, eds. *Prehistoric Pastoralism in Southern Africa.* Goodwin Series 5. The South African Archaeological Society. Vlaeberg, 1986.

Hambly, Wilfrid. *The Ovimbundu of Angola.* Field Museum of Natural History, Anthropology Series 21:2. Chicago, 1934.

Hastings, Daniel Adolphus. "Ovimbundu Customs and Practices as Centered around the Principles of Kinship and Psychic Power." Thesis, Seminary Foundation. Hartford, 1933.

Hauenstein, Alfred. *Les Hanya. Description ethnique d'un groupe de l'Angola.* Wiesbaden, 1967.

———. "L'Ombala de Caluquembe." *A,* 58 (1963): 47–120.

———. "Le serpent dans les croyances de certaines tribus de l'est et du sud de l'Angola." *Estudos etnográficos* 2, no. 1 (1960): 221–31.

Haveaux, Georges L. *La tradition historique des Bapende orientaux.* ARSOM 37. 1st facsimile. Brussels, 1954.

Heine, Bernd. "Zur Genetischen Gliederung der Bantu-Sprachen." *Afrika und Uebersee* 56 (1973): 164–85.

Heine, Bernd, and Derek Nurse, eds. *African Languages: An Introduction.* Cambridge, 2000.

Heintze, Beatrix. *Alfred Schachtzabel's Reise nach Angola 1913–1914 und seine Sammlungen für das Museum für Völkerkunde in Berlin.* Afrika Archiv 1. Cologne, 1995.

———. "Beiträge zur Geschichte und Kultur der Kisama (Angola)." *Paideuma* 16 (1970): 159–86.

————. *Besessenheits-Phänomene im Mittleren Bantu Gebiet.* Studien zur Kulturkunde 25. Wiesbaden, 1970.

————. "Bestattung in Angola—eine Synchronische-diachronische Analyse." *Paideuma* 17 (1971): 184–93.

————. "Buschmänner und Ambo-Aspekte ihrere gegenseitiger Beziehungen." *Journal of the S. W. A. Wissenschaftliche Gesellschaft* 26 (1972): 45–56.

————. *Ethnographische Aneignungen: Deutsche Forschungsreisenden in Angola.* Frankfurt, 1999.

————. *Ethnographische Zeichnungen der Lwimbi/Ngangela (Zentral-Angola).* Sonderschriften des Frobenius-Instituts 5. Wiesbaden, 1988.

————, ed. *Fontes para a história de Angola do século XVII.* 2 vols. Wiesbaden, 1985, 1988.

————. "Gefährdetes Asyl: Chancen und Konsequenzen der Flucht angolanischer Sklaven im 17. Jahrhundert." *Paideuma* 39 (1993): 321–41.

————. "Historical Notes on the Kisama of Angola." *JAH* 13 (1972): 407–18.

————. "Die Steinnekropolen von Quibala." Unpublished manuscript. 2002.

————. *Studien zur Geschichte Angolas im 16. und 17. Jahrhundert. Ein Lesebuch.* Cologne, 1996.

Heintze, Beatrix, and Adam Jones, eds. *European Sources for Sub-Saharan Africa before 1900: Use and Abuse.* Stuttgart, 1988.

Herskovits, Melville. "The Cattle Complex in East Africa." *AA* 28 (1926): 230–72, 361–88, 494–528, 633–64.

————. "The Culture Areas of Africa." *Africa* 3 (1930): 59–77.

Heywood, Linda, and John Thornton. "African Fiscal Systems as Sources for Demographic History: The Case of Central Angola, 1799–1920." *JAH* 29 (1988): 213–28.

Hilton, Anne. *The Kingdom of Kongo.* Oxford, 1985.

Hirschberg, W. "Khoisan Sprechende Völker Südafrikas." *Die Völker Afrikas,* ed. Hermann Baumann, 1: 383–408. Wiesbaden, 1975.

Hitchcock, R. Renée, and Mary R. Smith, eds. *Proceedings of the Symposium on Settlement in Botswana: The Historical Development of a Human Landscape.* Wynberg, 1982.

Holdredge, Claire Parker, and Kimball Young. "Circumcision Rites among the Bajok." *AA* 29 (1927): 661–69.

Horton, Mark. *Shanga. The Archaeology of a Muslim Trading Community.* British Institute in Eastern Africa, Memoir 14. London, 1996.

Hoover, Jeffrey J. "The Seduction of Ruwej: Reconstructing Ruund History (The Nuclear Lunda; Zaire, Angola, Zambia)." 2 vols. Ph.D. diss., Yale University, 1978.

Huffman, Thomas. *Iron Age Migrations. The Ceramic Sequence in Southern Zambia. Excavations at Gundu and Ndonde.* Johannesburg, 1989.

"Hugo Hahn's Reise von Otjimbingue zum Cunene 1866." Part III of "Neueste Deutsche Forschungen in Süd-Afrika." *PM* 8 (1867): 284–97.

Inskeep, Raymond R. "Southern and Eastern Africa: History of Archaeology." In *Encyclopedia of Precolonial Africa,* ed. Joseph Vogel, pp. 75–84. Walnut Creek, 1997.

Irle, J. *Die Herero: Ein Beitrag zur Landes-, Volks-, und Missionskunde.* Gütersloh, 1906.

Jamieson, Ross, Sylvia Abonyi, and Neil Nirau, eds. *Culture and Environment.* Calgary, 1993.

Kanimba Misago. "Zaïre." In *Aux origines de l'Afrique Centrale,* ed. Lanfranchi Raymond and Clist Bernard, pp. 213–17. Libreville, 1990.

Kanyungulu, V. V. N. "The Early History of the Kings and Queens of the Cokwe People," ed. Robert Papstein. Manuscript, n.l., n.d. [ca. 1990].

Katanekwa, N. M. "The Iron Age in Zambia: Some New Evidence and Interpretations." Unpublished paper, 1995.

Keech McIntosh, Susan, ed. *Beyond Chiefdoms: Pathways to Complexity in Africa.* Cambridge, 1999.

Keiling, Luiz A. *Quarenta anos de Africa.* Braga, n.d. [1934].

Kinahan, John. *Pastoral Nomads of the Central Namib Desert: The People History Forgot.* Windhoek, 1991.

———. "The Rise and Fall of Nomadic Pastoralism in the Central Namib." In *The Archaeology of Africa,* ed. Thurstan Shaw et al., pp. 372–85. London, 1993.

Kinahan, John, and Joseph C. Vogel. "Recent Copper-working Sites on the !Khuiseb Drainage, Namibia." *SAAB* 37 (1982): 23–62.

Klein, Robert G. "The Prehistory of Stone Age Herders in the Cape Province of South Africa." In *Prehistoric Pastoralism in Southern Africa,* ed. Martin Hall, A. Hall, and Andrew B. Smith, pp. 5–12. Vlaeberg, 1986.

Kodi Muzong, Wanda. "A Pre-Colonial History of the Pende People (Republic of Zaire) from 1620 to 1900." 2 vols. Ph.D. diss., Northwestern University. Evanston, 1976.

Kolbe, Frederick William. *An English-Herero Dictionary . . .* Cape Town, 1883.

Kopytoff, Igor. "The African Frontier. In *The African Frontier,* ed. Igor Kopytoff, pp. 3–84. Bloomington, 1987.

———, ed. *The African Frontier.* Bloomington, 1987.

Kopytoff, Igor, and Suzanne Miers. "African 'Slavery' as an Institution of Marginality." In *Slavery in Africa,* ed. Igor Kopytoff and Suzanne Miers, pp. 3–81. Madison, 1977.

———, eds. *Slavery in Africa: Historical and Anthropological Perspectives.* Madison, 1977.

Kriger, Colleen. *Pride of Men: Ironworking in 19th Century West Central Africa.* Portsmouth, NH, 1999.

Kubik, Gerhard. *Makisi, Maskentraditionen im bantu-sprachigen Afrika.* Munich, 1993.

———. "Masks of the Mbwela." *Geographica* 5, no. 20 (1969): 4–17.

Kuvare, Silas. "Die Kaokoveld-Herero." In *Die Mbanderu*, ed. Theo Sundermeier, pp. 187–258. St. Augustin, 1977.

Lacerda, Paul Martins Pinheiro de. "Noticia da cidade de S. Felipe de Benguela e dos costumes dos gentes habitantes daquele sertão." In *Ao Sul do Cuanza*, 2 vols., ed. R. Delgado, 1: 639–43. Lisbon, 1944.

———. "Noticias do Paiz de Quisama." *Annaes* 6 (1846): 119–27.

"Ladislaus Magyar's Erforschung von Inner-Afrika." *PM* 6 (1860): 227–37.

"Ladislaus Magyar's Schilderung der Negerresidenz zu Nambambi." *Das Ausland* 30, no. 42 (1857): 1001–3. Reprinted from *Peßther Lloyd* (newspaper, Budapest).

Lancaster, Chet S. "Brideservice, Residence, and Authority among the Goba (N. Shona) of the Zambezi Valley." *Africa* 54 (1974): 46–64.

———. *The Goba of the Zambezi: Sex Roles, Economics and Change.* Norman, 1981.

Lanfranchi, Raymond, and Bernard Clist, eds. *Aux origines de l'Afrique centrale.* Libreville, 1991.

Lanfranchi, Raymond, Bernard Clist, and Dominique Schwartz, eds. *Paysages quaternaires de l'Afrique centrale atlantique.* Paris, 1990.

Lang, Afonso Maria, and C. Tastevin. *Ethnographie: La tribu des Va-Nyaneka. Angola et Rhodesia (1912–14).* Mission Rohan-Chabot. Vol. 5. Corbeil, 1938.

Lau, Brigitte. "Conflict and Power in Nineteenth Century Namibia." *JAH* 27 (1986): 29–40.

Lee, Richard B. *The !Kung San: Men, Women and Work in a Foraging Society.* Cambridge, 1979.

Leguzzano, Graziano de, trans. and ed. *Descrição histórica dos três reinos Congo, Matamba e Angola,* by António Cavazzi de Montecúccolo, 2 vols. Lisbon, 1965.

Leroux, P. "Quelques coutumes pastorales de Kuvale." *BSNG* 67 (1939–40): 52–61.

Leslie, Mary, and Tim Maggs, eds. *African Naissance: The Limpopo Valley 1000 Years Ago.* The South African Archaeological Society. Goodwin Series 8. Cape Town, 2000.

Lima, Mesquitela de. *Os Kiaka de Angola: História, parentesco, organização política e territorial.* 3 vols. Lisbon, 1988–90.

Livingstone, David. *Missionary Travels.* London, 1857.

Loeb, Edwin M. *In Feudal Africa. International Journal of American Linguistics,* Part 2, 28 (3). Bloomington, IN, 1962.

Luttig, Hendrik Gerhardus. *The Religious System and Social Organization of the Herero. A Study in Bantu Culture.* Utrecht, 1933.

MacCalman, H. R., and B. J. Grobbelaar. "Preliminary Report on Two Stone-working Ovatjimba Groups in the Northern Kaokoveld of South West Africa." *Cimbebasia* 13 (1965): 1–39.

Madeira, Maria Emilia, ed. *Viagens e apontamentos de um Portuense em Africa. Diário,* vol. I (the only one published). By António Francisco Ferreira da Silva Porto. Coimbra, 1986.

Magyar, Ladislaus. *Reisen in Süd-Afrika in den Jahren 1849–1857,* trans. and ed. Johann Hunfalvy. Pest/Leipzig, 1859.

Martins, João Vicente. "Arqueologia." In Diamang, *Annual Reports* (1967): 10–12 and 12 plates.

Maley J. "Conclusions de la quatrième partie: Synthèse sur le domaine forestier africain au quaternaire récent." In *Paysages quaternaires de l'Afrique centrale atlantique,* ed. Raymond Lanfranchi and Dominique Schwartz, pp. 383–89. Paris, 1990.

Mazzaoui, Maureen F., ed. *Textiles: Production, Trade and Demand.* An Expanding World 12. Aldershot, 1998.

Mbida Mindzie, Christophe et al. "First Archaeological Evidence of Banana Cultivation in Central Africa during the Third Millennium before Present." *Vegetation History and Archaeobotany* 10 (2001): 1–6.

McCulloch, Merran. *The Ovimbundu of Angola.* Ethnographic Survey of Africa: West Central Africa, 2. London, 1952.

———. *The Southern Lunda and Related Peoples.* Ethnographic Survey of Africa: West Central Africa, 1. London, 1951.

McGurk, Cecilia R. "The Sambiyu." In *The Kavango Peoples,* ed. Gordon D. Gibson et al., pp. 97–157. Wiesbaden, 1981.

Medeiros, Carlos Laranjo. *Vakwandu: History, Kinship and Systems of Production of an Herero People of South-West Angola.* Lisbon, 1981.

Meeussen, Emiel. *Bantu Lexical Reconstructions. MRAC.* Archives d'anthropologie 27. Tervuren 1980.

Miller, Duncan. *The Tsodilo Jewellery: Metal Work from Northern Botswana.* Rondebosch, 1996.

Miller, Joseph Calder. *Cokwe Expansion 1850–1900.* African Studies Program. Jordan Prize 2. Madison, 1974.

———. *Kings and Kinsmen.* Oxford, 1976.

———. "Requiem for the Jaga." *CEA* 13, no. 49 (1973): 121–49.

———. "The Significance of Drought, Disease and Famine in the Agricultural Marginal Zones of West Central Africa." *JAH* 23 (1982): 17–61.

———. "Thanatopsis." *CEA* 18, nos. 69/70 (1978): 229–31.

———. *Way of Death: Merchant Capitalism and the Angolan Slave Trade, 1730–1830.* Madison, 1988.

Miller. Sheryl F. "A New Look at the Tshitolian." *AT* 18 (1972): 86–89.

Missionários do Espiritu Santo. *Vocabulario de Português-Kimbundu.* Mimeograph. Malange, n.d. [1980].

Möhlig, Wilhelm. *Die Sprache der Dciriku: Phonologie, Prosodologie und Morphologie.* Cologne, 1967.

Moura, Júlio Diamantino de. "Uma história entre lendas." *Boletim do Instituto de Angola* 10 (1957): 55–75.

Murdock, George. *Africa: A Culture History.* New York, 1959.

Murphy, L. A., Michael L. Murphy, Lawrence H. Robbins, and Alex C. Campbell. "Pottery from the White Paintings Rock Shelter, Tsodilo Hills, Botswana." *NA* 55 (2001): 2–7.

Musasa Samal, Mwinkatim, Dizez. "Comment les Kanintshin jettent une lumière sur les origines de l'empire lunda et des légendes qui entourent ces origines." Mimeograph. n.l., [1977].

———. "Les États Lunda, Genèse, évolution, perspective." Manuscript. Mweka, 1977.

Ndaywel e Nziem, [Isidore]. "The Political System of the Luba and Lunda: Its Emergence and Expansion." In *Africa from the Sixteenth to the Nineteenth Century,* ed. Bethwell Ogot, pp. 588–607. Berkeley, 1992.

Neves, António Rodrigues. *Memoria da expedição a Cassange commandada pelo major graduato Francisco de Salles Ferreira em 1850 . . . .* Lisbon, 1854.

Niangi, Batulukisi. "La sculpture des Holo (République démocratique du Congo). Étude socio-morphologique et stylistique." 3 vols. Ph.D. diss., Louvain-la Neuve, 1998.

Nogueira, António Ferreira. *A Raça negra Sob o ponto de vista da Civilisação da Africa: Usos e costumes de alguns povos gentîlicos do interior de Mossamedes e as colonias portuguezas.* Lisbon, 1880.

———. "O Lu'N Kumbi: Dialecto do grupo o'n Bundo que se fall no interior de Mossamedes." *Boletim da Sociedade de Geografia de Lisboa* 5, no. 4 (1885): 181–261.

Nsuka Nkutsi, François, and Pierre de Maret. "Étude comparative de quelques termes métallurgiques dans les langues bantoues." In *L'expansion bantoue, Actes du Colloque International du C.N.R.S. Viviers,* ed. Luc Bouquiaux, 3 vols., 3: 731–42. Paris, 1980.

Ogot, Bethwell Allan, ed. *Africa from the Sixteenth to the Eighteenth Century.* Vol. 7 of *The General History of Africa.* Berkeley, 1992.

Oliveira, Jorge V. *Projetar o passado.* Lisbon, 1987.

"Ovanthu Vatetekela memo n'Otyilenge" [The People Who First Came to to Ocilenge], trans. Julio Beio Henrique. Manuscript, five pages. Quihita?, before 1954.

Palmer, Robin, and Q. Neil Parsons, eds. *The Roots of Rural Poverty in Central and Southern Africa.* London, 1977.

Papstein, Robert. "The Upper Zambezi: A History of the Luvale People, 1000–1900." Ph.D. diss., University of California, Los Angeles, 1978.

Passarge, Siegfried. *The Kalahari Ethnographies (1896–1898) of Siegfried Passarge: Nineteenth-century Khoisan- and Bantu-speaking Peoples.* Ed. and trans. Edwin N. Wilmsen. Quellen zur Khoisan-Forschung 13. Cologne, 1997.

Pearson, Emil. *People of the Aurora.* San Diego, 1972.

Petermann, August. "Die Reisen von Ladislaus Magyar in Süd-Afrika, Nach Bruchstücken seines Tagebuches." *PM* 3 (1857): 181–99.

Pierot, Fabrice. "Étude ethnoarchéologique du site de Mashita Mbanza Zaïre." Mémoire de licence de l'université libre de Bruxelles. Brussels, 1987.

Pigafetta, Filippo, and Duarte Lopes. *Description du Royaume de Congo et des contrées environnantes*. Trans. and ed. Willy Bal. Paris, 1965. 2d ed.

Pinçon, Bruno. "L'archéologie du monde teke." In *Aux origines de l'Afrique centrale*, ed. Raymond Lanfranchi and Bernard Clist, pp. 243–52. Libreville, 1991.

Pinto, Serpa. *How I Crossed Africa*, 2 vols. Trans. Alfred Elwes. New York, 1971. 2d ed.

Piron, Colette. "Classification interne du groupe Bantoide." Ph.D. diss., Université libre de Bruxelles. 3 vols. Mimeograph. Brussels, 1996.

Phillipson, David. *African Archaeology*. Cambridge, 1993. 2d ed.

Plancquaert, Marcel. *Les sociétés secrètes chez les Bayaka*. Bibliothèque Congo 31. Louvain, 1930.

Plug, Ina. "Domestic Animals during the Early Iron Age in Southern Africa." In *Aspects of African Archaeology*, ed. Gilbert Pwiti and Robert Soper, pp. 515–20. Harare, 1996.

Pogge, Paul. *Im Reiche des Mwata Yamwo. Tagebuch . . . in die Lunda-Staaten unternommen Reise*. Berlin, 1880.

Porter, P. W. "Environmental Potentials and Economic Opportunities." *AA* 67 (1965): 402–20.

Porto, António Francisco Ferreira da Silva. "Uma viagem de Angola em direcção à contra-costa." *Annaes* (October–December 1856): 273–92, 297–300, 304–08, 314–16; (May) 1858: 467–70.

———. *Viagens e apontamentos de um Portuense em Africa. Diário*. Ed. Maria Emília Madeira Santos. Vol. I (the only one published). Coimbra, 1986.

Pritchett, James A. *The Lunda-Ndembu. Style, Change and Social Transformation in South Central Africa*. Madison, 2001.

———. *Ubwambu*. Forthcoming.

Pruitt, Jr., William F. "An Independent People: History of the Sala Mpasu of Zaire and Their Neighbors." Ph.D. diss., Northwestern University. Evanston, 1973.

Pwiti, Gilbert, and Robert Soper, eds. *Aspects of African Archaeology. Papers from the 10th Congress of the Panafrican Association for Prehistory and Related Studies*. Harare, 1996.

Randles, William. *L'ancien royaume du Congo des origines à la fin du XIXe siècle*. Paris, 1968.

Ravenstein, E. G., ed. *The Strange Adventures of Andrew Battell of Leigh, in Angola and the Adjoining Regions. Reprinted from 'Purchas his Pilgrimes'*, by Andrew Battell. London, 1901.

Read, Frank R. "Iron-smelting and Native Blacksmithing in Ondulu County, South-east Angola." *Journal of the African Society* 5 (1902): 44–49.

Redinha, José. *Distribução Etnica da Província de Angola*. Luanda, 1969. 5th ed.

Reefe, Thomas Q. *The Rainbow and the Kings: A History of the Luba Empire to 1891*. Berkeley, 1981.

Reid, Andrew, and Segobye, Alinah. "Politics, Society and Trade on the Eastern Margins of the Kalahari." In *African Naissance,* ed. Mary Leslie and Tim Maggs, pp. 58–68. Cape Town, 2000.

"Relacam da Viagem que fez João Pilarte da Silva as Prayas das Macorocas, Huila 1770." In *Angola,* ed. Alfredo de Albuquerque Felner, 1: 177–86. Lisbon, 1940.

"Relatório de Gregório Mendes de 1 de Janeiro de 1786." In *Ao Sul do Cuanza* ed. Ralph Delgado, 2: 562–75. Lisbon, 1944.

Ribas, Oscar. *Ilundo.* Luanda, 1958.

Robbins, Lawrence H., et al. "Archaeology, Palaeoenvironment and Chronology of the Tsodilo Hills White Paintings Rock Shelter, Northwest Kalahari desert, Botswana." *Journal of Archaeological Science* 27, no. 11 (2000): 1086–111.

Robbins, Lawrence H., and Alex Campbell. "Prehistory of Mongongo Nut Exploitation in the Western Kalahari Desert, Botswana." *BNR* 222 (1990): 37–41.

Robbins, Lawrence H., Michael Murphy, Alex Campbell, and George Brook. "Intensive Mining of Specular Hematite in the Kalahari A.D. 800–1000." *CA* 39 (1998): 144–50.

Roberts, Andrew. *A History of Zambia.* London, 1976.

Robertson, John H. "Disease and Culture Change in South Central Africa." In *Culture and Environment,* ed. Ross Jamieson et al., pp. 165–73. Calgary, 1993.

———. "Early Iron Age Archaeology in Central Zambia." *Azania* 35 (2000): 147–82.

———. "A New Iron Age Pottery Tradition from South-Central Africa." *NA* 32 (1989): 59–64.

Robertson, John H., and Rebecca Bradley. "A New Paradigm: The African Early Age without Bantu Migrations." *HA* 27 (2000): 287–323.

Rodrigues, Adriano Vasco. "Construções bantas de pedra em Angola." *Boletim do Instituto de Investigações científicas de Angola* 5 (1968): 169–89, 23 plates and map.

Roelandts, Administrateur de territoire. "Die Bevölkerung des Landes Kahemba." Manuscript. Translated from the French. n.l. [Kahemba], March 1936.

Rossel, Gerda, *Taxonomic-Linguistic Study of Plantain in Africa.* Leiden, 1998.

Rudner, J. "An Archaeological Reconnaissance Tour of Angola." *SAAB* 31 (1994): 99–111.

Sadr, Karim. "Kalahari Archaeology and the Bushman Debate." *CA* 38 (1997): 104–12.

———. "The First Herders at the Cape of Good Hope." *AAR* 15 (1998): 101–32.

Sahlins, Marshall. *Stone Age Economics.* Chicago, 1972.

Sandelowsky, B. H. "Kapako and Vungu Vungu: Iron Age Sites on the Kavango River." In *Goodwin Series* South African Archaeological Society, ed. Nikolaas J. Van der Merwe and T. N. Huffmann, 3: 52–61. Cape Town, 1979.

Sangambo, Mose Kaputungu. *The History of the Luvale People and Their Chieftainship.* Ed. Art Hanson and Robert Papstein. Los Angeles, 1979.

Santos, J. R. Junior dos, and Carlos M. N. Ervedosa. "A estação arqueológica de Benfica. Luanda-Angola." *Sciencias Biologicas* 1, no. 2 (1970): 33–51, 36 plates.

Santos, Maria Emília Madeira, ed. *Viagens e apontamentos de um Portuense em Africa. Diário,* vol. I (the only one published). By António Francisco Ferreira da Silva Porto. Coimbra, 1986.

Sarmento, Alfredo de, *Os sertões d'Africa (Apontaméntos de viagem).* Lisbon, 1880.

Schadeberg, Thilo. "Progress in Bantu Lexical Reconstruction." *Journal of African Languages and Linguistics* 23 (2002): 183–95.

———. *Sketch of Umbundu.* Cologne, 1990.

Schecter, Edmund Robert. "History and Historiography on a Frontier of Lunda Expansion: The Origins and Early Development of the Kanongesha." Ph.D. diss., University of Wisconsin–Madison, 1976.

Schoenbrun, David Lee. *A Green Place, A Good Place: Agrarian Change, Gender, and Social Identity in the Great Lakes Region to the 15th Century.* Portsmouth, NH, 1998.

Schwartz, Dominique, Bernard Guillet, and Robert Deschamps. "Étude de deux flores forestières mi-holocène (6000–3000 BP) et subactuelle (500 BP) conservées in situ sur le littoral ponténégrin (Congo)." In *Paysages quaternaires de l'Afrique centrale atlantique,* ed. Raymond Lanfranchi and Dominique Schwartz, pp. 283–94. Paris, 1990.

Scudder, Thayer. *Gathering among African Woodland Savannah Cultivators: A Case Study of the Gwembe Tonga.* Zambia Papers no. 5, Lusaka, 1971.

Sebestyén, Evá, and Jan Vansina. "Angola's Eastern Hinterland in the 1750s: A Text Edition and Translation of Manoel Correia Leitão's 'Voyage' 1755–1756." *HA* 26 (1999): 299–364.

Sharma Saitowitz, Jeannette, Nikolaas J. Van der Merwe, and Carol Kaufmann. "Chevron Beads in an Iron Age Context: A Unique Find from Central Angola." *Muntu* 9 (1994): 125–56.

Shaw, Thurstan, Paul Sinclair, Bassey Andah, and Alex Okpoko, eds. *The Archaeology of Africa: Food, Metals and Towns.* London, 1993.

Siiskonen, Harr. *Trade and Socioeconomic Change in Ovamboland 1850–1906.* Studia Historica 35. Societas Historica Fennica. Helsinki, 1990.

Silva, José António Lopes da, and António Romano Franco. "Annaes do Municipio de Mossamedes . . ." *Annaes* (June 1858): 485–90.

Simoons, Frederick. "The Non-Milking Area of Africa." *Anthropos* 49 (1954): 58–66.

Smith, Andrew B. "Early Domestic Stock in Southern Africa: A Commentary." *AAR* 15 1998: 151–56.

Sommer, Gabriele. *Ethnographie des Sprachwechsels. Sozialer Wandel und Sprachverhalten bei den Yeyi (Botswana).* Sprachkontakt in Afrika 2. Cologne, 1995.

Strother, Zoe S. *Inventing Masks: Agency and History in the Art of the Central Pende.* Chicago, 1998.

Sundermeier, Theo, and Silas Kuvare. *Die Mbanderu. Studien zur ihrer Geschichte und Kultur.* Collectanea Instituti Anthropos 14. St. Augustin, 1977.

Teixeira, Alexandre da Silva. "Relação da viage . . . para as do lovar, no anno de 1794." In *Angola,* ed. Alfredo de Albuquerque Felner, 1: 236–37. Lisbon, 1940. Also in *Arquivos de Angola* 1:4 (1933), document X.

Tönjes, Hermann. *Ovamboland. Country, People, Mission. With Particular Reference to the Largest Tribe, the Kwanyama.* Trans. Peter Reiner. Windhoek, 1996.

Thornton, John. *The Kongolese Saint Anthony. Dona Beatriz Kimpa Vita and the Antonian Movement, 1684–1706.* Cambridge, 1998.

———. "The Origins and Early History of the Kingdom of Kongo." *IJAHS* 34 (2001): 89–120.

———. "A Resurrection for the Jaga." *CEA* 18, nos. 69/70 (1978): 223–27.

Torday, Emil. *Camp and Tramp in African Wilds.* London, 1913.

Turner, Gil. "Early Iron Age Herders in Northwestern Botswana: The Faunal Evidence." *BNR* 19 (987): 7–23.

———. "Hunters and Herders of the Okavango Delta, Northern Botswana." *BNR* 19 (1987): 25–40.

Turner, Victor W. *Schism and Continuity in an African Society: A Study of Ndembu Village Life.* Manchester, 1957.

Tuupainen, Maija. *Marriage in a Matrilineal African Tribe: A Social Anthropological Study of Marriage in the Ondonga Tribe in Ovamboland.* Transactions of the Westermarck Society 18. Helsinki, 1970.

Urquhart, Alvin W. *Patterns of Settlement and Subsistence in Southwestern Angola.* Washington, 1963.

Van Chi-Bonnardel, Régine. *The Atlas of Africa.* Paris, 1973.

Van Coillie, G. "Grepen uit de Mbagani–traditie." *Aequatoria* 10 (1947): 89–101, 122–29.

Van Koolwijk, Martinho. "Entre os Ganguellas III. Entronização de um Soba Ganguela." *Portugal em Africa* 23 (1966): 193–201.

Van Noten, Francis. "La plus ancienne sculpture sur bois de l'Afrique centrale?" *AT* 18 (1972): 133–36.

Vansina, Jan. "Antécédents des royaumes kongo et teke." *Muntu* 9 (1994): 7–49.

———. "Bananas in Cameroon ca. 500 BCE? Not Proven." *Azania* 38 (2004): 174–76.

———. "Bells of Kings." *JAH* 10 (1969): 187–97.

———. "Du nouveau sur la conquête lunda au Kwango." *Congo Afrique* 341 (2000): 45–58.

———. "Government in Kasai before the Lunda." *IJAHS* 31 (1998): 1–22.

———. "It Never Happened: Kinguri's Exodus and Its Consequences." *HA* 25 (1998): 387–403.

———. "Le régime foncier dans la société kuba." *Zaire* 9 (1956): 899–926.

———. "New linguistic evidence and 'the Bantu expansion.'" *JAH* 36 (1995): 173–95.

——. *Paths in the Rainforest: Toward a History of Political Tradition in Equatorial Africa.* Madison, 1990.

——. "Raffia Cloth in West Central Africa, 1500–1800." In *Textiles, Production, Trade and Demand,* ed. Maureen Mazzaoui, pp. 263–81. Brookfield, 1998.

——. "A Slow Revolution: Farming in Subequatorial Africa." *Azania* 29/30 (1994/95): 15–26.

Vasconcellos, Alexandre José Botelho de. "Anno de 1799. Descripção da capitania de Benguella." *Annaes* 4 (1844): 147–61.

Vedder, Heinrich. *Die Bergdama.* Abhandlungen aus dem Gebiet der Auslandskunde 11. Hamburgische Universität. 2 vols. Hamburg, 1923.

——. "The Berg Damara." In *The Native Tribes of South West Africa,* ed. Carl Hugo L. Hahn, Heinrich Vedder, and L. Fourie, pp. 37–78. London, 1966. 2d ed.

——. "The Herero." *The Native Tribes of South West Africa,* ed. Carl Hugo L. Hahn, Heinrich Vedder, and L. Fourie, pp. 153–208. London, 1966. 2d ed.

——. *South West Africa in Early Times.* Trans. and ed. Cyril G. Hall. London, 1966. 2d ed.

Vellut, Jean-Luc. "Diversification de l'économie de la ceuillette: Miel et cire dans les sociétés de la forêt claire d'Afrique centrale." *AEH* 7 (1979): 93–112.

Vidal, João Evangelista Lima. *Por Terras de Angola.* Coimbra, 1916.

Verbeken, A. "Succession au pouvoir chez certaines tribus du Congo par système électif." *Congo* (1933/2): 653–75.

Vivelo, Frank R. *The Herero of Western Botswana: Aspects of Change in a Group of Bantu-Speaking Cattle Herders.* Monograph 61 of The American Ethnological Society. St. Paul, 1977.

Vogel, Joseph C., ed. *Encyclopedia of Precolonial Africa: Archaeology, History, Languages, Cultures and Environments.* Walnut Creek, 1997.

——. "Eastern and South-Central African Iron Age." In *Encyclopaedia of Precolonial Africa,* ed. Joseph Vogel, pp. 439–44. Walnut Creek, 1997.

Vogelsang, Ralph. "Archaeological Investigations in the Kaokoland: Survey and Excavations in 1999 and 2000." *NA* 54 (2001): 25–28.

——. "An Archaeological Survey in the Kaokoveld, Namibia." *NA* 50 (1998): 22–24.

von Oppen, Achim. *Terms of Trade and Terms of Trust: The History and Contexts of Pre-colonial Market Production around the Upper Zambezi and Kasai.* Studien zur Afrikanischen Geschichte 6. Münster, 1993.

Vossen, Rainer. "Studying the Linguistic and Ethnohistory of the Khoe-speaking (central Khoisan) Peoples of Botswana: Research in Progress." *BNR* 16 (1984): 19–35.

Vossen, Rainer, and Keuthmann Klauss. *Contemporary Studies on Khoisan I.* Quellen zur Khoisan-Forschung 5.1. Hamburg, n.d. [1987?].

Vuyck, Trudeke. *Children of One Womb: Descent, Marriage, and Gender in Central African Societies.* Leiden, 1991.

White, Charles M. N. *An Outline of Luvale Social and Political Organization.* The Rhodes Livingstone Papers 30. Manchester, 1960.

———. "Notes on the Mungongi Ritual of the Balovale Tribes." *African Studies* 13 (1954): 108–16.

Wiessner, Pauline. "*Hxaro:* A Regional System of Reciprocity for Reducing Risk among the !Kung San." Ph.D. diss., University of Michigan, 2 vols. Ann Arbor, 1977.

Wilmet, Jules. "Essai d'une écologie humaine au Territoire de Luiza, Kasaï, Congo Belge." *Bulletin de la société belge d'études géographiques* 27, no. 2 (1958): 307–63.

Wilmsen, Edwin N. "Exchange, Interaction and Settlement in North-Western Botswana: Past and Present Perspectives." In *Proceedings . . . Settlement in Botswana,* ed. R. Renée Hitchcock and Mary R. Smith, pp. 98–110. Wynberg, 1982.

———, ed. and trans. *The Kalahari Ethnographies (1896–1898) of Siegfried Passarge: Nineteenth-century Khoisan- and Bantu-speaking Peoples.* Quellen zur Khoisan-Forschung 13. Cologne, 1997.

———. *Land Filled with Flies: A Political Economy of the Kalahari.* Chicago, 1989.

Wittfogel, Karl A. *Oriental Despotism: A Comparative Study of Total Power.* New Haven, 1957.

Wunenberger, Charles. "La Mission et le royaume de Humbe sur les bords du Cunène." *Les Missions Catholiques* 20 (1888): 224–25, 234–36, 250–52, 261–64, 269–72.

INDEX

actors, humans as, 13–14, 67–68, 204–5, 223, 272

agate, 113

age, 50; and division of labor, 97, 99; and sodality, 120, 216, 220, 229, 231, 254, 260, 262

age set, 148, 159, 219–23, 229, 234, 253, 257, 259, 265, 267

agriculture, 16–18, 19, 93; adoption of, 23, 101, 156, 263; and keeping cattle, 83–85; and natural conditions, 107, 117, 118, 206, 259, 264; on the planalto, 178; in the Cuanza basin, 187, 188; intensification of, 203, 204, 211. *See also* agropastoralism; cereal farming; fields; horticulture; irrigation

agropastoralism, 87, 132–53, 156–58; and descent systems, 85, 88, 92–93, 95, 96, 217; at Nqoma, 115; and pastoralists, 117, 118, 119, 123; and trade in cattle, 154, 178, 213; and chieftaincy, 163; and Feti, 173; and fascination with cattle, 200, 205

alliance: between clans, 49, 126, 130, 155; within clans, 85, 99, 140, 141; between polities, 131, 144, 149, 169, 202, 232, 248–50; between generations, 220, 229

amaranth, 34, 43

Ambaca, fort, 160

Ambaquista, 244

Ambo languages, 108, 134; speakers of, 110, 116, 123, 127, 143, 183, 185

Ambundu: polities, 83, 188, 201, 202–3, 270–71; people, 96, 180, 181

ancestor spirits: nomenclature, 48, 51; cult for, 123–24, 130, 199, 247; embodiment of, 124, 147, 174–75; cattle dedicated to, 125, 266; and nature spirits, 167, 231; and charms, 167, 190, 192–94, 242; protective paternal, 240; of clans, 252, 253

Angola, colony of, 2, 75, 267; history of, 171, 196, 197

Angolo, 144

apprentices, 35, 63, 64, 115, 211

arbitration, 147, 149, 163–65, 167, 237, 269. *See also* palavers

army, 197, 199, 249

assembly, 52, 164, 195, 269, 271

assimilation process, 54, 59, 60, 103, 282

association, 96, 226n56, 231; of experts, 167, 178, 211, 232–33, 234

authority: exercised over, 101, 195; as arbitrator, 163; nomenclature, 165, 231, 246; spiritual backing for, 167, 190, 242; of experts, 168–69, 178, 269; recognized, 209, 234, 258; collective, 231–32

autochtons, 1, 23, 40, 118, 206, 207; differences between, 41, 207; as teachers, 47, 121; Mbwela as, 225, 250; languages, 263

autonomy, 101, 114, 222; in cattle-keeping regions, 119, 130, 143, 158; in middle Angola, 201–2, 203, 204; in Moxico, 247, 251, 259

Bailundu, polity, 172, 175, 176, 182, 189, 236

balance of power, 143, 170, 233

Bambata, cave, 39, 281

founders, 89–90, 165, 217–18, 230, 236, 242, 248, 254
friendship, 127–28, 159, 219–20, 224; friends, 51n95, 214, 269
frontier, 185–86
fruits, 28, 35, 212
funerals, 154, 155, 220, 233, 253
fur, 65, 111, 113, 179
furnace, 64, 212
Furtado, Pinheiro, 145

Gaga, leader, 199
Gagas, people, 197
Gambo, *mwene*, 224–25
game, 27, 28–29, 31, 70, 110, 117, 173, 212; abundance of, 28, 37, 206, 211, 262; exchange of, 111, 113, 183; as offering, 143, 240, 242, 245, 253
gathering: by foragers, 27–28, 31, 35–36, 45; by farmers, 47, 58, 77, 182, 211, 212, 219
gender relations, 50, 79, 119, 148; and division of labor, 36, 99, 137, 262; and sodalities, 209, 216, 219, 220, 221, 229
genealogy, 89, 252, 259, 272
generations, relations between, 50, 88–89, 220, 229; and change, 28, 52, 73, 77–78; alternate, 220, 229
Genesis, traditions of, 10, 80, 126
ghosts. *See* ancestor spirits
Giagas, people, 197
Gindes, people, 197
glottochronology, 8, 42n52, 279–80
goats, 70, 82, 87, 91, 281–82; and proto-Njila speakers, 25, 37, 40, 41, 45, 65, 68; trade in, 65, 113, 115; and environments, 117, 119, 156, 179; as wealth, 230, 236. *See also* flocks
God, 174n37, 193
Gokomere ware, 109
gold, 115
gossip, 269, 271
gourds, 28, 37–38, 57, 213, 256
governance. *See* centralized governance; collective governance; overarching institutions of governance

grasslands, 19, 20, 28, 33, 76n32, 87, 119, 206, 223; and fields, 43, 46; *mopane*, 40, 68, 281
groundnuts, 34, 38–39, 43, 57, 58, 77
Guinda, people, 196
guns, 252
Gutierrez, Manuel, 5

Haco, region, 190
Handa, polity, 150, 183
Hausa potato, 34, 43
headhunters, 231
healers, 51, 223
healing, 2, 122n43, 131, 153, 257
herders, cattle, 12, 14, 53, 101–3, 116, 156, 264, 268; and transhumance, 83, 86, 119, 124, 126
herding, 23, 30, 68, 90, 93; cattle, 23, 58, 74, 116, 117, 119, 129, 147, 156, 182, 184, 187
Herero language, 41–42, 141; speakers of, 10, 41–42, 108, 110, 120–31, 151, 282
hierarchy: territorial, 49, 114, 152; social, 50, 116, 176–77, 262, 264; of initiations, 231, 233, 234, 255, 257, 265; of titles, 258, 263
Himba, people, 53
hoards, 80, 116, 128, 173, 236
hoes: and agriculture, 66, 74, 75, 77, 79, 262; trade in, 80, 178, 188, 212; two-handed, 81, 178; as wealth, 95, 172, 173, 230, 236; as charm, 192
Holo, people, 192, 249–50
homesteads, 37–38, 141, 142, 143, 149, 155
honey, 45, 183, 212
Hoover, Jeffrey, 276
horticulture: introduction of, 12, 23, 25, 33–34, 36–39, 67, 235; and environmental barrier, 41, 55–56, 59, 68, 87, 261–62; and proto-Njila speakers, 42–45, 59–60, 66, 102, 216, 218; and foragers, 47, 52, 54–55; and diffusion of cereals, 78, 227–28, 236
House, 229, 230, 255, 256
households, 23, 178, 267; proto-Njila, 47, 49, 52, 54; and Tsodilo sites, 72, 109, 115;

to chiefdom, 244, 247; and dynastic web, 248–51, 254; Rund, 255, 257

villages, 234, 274; and rise of larger groups, 3, 101, 102, 163–65; first appearance of, 13, 80, 98; early, 47–50, 52, 88, 89, 235; and foragers, 53–55, 58, 64, 272; Divuyu, 69–72, 73, 74; mobility, 74, 122; and matrilineage, 97, 209, 236–37; in middle Angola, 177, 195, 196; and vicinage, 206, 210–26; in the Lweta region, 227–28, 230, 231, 233

Viye, polity, 180–81, 182

Vungu Vungu, site, 2n4, 154, 183

Wambu, polity, 179–80, 181, 182

warfare, 63, 122; and cattle herds 110; in southern Angola, 147, 149; and Portuguese, 160, 199; on the planalto, 170; and slaves, 178, 201, 238, 239; and Ndongo, 189, 193, 195, 196; and Jaga, 199–201; and Lweta speakers, 231; in middle Kwilu, 243

warlords, 122, 131

warriors, 150–51, 231, 244, 255, 257

water supply: surface, 107, 108, 111, 124, 138; waterhole, 117, 119, 129, 139; pan, 118; reservoir, 134, 151–52

wax, 252

wealth, 96, 116, 159; in metal, 66, 79, 80, 95, 99, 173, 183; in cattle, 85, 88, 95, 99, 110, 119, 156, 262; in other valuables, 137, 230, 236, 238; and trade, 188; and political office, 231, 234, 238; management of, 239, 240

West Central Africa, as a historical region, 32, 33, 39, 40, 41, 61, 67–68, 99, 263

Wiessner, Polly, 113

wives, 64, 80, 125, 195, 217, 239, 240; and sacred fire, 124; sharing, 127; of spirit, 168–69

Wilmsen, Edwin, 5, 6

Wilton industry, 27, 32

witchcraft, 51, 177, 178, 268–69

Wittfogel, Karl, 151

women, 14, 40, 86, 124, 194, 232; gatherers, 28, 29, 35, 212, 219; mobility of, 30, 215, 247; producers, 35, 265; potters, 35, 37, 213, 262; farmers, 36, 91, 137, 228, 262; unequal status of, 88, 229, 239, 262; sodalities, 122n43, 148, 219, 229, 232, 237, 259, 265; and high office, 148, 195–96, 224–25, 254; self-governance, 229, 232

words and things, 5–9, 11, 13, 176–77n47

worldview, 1, 41, 122n43, 169, 201

written evidence, 1, 4, 10, 78, 115, 132, 163, 238, 279

Xam, people, 92

Xaro, site, 73

Yagua, people, 196

Yaka, polity, 244, 258

yams, 8, 19; water, 8, 78n37, 178, 211, 236; and horticulture, 34, 43, 46, 78, 206, 263; wild, 35–36; limits of, 37–38, 55–56, 207; and cereals, 78, 227–28

Yauma, people and ruler, 224

Yeyi, people, 53

Zama, people, 32

Zimbabwe Great, site, 111, 170